AF773460

Megan Maruschke
Portals of Globalization

Dialectics of the Global

Edited by
Matthias Middell

Volume 2

Megan Maruschke

Portals of Globalization

Repositioning Mumbai's Ports and Zones, 1833–2014

DE GRUYTER
OLDENBOURG

Funded with help of the DFG, a product of the SFB 1199

ISBN 978-3-11-061221-9
e-ISBN (PDF) 978-3-11-061513-5
e-ISBN (EPUB) 978-3-11-061243-1

Library of Congress Control Number: 2019931409

Bibliographic information published by the Deutsche Nationalbibliothek
The Deutsche Nationalbibliothek lists this publication in the Deutsche Nationalbibliografie; detailed bibliographic data are available on the Internet at http://dnb.dnb.de.

© 2019 Walter de Gruyter GmbH, Berlin/Boston
Cover image: © The British Library Board, X.1190.
Typesetting: Integra Software Services Pvt. Ltd.
Printing and binding: CPI books GmbH, Leck

www.degruyter.com

Preface

Ever since the 1990s, "globalization" has been a dominant idea and, indeed, ideology. The metanarratives of Cold War victory by the West, the expansion of the market economy, and the boost in productivity through internationalization, digitization, and the increasing dominance of the finance industry became associated with the promise of a global trickle-down effect that would lead to greater prosperity for ever more people worldwide. Any criticism of this viewpoint was countered with the argument that there was no alternative; globalization was too powerful and thus irreversible. Today, the ideology of "globalization" meets with growing scepticism. An era of exaggerated optimism for global integration has been replaced by an era of doubt and a quest for a return to particularistic sovereignty. However, processes of global integration have not dissipated, and the rejection of "globalization" as ideology has not diminished the need to make sense of both the actually existing high level of interdependence and the ideology that gave meaning and justification to it.

The following three dialectics of the global are in the focus of this series: Multiplicity and Co-presence: "Globalization" is neither a natural occurrence nor a singular process; on the contrary, there are competing projects of globalization, which must be explained in their own right and compared in order to examine their layering and their interactive composition.

Integration and Fragmentation: Global processes result in de- as well as reterritorialization. They go hand in hand with the dissolution of boundaries, while also producing a respatialization of the world.

Universalism and Particularism: Globalization projects are justified and legitimized through universal claims of validity; however, at the same time they reflect the worldview and/or interest of particular actors.

https://doi.org/10.1515/9783110615135-201

Acknowledgements

Research for this book began in 2012 as a dissertation at Leipzig University and was generously funded by the German Research Foundation (DFG) Research Training Group (GK) 1261, "Critical Junctures of Globalization." I also received financial support from the German Academic Exchange Service (DAAD) to carry out field research in India under the "New Passages to India" scholarship. The DFG Collaborative Research Centre (SFB) 1199 "Processes of Spatialization under the Global Condition" allowed me the time and resources to publish this book and provided a stimulating academic environment that made this research possible.

I would like to extend my thanks to all the staff and students at the Global and European Studies Institute, the Research Training Group 1261, and the Collaborative Research Centre 1199 at Leipzig University. In particular, I would like to thank Ulf Engel, the speaker of the research training group, and my dissertation supervisor, Matthias Middell, for his continuous support and guidance over the years and for his encouraging comments on many drafts. I am also grateful for Valentina Padula's (University of California Santa Barbara) early support. In particular, a number of colleagues have provided valuable feedback during the writing process, especially the members of the global and transnational history working group. Steffi Marung always gave thoughtful and thorough comments on my writing as well as organized activities to keep my writing on track. I am also grateful to Claudia Baumann, Geert Castryck, Antje Dietze, and Katja Naumann for our collaboration and exchange on portals of globalization over the years.

This project might never have taken the form it did without the help I received during my field research. I am thankful for Marie-Lou Fernandes and her lovely friends and family, especially Vishal Modi, for their kindness, hospitality, stimulating conversation, and networking. Jayaram Hegde of Wilhelmsen Ships' Services went above and beyond in assisting my inquiries into the current state of Mumbai's ports and shipping industry. In researching Mumbai Port's past, I thank the staff of the Asia and Africa reading room of the British Library; the Leipzig University library staff; Swapna Sathe, librarian at the Indian Merchants' Chamber in Mumbai; and the staff at the Central Secretariat Library in New Delhi. The Maharashtra State Archives and the Asiatic Society of Mumbai also generously allowed me to browse their holdings. Additionally, a number of institutions were helpful over the course of this research: the Bombay Chamber of Commerce and Industry; Mumbai Port Trust; Jawaharlal Nehru Port Trust; Wilhelmsen Ships' Services; Mumbai First; Forbes and Co.; Ernst & Young, Mumbai; C. H. Robinson; the Centre for Policy Research in New Delhi; and the Consul General for the Kingdom of the Netherlands in Mumbai.

https://doi.org/10.1515/9783110615135-202

I have benefited greatly from feedback on this research. In addition to the many events in Leipzig, I received helpful comments at a number of international conferences, including the "Seaports in Transition: Global Change and the Role of Seaports since the 1950s" conference at the Forschungsstelle für Zeitgeschichte in Hamburg, Germany (2014); the Flying University of Transnational Humanities conference at the University of Pittsburgh, USA (2014); the European Social Science and History conference at Valencia University, Spain (2015); and the "Mutants of Development? Special Economic Zones, Economic Corridors, and the Changing Geographies of Capitalism" workshop at the University of Amsterdam, in the Netherlands (2016).

My students were also a great inspiration. They came from all over the world and unbeknownst to them, *they* were teaching *me* about zones in a global context. Agnieszka Paciorek and Wakana Sato assisted me with texts written in Polish and Japanese.

Finally, I would like to thank my wonderful family and friends, especially my parents, Scott and Caron Campbell, and my husband, Manuel Maruschke, for their love and support.

Contents

Abbreviations

ASEAN	Association of Southeast Asian Nations
BISN	British India Steam and Navigation
BPT	Bombay Port Trust
BRIC	Brazil, Russia, India, China
CIDCO	City and Industrial Development Corporation of Maharashtra
DMIC	Delhi Mumbai Industrial Corridor
EIC	East India Company
EPZ	Export Processing Zone
FDI	Foreign Direct Investment
FTZ	Foreign-Trade Zone
FTZ	Free Trade Zone
ILO	International Labour Organization
IMF	International Monetary Fund
INSTC	International North-South Transport Corridor
JETRO	Japan External Trade Organization
JNNURM	Jawaharlal Nehru National Urban Renewal Mission
JNPT	Jawaharlal Nehru Port Trust
KFTZ	Kandla Free Trade Zone
KPT	Kandla Port Trust
MEDC	Maharashtra Economic Development Council
MHADA	Maharashtra Housing and Area Development Authority
MIDC	Maharashtra Industrial Development Corporation
MMR	Mumbai Metropolitan Region
MMRDA	Mumbai Metropolitan Regional Development Authority
MPT	Mumbai Port Trust
NAM	Non-Aligned Movement
NIDL	New International Division of Labour
NMIZ	National Manufacturing Investment Zone
NRI	Non-resident Indian
OECD	Organisation for Economic Co-operation and Development
PSA	Port of Singapore Authority
SAARC	South Asian Association for Regional Cooperation
SAFTA	South Asian Free Trade Area
SEEPZ	Santacruz Electronics Export Processing Zone
SEZ	Special Economic Zone
SWIFT	Society for Worldwide Interbank Financial Telecommunications
TAMP	Tariff Authority for Major Ports
UK	United Kingdom
UN	United Nations
UNCTAD	United Nations Conference on Trade and Development
UNIDO	United Nations Industrial Development Organization
US	United States

https://doi.org/10.1515/9783110615135-203

USAID	United States Agency for International Development
USD	United States Dollar
USSR	Union of Soviet Socialist Republics
WB	World Bank

1 Introduction

Globalization rhetoric, especially in the 1990s, described a flat, interconnected world comprised of capital flows, human mobility, and international trade. In this narrative, the world grows smaller as new technologies enable high-speed communication and transport, and larger as occurrences in far-away places not only feel close but also have immediate impact on other distant parts of the world. In this description, the nation state, once so central to explanations of societal cohesion and political order, constituted by territoriality, has been deterritorialized by global cities, special economic zones (SEZs), global corporations, supply chains, and other transnational actors and spaces that the state no longer controls.

Research in global history, however, has shown that state territoriality as a powerful spatial format for societal organization became ever more complete alongside increasing global connectedness over the course of the nineteenth century. Territoriality dates back to the seventeenth century, but it achieved added relevance with new technologies that enabled connectivity, advances in cartography, and the significance of the nation as a political unit in both empires and states. The nation state and territorial forms of organization emerged as world trade and migration increased, suggesting that this form of state control, which consists in its ideal type of borders and the even integration of state space, developed as a strategy to deal with flows of goods, capital, and people.[1] Likewise, political geographers have also been historically informed about the changing nature of the state as only one form of state spatiality in history.[2] Such

1 C. Maier, "Consigning the 20th Century to History: Alternative Narratives for the Modern Era", *American Historical Review* 105 (2000) 3, pp. 807–831; C. Maier, "Transformations of Territoriality, 1600–2000", in: G. Budde, S. Conrad and O. Janz (eds.), *Transnationale Geschichte: Themen, Tendenzen und Theorien*, Göttingen: Vandenhoeck & Ruprecht, 2006, pp. 32–55; C. Maier, *Once within Borders: Territories of Power, Wealth, and Belonging since 1500*, Cambridge, MA: Harvard University Press, 2016. For a discussion on Maier's work and the term "regimes of territoriality", see: M. Middell and K. Naumann, "Global History and the Spatial Turn: From the Impact of Area Studies to the Study of Critical Junctures of Globalization", *Journal of Global History* 5 (2010) 1, pp. 149–170, at 163–166. See also: C. Mukerji, *Territorial Ambitions and the Gardens of Versailles*, Cambridge: Cambridge University Press, 1997; S. Elden, *The Birth of Territory*, Chicago: The University of Chicago Press, 2013.

2 J. Agnew, "The Territorial Trap: The Geographical Assumptions of International Relations Theory", *Review of International Political Economy* 1 (1994) 1, pp. 53–80; J. Agnew, *Globalization and Sovereignty*, Lanham, MD: Rowman & Littlefield, 2009; N. Brenner, "Between Fixity and Motion: Accumulation, Territorial Organization and the Historical Geography of Spatial Scales", *Environment and Planning D. Society and Space* 16 (1998) 4, pp. 459–481; N. Brenner,

https://doi.org/10.1515/9783110615135-001

discussions inform discourses in related disciplines on the emergence of new spatial formats and fuel research on the forms of political and economic organization such as the empires within which nation states emerged.[3] Ulf Engel and Matthias Middell have linked synchronic changes in dominant modes of spatial organization to crises on a global scale, which they call critical junctures of globalization.[4] In short, the nation state is not the end or beginning of history; instead, the nation state has become the dominant spatial format of social organization for a certain part of the world during a specific historical period and is not likely to prevail indefinitely. Other spatial formats such as regional organizations, global cities, and SEZs, to name but a few, have become more prevalent in the last several decades, though nation states remain relevant in the current global spatial order.

In particular, SEZs have attracted attention within the above narrative on the decline of the nation state. Such zones are associated with neoliberalism, enclaving, and offshoring that have deregulated certain economic sectors in particular places, thereby removing state sovereignty over parts of its own economy and territory. While most authors dealing with the rising number of such zones take them as further proof of a deterritorializing world since the late twentieth century, several scholars have shown the usefulness of these zones to the state beyond Western contexts. Aihwa Ong argues that neoliberalism in Southeast Asia takes a different form than it does in the West. Likewise, Loraine Kennedy shows that state rescaling in India, of which a rising number of SEZs appear to be a symptom, is an active state-based strategy in comparison to

---

"Beyond State-Centrism? Space, Territoriality, and Geographical Scale in Globalization Studies", *Theory and Society* 28 (1999) 1, pp. 39–78; N. Brenner, *New State Spaces: Urban Governance and the Rescaling of Statehood*, Oxford: Oxford University Press, 2004.

3 For new spaces, see: A. Appadurai, "Sovereignty without Territoriality: Notes for a Post-National Geography", in: P. Yaeger (ed.), *The Geography of Identity: Notes for a Postnational Geography*, Ann Arbor: University of Michigan Press, 1996, pp. 40–58; S. Sassen, "When Territory Deborders Territoriality", *Territory, Politics, Governance* 1 (2013) 1, pp. 21–45. For empires, see: J. Burbank and F. Cooper, *Empires in World History: Power and the Politics of Difference*, Princeton, NJ: Princeton University Press, 2010; K. Kumar, "Nation-States as Empires, Empires as Nation-States. Two Principles, One Practice?", *Theory and Society* 39 (2010) 2, pp. 119–143; C. S. Maier, *Among Empires: American Ascendancy and Its Predecessors*, Cambridge, MA: Harvard University Press, 2006. For a discussion on globalization and an analysis of empires, see: J. Darwin, *After Tamerlane: The Rise and Fall of Global Empires, 1400–2000*, New York: Bloomsbury Press, 2007.

4 U. Engel and M. Middell, "Bruchzonen der Globalisierung, globale Krisen und Territorialitätsregimes – Kategorien einer Globalgeschichtsschreibung", *Comparativ: Zeitschrift für Globalgeschichte und vergleichende Gesellschaftsforschung* 15 (2005) 5–6, pp. 5–38. These critical junctures may constitute periodizations of global spatial orders.

Western cases in which state rescaling emerged under crisis.[5] This book furthers research that argues that zones and states have a more complex and ambivalent relationship than the standard narrative describes. Furthermore, this book, through the example of Mumbai, India, shows a longer history of using place and creating enclaves as part of both territorializing and globalizing projects pursued by a number of actors for much longer than the current research suggests, thereby examining the variety of spaces and processes of respatialization that have constituted the state and its reformulation under globalization since the mid-nineteenth century.

This book contributes to research on globalization by observing it "in action." It unravels the past and present of zones and ports in India's major trading city, Mumbai (formerly Bombay). This port city was chosen for this study due to its significance to India since the mid-nineteenth century, though in terms of world trade its positionality has remained secondary. In addition to hosting zones for many decades, Mumbai offers a rich look at various projects to reassert its dominance in shifting global, regional, and national frameworks, including through zone and port projects. This study demonstrates the importance of place and the role of various actors, including state agencies, in the production of globalization and territorialization in Mumbai from the interventions of Britain's East India Company (EIC) to India's Prime Minister Narendra Modi's agenda (from ca. 1833 to 2014). This book investigates the planning of ports and zones, focusing on periods of global and regional change: the British Raj (1858), the period when India gained national independence and developed its particular economic strategy to cope with the world of Cold War competition (1947), and finally more recent attempts at economic liberalization (1991). Mumbai's ports and free trade zones (FTZs) are sites through which state and non-state actors have channelled their globalization and territorialization projects; this book asks how they have negotiated shifting world orders and dealt with new national strategies at a local level.

The port and zone plans illustrated here, whether realized or stalled, demonstrate how state and non-state actors have repositioned the city within shifting global, regional, and national frameworks. This history calls master narratives on SEZs, often seen as Western projects to deterritorialize developing states, into question, showing the complexity of the zone's usefulness to a variety of actors and its association with territorial forms of organization. This book

5 A. Ong, *Neoliberalism as Exception: Mutations in Citizenship and Sovereignty*, Durham, NC: Duke University Press, 2006; L. Kennedy, *The Politics of Economic Restructuring in India: Economic Governance and State Spatial Rescaling*, Abingdon: Routledge, 2014.

argues that the global history concept of portals of globalization – places in which global flows are particularly dense and institutions have been established to deal with global connectivity – is an important lens for analysing the implementation of globalization projects in local places and the repositioning of these sites in global spatial orders.

Sites of Globalization: Ports and Zones

Although research on globalization tends to focus on flows, connectivity, and circulation, these mobilities are difficult to observe.[6] Processes of globalization become tangible in particular sites such as metropolises, border checkpoints, trading centres, ports, and SEZs. These sites perform a regulatory function in managing globalization. They are the location where various actors with competing projects meet and where these actors institutionalize their competencies in dealing with "the global." Furthermore, these sites may become symbolic points of reference in debates on what it means to live in a global age and how to deal with a global past. Place is, therefore, a methodological entry point to observe globalization projects in action and their effects.

Among studies on place and globalization, Saskia Sassen's work on what she calls global cities is well known. She has closely focused on fixed infrastructure that fosters global mobility.[7] Her work was a major contribution to globalization research because it explained why a world globally connected by, for example, digital networks, remains so place bound. She maintains that globalization is not an all-encompassing "flattening" process but an uneven and partial strategy.[8] Sassen writes: "Global processes are often strategically located/constituted in national spaces, where they are implemented usually with the help of legal measures taken by state institutions. The material and legal infrastructure that makes possible the global circulation of financial capital, for example, is often produced as 'national' infrastructure – even though increasingly shaped

6 For a conceptual discussion on circulation and connections, see: S. Gänger, "Circulation: Reflections on Circularity, Entity, and Liquidity in the Language of Global History", *Journal of Global History* 12 (2017) 3, pp. 303–318; R. Wenzlhuemer, "The Ship, the Media, and the World: Conceptualizing Connections in Global History", *Journal of Global History* 11 (2016) 2, pp. 163–186.

7 S. Sassen, *The Global City: New York, London, Tokyo*, Princeton, NJ: Princeton University Press, 2001; Brenner, *New State Spaces*; D. Harvey, *Spaces of Global Capitalism: Towards a Theory of Uneven Geographical Development*, London: Verso Books, 2006.

8 S. Sassen, "Spatialities and Temporalities of the Global: Elements for a Theorization", *Public Culture* 12 (2000) 1, pp. 215–232, at 219.

by global agendas."[9] She describes the insertion of global agendas into the national as an "unbundling" of national space. This unbundling is both a strategic move by the state (or *nation*, the term she typically uses) to connect the nation's cities to "global circuits", but this unbundling is also an effect of globalization processes that the nation cannot control.[10] In addition to global cities, Sassen writes about other infrastructural forms, namely, the export processing zone (EPZ) or SEZ, originally set up by the state, which have also led to its unbundling but are part of state-based globalization projects. She notes that these sites are also nodal points through which global capital and trade flows are managed.[11]

By the late 1990s, as globalization became a household term, images of EPZs and sweatshops were used as a rallying cry in the alter-globalization movement, popularized by Naomi Klein's book, *No Logo*.[12] Klein explored similar themes of exploitation in her next book, *The Shock Doctrine*.[13] These popular works, however, followed decades of criticism that stemmed from research in the 1970s that identified the zone as a key feature enabling a shift from manufacturing raw materials in the developed world towards low-cost manufacturing in the developing world, that is, the new international division of labour (NIDL).[14] This criticism, which focused on lost employment opportunities in the West, was supported by claims that the zone was a tool for neo-colonial

---

9 Sassen, "Spatialities and Temporalities", p. 218.

10 This argument is best outlined in her book, *Territory, Authority, Rights*, in which she discusses how globalization can be understood as "denationalization": The infrastructures and institutions enabling globalization were originally developed by the state for national purposes but are now used by non-state actors. See: S. Sassen, *Territory, Authority, Rights: From Medieval to Global Assemblages*, Princeton, NJ: Princeton University Press, 2008.

11 S. Sassen, "The Global City: Introducing a Concept", *Brown Journal of World Affairs* 9 (2009) 2, pp. 27–43.

12 N. Klein, *No Logo: Taking Aim at the Brand Bullies*, 2nd edition, New York: Picador, 2002, pp. 195–229. The citation refers to the Picador edition, which describes the practices within a free trade zone in the Philippines in the late 1990s. The publication of this book followed shortly after the 1999 "Battle of Seattle" World Trade Organization protest and became an international bestseller, informing the so-called anti-/alter-globalization movements.

13 N. Klein, *The Shock Doctrine: The Rise of Disaster Capitalism*, New York: Metropolitan Books, 2007.

14 F. Fröbel, J. Heinrichs and O. Kreye, *The New International Division of Labour: Structural Unemployment in Industrialised Countries and Industrialisation in Developing Countries*, Cambridge: Cambridge University Press, 1981. The book was first published in German in 1977 under the title *Die neue internationale Arbeitsteilung: Strukturelle Arbeitslosigkeit in den Industrieländern und die Industrialisierung der Entwicklungsländer*, Reinbek bei Hamburg: Rowohlt, 1977.

practices in former colonies.[15] At the turn of the twenty-first century, criticisms of zones as part of a neo-imperial framework were still prevalent.[16] Historians have looked at the rise of sweatshop labour and its implications for changing patterns of trade and employment.[17] News of objectionable practices in zones and factories can travel quickly through today's social media platforms. Examples include the series of suicides in China's Shenzhen in 2010 and the deadly fire in a Bangladesh factory in 2012.[18] FTZs have been sites in which the inequality produced by global trade and transregional value chains becomes particularly visible.

These zones, EPZs and SEZs, are designated areas in which the state eliminates certain national and local laws and taxes, often to attract foreign investment in the zone in order to generate exports and thereby foreign exchange earnings. Import and export tariffs on goods and other taxes are reduced or removed, and contemporary zones may be associated with tax havens.[19] They are often fenced in and entry and exit is guarded. A study from the International Confederation of Free Trade Unions found that most zones operate in countries with weak labour laws where production in industrial sectors relies on a (usually female) "cheap and compliant workforce."[20] The report notes that, in some instances, the EPZ as a policy tool exempts corporations operating inside the zone from complying with existing national and local labour laws as an inducement to attract foreign investors; however, the report states that the majority of the time governments simply decline to enforce labour laws in zones as part of an informal concession to corporations. These zones are thereby known as

15 T. Takeo, "Free Trade Zones in Southeast Asia", *Monthly Review* 29 (1978) 9, pp. 29–41, at 30; T. Takeo (ed.), *AMPO: Japan–Asia Quarterly Review* 8 and 9 (Special Issue: Free Trade Zones and Industrialization of Asia, 1977) 4, 1–2; A. G. Frank, "Third World Manufacturing Export Production", *The South East Asian Economic Review* 1 (1980) 2, pp. 83–105.

16 For the Indian context, see: S. Ananthanarayanan, "New Mechanisms of Imperialism in India: The Special Economic Zones", *Socialism and Democracy* 22 (2008) 1, pp. 35–60.

17 J. Cowie, *Capital Moves: RCA's Seventy-Year Quest for Cheap Labor*, Ithaca, NY: Cornell University Press, 1999; E. Rosen, *Making Sweatshops: The Globalization of the U.S. Apparel Industry*, Berkeley: University of California Press, 2002.

18 Both of these events received enough media coverage to have dedicated Wikipedia pages: "2012 Dhaka Fire", Wikipedia, https://en.wikipedia.org/wiki/2012_Dhaka_fire (accessed 29 January 2016); "Foxconn Suicides", Wikipedia, https://en.wikipedia.org/wiki/Foxconn_suicides (accessed 29 January 2016).

19 For zones linked to tax havens, see: K. Easterling, *Extrastatecraft: The Power of Infrastructure Space*, London: Verso, 2014, pp. 59–60; R. Palan, *The Offshore World, Sovereign Markets, Virtual Places, and Nomad Millionaires*, Ithaca, NY: Cornell University Press, 2003.

20 S. Perman et al., "Behind the Brand Names: Working Conditions and Labour Rights in Export Processing Zones", International Confederation of Free Trade Unions, 2004, p. 7.

deterritorialized spaces that are cut off from the nation state's authority. They are enclaves that carve out a state's territory for investors.

When zones are generally considered problematic for the sovereignty of nation states, why do states continue to pursue them? The International Labour Organization (ILO) estimates that there were 79 zones in 25 countries in 1975. By 2006, the ILO recorded approximately 3,500 EPZs/SEZs in 130 countries, employing 66 million people.[21] Two articles from 2015 in *The Economist* put the global estimate at 4,300 zones and rising.[22] They have become so ubiquitous that tax enclaves like the Canary Islands have created their own zones.[23] Zones are also currently associated with the tendency towards business service offshoring to the developing world, meaning they are no longer only associated with manufacturing and transport logistics as they were several decades ago.[24] According to the ILO report, the majority of zones can be found in Asia even though as *The Economist* articles highlight, three in four countries host them.

Many of these zones manufacture for export. Ports are often connected to zones in order to enable their exports. Research in economic geography has focused on the links between ports and zones.[25] The most dynamic research with this focus has looked at the port and zone combination as a "space of global articulation" that connects the state and its manufactured exports to global and regional trade routes.[26] These studies are concerned with the changing geographies of ports and how they are embedded in other spaces of power such as states, urban spaces, and regional trade agreements. While ports have historically been understood in terms of their embeddedness within states, the emergence of private terminal operators in the last two decades has shifted the scale

21 J. P. Singa Boyenge, "ILO Database on Export Processing Zones (Revised)", International Labour Office working paper, Geneva, 2007, p. 1.

22 "Special Economic Zones: Political Priority, Economic Gamble", *Economist*, 4 April 2015, http://www.economist.com/news/finance-and-economics/21647630-free-trade-zones-are-more-popular-everwith-politicians-if-not; "Special Economic Zones: Not So Special", *Economist*, 4 April 2015, http://www.economist.com/news/leaders/21647615-world-awash-free-trade-zones-and-their-offshoots-many-are-not-worth-effort-not.

23 ZEC: Zona Especial Canaria/Canary Islands Special Zone website, http://www.zec.org/en/ (accessed 22 September 2015).

24 J. M. Kleibert, "Islands of Globalisation: Offshore Services and the Changing Spatial Divisions of Labour", *Environment and Planning A* 47 (2015) 4, pp. 884–902.

25 E. E. Pollock, "Free Ports, Free Trade Zones, Export Processing Zones and Economic Development", in: B. S. Hoyle and D. Pinder (eds.), *Cityport Industrialization and Regional Development*, Oxford: Pergamon Press, 1981, pp. 37–45; R. J. McCalla, "The Geographical Spread of Free Zones Associated with Ports", *Geoforum* 21 (1990) 1, pp. 121–134.

26 J. J. Wang and D. Olivier, "Port-FEZ Bundles as Spaces of Global Articulation: The Case of Tianjin, China", *Environment and Planning A* 38 (2006) 8, pp. 1487–1503.

of analysis from the port to the terminal and the corporate networks of the terminal operator.[27]

Several authors have linked zones to offshoring practices. James Sidaway has connected EPZs to enclaves, which enables a broader understanding of the space and its association with uneven patterns of development.[28] The EPZ or SEZ is only one form associated with offshoring and enclaving within cities (e.g., gated communities). Likewise, and in more detail, Ronen Palan links the zone to multiple practices of offshoring, which he associates with tax havens and flags of convenience.[29] All of these practices, according to Palan, can be understood as state-based practices, which are highlighted in his work on tax havens, the majority of which are still loosely associated with the British Empire. This form of sovereignty provides investors with a form of security associated with the United Kingdom (UK) and its legal system that cannot be guaranteed in "pure" tax havens.[30] Vanessa Ogle also links the rise of tax havens in the mid-twentieth century with the dismantling of the British Empire.[31] While some elements of her study apply to zones, her work concentrates on finance and tax havens more than the EPZ or SEZ and their physical sites of production. Furthermore, it focuses on the implementation of tax havens in states such as Liberia or the Bahamas but does not address how larger states such as China and India may have dealt with the decline of empire through zones.

In seeking to understand today's connectivity, port cities in particular have been the subject of interdisciplinary scholarship, ranging from ethnographic to historical perspectives. In his history of European port cities and their networks, Michael Miller argues that these ports offer a lens for understanding the history of globalization, that is, how ports, shipping, and trade companies and their networks spanned the globe, and how technology rendered their connectivity possible. Through the lens of port cities and merchant shipping networks, Miller demonstrates the experienced transformation of the world economy over the course of the twentieth century.[32] Building partly on his historical

27 D. Olivier and B. Slack, "Rethinking the Port", *Environment and Planning A* 38 (2006) 8, pp. 1409–1427.

28 J. Sidaway, "Enclave Space: A New Metageography of Development?", *Area* 39 (2007) 3, pp. 331–339.

29 Palan, *Offshore World*.

30 R. Palan, "International Financial Centers: The British-Empire, City-States and Commercially Oriented Politics", *Theoretical Inquiries in Law* 11 (2010) 1, pp. 149–176.

31 V. Ogle, "Archipelago Capitalism: Tax Havens, Offshore Money, and the State, 1950s–1970s", *American Historical Review* 122 (2017) 5, pp. 1431–1458.

32 M. Miller, *Europe and the Maritime World: A Twentieth Century History*, Cambridge: Cambridge University Press, 2012.

approach, sociologist Alice Mah examined how former imperial port cities experience the decline in their global networks and centrality long after the age of empire, showing how the legacy of having once been global is currently articulated at a local scale.[33] Ports and port cities, in these works, are vantage points for understanding local and transnational actors' experiences with shifting global processes. In short, they are sites through which processes of globalization become tangible.

These interdisciplinary and historical works offer port cities as vantage points for understanding shifts in processes of globalization. For these scholars, globalization has not emerged in the last four decades. Through these sites one can observe the history of increasing economic and cultural connectedness on a global scale. Therefore, while the SEZ is associated predominantly with the current phase of globalization, it is worth investigating how creating sites of exception to facilitate global trade have been carried out in the past. Those working on the history of the EPZ specifically have not yet focused on how globalization processes are managed through these sites or how they are connected to the rise of other spatial formats like regional blocs or nation states. Yet, SEZs do have a longer history than much of the current social science research suggests.

Despite a focus on the present, a narrative that contemporary zones have their origins in past colonial free ports, treaty ports, and Hanseatic league ports is common in academic texts on the zone, not to mention news accounts in the media. However, this statement is not a historical claim, but an anecdote meant to engage the reader.[34] A historical work on Livorno's free port ca. 1600 also refers to this free port system as an early example of today's SEZ.[35] These

---

33 A. Mah, *Port Cities and Global Legacies: Urban Identity, Waterfront Work, and Radicalism*, Basingstoke: Palgrave Macmillan, 2014.

34 For example, see: Takeo, "Free Trade Zones", p. 30; K. Y. Wong and D. K. Y. Chu, "Export Processing Zones and Special Economic Zones as Generators of Economic Development: The Asian Experience", *Geografiska Annaler. Series B, Human Geography* 66 (1984) 1, pp. 1–16, at 1; M. Guangwen, "The Theory and Practice of Free Economic Zones: A Case Study of Tianjin, People's Republic of China", PhD dissertation, Ruprecht-Karls University of Heidelberg, 2003; Wang and Olivier, "Port-FEZ Bundles", p. 1487; Ong, *Neoliberalism as Exception*, p. 103; P. Amitendu and S. Bhattacharjee, *Special Economic Zones in India: Myths and Realities*, New Delhi: Anthem Press India, 2008, p. 1; "J. Bach, "Modernity and the Urban Imagination in Economic Zones", *Theory, Culture & Society* 28 (2011) 5, pp. 98–122, at 98–99; A. Aggarwal, *Social and Economic Impact of SEZs in India*, New Delhi: Oxford University Press, 2012, pp. 15–36; K. Easterling, *Extrastatecraft*, pp. 25–69; P. Khanna, *Connectography: Mapping the Global Network Revolution*, New York: Random House, 2016, pp. 279–280.

35 C. Tazzara, *The Free Port of Livorno and the Transformation of the Mediterranean World, 1574–1790*, Oxford: Oxford University Press, 2017.

references between free ports and zones are not grounded in historical research that demonstrates how the free port of the past gave way to the modern SEZ.[36] Instead, historical research on the origins of the zone policy shows that multiple prior policies – such as the United States (US) foreign-trade zone of the 1930s and Puerto Rico's operation bootstrap, among other local inspirations – gave way to a single zone model by the 1970s through the attempts at standardization of various agencies of the United Nations (UN).[37] However, these anecdotes point to an awareness that specific places like ports, metropolitan centres, and zones have served and continue to serve as key nodal points in a globalizing economy. Furthermore, these sites' functionality and character change over time as they are repositioned – and as new actors seek to use these sites to reposition themselves – in new global orders.

Portals of Globalization

This book advances the concept of portals of globalization as an analytical perspective introduced in global history to investigate how global interactions are anchored and managed in particular places. Importantly, this approach has also emerged as a critique of concepts that focus on the novelty of globalization and the global city. This research perspective seeks a nuanced understanding of the history of globalization as well as the key sites that have enabled global connectedness with a particular focus on Mumbai, India.

36 An exception is Corey Tazzara's analysis of zones and past free ports in "Capitalism and the Special Economic Zone, 1590–2014", in: R. Fredona and S. Reinert (eds.), *New Perspectives on the History of Political Economy*, Basingstoke: Palgrave Macmillan, 2018, pp. 75–102.

37 For foreign trade zones, including their ties to free ports, see: R. S. Thoman, *Free Ports and Foreign-Trade Zones*, Cambridge, MD: Cornell Maritime Press, 1956; A. L. Lomax, *The Foreign Trade Zone*, Eugene: University of Oregon, 1947; D. Orenstein, "Foreign-Trade Zones and the Cultural Logic of Frictionless Production", *Radical History Review* (Winter 2011) 109, pp. 36–61. For Puerto Rico, see: P. Neveling, "Export Processing Zones, Special Economic Zones and the Long March of Capitalist Development Policies During the Cold War", in: L. James and E. Leake (eds.), *Negotiating Independence: New Directions in the Histories of the Cold War and Decolonisation*, London: Bloomsbury, 2015, pp. 63–84. For a critique of World Bank narratives of zone origins in free ports, see: P. Neveling, "Free Trade Zones, Export Processing Zones, Special Economic Zones and Global Imperial Formations 200 BCE to 2015 CE", in: I. Ness and Z. Cope (eds.), *The Palgrave Encyclopedia of Imperialism and Anti-imperialism*, Basingstoke: Palgrave Macmillan, 2015, pp. 1007–1016. For the 1970s as a decade of consolidation, see: P. Neveling, "The Global Spread of Export Processing Zones, and the 1970s as a Decade of Consolidation", in: K. Andresen and S. Müller (eds.), *Contesting Deregulation: Debates, Practices and Developments in the West since the 1970s*, Oxford: Berghahn Books, 2017, pp. 23–40.

Building on insights from various disciplines, Ulf Engel and Matthias Middell developed a transdisciplinary research agenda to study contemporary and historical regimes of territorialization and globalization, focusing on the dialectics between these two processes.[38] Globalization is thereby understood as a process of de- and reterritorialization as economic and political actors expand their activities to new markets while also protecting their own markets from competition.[39] In other words, globalization indicates an increase in "flows" in conjunction with attempts to regain control over these flows by various actors. Similarly, Arjun Appadurai describes five cultural flows of globalization, which act as frameworks for how individuals and groups conceive of their own movement and space within the global condition.[40] It is also through these imaginations that we can see globalization as the interplay of flows and controls, which lead to new spatial realities.[41] Globalization can be understood in another sense: as an active political strategy to foster, manage, and perhaps limit changing global connectedness. As Matthias Middell summarizes, "[i]t therefore seems helpful to distinguish between the 'global condition' and 'globalizations'; the first refers to the structural preconditions under which such strategies became and become meaningful, the latter encourages a close analysis of individual and collective reactions to the global condition."[42] Such an understanding of globalization as a strategy rather than a passive process emerging as an effect of (neo)liberalization, the elimination of borders, and technological innovations is based on research in political geography and global history. This understanding forms the basis of portals of globalization: portals are a lens through which not only processes of globalization become tangible, but also where the actors, strategies, and institutions that seek to control flows become visible.

---

38 Engel and Middell, "Bruchzonen der Globalisierung."

39 N. Brenner, "Globalisierung und Reterritorialisierung: Städte, Staaten und die Politik der räumlichen Redemensionierung im heutigen Europa", *WeltTrends* 17 (Winter 1997), pp. 7–30, at 8; Brenner, "Between Fixity and Motion."

40 A. Appadurai, *Modernity at Large: Cultural Dimensions of Globalization*, Minneapolis: University of Minnesota Press, 1996, pp. 27–47.

41 A. Appadurai, "Grassroots Globalization and the Research Imagination", in: A. Appadurai (ed.), *Globalization*, Durham: Duke University Press, 2001, pp. 1–21, at 6–7.

42 M. Middell, "What is Global Studies All About?" *Global Europe: Basel Papers on Europe in a Global Perspective* (2014) 105, pp. 38–49, at 40, https://europa.unibas.ch/fileadmin/europa/redaktion/PDF_Basler_Schriften/BS105.pdf. A similar argument is made in Middell and Naumann, "Global History", p. 152: the authors discuss two meanings of the term globalization, "first, as an objective situation; and second, as a multitude of political projects to redetermine what is meant by interdependence and sovereignty."

Subsequent to Engel and Middell's institutional efforts to promote transdisciplinary research on historical and contemporary globalization and shifting regimes of territorialization, several authors further elaborated on the place in which globalization and regimes of territorialization are negotiated (i.e., portals of globalization) and began to define the concept. Michael Geyer highlights how global flows were channelled and managed as they entered and exited modern societies. He argues that the way in which flows were controlled changed substantially over the course of the nineteenth century with the rise of the nation state.[43] Separately, Matthias Middell emphasizes the institutionalization of portal functions – that is, the accumulation of experience and knowledge in dealing with global connectivity – in certain places such as port cities, metropoles, and financial centres. As a result of the institutionalization of these capacities, these places develop a particular character and may become sites of memory (*lieux de mémoire*) for not only past spatial orders such as empire or commercial networks, but also transnational legacies such as the slave trade.[44]

A further work by Matthias Middell and Katja Naumann closely relates the aforementioned publications with a more concrete research agenda in global history in light of the spatial turn.[45] Their research agenda proposes looking at places where these spaces are negotiated and renegotiated by various actors, which they call portals of globalization.[46] In addition to cities, other places and institutions where "practices for dealing with global connectedness have been developed" such as ports and museums become the location of the research while the focus remains on the actors operating within, beyond, and between such places.[47] They thereby draw from transnational history research methods that responded to the global condition by focusing on connections and entanglements, including in comparative historical analyses.[48] Middell and Naumann write that

43 M. Geyer, "Portals of Globalization", in: W. Eberhard and C. Lübke (eds.), *The Plurality of Europe: Identities and Spaces*, Leipzig: Leipziger Universitätsverlag, 2010, pp. 509–520.

44 M. Middell, "Erinnerung an die Globalisierung? Die Portale der Globalisierung als *lieux de mémoire*. Ein Versuch", in: K. Buchunger (ed.), *Europäische Erinnerungsräume*, Frankfurt am Main: Campus-Verlag, 2009, pp. 296–308.

45 For one of the key works inspiring the spatial turn, see: H. Lefebvre, *La production de l'espace* [*The Production of Space*], D. Nicholson-Smith (trans.), Oxford: Blackwell Publishers, 1991 [1974].

46 Middell and Naumann, "Global History."

47 Ibid., p. 162.

48 J. Kocka and H. Haupt, *Comparative and Transnational History: Central European Approaches and New Perspectives*, New York: Berghahn Books, 2009; M. Werner and B. Zimmerman, "Beyond Comparison: Histoire Croisée and the Challenge of Reflexivity", *History and Theory* 45 (2006) 1, pp. 30–50; M. Espagne, "Comparison and Transfer", in: M. Middell and L. Roura (eds.), *Transnational Challenges to National History Writing*, Basingstoke: Palgrave

such an agenda examines the portal as a "means by which elites try to channel and therefore control the effects of global connectivity (among others, by the creation of political structures and social control)",[49] extending this investigation to past and present sites of global connectivity.[50] Most importantly, what the portals of globalization concept adds to previous spatial turn approaches is the role of actors within particular spaces. It is thereby a lens through which to witness how new spatial orders unravel and how actors manage and are participant in these shifts.

The portals of globalization concept contributes to four key debates regarding globalization. First, it seeks to overcome a narrative of novelty in globalization research by historicizing places in which global interactions are particularly dense.[51] Second, it goes beyond a focus on European actors in directing these processes – as well as moving beyond the inevitability of globalization – to examine connections in other world regions, drawing from Area Studies. Third, the approach does not assume globalization is a process that challenges the nation state. In some cases, opening up certain sites to global capital and trade flows, not to mention human and cultural connections, may be an active state-based strategy. In short, nation states may also be actors driving globalization.[52] While partaking in processes of globalization and seeking to manage connectedness, the nation state has remained a relevant format for societal organization.[53] Finally, the concept of portals of globalization overcomes the much too narrow focus on global and local interactions that characterizes much of global history and global studies research, which tends to bypass the relationship between the local scale and other spatial units. Portals

Macmillan, 2013, pp. 36–53; M. Middell, "Kulturtransfer und Historische Komparatistik – Thesen zu ihrem Verhältnis", *Comparativ: Zeitschrift für Globalgeschichte und vergleichende Gesellschaftsforschung* 10 (2000) 1, pp. 7–41; T. Adam, *Intercultural Transfers and the Making of the Modern World, 1800–2000: Sources and Context*, Basingstoke: Palgrave Macmillan, 2012.

49 Middell and Naumann, "Global History", p. 162.

50 An example of such a perspective is: Y. Cassis, *Capitals of Capital: A History of International Financial Centres, 1780–2005*, Cambridge, Cambridge University Press, 2006. Cassis describes the strategies employed by individual bankers to deal with changing world economic orders within the framework of banking institutions, financial centres (cities), family networks, and the state/empire in which they are embedded. See, for example, pp. 11–15.

51 P. Y. Saunier and S. Ewen (eds.), *Another Global City: Historical Explorations into the Transnational Municipal Moment, 1850–2000*, Basingstoke: Palgrave Macmillan, 2008; A. K. Sandoval-Strausz and N. H. Kwak (eds.), *Making Cities Global: The Transnational Turn in Urban History*, Philadelphia: University of Pennsylvania Press, 2017.

52 Kennedy, *Politics of Economic Restructuring*.

53 I. Löhr and R. Wenzlhuemer (eds.), *The Nation State and Beyond: Governing Globalization Processes in the Nineteenth and Early Twentieth Centuries*, Heidelberg: Springer, 2013.

as a research lens pay close "attention to historically changing, regionally specific, and spatially complex ways in which this relationship between place and global networks takes place."[54]

This approach in global history has drawn inspiration from the spatial turn in history as well as approaches in critical political geography. Much of the literature that focuses on the changing relevance of various spatial scales in the global economy is rooted in neo-Marxist perspectives that seek to understand changes in capitalism, the global economy, and the welfare state in Western countries since the 1970s. David Harvey's work examines the shift from national to subnational scales, as cities became one of the key sites of capital accumulation when city governments shifted their focus from managing the city's services to growth and job creation.[55] Highlighting the specific ways in which states shift their policies in a strategic manner to facilitate connections between local spaces and global markets, Erik Swyngedouw discusses "glocal states"[56] and "glocalization"[57] while Neil Brenner describes "glocal fixes",[58] relating glocal states to global cities. These perspectives form part of broader research approaches to state rescaling, which seek to understand the scalar restructuring within and beyond states as new geographies of power emerge such as global, regional, and urban spaces.[59] Such research focuses on understanding the interactions between these spaces – territories, places, scales, and networks – and seeks to transcend approaches that prioritize one scale while neglecting their relation to one another.[60]

54 C. Baumman, A. Dietze, and M. Maruschke, "Portals of Globalization – An Introduction", *Comparativ: Zeitschrift für Globalgeschichte und vergleichende Gesellschaftsforschung* 27 (2017) 3–4, pp. 7–20, at 9.

55 D. Harvey, "From Managerialism to Entrepreneurialism: The Transformation in Urban Governance in Late Capitalism", *Geografiska Annaler. Series B* 71 (1989) 1, pp. 3–17; D. Harvey, *Spaces of Capital: Towards a Critical Geography*, Edinburgh: Edinburgh University Press, 2001.

56 E. Swyngedouw, "Reconstructing Citizenship, the Re-scaling of the State and the New Authoritarianism: Closing the Belgian Mines", *Urban Studies* 33 (1996) 8, pp. 1499–1521.

57 E. Swyngedouw, "The Mammon Quest: 'Glocalisation,' Interspatial Competition and the Monetary Order – the Construction of New Scales", in: M. Dunford and G. Kafkalas (eds.), *Cities and Regions in the New Europe: The Global-Local Interplay and Spatial Development Strategies*, London: Belhaven Press, 1992, pp. 39–67.

58 N. Brenner, "Global Cities, Glocal States: Global City Formation and State Territorial Restructuring in Contemporary Europe", *Review of International Political Economy* 5 (1998) 1, pp. 1–37.

59 N. Brenner, et al., *State/Space: A Reader*, Malden MA and Oxford: Blackwell, 2003.

60 B. Jessop, N. Brenner and M. Jones, "Theorizing Sociospatial Relations", *Environment and Planning D: Society and Space* 26 (2008) 3, pp. 389–401.

This book contributes to a growing body of empirical research that has emerged following the call to research portals of globalization.[61] It uses portals of globalization as a research lens that helps to focus on the zone and port as state-planned spaces of reterritorialization through which private actors and the state channel their globalization strategies. This research enhances the concept and finds that the state may create "portals" for its own purposes, but it also relies on the individual users of that space to enable its goals. These corporations, investors, and shippers may have very different agendas than the state. Such a perspective shifts the view presented here between the zone or port and the actors who operate within and beyond those spaces. This study helps to clarify how ports and zones are also given meaning through their changing relationality with India's state space, understood here as more than territoriality.[62] That is to say that Mumbai's ports and zones have various and changing scalar connections to India's state space and transnational articulations in ways that are not exclusively glocal.

Several authors from various fields have also seen the zone as a multi-layered site of agency. Jamie Cross, for instance, sees the zone through the lens of many actors and examines the motivations of workers, managers, subnational state officials, and villagers in Andhra Pradesh, India.[63] Jonathan Bach examines how villagers in Shenzhen, China, used the dual legal structure of Chinese citizenship and the fragmented zone space to their financial advantage through playing an important role in the city-zone's growth, a vision not foreseen and even initially unwanted by Chinese officials.[64] Those Chinese officials as well as city managers have since altered the zone policy to informally and formally allow some of these practices. Aihwa Ong has examined the role of women in EPZ manufacturing and the way in which they use the structure of the zone to

---

61 For several special issues and volumes on the concept, each containing numerous empirical articles, see: C. Baumann (ed.), *Universities as Portals of Globalization: Crossroads of Internationalization and Area Studies*, Leipzig: Leipziger Universitätsverlag, 2014; G. Castryck, "Introduction: From Railway Juncture to Portal of Globalization: Making Globalization Work in African and South Asian Railway Towns", *Comparativ: Zeitschrift für Globalgeschichte und vergleichende Gesellschaftsforschung* 25 (2015) 4, pp. 7–16; A. Bashford (ed.), *Quarantine: Local and Global Histories*, Basingstoke: Palgrave Macmillan, 2016; H. Weiss (ed.), *Ports of Globalization, Places of Creolisation: Nordic Possessions in the Atlantic World during the Era of the Slave Trade*, Leiden: Brill, 2016; Baumann, Dietze and Maruschke, "Portals of Globalization."

62 Brenner et al., *State/Space*, p. 9.

63 J. Cross, *Dream Zones: Anticipating Capitalism and Development in India*, London: Pluto Press, 2014.

64 J. Bach, "'They Come in Peasants and Leave Citizens': Urban Villages and the Making of Shenzhen, China", *Cultural Anthropology* 25 (2010) 3, pp. 421–458.

pursue their own goals.[65] This last observation is of course a contested one in that focusing on workers' agency makes them complicit in their own exploitation. What these authors have in common is that the zone is not only a state space or a corporate space of exploitation. It is a space in which individuals channel their own goals. This book builds on these perspectives to show how individuals, corporations, subnational states, and government ministries use the ports and zones in Mumbai area to manage their own transregional agendas.

Investigating Mumbai's ports and zones through the lens of portals of globalization attaches a different meaning to the relevance of the zone and its relation to port projects. The ubiquitous practice of carving out spaces within a territory not only promotes corporate deterritorialization through capital flows.[66] Such a space might also be an active strategy to deal with global connectedness: it can foster new and additional connections between the internal and external while simultaneously seeking to limit the externalities of such global connectedness on the internal (i.e., the rest of the state). Finally, the zone makes the separation of internal and external difficult in that foreign policy and domestic policy become linked through the zone.[67] Though this book does not focus on workers' experiences directly as do many sociologists and anthropologists, portals of globalization perspective is complimentary in that it eliminates the assumed inevitability of such exploitative practices by focusing on the strategic (planned) nature of the zone.

Portals of globalization as a research agenda is also an effort to bring the spatial perspectives of globalization research to the understanding of cultural connections. Though the present enquiry appears to be an economic one, it is interested in the knowledge, the policies, and the practices that emerged in Mumbai to control economic connectivity in a concerted way. These approaches in transnational history are useful in overcoming perspectives that prioritize the nation as the container in which history unfolds; they are also useful in overcoming diffusionist perspectives in public policy and international relations that view policy transfers as occurring between nations and

---

65 A. Ong, *Spirits of Resistance and Capitalist Discipline: Factory Women in Malaysia*, Albany NY: State University of New York Press, 1987.

66 Klein, *No Logo*. For example, an ILO report identifies the EPZ as an "important feature of globalization", indicating that such an inevitable association between the zone and globalization calls for monitoring labour practices in zones by the ILO: International Labour Organization "Employment and Social Policy in Respect of Export Processing Zones (EPZs)", 2003, p. 1, http://www.ilo.org/public/libdoc/ilo/GB/286/GB.286_esp_3_engl.pdf.

67 Agnew, "Territorial Trap."

tend to focus on the act of transfer rather than its content.[68] Portals of globalization have been understood as sites of intercultural transfers as well as places that produce the cultural capital to enable such further transfers.[69] In this book, the zone is seen as a space that has been institutionalized as a particular strategy to deal with global flows. It is also an object of intercultural transfer rather than simply its enabler as state planners look to a variety of zone models around the world and past practices.

Mumbai's Ports and Zones

Mumbai has a particular history that allowed for research on the various applications of the zone and port projects over time and how they relate to shifting spatial orders. Ports offer an interesting vantage point as their planning from a local perspective is rooted in their trading networks, their competition, and their attachments to a state. They must look onwards to their forward and backward linkages as well.[70] In order to be competitive, ports require specific infrastructure to meet shippers' requirements and must maintain competitive tariffs in relation to transit ports or those that also service their hinterlands. In addition to being a port city, Mumbai was originally an archipelago, which has since been filled in to form a peninsula. "Island spatiality" identifies islands as a form that has historically encouraged the establishment of seats of government and trading posts, resulting in major cities.[71] An island city like Mumbai can offer insight into the interplay between how spatialities of power and elites seek to project their economic reach outwards through the transport advantages that the port city offers.

Mumbai is India's primary business city and hosts an important commercial and navel port. The islands that make up Mumbai were settled and claimed by various dynasties and kingdoms. Its importance as a trade centre grew with the Portuguese takeover of the islands in the sixteenth century before they were relinquished to the British Crown in 1659. Soon after, the EIC began offering concessions to entice traders to settle in Bombay and introduced a number of

68 D. Stone, "Transfer Agents and Global Networks in the 'Transnationalization' of Policy", *Journal of European Public Policy* 11 (2004) 3, pp. 545–566.
69 Middell, "Erinnerung an die Globalisierung?" For intercultural transfers, see: Adam, *Intercultural Transfers*.
70 R. Mukherjee (ed.), *Vanguards of Globalization: Port-Cities from the Classical to the Modern*, New Delhi: Primus Books, 2014.
71 A. Grydejøj, "Island City Formation and Urban Island Studies", *Area* 47 (2015) 4, pp. 429–435.

institutions and measures to manage trade. The port city became increasingly central over the course of the nineteenth century to Britain's Indian Ocean trade as the EIC's rule became more territorial. Bombay transitioned from a British enclave along India's western coastline (then ruled by the Maratha Empire) to incorporate the hinterlands. In the 1840s, Bombay became the capital of the Bombay Presidency and more institutions were developed to enhance the port's trade, especially in opium and cotton. In addition to instituting a port trust in the 1870s, a number of institutions such as the University of Bombay were developed in the city during the mid-nineteenth century. After Indian independence in 1947, Bombay became the capital of the state of Bombay and later Maharashtra. The city remained India's primary business city and the port received a "major" port classification, meaning that its status as a port trust remained under the central government's authority but was independently administered. Bombay Port also endured as a naval port for the Indian navy. This classification has remained until today.[72]

Throughout these transitions, Mumbai maintained a degree of significance for the various territorial entities to which the city was attached. However, its positionality within these structures – the British Empire and British India as well as post-1947 independent India – was as uncertain as its positionality within trading networks. As Meera Kosambi stresses, the city's positionality was not just natural, though it did have a protected harbour. It became important due to the growing political power of the EIC on India's west coast.[73] The city not only survived transitions in a national context but also on a global and regional scale over the last century and a half: the implementation of "free trade" within the British Empire, decolonization and the Cold War, as well as neoliberalization and the introduction of the South Asian Free Trade Area (SAFTA). Planners at various levels of government, merchants, and businesses responded to these shifting spatial orders and sought to retain or regain the

---

72 For histories of the city, see: M. Kosambi, *Bombay in Transition: The Growth and Social Ecology of a Colonial City, 1880–1980*, Stockholm: Almqvist & Wiksell International, 1986; M. Kosambi, "Bombay and Poona: A Socio-Ecological Study of Two Indian Cities, 1650–1900", PhD diss., Stockholm University, 1980; N. Fernandes, *City Adrift: A Short Biography of Bombay*, New Delhi: Aleph, 2013; Frank Broeze, "The External Dynamics of Port City Morphology: Bombay 1815–1914", in: I. Banga (ed.), *Ports and Their Hinterlands in India (1700–1950)*, New Delhi: Manohar Publications, 1992, pp. 247–272; S. Hazareesingh, *The Colonial City and the Challenge of Modernity: Urban Hegemonies and Civic Contestations in Bombay City (1900–1925)*, Hyderabad: Orient Longman, 2007.
73 For texts on the city's positionality, see: M. Kosambi, "Commerce, Conquest and the Colonial City: Role of Locational Factors in the Rise of Bombay", *Economic and Political Weekly* 20 (1985) 1, pp. 32–37; J. Masselos, "Changing Definitions of Bombay: City State to Capital City", in: Banga (ed.), *Ports and Their Hinterlands*, pp. 273–316.

city's positionality under new circumstances. Some of these plans involved preparing new port infrastructure, building new ports, and implementing FTZs or other incentives. Mumbai's ports and zones are a lens through which to understand how a variety of actors use place to enable their globalization projects, how these projects connect to local initiatives, and in what way they are entwined with territorial strategies.

India's SEZ Act from 2005 signalled India's plans to enhance and control global flows of capital and goods into and out of India in specific locations.[74] This act was also a shift from the prior use of EPZs in India in terms of policy and its scope. In 1965, India's first zone was established at Kandla, and several zones were subsequently established throughout India, including in Bombay. These zones were developed by the central government and gave businesses that operated inside the zones tax incentives to manufacture for export. Under changing circumstances, the zone policy has shifted considerably. Under the current act, private developers are now encouraged to acquire land for SEZ projects and develop the infrastructure for their own private profit, sometimes in collaboration with public companies. The space within the SEZ can include a non-processing area including residential areas, commercial space, and social infrastructure. Since 2015, the non-processing area's social infrastructure may also be used by persons and entities outside the zone, that is, dual use infrastructure. In terms of quantity, until the 1980s, there were just two EPZs in India. Before the 2000s, there were only seven EPZs. Since the announcement of the 2005 SEZ policy, as of 31 March 2018, there are 223 operational SEZs around India and hundreds more in the planning phase, according to India's Ministry of Commerce.[75]

Research on Indian SEZs has been more concerned with the current development of the policy than with the policy's history in India. Current SEZ research has been dynamically connected to state-based strategies for dealing with and fostering globalization. The SEZ policy is seen as part of a state rescaling strategy, linked to India's ongoing economic liberalization since the 1980s.[76] Such an approach is fruitful for understanding the SEZ as a form of an active state-based strategy for dealing with global connectedness.[77] Loraine Kennedy's research on India's political economy helps explain why the SEZ emerged as part of India's territorial restructuring as a strategy to increase

---

74 For the 2005 act, see: Aggarwal, *Social and Economic Impact.*

75 "Fact Sheet on Special Economic Zones", Special Economic Zones in India website, http://sezindia.nic.in/upload/5b16778e5e714FACTSHEETupdationonSEZIndia.pdf (accessed 23 July 2018).

76 Kennedy, *Politics of Economic Restructuring.*

77 Brenner, *New State Spaces.*

private (foreign and domestic) investment in key areas. On the surface, the policy seems neoliberal, or at the very least like a deterritorialization process whereby enclaves within India are carved out by major corporations that use the space for their own profit. However, as Kennedy argues, the state still has a strong, central regulatory authority over such private or public-private spaces. Furthermore, the policy framework for the SEZ plays out differently in India's subnational states.[78] Each represents different political spaces, and the various ways in which the SEZ policy is implemented reflects India's federal democracy, which sets the Indian SEZ apart from zones in other contexts. Such perspectives overcome assumptions that India's economic liberalization (and the associated SEZ policy) has been imposed or that the outcomes of these liberalization policies were not intentional.[79] This research supports Aihwa Ong's argument that neoliberalism can take on different forms in non-Western contexts. The state may use the rhetoric of market rationality to govern its population and territory in particular ways.[80]

Mumbai hosts one of India's larger ports as well as one of its first SEZs. Mumbai Port's docks were built on the current site starting in the 1870s, though a number of private ports lined the shoreline prior to that period. As early as the 1830s, plans for designating Bombay a free port were drafted. Later, land companies speculated on reclaimed land and built a series of for-profit docks along the foreshore. The port trust was established in 1873 to centralize the harbour's management. During the course of British rule, Bombay became the "gateway to India." Post-independence, the port's docks as well as the city's expansion led to constraints on the harbour space. Committees soon thereafter explored sites for a future port expansion, which culminated in not only Kandla Port Trust (KPT) and zone in Gujarat during the 1950s and 1960s, which were meant to relieve pressure on Bombay Port, but later a port at Nhava Sheva across Mumbai's harbour (1989), which now plans to establish an SEZ for manufacturing.[81] Mumbai has hosted Santacruz Electronics Export Processing Zone (SEEPZ) since 1973. It was the second zone established in India after the one near Kandla Port.

This book's perspective is historical, though it relies on Kennedy's contemporary assessment of zones as strategic state spaces. Though Kennedy identifies

78 R. Jenkins, L. Kennedy, and P. Mukhopadhyay (eds.), *Power, Policy, and Protest: The Politics of India's Special Economic Zones*, New Delhi: Oxford University Press, 2014.

79 Kennedy, *Politics of Economic Restructuring*, p. 3.

80 Ong, *Neoliberalism as Exception.*

81 Kandla Port Trust has been recently renamed to Deendayal Port Trust.

the zone as an internal restructuring of the state that is part of a strategy to deal with global connectivity, such a view can be extended to understanding the use of the zone as a tool to resituate Mumbai or India in different contexts and time periods within prevailing world orders and regional arenas. Such an approach understands the zone as a state-based spatial policy to deal with global connectedness in periods beyond the temporal scope of neoliberalism as a governing and market expanding strategy since the 1980s. Instead, creating enclaves, carving out spaces, and making exceptions is part of a wider practice of how territorial regimes seek to articulate and manage global and regional connectedness by channelling that connectedness through particular places.

The Structure of This Book and Its Sources

After discussing the first failed attempt by local merchants to implement a free port in Bombay in 1833, Chapters 2 and 3 look at plans in the 1860s to try to enhance the port's infrastructure by giving concessions to private firms to build port facilities. The newly consolidated Government of India took control of the port in the 1870s, creating the port trust model that still operates India's public ports today. Chapters 4 and 5 analyse the first two FTZs in India at Kandla and Bombay. Though UN agencies promoted a single-model zone in the 1970s, India's zones never completely conformed to these standards. Through the lens of zones and ports in Bombay and India's west coast, multiple model zones rather than a single policy model become evident, and India's zones emerged without significant policy interventions from Western development agencies. Though the Government of India had hoped that companies established by Indians living abroad could use the zones to export to Western countries, these family networks also used the zones to trade with the Soviet Union (USSR) through India's trade agreement with Eastern Europe. Chapters 6 and 7 discuss the 2000/2005 SEZ policy in light of a number of new trade incentives. Abroad, the Government of India is using the SEZ in its foreign policy to enhance trans-regional trade connections through Iran and Afghanistan, linked to Mumbai. Domestically, the government uses zones to encourage investment from Japanese firms in India. While the central government focuses on facilitating these connections, particularly through Mumbai, the local business elite and the state government in Mumbai are more concerned with using these zones to promote Mumbai as a global city by rebuilding its infrastructure and potentially eliminating its port to open up prime real estate along the foreshore.

Together, these six chapters highlight the interplay between overlapping and at times competing globalization and territorialization projects unfolding in Mumbai. They show how actors from different scales and sectors use sites and policies like zones and ports to further their goals. The long timespan accompanied by a focus on moments of change – the British Raj, independence, liberalization – in addition to global and regional shifts – such as free trade, an expanding British Empire, decolonization, the Cold War, the advent of neoliberalism, and the rise of regional blocs – can also be observed from this vantage point. These chapters demonstrate that these sites of transregional connectivity not only respond to shifts but also seek to alter them. Individuals, corporations, subnational states, and government ministries use the ports and zones in the Mumbai area to channel their own globalization agendas. These agendas are not opposed to territorialization but are also part of this process. However, this book's contribution highlights that different actors drive these processes. Though the state seeks to forge transregional connections, it relies on non-state actors to do so, adding to the contingency of these projects.

This book's timespan and multi-scalar approach necessitated research in multiple locations and archives, notably in the British Library's India Office Records, the Central Secretariat Library in New Delhi, and various institutions in Mumbai, including the business library at the Indian Merchants' Chamber named the F.E. Dinshaw Commercial and Financial Reference Library.[82] Annual reports by Indian government ministries and Mumbai business chambers were also consulted. These annual reports support a variety of other sources from subnational states, international agencies, and foreign trade organizations. Newspaper articles and industry periodicals were an additional source used in the last two chapters, which follow the developments of the SEZ and Indian ports since the early 2000s.[83]

Business chambers are key institutions that collect trade, market, and economic data in local, national, regional, and global contexts. They also seek to coordinate policy development with governments, serving as an interface between government and prominent business houses and trade organizations. In India, they operate as private institutions and are not state mandated as in

82 This organization has recently changed its name to IMC Chamber of Commerce and Industry.

83 Since the 1980s, annual reports of business chambers and ministries became increasingly superficial. Rather than detailing meetings over several pages, a brief sentence might indicate the date of a meeting and the topic without specifying its contents. This became especially apparent in business chambers' reports. Presumably, new technology makes letter writing a less relevant style of communication between the chambers and government, and these conversations may not be captured and archived for future reference. To help supplement the loss of information from annual reports, the final two chapters refer extensively to newspaper articles found online and in trade journals.

many European countries. For the earliest sections of this history before Indian independence in 1947, reports from the Bombay Chamber of Commerce through the 1880s were used. This business chamber was founded in the late 1830s, but lost its favourable position following independence in 1947. The Bombay Port Trust annual reports were also accessed as well as those from private intuitions like the Elphinstone Land and Press Company, which built private ports in Bombay. The Indian Merchants' Chamber, which has represented Indian merchants in Mumbai since the early 1900s, gained legitimacy as one of city's key business institutions following independence. The Bombay Chamber of Commerce and Industry fell out of favour with the government during the period following independence due to its previous close connection with British business houses and the colonial government. The Indian Merchants' Chamber's annual reports from the 1940s onwards provide a rich understanding of India's and Mumbai's business and economic history written from a contemporary perspective. Both the Bombay Chamber of Commerce and Industry and the Indian Merchants' Chamber compiled correspondence between the chamber and government, which detailed Indian economic policy debates, including debates on FTZs and free ports and updates to the port sector.

The portals of globalization lens looks at ports and zones as strategies exercised by state agents, local administrators, and economic elites. This book thereby also relies on government reports from multiple ministries. Contrasting these reports also opens up the state to show the multiple actors and ministries on several levels of government that at times conflict in their strategies to deal with India and Mumbai's place in the world. These documents include the Bombay/Mumbai Port Trust annual reports, the Ministry of Commerce export promotion committee documents, the KPT annual reports, the Jawaharlal Nehru Port Trust annual reports, the Ministry of Transport (now Ministry of Shipping) annual reports, and various individual reports on EPZs from the Ministry of Electronics, the Ministry of Finance, and the Ministry of Mining and Steel. Each chapter indicates, where necessary, the implications of using particular sources or the shortcomings of these documents. In several cases, it was possible to establish a relatively reliable view of each institution since its founding, which includes in some contexts both the British Indian ministry and its continuation after independence.

In researching this book, I also talked to people at relevant institutions in Mumbai, which was helpful in gaining background insight from local economic elite. These interviews are not cited because, though I received permission to cite certain individuals, the material was not directly related or not the only source of information and could be found in official reports. Indirectly, these meetings were vital for understanding the dynamics of the city, India, and its ports. Between 2012 and 2014, I met with the traffic manager of Mumbai Port Trust and twice with the legal department at the Jawaharlal Nehru Port Trust. I also met with three local teams of third-party logistics companies. Additionally, I met with representatives from Forbes and Co., one of the oldest business houses in the city, the Indian Merchants' Chamber, the Bombay Chamber of Commerce and Industry, Mumbai First, Ernst & Young, environmental advocates, and the Consul General for the Netherlands. These meetings were also complemented by business events at Mumbai's stock exchange and academic talks throughout the city. These discussions helped to inform the views reflected here and indirectly contributed to this research.

Recognizing the constructed nature of space within these sources has been key to reading them. Spatial frameworks are defined not only by historical actors but also by historians who may, through the lens of their own time, impose their views of the present day on the past. The term spatial framework is used here to indicate ideas of space and how they are categorized based on normative ideas framed within a spatial order. The aforementioned sources, too, have at times justified ministerial and government projects through such spatial frameworks. The way in which space is categorized can have a considerable impact on economies, citizenship rights, and access to social services. Some of these issues are discussed in this book. These different ways of categorizing space, that is, producing spatial frameworks, enriches this book by highlighting the flexibility of the zone in enabling interactions with perceived spatial frameworks that may work towards the development of new spatial orders. In short, through portals of globalization we may witness how new spatial orders emerge and how actors seek to reposition their societies within them.

This book originates from a PhD dissertation in Global Studies at Leipzig University in 2016. It has been substantially reworked for the Collaborative Research Centre "Processes of Spatialization under the Global Condition", established in 2016 at Leipzig University with the generous support of the German Research Foundation (DFG). This empirical study, based on field and archival work in India's vibrant economic metropolis, combines a *longue durée* observation of the concrete practice of formatting space with the theoretical ambition of formulating categories for an innovative interpretation of processes of respatialization inspired by recent developments in the growing field of global history.

2 Freeing the Port and Winning Land, 1830s–1860s

Bombay's rise to British India's primary port has been a key point of enquiry addressed by a number of scholars.[84] The first English factory was established on the island in 1668, but the port did not become central to British trade on India's west coast until over a century later. Port historians point out that the harbour was naturally protected from weather conditions and its central location on India's coastline made it ideally suited as the site of British commerce in India. However, nature had not positioned the port ideally within British imperial trade networks. The growing political power of the EIC turned it into the thriving commercial city it eventually became by the early nineteenth century.[85]

The early nineteenth century is also the start of another tendency in the company's history, which involved the shift from controlling coastal enclaves and forging trade deals to controlling territory. Some scholars have researched how the EIC overtime began to operate as a hybrid state-corporation that, on the one hand, paid its shareholders and, on the other hand, minted coins, built cities, and entered into negotiations with foreign powers.[86] Recently, Rupali Mishra's account of the company's early history shows that the EIC was from the start inseparable from the English state.[87] However, for India and Bombay, becoming territorial changed the city's position within the company's trading networks. Manu Goswami writes that "[t]erritorial consolidation involved the attempted monopolization of regulatory powers by an increasingly centralized apparatus, the development of an elaborate, hierarchical bureaucracy that surveyed, mapped, and measured both land and people, the deepening and widening of the administrative and military reach of the state, and a determined reinvestment in epistemic modalities of rule."[88] By the early nineteenth century, British rule in India became increasingly territorial and by 1857 the

---

84 A section of this chapter has been previously published in M. Maruschke, "Managing Shifting Spatial Orders: Planning Bombay's Free Port and Free Zone, 1830s–1980s", *Comparativ: Zeitschrift für Globalgeschichte und vergleichende Gesellschaftsforschung* 27 (2017) 3–4, pp. 21–40.

85 Kosambi, "Commerce, Conquest and the Colonial City."

86 P. J. Stern, *The Company-State: Corporate Sovereignty and the Early Modern Foundations of the British Empire in India*, New York: Oxford University Press, 2011.

87 R. Mishra, *A Business of State: Commerce, Politics, and the Birth of the East India Company*, Cambridge, MA: Harvard University Press, 2018.

88 M. Goswami, *Producing India: From Colonial Economy to National Space*, Chicago: University of Chicago Press, 2004, p. 31.

https://doi.org/10.1515/9783110615135-002

"colonial regime made territorially comprehensive claims to rule" in India, at which point the EIC was relieved of its position as colonial administrator of India.[89] This process of "producing India" resulted in a highly uneven and fragmented state space.

The production of a state space in India did not happen overnight but rather over the course of the nineteenth century. Bombay, too, transitioned from a city with trade connections to specific ports to a city that was also part of a scalar hierarchical structure of governance and a seat of political power. During the early 1800s, the EIC acquired Gujarat and soon after the Maratha territory came under the control of the company.[90] This transition motivated many merchants to move to Bombay to establish their new base. According to Jim Masselos, "Bombay Town in consequence became the seat for the control of a widespread Presidency, the city state was no longer confined within a minute surrounding area, it had become the capital of a major region."[91] This transformation of Bombay's territory coincided with a political transition in which Bombay was no longer an isolated port but a capital city. As a result, Bombay's inland areas became the port's hinterland rather than its maritime network of forward and backward linkages. Until that time, the hinterlands could be described as the coastal ports such as those in Gujarat that served as feeder ports, sending raw cotton to Bombay, which would then be shipped to Britain or China. This transition from port city to presidency capital was part of a wider trend in the British Indian Ocean; the first phase included gaining control of the port, much like previous European maritime powers such as the Dutch East India Company, before later controlling (industrialized) production, which entailed taking control of territory in order to direct the production process.[92]

As part of this transition, Bombay's economic elite and government officials – both in bureaucratic and technical capacities – began to strategize the town's shifting positionality in British imperial space. Some of these competing strategies involved trade incentives for merchants. Others involved financial incentives for the development of the "necessary" land and infrastructure for Bombay to thrive in a new imperial order. This chapter describes both projects from the 1830s and the 1860s, respectively. It shows that while the first plan sought to enhance

89 Ibid., p. 31.

90 Lakshmi Subramanian provides a more detailed overview of the changing political situation on India's west coast and the effects on Indian merchants operating there: L. Subramanian, *Three Merchants of Bombay: Doing Business in Times of Change*, New Delhi: Penguin Books India, 2012, pp. 17–30.

91 Masselos, "Changing Definitions of Bombay", p. 287.

92 M. Pearson, *The Indian Ocean*, Abingdon: Routledge, 2003, p. 192.

Bombay's connectedness within a British imperial trade framework, the second plan, while based on the cotton boom and enhanced trade between Bombay and Lancashire, increasingly looked inward as infrastructure development itself became profitable. Both plans, however, make evident the tension between the territorializing and globalizing plans of government officials and merchants. Both plans sought to reposition the city by forging external connections and by better linking the city to (or raising its profile within) a territorializing multi-scalar government in India.

A Free Port for Bombay?

In 1813 and 1833, changes within the company reshaped the way trade was carried out throughout the empire. As a chartered company, the EIC controlled British trade between the so-called East Indies and Britain. Private merchants operated the trade within the East Indies, basically, any intra-Asian trade, including that between China and India.[93] The EIC, unlike other European trading companies, allowed extensive private participation in trade, making the organization extremely flexible.[94] Through the company's later territorial expansion, it was able to control trade flows while not always participating directly in that trade itself.

Controlling the opium trade was one important factor driving the company's territorial expansion. Opium grown in Malwa, part of the Maratha territory, was being exported through Portuguese-controlled outposts such as Goa and then shipped to Macao, which depressed the price of the company's Bengal opium. After unsuccessfully trying to control the Malwa trade, the company allowed Malwa opium to be transported to Bombay for a small transit duty. By 1831, 90 per cent of the Malwa opium passed through Bombay. Exports of opium from India to China grew from approximately 4,000 chests at the turn of the nineteenth century to 23,000 chests by 1833. By 1843, the company

93 K. N. Chaudhuri, *The English East India Company: The Study of an Early Joint-Stock Company 1600–1640*, London: Routledge/Thoemmes Press, 1999 [1965]; K. N. Chaudhuri, *The Trading World of Asia and the English East India Company, 1660–1760*, Cambridge: Cambridge University Press, 2006 [1978].

94 P. Marshall, "Private British Trade in the Indian Ocean before 1800", in: A. Das Gupta and M. N. Pearson (eds.), *India and the Indian Ocean, 1500–1800*, Calcutta: Oxford University Press, 1987, pp. 276–300; O. Prakash, "The English East India Company and India", in: H. V. Bowen, M. Lincoln and N. Rigby (eds.), *The Worlds of the East India Company*, Suffolk: The Boydell Press, 2002, pp. 1–18.

conquered Sind, the territory with the only remaining ports in India that shipped non-company opium.[95] Territorialization is generally ascribed to the late nineteenth century and the emergence of new technologies such as extensive railroads. Asserting control over commodities was also part of the process of integrating India's inland areas to British political and economic control along coastal enclaves.

Though the company controlled the production of opium in India, it did not actually ship opium itself. By 1813 the EIC had lost its exclusive trading rights to and from Asia due to the "free trade" lobby at Lancashire's manufacturing industries.[96] The profitable tea trade from China to England was the last remaining commodity to which the company had exclusive rights. Opium was only a means to an end as it was meant to balance trade in order to purchase tea, which was in heavy demand in Britain. If the company had participated directly in shipping opium, it would have jeopardized the company's trading rights in China. Instead, Parsi (Zoroastrians of Persian descent living in India, especially Bombay) and European agency houses, including many in Bombay, procured the opium crop and shipped it to China, a practice that had become highly profitable by 1820.[97] Bombay was an important node in the opium network along with Singapore, where opium was transshipped, and Canton, its final destination. The constructed regional and transregional division of trade at this time is worth noting: "Asians" could participate openly in trade within the Indian Ocean (including both Asia and the eastern coast of Africa), while Europeans participated in the trade between Asia and Europe. Bombay's positionality in this system ensured both the accumulation of wealth by the city's merchants and the need to create more and better docking facilities on the island.

The Charter Act of 1833 reorganized the EIC's control over India. It not only limited the legislative powers of the governors of Madras and Bombay but also turned the Governor General of Bengal into the Governor General of India. Thus, a process of state building was underway, which could be considered a combination of territorial expansion, upscaling, and simultaneous state decentralization.[98] As more competencies fell under the authority of a growing

---

95 N. Robins, *The Corporation that Changed the World: How the East India Company Shaped the Modern Multinational*, London: Pluto Press, 2012, pp. 159, 166.
96 J. Keay, *The Honourable Company: A History of the English East India Company*, New York: Macmillan Publishing House, 1991, pp. 451–453.
97 Ibid., pp. 454–455.
98 E. Thompson and G. T. Garratt, *Rise and Fulfilment of British Rule in India*, Allahabad: Central Book Depot, 1962, p. 473.

Government of India, the Government of India was also in a process of decentralizing itself financially from Bengal Presidency. These transitions produced not only many opportunities but also anxieties in Bombay.

The way trade was managed within the newly forming India and in the empire as a whole were major factors pushing for changing port practices in Bombay. Local merchants advocated siting a free port in Bombay based on changes in shipping within the empire, the territorial restructuring of India, as well as specific problems with shipping charges in Canton. Mariam Dossal writes that "Bombay merchants felt they would be able to hold their own if trade incentives were provided, import and export duties withdrawn, and Bombay declared a free port."[99] Merchants floated three proposals to the government, all of which involved changes in warehousing at the docks and customs fees. The most extensive proposal and the one perceived to be most useful was named the "Free Port or Entrepôt for China Goods" model. Doveton and Bruce, the firm that formed the committee to consider the plan, described the situation in Canton and port competition as motivating factors. These factors external to Bombay prompted the city's merchants to search for models to reorganize local port and customs procedures. However, their enthusiasm was hindered by Bombay's incorporation into India, a territorializing state.

The plan was meant to reorganize trade between Canton and Bombay and ultimately between Bombay and British ports. Although Bombay was an important port in the opium trade with Canton, there were few goods traders could bring back to Bombay, which meant that ships were only fully laden in one direction. Furthermore, the way that ships were charged customs fees at Canton was favourable to larger vessels because ships paid similar fees regardless of size.[100] These merchants proposed that, by allowing goods to be imported and (re)exported from Bombay freely with very limited charges to cover costs, Bombay could become an entrepôt between China and Britain. Opium traders could ship opium to Canton and return to Bombay with tea. Traders from Britain would only have to sail as far as Bombay for tea rather than to China.

The Government of Bombay was not entirely drawn in by the proposal but recognized that in wake of the change to a free trade system a new business environment was emerging. In 1834, the Government of Bombay sent a questionnaire to various firms to seek their opinion on the matter. Replies were

---

99 M. Dossal, *Imperial Designs and Indian Realities: The Planning of Bombay City, 1845–1875*, New Delhi: Oxford University Press, 1991, pp. 143–144.

100 B. Doveton and W. C. Bruce to L. R. Reid, 20 January 1834, p. 3 (Z/E/4/14/D557, 1834–1837), India Separate Revenue Department (ISRD), General Correspondence (GC), India Office Records (IOR), British Library (BL).

received from some of the most prominent businesses such as Forbes and Co., Remington and Co., Nicol and Co., B. and A. Hormusjee and Co., Leckie and Co., Adam Skinner and Co., Thomas Crawford, Roger de Faria and Co., and Jamsetjee Jejeebhoy and Co.[101] Just a few years later, many of these individuals and firms founded the Bombay Chamber of Commerce and Industry, which pushed for several of the future key port developments. The questionnaire asked merchants to analyse the trade situation not only in Bombay but also within the trading network of the empire. These questions related to their experience and knowledge of Singapore as a model free port and whether such a system in Singapore was harmful to Bombay's trade, or whether Bombay should form part of a system of free ports that would link it to Singapore.[102] The questions also dealt with how to balance the interests of private traders who were vital to the city and presidency's success with the need for public revenue under the current shifting circumstances of Bombay as a seat of presidency.[103]

They were in search of a model, but each group of actors had different motivations for controlling trade in Bombay, and no model could truly satisfy all interests. Popular opinion among Indian and European merchants, at least those prominent enough to be sent the questionnaire, was in favour of turning Bombay into a free port. Despite references to Singapore, the proposal suggested something along the lines of a modified bonded warehouse. The bonded warehouse system had been implemented at several ports in Britain since the early 1800s, which could be tailored to Bombay. Bombay's merchants advocated a bonded warehouse for all goods meant for re-export. In contrast, the Government of Bombay advocated a bonded warehouse specifically for "China goods" that were to be re-exported, thus directing very specific trade flows without losing customs revenue.[104] The debates within these letters between Bombay merchants, the Government of Bombay, and the Government of India relate to whether this system should be confined to "China goods"; whether only Bombay or a system of ports should be reformed; or whether other locations might be more favourable. These letters compared port practices in Calcutta and Madras to Bombay, Singapore, Canton, Cape Town, and British "home ports."

101 Dossal, *Imperial Designs*, p. 144.

102 The survey never specified what respondents knew of Singapore, but it was assumed to be a system with both few trade restrictions and few levies on trade.

103 "Queries for Answers", Fort William, 19 May, no. 5. Govt. Dept. 1834, ISRD, GC, IOR, BL.

104 Separate Department letter to the Court of Directors of the East India Company, 25 July 1834, ISRD, GC, IOR, BL.

By 1833, the Government of Bombay could no longer act entirely on its own to implement such a scheme but needed to defer to the Government of India. The latter validated the argument that converting Bombay into a free port by eliminating import and export duties would increase shipping and trade, but it objected to providing specific incentives at one port without taking into consideration its acquired territory as a whole. It was deemed more expedient by the Government of India to become acquainted with the various systems of ports within the three presidencies that formed the "British Territories in India" so that it could reform customs practices as a single, unified system rather than a piecemeal promotion.[105] This view changed Bombay's position from a port within a system of ports connected together through their trading patterns to a port controlled by a territorial power with an interest in controlling its activities. Its practices no longer needed to be connected to practices in "foreign" ports such as Canton, Singapore, or British homeports, but rather to other "Indian" ports. Therefore, while merchants in Bombay still saw Bombay as a port connected to its trading networks, the government began to see it as part of a territorial system that required uniform management.

Regardless of the decision to turn down the free port proposal, by the 1850s, Bombay had become an entrepôt for the export of opium to China and the cotton trade to and from India, despite not having ever been a free port. Bombay's first cotton mills were established by local entrepreneurs using the proceeds of this trade. The extension of the company's territorializing rule in Bombay was paramount to the establishment of Bombay as the main port on India's west coast in both the opium and the cotton trade. However, incorporating this territory into a larger scalar framework had also hindered local plans to promote the port's trade.

The Cotton Connection

Despite having failed to implement their free port plan, merchants, shippers, and financiers often referred to the docks provided by the Government of Bombay as a free port, though many items required the payment of customs duties. They did so because the government docks in Bombay were provided free of charge to merchants regardless of trade. They did not pay docking fees to use the facilities and only paid for storage at the government godowns (warehouses) if the goods stayed

105 "Note prepared by the Secretary to Government in the General Department", 25 April 1834, ISRD, GC, IOR, BL.

there longer than the allotted period of several days. Therefore, the charge was not really a service fee, but rather an incentive to quickly clear goods from the godowns. The port was free in a different manner; it still allowed for the collection of customs. The term "free port" was not really a standardized policy but referred to a number of ways to make a port "free." European and Indian merchants active in Bombay viewed these services as a right and referred to Bombay colloquially as a free port. Though Bombay did not become a free port – that is, one considered free by the government – the port was booming and merchants needed additional docking and warehouse space in the harbour.

In 1857, after the Indian Rebellion, also known as the Sepoy Mutiny, in northern and central India, an uprising that challenged British rule, Britain reorganized its control over the Indian subcontinent. The EIC was dissolved, and the British Crown directly controlled India under a reorganized administration in 1858, though the first non-company governor was appointed to Bombay only in 1862. Bombay was untouched by the rebellion itself. In terms of administration, however, the Bombay Presidency had to contend with a stronger Government of India run out of Calcutta. In effect, much of the bureaucracy left by the EIC remained but was rebranded under the creation of the India Office in London, the Secretary of State for India, and the Viceroy of India, formerly the Governor General of India that had been formed in 1833. In terms of planning, documented correspondence in the records of the Bombay Chamber of Commerce point to an alleged rivalry between the two governments and the prioritization of Calcutta in terms of planning while Bombay, according to the members of the chamber, was left to deal with global and imperial changes in trade and shipping on its own terms.[106]

Coinciding with the administrative shifts in India, the outbreak of the American Civil War (1861–1865) gave Bombay traders an economic opportunity. The first boon for Indian producers came at the end of the eighteenth century, along with a shortfall in Chinese agriculture. Merchants from Bombay were able to fill the gap with exports of raw cotton. Agency houses in Bombay were established to handle this trade and maintained representatives at their branch offices in Canton.[107] Parsis who had heretofore profited from the opium trade

106 Annual reports from the Bombay Chamber of Commerce point to a suspected conspiracy to interfere with telegrams between London and Bombay (in effect when steamers reached Suez) to the benefit of merchants in Calcutta. The chamber claimed that every time a steamer carrying telegrams was announced, interruptions on the line immediately followed. The chamber even offered a reward for the parties responsible. See: Bombay Chamber of Commerce and Industry, 1864–1865, Annual Report, pp. xxxvii–xl, Asia Pacific & Africa (APA), BL.
107 Ibid., pp. 430–431.

shifted to the cotton trade during the mid-1800s, just as they had previously shifted from cotton to opium at the turn of the nineteenth century.[108] In the early 1860s, as American cotton was no longer accessible, Bombay's cotton trade became central to local export promotion schemes and port policies.

Britain was the largest consumer of American cotton, woven in the textile mills of Lancashire. Prior to the American Civil War, US cotton accounted for 77 per cent of the cotton consumed in Britain, 90 per cent of cotton in France, 60 per cent in Germany, and 92 per cent in Russia.[109] During the American Civil War, not only was cotton production in the American South compromised, but also the blockade of southern ports meant that cotton could not be shipped to Lancashire. Egyptian cotton was considered the best replacement for the supply shortfall, but Indian cotton (short-staple as opposed to long-staple) was also a decent substitute. By the mid-1860s, 71 per cent of Britain's cotton imports came from India, compared to just 12 per cent before the war.[110] The war boosted the entire British imperial economy by shifting cotton supply chains.[111] The war in America created a massive opportunity for entrepreneurs in India, especially in Bombay.

During the decades preceding the war, efforts had already been made to increase and improve Bombay's cotton supply. Bombay, however, did not only export raw cotton. The first weavers had already arrived in Bombay in 1668 and were supported by the government early on.[112] The first steam-powered cotton press and cotton textile mill in India were established in Bombay in 1854 by Cowasji Nanabhoy Davar, a Parsi who had his own firm in the China trade.[113] Along with other Parsis, he was one of the main investors in the Indian-owned Bombay Steam Navigation Company. Several prominent Indian

108 See: J. S. Palsetia, *The Parsis of India: Preservation of Identity in Bombay City*, Leiden: Brill, 2001, pp. 53–56. It became very difficult for merchants to repatriate the profits of the opium trade in Canton to Bombay. The Opium Wars also bankrupted merchants. Other Indian communities from Bombay or who settled in Bombay, such as Jews and Guajaratis, were involved in these trades alongside Americans and other nationalities. The Parsi silk trade from Canton to Bombay was also somewhat profitable.

109 S. Beckert, "Emancipation and Empire: Reconstructing the Worldwide Web of Cotton Production in the Age of the American Civil War", *American Historical Review* 109 (2004) 5, pp. 1405–1438, at 1408–1409.

110 S. Hazareesingh, "Interconnected Synchronicities: The Production of Bombay and Glasgow as Modern Global Ports, c. 1850–1880", *Journal of Global History* 4 (2009) 1, pp. 7–31, at 21.

111 C. A. Bayly, *The Birth of the Modern World 1780–1914: Global Connections and Comparisons*, Malden, MA: Blackwell Publishing, 2004, p. 162.

112 S. T. Sheppard, *Bombay*, Bombay: The Times of India Press, 1932, p. 88.

113 Palsetia, *Parsis of India*, p. 58.

families – including the Sassoons, the Wadias, the Tatas, and the Petits – made their fortunes from the early cotton mills. In 1874, "there were 17 Indian-promoted mills to one British dominated project. Of the 95 mills established before 1914, Parsis promoted 34, Hindus 27, Europeans 15, Muslims 10, Jewish businessmen 4, with four listed as uncertain."[114] Several mill owners travelled to Manchester and Lancashire to study mill operations before starting their own mills in Bombay. Although these finished goods could be exported by Gujarati merchants throughout the western Indian Ocean and China, exports suffered heavily from Japanese competition in the early 1900s.[115] This is to say that Bombay merchants did not only exclusively export raw cotton to the Lancashire, but also established mills of their own.

The US Civil War brought lasting change to Bombay's economy. Sven Beckert writes that "perhaps the most important effect of the American Civil War was that the cotton manufacturers realized how dangerous it was to depend on a single and also a politically unreliable source of raw cotton."[116] A global shift occurred as manufacturers in aforementioned states like Russia, France, and Britain relied more heavily on colonial and thus politically stable cotton sources. Interest groups such as the Manchester Cotton Supply Association played an important role in lobbying for more political control and intervention in the cotton market. Thus, when we see the American Civil War as a global rather than a national event, the paradox of its effects becomes evident: "the liberation of 4 million slaves in North America and the extension and intensification of imperial control over potential cotton-growing regions in Asia and Africa."[117] In Britain, raw cotton was increasingly sourced from Egypt, Sudan, and India. The state intervened heavily in the market through direct political control of these territories and by raising tariffs on raw cotton imports.[118]

The end of the American Civil War in 1865 led to a market crash in Bombay. The cause of the crash was attributed to the fall in cotton prices when the war ended, though cotton exports remained high. The financial crash involved land speculation. Following the crash, cotton remained an important commodity in

114 Ibid., p. 59. The numbers of mills listed here amount to 94 mills, not the 95 quoted here.
115 Ibid., pp. 90–91.
116 "Der vielleicht wichtigste Effekt des amerikanischen Bürgerkriegs war, dass die Baumwollfabrikaten begriffen, wie gefährlich es war, sich von einer einzigen und zudem noch politisch unzuverlässigen Quelle für Rohbaumwolle abhängig zu machen" (translated by author). S. Beckert, "Das Reich der Baumwolle: eine globale Geschichte", in: S. Conrad and J. Osterhammel (eds.), *Das Kaiserreich transnational: Deutschland in der Welt 1871–1914*, Göttingen: Vandenhoeck & Ruprecht, 2006, pp. 280–301, at 296.
117 Beckert, "Emancipation and Empire", p. 1406.
118 Beckert, "Das Reich der Baumwolle", p. 296.

terms of the city's economic and social development, including the structure of the port and the use of land within the city until the present day. The mills remained the backbone of Bombay's economy until their mass closure in the 1980s.[119] Along with private firms, the Government of Bombay sought to enhance the connectivity within Bombay to secure the most effective route between the source of cotton, the cotton presses and mills, and the docking facilities from which cotton was exported.

Winning Land and Reforming Ports

Land reclamation played a central role in providing docking places for the aforementioned trade in various commodities, especially cotton and opium. Bombay had originally been a series of islands. From the time the British first occupied the islands in 1668, "the English saw not only the value of their new possession but the possibility of improving it by winning land from the sea."[120] By 1858, levelling the islands' hilly terrain had since filled in the sea between the islands, and Bombay took the general shape that it is recognized for today. During the decade following 1862, Bombay expanded in size by four square miles (10.36 km), and environmental groups active in the city today estimate that land is still reclaimed from the sea every year.[121] The making of Bombay has been a continuous project.

Unlike other colonial port cities at this time, Bombay's port did not need to be constructed entirely from scratch. Docks that had served the EIC were already in existence prior to the construction of the first docks for steam shipping companies between 1845 and 1859.[122] The original dockyard was established in the mid-eighteenth century on the eastern side of the foreshore, which over time spread into additional bunders (a docking place or a wharf) and godowns.[123] Yet, most places for landing goods and passengers were not satisfactory. Bombay's landing places for sailing ships at the start of the nineteenth

---

119 Though many of Bombay's cotton mills have been closed for about three decades, debates on the use of the land and the social effects of the mill closures are still an ongoing controversy. See: D. D'Monte, *Ripping the Fabric: The Decline of Mumbai and Its Mills*, New Delhi: Oxford University Press, 2002; N. Adarkar and V. K. Phatak, "Recycling Mill Lands: Tumultuous Experience of Mumbai", *Economic and Political Weekly* 40 (2005) 51, http://www.epw.in/journal/2005/51/commentary/recycling-mill-land.html.

120 Sheppard, *Bombay*, p. 60.

121 Broeze, "External Dynamics", p. 260.

122 Ibid, p. 254.

123 Hazareesingh, *Colonial City*, p. 17.

century "could only be used intermittently during some parts of the day while at low tide goods and passengers had to be carried through the mud."[124] Soon enough, small piers were erected including Wellington Pier at Apollo Bunder in 1819, which continues to be used as a passenger terminal today.[125]

Although Bombay's islands had been consolidated by reclamation before 1858, very little of the foreshore had been extended. Official reclamation work was started on the foreshore in the 1830s, but private individuals had, from the very early days of British Bombay, been "reclaiming small plots of land for themselves."[126] The extent of that private reclamation warranted a tax on such land by the turn of the eighteenth century. Thus, it is important to note that these reclamations were not all government projects from their inception. Large-scale public and private reclamation projects on the foreshore did not make a lot of headway until the 1860s. The very "first mention of a private land-reclamation company being formed was made in 1837, while in 1857 the Mody Bay Land Reclamation Scheme was put forward."[127] Yet, the earlier schemes had not been supported, as there was a difference of opinion between the Supreme Government in Calcutta and the Government of Bombay regarding the usefulness of public-private partnerships.

Upon transition to British Crown rule, Bartle Frere, the first crown governor of Bombay from 1862 to 1867, was instrumental in pushing forward major civil engineering works in the city through public-private partnerships and private enterprise. He was a career colonial administrator who had first worked in Sind and Calcutta before his appointment as Governor of Bombay. After 1867, he returned briefly to England before being sent as governor to the Cape Colony, a role that earned him infamy for the Zulu War massacre of 1879.[128] According to Lakshmi Subramanian, Bartle Frere was able to convince his superiors in Calcutta and London of the importance of involving private corporations in public reclamation schemes in order to overcome the financial impotence and incompetence of government works:

> It is this uncertainty, which makes me despair of ever getting much of these profitable reclamations done by government on their own account. In a general way, a rupee spent

124 Ibid.
125 Wellington Pier hosts a jetty service between South Mumbai and Jawaharlal Nehru Port Trust (Navi Mumbai/mainland side of the harbour) and a tourist jetty to Elephanta Island.
126 Sheppard, *Bombay*, pp. 63, 76.
127 Subramanian, *Three Merchants of Bombay*, p. 164.
128 "Sir Bartle Frere 1st Baronet", *Encyclopaedia Britannica*, http://www.britannica.com/EBchecked/topic/219678/Sir-Bartle-Frere-1st-Baronet, (accessed 2 December 2014); J. Darwin, *Unfinished Empire: The Global Expansion of Britain*, London: Penguin Books, 2012, pp. 141–144.

> in reclamation near the Town yields Rs 3 worth of land – if the work be well planned, and well and quickly done. But the capital required is large and if we have nothing to spend, but what we can clip from canals in Sind or cotton roads in Deccan, our reclamation get on but slowly – and because slowly, very expensively, for slower the work, the more costly it is, the returns are longer postponed, and interest accumulates on capital sunk.[129]

Bartle Frere's support of these private projects was all the more convincing since the cost of suppressing the 1857 rebellion put a strain on government coffers in Calcutta. While in Britain a budget deficit might have been accepted, in India, there were no policies in place to allow a deficit or to imagine that India had credit. New taxes were introduced to fund public works, but even these were insufficient.[130]

Out of these arguments, most of the major work on the foreshore started in the 1860s when land companies sprang up in order to make a quick profit by speculating on land prices during the US Civil War. Land companies were common in many of the colonies at this time, especially settlement colonies like Australia.[131] What was unique about Bombay's land companies was that they were land reclamation companies that speculated on land that did not yet exist but once it had been reclaimed could be sold for a profit based on the expectation of rising land values from the booming cotton trade. The most successful projects were realized on the harbour/eastern side of the islands where most docking facilities existed.

The Bombay Chamber of Commerce and Industry, established in 1836 by John Skinner, a Scotsman, and founder of Jardine, Skinner and Company, became an important advocate for the wealthy European and Indian commercial communities in Bombay.[132] Early on, the chamber gave voice to the growing concerns about the state of the port. While the sanitary condition and the state of the various government and private docks were poor, safety within the harbour was also a concern. This particular part of a ship's journey – docking and undocking – was dangerous, and fatalities occurred regularly. Theft and plundering were also prevalent within the harbour. Part of the problem with the facilities and the lack of organization can be attributed to the structure of how the government dock, the pilotage, and the harbour lighting were run under the Indian navy. The master attendant, appointed by the naval commander-in-chief,

---

129 Bartle Frere quoted in both M. Dossal and L. Subramanian, *Imperial Designs and Indian Realities*, p. 153; Subramanian, *Three Merchants of Bombay*, p. 164.

130 Thompson and Garratt, *Rise and Fulfillment*, pp. 472–474.

131 Darwin, *Unfinished Empire*, p. 97.

132 R. J. F. Sulivan, *One Hundred Years of Bombay: History of the Bombay Chamber of Commerce, 1836–1936*, Bombay: Uchitha Graphic Printers, 1937 [reprinted 2012], p. 1.

also appointed his own assistants to manage the dockyard. All port expenses were charged to general revenue and were therefore not obtained by the mercantile community specifically.[133] As a result, the navy was not accountable to the needs of merchants.

In the 1850s, two bills were passed that changed the way in which the port was financed.[134] The upkeep of the harbour's lights, buoys, and other fixtures were charged on shipping and not general revenues. As a result, ship owners and merchants had an expectation that whatever fees were collected from them be used exclusively for mercantile purposes and not naval purposes. The Chamber of Commerce suggested the creation of a harbour board to better manage the harbour; the Government of Bombay "agreed that the duties of Master Attendant should in future be wholly disconnected from those of the Dockyard but refused to concur in the proposal for a Harbour Board."[135] A harbour board had, during those years, been instituted at Mersey Docks in Liverpool, also pushed through out of merchants' frustration with fees going towards maintenance of the city of Liverpool and not the docks. The structure implemented at Liverpool is considered the first port with a predecessor to a port authority, the way in which most ports around the world are still run today. These tensions led merchants to advocate a restructuring of the port space through the Bombay Chamber of Commerce.

Numerous land companies were founded during the US Civil War. Their activities were particularly directed to the city's harbour space. As stated, these land companies were based on the premise of reclaiming land from the sea with the expectation of selling the land for a profit based on rising land values. These companies issued shares, but their activities involved a mixture of two tendencies: one was pure speculation and the other was land acquisition and infrastructure development. Most companies fell somewhere between the two objectives, though some companies tended more towards one direction. Such companies included the Colaba Land Company, the Frere Land Company, the Bombay Reclamation Company (commonly referred to as the Back Bay Company), and the Elphinstone Land and Press Company. The Mazagon, Colaba, and Frere companies all had wharves on the foreshore by 1864, as did the Elphinstone Land and Press Company, the United Victoria and Colaba Company, and the Apollo Bunder Warehouse Co.[136]

---

133 Ibid., p. 36.

134 Act 22 of 1855 for the Regulation of Ports and Port Dues and Act 31 of 1857 for the Levy of Port Dues and Fees in the Port of Bombay.

135 Sulivan, *One Hundred Years*, p. 37.

136 Bombay Chamber of Commerce and Industry, 1864–1865, Annual Report, APA, BL, pp. 130–135.

All these companies were what Dinesh Edulji Wacha, the president of the Indian Merchants' Chamber in 1915, termed "triangulated concerns." Each land company was supported by a bank and a financial institution with usually the same board of directors for all three companies.[137] The most well documented of these is the Elphinstone Company, which was also the most successful in terms of actually carrying out its land reclamation projects and was one of the land companies on the infrastructure development and expansion side of the spectrum. This company built for-profit facilities like godowns and bunders on its land while it continued reclamations for itself and for the government. The Elphinstone Company's supporters were William Nicol and Co.

The Elphinstone Land and Press Company

Bombay's commercial elite sought to expand and improve the port facilities through private means for three reasons. First, port expansion was necessary to cater to the growing trade in which these companies and individuals were already involved. Second, due to the "prevailing ideological climate and financial impotence of the Indian government, all new projects had to be instigated and financed by private firms and companies."[138] Third, the individuals who formed these companies realized that developing docking facilities and godowns could be profitable. Developing transport infrastructure was not just a means to an end but an end in itself.

William Nicol and Co. was one of the most important companies in Bombay in the nineteenth century and one of the founding members of the Bombay Chamber of Commerce in 1836. It also served as the main accountant for the chamber and was led by John and James Nicol Fleming, two brothers from Glasgow.[139] The Fleming brothers founded the Elphinstone Land and Press Company in 1858. John Fleming "straddled the commercial worlds of Bombay, Glasgow, and the city of London with equal ease", and had a shipping "network that extended to Karachi, Colombo, and Rangoon."[140] Like many

137 D. E. Wacha, *A Financial Chapter in the History of Bombay City*, Bombay: A. J. Combridge & Co., 1910, p. 36.

138 Broeze, "External Dynamics", p. 255.

139 S. Hazareesingh, "'Chasing Commodities over the Whole Surface of the Globe': Shipping, Port Development, and the Making of Networks Between Glasgow and Bombay, c. 1850–1880", Working paper, The Open University, 2007, p. 11.

140 Hazareesingh, "Interconnected Synchronicities", p. 22.

companies in Bombay, the most prominent merchant classes were members of the Elphinstone company's board: Scottish, Parsi, and Arab Jews.[141]

The company's reclamation of the foreshore began in October 1858 and by August 1859, the first bunder, the Elphinstone Bunder, was opened for traffic.[142] The right to establish a private dock was at first objected to by the Government of Bombay. The government later allowed the company to retain the right to land and ship goods from the new wharf under the condition that no further claims were made based on this understanding. Furthermore, the company needed to pay for and maintain a customs office on their property, set up by the commissioner of customs, in order to control that town dues were paid on goods landed at the bunder.[143] Though their rights to further development had been curtailed, the Elphinstone Company entered into negotiations with the government for additional bunders the next year. The company subsequently offered to reclaim land needed for a rail terminus for the government in exchange for rights to the foreshore, including land reclamation for bunders.[144]

The goods terminus for the Great Indian Peninsula Railway Company was to be located at Wari Bunder, adjacent to the Elphinstone Bunder. The government created a commission to negotiate the terms and conditions with the company. The final arrangements stipulated that for each acre of the company's current property that was relinquished to the railway company, the Elphinstone Company received the rights to three and a half acres of the foreshore. For each acre that the company reclaimed on behalf of the railway, they had rights to two acres of the foreshore.[145] Based on these stipulations, the company was hired to reclaim 100 acres of land for the rail terminus in exchange for the right to develop 250 acres for its own commercial benefit. In the same year, the company expanded by entering into negotiations to purchase the Clare and Carnac Bunders in order to reclaim those properties as well.[146] As long as the company continued to provide the land for the railway that would connect Bombay's port to its hinterland, it could continue to reclaim the foreshore and, therefore, expand its right to profit from landing and shipping goods in Bombay's harbour.

---

141 Elphinstone Land & Press Company Limited, "Report of the Directors to the Shareholders at the First Annual General Meeting", 1860, APA, BL.

142 Ibid., p. 1.

143 Ibid., p. 2.

144 Elphinstone Land & Press Company Limited, "Report of the Directors to the Shareholders at the Second Annual General Meeting", 1861, APA, BL, pp. 2–3.

145 Ibid., p. 3.

146 Ibid., p. 2; Elphinstone Land & Press Company Limited, "Report of the Directors to the Shareholders at the Third Annual General Meeting", 1862, APA, BL, p. 2.

The company built godowns, roads, and other buildings on this new land. It leased parts of its property to other companies as part of its business since proximity to docks was in demand. Furthermore, the company attempted to provide additional facilities to traders for its own profit. It therefore operated as a landlord, seeking rents for the prime location along the foreshore. By 1862, the directors of the company were aware that the "present crisis of affairs in America" resulted in an unprecedented opportunity for Bombay's merchants in general, and thereby also an opportunity for this company to profit from the increase in trade and the demand for docks necessary for shipping and landing.[147]

The company combined additional services and on-site processing such as cotton pressing in combination with docking and warehousing facilities. This style was unusual; other land companies were either unwilling or unable to make their land profitable while reclamation was underway. Instead, other land companies relied on issuing shares to reclaim land that would, at a later date, be sold based on the assumption of rising land values, which is why many schemes collapsed along with their financial backers at the end of the American Civil War in 1865.

These services rendered from bunders and godowns became the main source of the company's revenues, though their cotton presses remained unprofitable.[148] The company held land that was rising in value and continued to gain land through reclamation, but profit from the land could not be made until it was fully reclaimed and/or sold. The directors of the company held meetings with traders to figure out how to make their wharves the most frequented in Bombay. Their revenue came from bunder fees, and there was stiff competition with the free government bunders:

> Adjacently, Government owns a wharf, the use of which is allowed gratis to the public, even to importers who do not on their importations pay directly a single rupee to the revenues of the State. The Directors, however, trust that ere long Government may abandon the present system, and admit the principle that, at any rate for goods free of duty, suitable and convenient wharves, erected at great cost, are entitled to claim a fair and reasonable return for the outlay on them in the form of fees from those who use them, and that the Government wharves shall at least be reserved for the accommodation of those who pay to the revenues of the country.[149]

147 Ibid., p. 4.
148 Elphinstone Land & Press Company Limited, "Report of the Directors to the Shareholders at the Fourth Annual General Meeting", 1863, APA, BL, p. 1.
149 Ibid., p. 2.

Since these bunder fees allowed the company to continue reclamations and prevent financial ruin, the company needed to be inventive. One way it could compete with a free government services was by offering the best facilities.

Though the idea of creating a bonded warehouse in Bombay had been abandoned in the 1830s, in 1863, the directors discussed implementing bonded warehouses on the recently acquired Carnac Bunder. The first version of this warehousing system started with certain traded commodities in 1803 at London's docks, and was implemented in Liverpool as early as 1805 following the 1803 Warehousing Act. This system became solidified in Liverpool after the repeal of the Navigation Acts in 1839, which ended the monopoly of the EIC, at the Albert complex on the Albert Docks in 1846.[150] The Elphinstone Company's chief engineer, James Scott, travelled to Liverpool to view these facilities and to see first hand how they functioned in order to advise on how they might be implemented on the Elphinstone property.[151] The directors studied the idea intensely, but while a bonded warehouse had previously been a question of directing very specific trade to Bombay (between China and Britain), the scheme now focused on attracting merchants and shippers to the Elphinstone property within Bombay's harbour space to use (and pay for) their other services. With this scheme, the company sought to reposition itself within Bombay's harbour space rather than within imperial networks.

James Scott, the Elphinstone Company's chief engineer, reported that the basic system in Liverpool allowed an importer of merchandise that was subject to duties to store his goods in a bonded warehouse under the supervision of a bonded warehouse manager. The manager handled all receiving and storage of goods until the goods were removed, at which point the importer paid the duty.[152] This system allowed an importer to pay the duty once the goods had been sold rather than having to pay the duty upfront, which was difficult without surplus capital. This also differed from the previous 1833 proposal, which focused on removing duties entirely for transshipment. Though the value to importers was mentioned in the Elphinstone reports, the system also functioned well in entrepôt trade and allowed a certain amount of processing and manufacturing: "Owners of goods were allowed to repack, to manufacture *in* bond, and to carry out certain operations under bond [. . .]. Lastly, extensive facilities were granted for the removal of goods in transit, e.g. from Hull to Liverpool, under general bonds, and even for transhipment from vessel to vessel,

150 G. J. Milne, *Trade and Traders in Mid-Victorian Liverpool: Mercantile Business and the Making of a World Port*, Liverpool: Liverpool University Press, 2000, p. 80.
151 Ibid.
152 Ibid.

without any entry other than that of quantity for statistical purposes."[153] This system was similar to the system of free ports that developed in mainland Europe between the 1880s and the 1930s, a period characterized by territorializing empires and nation states. In comparison to free ports, these warehouses became common throughout Britain and the British Empire precisely because tariffs were not high, so bonded warehouses were usually useful for a limited number of goods.[154]

During his visit to Liverpool, James Scott would have found that secure and dry warehouses, a rarity, provided a steady source of income for the port. Without trade monopolies, ports needed to attract merchants by providing desired services for the lowest fees possible. During the 1840s, Liverpool was able to decrease dock dues to attract traffic while providing secure warehouses for the docks for a fee.[155] While the Albert Dock itself was not particularly profitable, the adjacent warehouses that stored the goods landed at that dock were. The Albert Dock warehouses were built by the port's harbour committee and were in competition with other private warehouses operating at the port. Dry and secure warehouses were something merchants were willing to pay for.

Before the negotiations over the Clare and Carnac bunders ended, James Scott left the Elphinstone Company to work for the Bombay Reclamation Company in 1864. Though many warehouses were built, it is not clear if the bonded warehouse on the Elphinstone property was ever constructed. However, the Elphinstone property was later purchased by and transferred to the government in 1870. The Bombay Port Trust (BPT) was formed out of this purchase in 1873. The Port Trust's annual reports indicate the existence of a bonded warehouse on the port trust property, which annually provided the port with steady revenue.[156] The bonded warehouse may very well have been a facility carried over from the purchase of the private docking and warehouse facilities of the Elphinstone Company. This system, considered a "limited free port", is still used all over the world today, including at Greater Mumbai's newest port.[157]

---

153 E. H. Rideout, "The Development of the Liverpool Warehousing System", *Transactions of the Historic Society of Lancashire & Cheshire* 82 (1930), p. 1–41, at 40.

154 Thoman, *Free Ports*, pp. 131–132.

155 Milne, *Traders in Mid-Victorian Liverpool*, p. 205.

156 Bombay Port Trust, "Administration Report to the 31st March 1875", p. 23, IOR, BL.

157 "Bonded Warehouses", Maharashtra State Warehousing Corporation website, http://mswarehousing.com/english/bonde-ware.htm (accessed 12 April 2015).

Private Bunders under Empire

In 1865, engineer Thomas Ormiston was hired to replace James Scott. Ormiston, like many British civil engineers at this time, was Scottish and had previously worked for the Clyde Navigation Trust (a port trust just downstream from Glasgow active in the sugar and herring trade, known today as Clydeport) and he had been "responsible for the design of Glasgow's big steam cranes."[158] He became a shareholder in his new employer's firm. In the company's annual reports, Thomas Ormiston began including an extensive engineer's report of the works already underway and those which could be undertaken by the company. He offered suggestions to the board of directors on what could be done to better the property and increase profits. In his reports, he made frequent reference to engineering projects in England, mainly port facilities in Liverpool and Cardiff, but also railways in Birmingham, in some cases even drawing parallels and comparisons between government agencies "at home" and government agencies in Bombay.[159] Many engineers worked in Bombay, but only a few became as influential as Thomas Ormiston.

In 1864, the company hired John Ryan, a bunder superintendent who oversaw and managed the traffic to and from the property. Like Thomas Ormiston, John Ryan also attached his own statement to the annual report, which generally described the type of traffic the company received and what could be done to increase traffic to the Elphinstone bunders. John Ryan was likely the first person to hold the position of traffic manager in Bombay, though the naval position of master attendant to the docks also involved similar functions. Government docks until this time had been managed by the navy. Ryan's job was to oversee and manage the organization of port traffic, pushing it towards efficiency. The most important part of his reports were assessments of which facilities were truly being used by the public, which were in demand, and which were profitable.

Both Thomas Ormiston and John Ryan remained at the Elphinstone Land and Press Company until the company dissolved in 1870. Despite their technical jobs, these men held significant positions at the Elphinstone Land and Press Company and later at the BPT. Thomas Ormiston argued for facilities and became a strong advocate for a wet dock in Bombay. John Ryan became influential in studying traffic in Bombay and schemes in other ports to profit from trade, including integrating land management into port revenue.

158 Hazareesingh, *Colonial City*, p. 24.

159 For example: Elphinstone Land & Press Company Limited, "Report of the Directors to the Shareholders at the Seventh Annual General Meeting", 1866, APA, BL, pp. 12–13 and 22.

There was tension between this private company, operating for profit, and the Government of Bombay, which had benefited from the private scheme in a private-public bargain. Though the Elphinstone property was a type of public benefit – indeed, it was ideally situated near the so-called native town, the perfect location for many merchants, and had wharves and docks to offer – it still operated on a profit basis. Therefore, it was not for the public good that these works were completed, but to benefit the shareholders. In reference to the goods terminus provided by the company to government in exchange for the rights to the foreshore, Thomas Ormiston wrote:

> The result has been that the Government has got for nothing the site of a goods station worth a million sterling; and, as in our case it was unguaranteed capital that was to be spent, Government has also made a good bargain for the Municipality, by which I mean the public, who will have in addition to the commodious and well-situated wharfs, a large and wholesome ground, instead of a pestilential foreshore reeking with all sorts of abominations, and adjoining to a large population crammed three times closer than the East London Union, the most densely populated district in London.[160]

In some respects, the annual reports issued by the company propagated an image of civic pride and duty, as though they had a mission to fulfil a public service. However, the reports are simultaneously profit-oriented and resentful of attempts by the government to curtail the company's right to profit from what was perceived in Bombay to be the public right to free docking at government bunders. The debate between corporate and individual rights played out on a number of issues between the Elphinstone Company and the Government of Bombay, where the Elphinstone Company claimed to back "public rights" by requesting that the government fund certain schemes to improve access to its own facilities.[161]

Despite complaints, the company did enjoy close ties to the colonial government, as evidenced by their increase in steamship accommodations. The first steamers arrived in Bombay by the 1830s. In 1866, steamers first began to use the company's bunders. The lines included the British India Steam and Navigation (BISN), the Coast and River, and the Ferry Company. Most of the steam traffic at this time was in the mail or passenger services; very little of it involved goods. BISN was founded by a Scotsman, William Mackinnon, who had close ties to the government. William Mackinnon first started his shipping operations in Calcutta in the 1850s, but by the late 1850s, he moved the management of his operations to Glasgow. At the start of the US Civil War, he

160 Ibid., p. 17.
161 Ibid., p. 22.

decided that Bombay would be a profitable location for his business.[162] Nicol and Co. provided weekly "Bombay Trade Reports" to the *Glasgow Herald* that summarized important market information for Scottish businesses. Nicol and Co. was, therefore, William Mackinnon's first stop in Bombay for local information about the city's business climate and access to political influence. According to Sandip Hazareesingh, William Mackinnon arrived in Bombay "just at a time when the colonial state, in a bid to cut down expenditure, had begun to privatise its maritime transport operations."[163]

Bartle Frere was a supporter of the use of private enterprise for governmental purposes and awarded BISN a contract in 1862 for three mail lines between Bombay and Cochin, Karachi, and Basra. Nicol and Co managed all three lines.[164] John Fleming owned shares in BISN and was the company's agent in Karachi.[165] That these lines were loaded and unloaded on the Elphinstone property, also managed by Nicol and Co., is no coincidence. The Karachi route had formerly been managed by the Bombay Steam Navigation Company, a Parsi-owned business. Though imperial interests in this case replaced Indian with Scottish business, BISN was unsuccessful in its bid to compete with the traffic of the so-called native craft that traded commodities along India's coast and between India and the western Indian Ocean, which remained dominated by Gujarati merchants.[166]

The Elphinstone Company invested in developing its property's infrastructure – built roads to integrate its facilities, focused on creating overpasses over the rail lines to link the estate with the town, built godowns, docks, and so on – but it was still a land company. Its main purpose was split between two approaches: the land estate and the dock estate. The dock estate was the property connected to the docks and godowns. The land estate was the inland section, bordering the railroads and the native town. Once all this land had been reclaimed, it could be sold. That was indeed the main purpose of land companies. The shareholders had decided that only the land estate was to be sold because the dock estate was profitable.[167] The land estate was located directly next to the native town, the

162 Hazareesingh, "Interconnected Synchronicities", p. 18.

163 Hazareesingh, "Chasing Commodities", p. 9.

164 Ibid., p. 10.

165 Hazareesingh, "Interconnected Synchronicities", p. 22.

166 Ibid., p. 19; for a history of Gujarati merchants in the eighteenth century and their institutions, knowledge, and might that channelled their dominance in Indian Ocean trade, see: C. Goswami, *Globalization before its Time: The Gujarati Merchants from Kachchh*, New Delhi: Penguin, 2016.

167 Elphinstone Land & Press Company Limited, "Report of the Directors of the Elphinstone Land & Press Company Limited to the Shareholders at the Eighth Annual General Meeting", 1867, APA, BL, p. 9.

most populated area of the city. This locational advantage served two benefits. First, the property could be sold for a premium and would be eagerly developed; the native town was the main location for Indian commerce. Second, this location was particularly valuable simply by neighbouring the dock estate. It was sandwiched between two high-traffic and high-trade areas.

Due to the financial and real estate crash with the end of the US Civil War, however, the Elphinstone property remained unsold and reclamation on it continued with the idea that one day the property could still be sold for a profit. Thomas Ormiston reported to the shareholders in 1867 that the cost of reclamation per square yard amounted to ten rupees, but "the shareholders must not [...] congratulate themselves on this being anything like the whole cost."[168] The company still had to develop the reclaimed land, manage the property, and pay interest. It was, therefore, to the company's benefit to sell this unproductive land. The shareholders had put up the capital for the development of the property based on the expectation of rising land value. After the market crash following the end of the US Civil War, it became difficult to justify such an investment as the returns on the property, which could only be expected after it was fully developed, seemed increasingly uncertain in turbulent economic times.

The professionalization and institutionalization of port management in Bombay emerged out of private enterprise. The engineer and traffic managers' jobs required an outward look to understand for which types of infrastructure and schedules merchants would need and be willing to pay. Their efforts rearranged the internal space of the harbour as a way to capture existing trade within prevailing frameworks. However, they also attempted to forge new connections, specifically to push for steamship facilities, even at a time when the majority of merchants would not need such infrastructure. The role of the Elphinstone Land and Press Company highlights the intertwined strategies of the Government of Bombay and merchant elite, but at the same time underscores the competition and diverging interests at stake in their outlooks.

Conclusion

This chapter outlined several specific attempts to incentivize trade in Bombay from approximately 1830 to 1870. In the first proposal to institute a free port in Bombay in 1833, Bombay's merchant community played an important role in

168 Elphinstone Land & Press Company Limited, "Report of the Directors to the Shareholders at the Seventh Annual General Meeting", 1866, APA, BL, p. 14.

directing trade to and from Bombay. The community had specific visions of situating Bombay between Canton and Britain by expanding trade in opium, cotton, and tea at what they hoped would become a "free port." This proposal reacted to the potential competition of "free trade" and how it would affect Bombay's positionality in trading networks. Instead of competing on an individual or firm level to direct trade to Bombay, these merchants sought to rescale competition to the port level by creating structural incentives for the port. Their agenda was hindered by the ongoing territorialization of India, whose officials began to consolidate a comprehensive state space, and saw India's ports as part of that space. Bombay was no longer to be envisioned as part of a network of ports along British trade routes; it became an Indian port that would be regulated according to an increasingly uniform "national" system, regardless of its trade networks.

Even so, the authorities in Calcutta, much less those in Bombay, did not have the means to enact such a uniform port system. To further both their goals of "territorializing" India – that is, connecting distant parts of colonial India and systematizing governance over that space – as well as to further trade goals such as increasing cotton and other exports, the government relied on private enterprise, primarily the same merchant community it had dismissed in 1833, to supply the infrastructure needed for such connectivity. The later development of the port under the Government of Bombay's watch led to tensions between the merchants who sought to direct trade to Bombay and the poor facilities provided for them. The government, therefore, gave incentives and concessions to private firms such as the Elphinstone Land and Press Company to develop the foreshore into well-equipped private docks. In contrast to the government and shippers who searched for specific routes and commodities, the objective of the Elphinstone Company was to profit from the infrastructure needed for this trade. Despite looking for models established elsewhere (e.g., Liverpool), they remained internally focused on Bombay's harbour space and on connecting their facilities to city and harbour infrastructure in a way that would bring about the most profit from international shippers.

The financial difficulty of sustaining extensive land development by private enterprise will strike the reader as one of the key issues faced by SEZs developers in India today. Bombay's land companies from the 1860s were in no way predecessors to today's SEZs, but it is worth noting that they were based on a similar premise. Yet, these land companies that operated docks, like zones, were a form of privatizing public infrastructure. The Elphinstone Land and Press Company endured many issues that developers deal with today, namely, how to link its the infrastructure to that of the public. The Elphinstone Company needed to build its own roads and bridges to connect its property to the native town and to overcome the burden of government railways near its property. The goal of port maintenance was, unlike for the government, not about a public good or enhancing or controlling specific connections. Rather, its sole purpose was the creation of infrastructure on its own. The incentives may look similar to the 2005 Special Economic Zone policy in India, which grants private firms extensive tax concessions to develop infrastructure in India.

In viewing the concessions given to this private firm to develop infrastructure in terms of portals of globalization, the following chapter elaborates on other actors' attempts to gain hold of these private gains and the resulting trade flows, namely, the creation of a government consolidated port and foreshore in Bombay. It is through this interplay between private actors, highlighted in this chapter, and the government's attempts to manage the port as a national and imperial strategic space that a combination of competing strategies to forge connections and manage trade flows becomes visible.

3 Territorializing Bombay Port, 1860s–1880s

This chapter deals with how the Government of Bombay, in negotiation with the Government of India, sought to control and manage trade to its own advantage as a source of revenue. Whereas trade was profitable under the EIC, these governments sought the tax revenues from trade rather than profit from trade on its own. The port was of local importance to its residents, both "settled" and "native."[169] The Government of Bombay slowly transitioned from a government that represented their interests to part of a larger entity with a greater imperial purpose. Rather than focusing on creating exceptions to promote trade flows through the erection of private docks, the government in effect brought the entire port trade under government oversight, creating what Michael Geyer terms a portal of globalization, a site through which cross-border flows, especially trade, come increasingly under state control.[170] This chapter shows how the character of the port changed as Bombay Port became a single port operated at the behest of government in the early 1870s.

Forming Bombay's multiple ports into a single port was a contentious process. Prior to the 1870s, there was not just one port of Bombay. Rather, there were multiple competing firms within the harbour space as well as a government port. Bombay Port, therefore, was not a single unit of analysis prior to this time. The outcomes of the disputes described here formed the BPT in 1873, which has become the model for how Bombay Port continues to operate today. This chapter illustrates the struggles of various actors to control the foreshore and its numerous docks and thereby institutionalize what today is thought of as a key institution of international trade: a port.

Port Competition in Bombay

By 1864, a number of private docks were operating on the foreshore alongside the Elphinstone Land & Press Company. According to the Bombay Chamber of Commerce and Industry, in 1864 government properties amounted to an area of 344,623 yards with a sea frontage of 7,518 feet compared to private wharves totalling an area of 288,064 yards and 11,716 feet of sea frontage.[171] The government wharves had a larger area than the private wharves combined. The

169 "Locals" describe all those who used Bombay as a home base for their business activities.
170 Geyer, "Portals of Globalization."
171 Bombay Chamber of Commerce and Industry, 1864–1865, Annual Report, APA, BL, p. 135.

https://doi.org/10.1515/9783110615135-003

private wharves continued to grow in number and size, thanks also to land reclamation. Though the government owned many wharves in name, some were little more than "swamps." The Fort Customs Bunder was an exception. Dutiable goods imported and exported from Bombay were handled there. Another functioning government bunder was the Masjid Bunder, which catered mostly to country craft.

In 1864, the Revenue Department of the Government of Bombay led an enquiry into the state of all bunders in order to determine wharfage fees at public and private ports and to ascertain "under what rules are these dues levied, and whether there appears to be any fixed principle in their regulation."[172] This report, in addition to describing each bunder's facilities and traffic, lists the various public and private properties operating on Bombay's foreshore. Bombay Port was not a single unit but comprised numerous properties. There was no overarching entity that managed traffic to and from Bombay. Rather than only competing with other ports in the Indian Ocean to entice traffic to Bombay, these port operators were also competing with each other within the harbour.

Port competition along the foreshore was possible due to the different types and qualities of infrastructure and different wharfage fees. The aforementioned 1864 committee was tasked with uncovering the wharfage fees levied by the Elphinstone Land Company, the Victoria Bunder, and the government bunders. The report found that all three had different fee rates, though the Elphinstone and Victoria bunders followed a similar logic. While these private bunders charged landing/wharfage fees for the use of the property, the government bunders were basically free in that the fees were only levied if goods sat on the wharves past a certain period of days "with the object not so much of producing revenue as of preventing obstruction."[173] The same principle was followed at Calcutta's government wharves, and "section 189 of the consolidate Customs Act VI of 1863 would seem, by the manner in which it has been worded, to contemplate such a course being adopted at all Government wharves."[174] This act was intended to standardize port practices across India. Yet, the government did not control all ports.

This committee's investigation speaks to an effort on behalf of the Government of Bombay to increase its regulation of local infrastructure and fees:

> The Committee are of opinion that the power of sanctioning from time to time as may be necessary, a maximum rate of landing fees to be levied by the owners of private Bunders should unmistakeably be vested in the hands of Government, and the consolidated

172 Ibid., p. 127.
173 Ibid., p. 136.
174 Ibid.

> Customs Act VI. of 1863 is silent on the subject, Section 189, relating apparently to Government wharves only, the Committee have to recommend that early Legislative action be taken in the matter, which should be made to meet the requirements of both existing and future wharves of this description.[175]

Despite protests from both the Elphinstone Company and the Victoria Company, the Government of Bombay instituted a cap on the wharfage fees these private companies could charge based on the fees that were levied at the Elphinstone bunders, and established its right to change that amount when it deemed fit.

In coming to this conclusion, the government also compared the fees of the two private companies with the government's fees as well as those collected in Liverpool and in London. The way in which Liverpool's port charged for certain services was extensively analysed, concluding that all the fees levied in Liverpool did not give merchants the right to store goods, as this was charged separately.[176] The comparison between "home" and Bombay was an omnipresent theme in government and chamber reports, but the authors usually qualified such reports by stating that "home" was an entirely different situation and could not be compared to Indian realities. They persisted in their comparisons nonetheless.

The Elphinstone Company later withdrew its protest of capped wharfage fees. The rates issued by the Elphinstone Land and Press Company were adopted as the standard rates. John Flemming of the Elphinstone Company signed the government report as a member of the government committee investigating wharfage fees.[177] Therefore, as a prominent member of the Bombay Chamber of Commerce with close government ties, Flemming was able to influence a favourable decision allowing such wharfage fees at the rate the company already charged to continue at private properties to his own financial benefit and to the detriment of the Indian community that provided the main source of traffic at his bunders during these years.[178]

Despite Flemming's influence, the government committee concluded that the government should protect the rights of merchants by holding on to as much foreshore property as possible:

> Finally, the Committee respectfully urge that Government should continue to hold all such portions of the foreshore of the harbour of Bombay as may still be in their own possession, thereby providing the only effective check against possible combinations and

175 Ibid., p. 139.
176 Ibid.
177 Ibid., p. 141.
178 Ibid., p. 132.

> exactions on the part of private wharf owners, and that no time be lost in commencing and prosecuting the various Government works mentioned in this report, so as to render them available for the purposes of trade at the earliest possible date.[179]

Governor Bartle Frere had stressed the importance of private enterprise in bettering the city's infrastructure, especially its port, but the government saw itself as a protector and promoter of trade, a check against the incursion of private enterprise in what merchants viewed as their right to free docking. The government used this argument throughout the next decade to justify its expanding holdings on the foreshore and the institutionalization and standardization of port practices in Bombay.

Indian and British merchants discussed the free landing of goods on government docks as a public right. The Masjid Bunder, adjacent to the Elphinstone Property, had been set up in the early nineteenth century through public subscriptions and was open to all merchants, but it was frequented in particular by country craft. The Elphinstone reclamations were to block the entrance to the bunder, as noted in the government investigation into the wharfage fees in 1864, so the company made arrangements to replace the bunder with a new one on a different location for the government.[180] The new Malet Bunder at Mazagon, the replacement bunder, was far from the native town and the Malet Bunder was not ready for traffic by the time the Masjid Bunder had been acquired by the Elphinstone Company in June 1867, leaving local native merchants little choice but to pay docking fees on other Elphinstone bunders to the ultimate benefit of the company.[181] The Indian public was especially at a disadvantage.[182] The entire Elphinstone property comprised the docking places nearest to the native town, meaning that Indian merchants' best option was to pay docking fees and land on the Elphinstone Estate.

Another subject of much controversy among Bombay's merchants was the Bombay Presidency Act V of 1870, otherwise known as the Bunder Fees Act.[183] The act stipulated that the government had the right to levy fees for docking at any government wharf, bunder, or landing place. John Ryan, the former traffic manager for the Elphinstone Company, was appointed by the government to

179 Ibid., p. 141.

180 Ibid., p. 133.

181 E. Pratt, *The Bombay Wharves; How the Right of Way over Them Was Lost to the Public and the Commerce of the Port*, London: J. Weare, 1881, pp. 30–31.

182 Hazareesingh, "Interconnected Synchronicities."

183 Act no. V. of 1870, An act for the levy of Fees for the use of the Government Bunders, Wharves, Landing Places, Piers and Hards in the City of Bombay, Bombay Presidency Acts, IOR, BL, pp. 12–13.

oversee the enforcement of these fees at government-owned properties. By the time this act came into effect in 1871, it was not clear whether a port trust would be instituted on government properties, as the negotiations were ongoing and not open to the public. The Bombay Chamber of Commerce, on behalf of the merchant community, wrote to the government to express dissatisfaction with the levying of fees on goods that had until then been free from any payment. It also expressed its frustration at remaining outside the negotiations over a port trust. A port trust had not yet been officially decided upon as a viable option to increase government oversight of trade and of revenues derived from trade.

The first fees were collected by the government under the claim of necessity to fund the upkeep of facilities. Yet, the fees were collected on the foreshore even where there was no landing or shipping accommodation provided.[184] Therefore, these fees were collected regardless of such facilities. The fees even included the loading and unloading of personal belongings of passengers landing in Bombay.[185] The wharfage rates were halved for transshipment of goods so as not to completely discourage the entrepôt trade.[186] Though these government fees began as an effort to increase funding for port facilities, they became a government source of revenue and control over Bombay's harbour space and its trade while reducing its competition with private ports.

An Indian Port Trust for Bombay

Fees levied by the government docks were connected to the question of setting up a port trust to manage the port's growth and modernization. As in Britain, disagreements over how fees levied on merchants were managed by government formed the impetus for the discussion of a port trust model, though many merchants, especially Indians, contested the legal right of the government to levy fees on a practice that had previously been a public right. The discussion of a port trust intensified following the financial collapse of several land reclamation companies along the foreshore following the market crash. The Back Bay Company is but one example of the properties received by the government.[187]

184 Bombay Chamber of Commerce and Industry, 1871–1872, Annual Report, APA, BL, p. 103.
185 Ibid., p. 32.
186 Bombay Chamber of Commerce and Industry, 1870–1871, Annual Report, APA, BL, p. 227.
187 P. Chopra, "A Joint Enterprise: The Creation of New Landscape in British Bombay (1839–1918)", in: *Mumbai Reader'10*, Mumbai: Urban Design Research Institute, 2010, pp. 320–347, at 333.

The most profitable of these land companies was sold to the government in 1870. Rather than keeping the profitable docking facilities and selling the land estate, the entire Elphinstone property was sold to the Government of India. Negotiations began between the Government of India, the Government of Bombay, which was in favour of the purchase, and the commercial community that was against the purchase, represented by the Bombay Chamber of Commerce. The manner in which the government handled the purchase also put the government docks in Bombay at a financial disadvantage. The nature of trade was dramatically altered as all bunders, including those run by the government, charged docking fees, and government and private ports competed with one another for traffic, generally to the government's disadvantage.

The Bombay Chamber of Commerce and Industry was opposed to the government's purchase of the Elphinstone Estate and the passing of the Bunder Fees Act. After the purchase and passage of that act, the chamber's opposition was channelled into protesting against further government management of Bombay's harbour. The chamber justified its opposition by analysing the amount of money put towards the property's docks. While the Elphinstone Company operated the Elphinstone Estate, annual expenditure for completing the reclamations works ended in 1869 at 1,931,274 rupees, down from 4,498,596 in 1865. When the property went into government hands, the government spent 1,123,738 rupees over a ten-month period in 1870, which fell to only 249,268 rupees by 1872, though reclamation was incomplete.[188] Thus, the purpose of bunder fees to fund government works in the same manner fees had been used by private companies was not adhered to. The merchant community was therefore against the pretense of paying for unrendered services.

The Bombay Chamber of Commerce took an active role in stressing its disagreement with wharfage fees imposed through the Bunder Fee Act and the possibility of creating a port trust by combining government bunders with the Elphinstone Estate. Neither the Government of India nor the Government of Bombay consulted the mercantile community in general or the Bombay Chamber of Commerce specifically, which may have contributed to the chamber's opposition. The Bunder Fee Act had been implemented quickly without seeking the opinion of Bombay's merchants, who had heretofore been the main sponsors of government plans. Prior to the negotiations for a port trust, these prominent local British and Parsi merchants shared their ideas with the Government

188 "Questions by Colonel Fraser, R.E., C.B., as to Deep Water Berthage for Ships and Steamers in Bombay; and Answers thereto by Mr. Ormiston, C.E." in: Bombay Chamber of Commerce and Industry, 1871–1872, Annual Report, 125, APA, BL, pp. 109–126.

of Bombay, which had been their advocate within the empire. In contrast, the negotiations over a port trust were carried out in secret between the Bombay Government and the Government of India over a period of at least three years. Despite the fact that the content of the discussions between the two governments had not been disclosed, it was widely understood that the prospect of a port trust was under discussion.

In January 1871, after the government had been debating a port trust for some time, the chamber held a special meeting with the mercantile community during which "resolutions were unanimously passed deprecating the settlement of the question before the mercantile community has an opportunity of expressing their views."[189] In order to form their opinion without the benefit of government correspondence or consultation on the matter, the chamber met with the chief engineer of the government reclamation works, Thomas Ormiston, the former chief engineer for the Elphinstone Land & Press Company. In 1872, Ormiston spent two days at the chamber answering questions regarding the current state of the port facilities and his plans for improving them. The purpose of the meeting was to ascertain whether a port trust would be beneficial to the merchants and the trade of the port so that the chamber could submit its views, regardless of whether or not the Government of India or the Government of Bombay were interested in its opinion.

The chamber concluded that a port trust would be beneficial for the port of Bombay. The chamber's prior opposition to the purchase of the Elphinstone Property and the resulting Bunder Fees Act of 1870 was that it "burdened the Port of Bombay with a debt of nearly two millions sterling." In order to pay the interest on their amount, the Government of Bombay passed the bill instituting bunder fees on all public landing places, "including those formerly free, thereby throwing fresh burdens on trade without rendering any additional service."[190] The chamber felt that bunder fees at government docks were an unfair burden on the mercantile community, of which they were the most prominent members. However, a port trust, in their opinion, would be an additional service and could make the payment of bunder fees justifiable if the facilities they offered would be beneficial to the city's trade.

The chamber's view of a potential port trust was that it would have a board made up of members with varying interests in the trade of the port. The trust would not be managed exclusively by government officials, but also by private individuals. In relation to this proposal, the chamber mentioned:

---

189 Bombay Chamber of Commerce and Industry, 1871–1872, Annual Report, APA, BL, p. 103.
190 Ibid., p. 130.

> Seven or eight years ago an Act was passed by the Government of Bengal, constituting a board of commissioners for the improvement on the port of Calcutta, and this board, – which consists of Government servants and merchants, the latter being the majority, – the Committee are informed, works well, and had already effected important improvements, especially in reference to the landing and shipping of cargo.[191]

Not only did the chamber indicate models elsewhere in India but also pointed to precedent in the UK that allowed merchants to constitute port trust boards:

> The Committee know of no case in the United Kingdom where the affairs of any harbour of the slightest importance are not managed by a trust or board of commissioners usually composed of persons for the most part unconnected with the Government of the public service, but having an interest in the trade and prosperity of the Port.[192]

The chamber proposed this model as the basis for the new port trust and supported the plan to form such a trust out of the government port property.

From the time of the purchase of the Elphinstone Estate by the Government of India, the Government of Bombay Public Works Department had urged the Government of India to form a port trust on the property and connect it with the adjacent government property at Mody Bay. The proposed plan put forward to the Government of India was to first form a "Board of Trust" made up of public servants and prominent merchants (nominated by the government); connect the government and Elphinstone estates; and then sell off portions of the land estate to pay off the debt imposed by the purchase while maintaining control over the dock estate.[193] The idea of selling parts of the land estate was repeated in later letters before the trust was finalized.[194] The government plan to sell the land estate was quite similar to the former Elphinstone Company's plan: keep the profitable docks and sell the land.

The financial terms proposed by the Secretary of the Public Works Department to the Government of Bombay were not favourable to the local government. The board of the proposed trust would take on the debt of the purchase of the Elphinstone Estate, with a 4.5 per cent interest over a period of 30 years.

---

191 Ibid., p. 128.

192 Ibid., p. 127.

193 "Letter from Colonel M.K. Kennedy, R.E., Secretary to the Government of Bombay, Public Works Department, to the Secretary to the Government of India, No. 78 E. – 201 M., February 1, 1869", in: Bombay Chamber of Commerce and Industry, 1871–1872, Annual Report, APA, BL, pp. 36–38.

194 "Letter from Colonel M.K. Kennedy, R.E., Secretary to the Government of Bombay, Public Works Department, to the Secretary to the Government of India, No. 179 A – 369, October 21, 1871", in: Bombay Chamber of Commerce and Industry, 1871–1872, Annual Report, APA, BL, p. 81.

Additionally, debt from past government reclamation and dock improvement projects would fall under the financial obligations of the newly formed board and would be taken off of government accounts.[195] The Elphinstone Company's reclamation for the government goods terminus, which had given the company rights to reclaim the foreshore and collect fees on their property, was also considered towards the new board's debt.[196] Thus, the Elphinstone Company prospered from this sale at the expense of the future port trust. The only concession finally agreed upon was that the 100,000 pounds sterling that had been paid to the Elphinstone Company by the Government of India for the release of their rights to collect wharfage fees not be added to the port trust account and that they would remain on the account of the Government of India.[197] The Elphinstone Company had profited twice from the collection of docking fees.

The Secretary to the Government of Bombay contested the Government of India's policy towards Bombay Port in comparison with Calcutta's public services:

> When the policy was pursued of giving over the foreshore of the first Port in India to private persons, it was, of course, the duty of Government to make the best terms, in the interests of the public, for the land that was to be sold; but even then it would have been difficult to justify the application of the proceeds of these sales to the provision of land on Imperial works like Railway stations, which in every other part of India have been paid for out of Imperial revenues. Now, however, that the former policy has been reversed, it can hardly be contended that the inhabitants of Bombay are to be taxed, to the extent of Rs. 1,80,000 every year, for the benefit of the general public of India, or that they should pay, as suggested by instalments in 30 years, 40 lakhs of Rupees to the Government of India, for a portion of their own foreshore. This Government believe it is only necessary for them to draw attention to the injustice of this demand, to ensure its immediate remission by the Government of India.[198]

---

195 Bombay Chamber of Commerce and Industry, 1871–1872, Annual Report, APA, BL, p. 42; "Letter from Colonel J.S. Trevor, R.E., Acting Secretary to the Government of Bombay, Public Works Department, to the Secretary to the Government of India, No. 139 A. – 935, May 3, 1870", in: Bombay Chamber of Commerce and Industry, 1871–1872, Annual Report, APA, BL, p. 48.

196 "Letter from Colonel J.S. Trevor, R.E., Acting Secretary to the Government of Bombay, Public Works Department, to the Secretary to the Government of India, No. 139 A. – 935, May 3, 1870", in: Bombay Chamber of Commerce and Industry, 1871–1872, Annual Report, APA, BL, pp. 47–48.

197 "Letter from R.B. Chapman, Esq., Secretary to the Government of India, Financial Department, to the Secretary to the Government of Bombay, in the Public Works Department, No. 3372, September 8, 1871", in: Bombay Chamber of Commerce and Industry, 1871–1872, Annual Report, APA, BL, p. 77.

198 "Letter from Colonel J.S. Trevor, R.E., Acting Secretary to the Government of Bombay, Public Works Department, to the Secretary to the Government of India, No. 139 A. – 935, May 3, 1870", in: Bombay Chamber of Commerce and Industry, 1871–1872, Annual Report, APA, BL, pp. 47–48.

The inconsistencies between imperial policies, imperfectly implemented and idiosyncratically administered, and local conditions were an ongoing part of the negotiations over the proposed trust and continued long after the trust was formed. The above quote brings to mind the general thesis of John Darwin's *Unfinished Empire*: the British Empire was never centrally planned from London, but was formed through individual initiatives and bundles of partially realized plans.[199]

The Government of Bombay concluded that wharfage fees at the newly formed trust would need to be implemented, perhaps with higher fees than usual, in order to fund this debt. This policy was considered beneficial to the Government of India but potentially detrimental to trade and merchants in Bombay: "His Excellency in Council [Governor of Bombay] desires to express, in the most emphatic terms, his repugnance to have recourse to this measure, for it would if it were adopted, be justly said that an increased burden had been placed on the commerce of the Port, at a time when no increased facilities were given in return for the enhanced charges."[200] The Public Works Department argued that should the Government of India advance a loan to complete upgrades to the port facilities (such as wet docks or deep tidal basins for steamships), the Government of Bombay would be willing to implement docking charges. However, simultaneous to the ongoing discussions over the purchase of the Elphinstone property, the Bunder Fees Act was passed in Bombay in 1870 and came into force by 1871, though the financial issues regarding the formation of the trust were not yet finalized and remained contested, as evidenced earlier.

Another point of disagreement between the Government of India in Calcutta and the Government of Bombay was the naval side of the port. The newly formed board, if it was to be profitable and pay off the imposed debt, did not need government troops landing for free at their docks or navy goods taking up space in government godowns. Under the Elphinstone Company, troops landed and stored goods at the Carnac Basin with a low annual fee of 8,000 rupees. The Government of Bombay's Public Works Department argued that, with the Government of India already profiting so much from this scheme, the government should pay the same fee charged to merchants to store goods and should pay a rupee a head for landing troops, which stood in the year 1869–1870, for example, at 29,115 troops, and their families who embarked or disembarked at

199 Darwin, *Unfinished Empire.*

200 "Letter from Colonel M.K. Kennedy, R.E., Secretary to the Government of Bombay, Public Works Department, to the Secretary to the Government of India, No. 93A. – 188A, May 30, 1871", in: Bombay Chamber of Commerce and Industry, 1871–1872, Annual Report, APA, BL, p. 68.

Bombay.[201] This rate scale of 1 rupee a head was accepted in the final draft of the Bombay Port Trust Bill.[202] Once the Port Trust was formed in 1873, this issue came up repeatedly as the Government of India profited from the port without taking financial responsibility for its benefit to the empire.[203]

The port trust model consisted of a self-sustaining institution that would channel profit back into the maintenance of the port's facilities and the construction of new facilities. The response of the Financial Department for the Government of India was favourable to the idea of advancing sums to cover the costs of additional works, but simultaneously indicated that increasing port dues would harm the port's trade. The rates at the time in Calcutta were 4 annas per tonne while in Bombay they were only 2 annas per tonne.[204] The arguments back and forth between the Government of India and the Government of Bombay continued through 1872. Essentially, the Government of Bombay delayed instituting a port trust that would impose additional fees on merchants in order to pay off the capital debt to the Government of India and would therefore not be able to serve its role as a port trust that served port users. The Government of Bombay insisted that even if dues were raised, the revenue would be funnelled back to the Government of India through interest payments rather than put towards improvements. As the estates stood in 1869–1872, the reclamations were not yet complete. The Government of Bombay insisted that the Government of India relieve some of the capital debt and provide additional funds for the construction of a deep-water basin or wet dock to accommodate

201 "Letter from Colonel J.S. Trevor, R.E., Acting Secretary to the Government of Bombay, Public Works Department, to the Secretary to the Government of India, No. 139 A. – 935, May 3, 1870", in: Bombay Chamber of Commerce and Industry, 1871–1872, Annual Report, APA, BL, p. 50; "Letter from Colonel M.K. Kennedy, R.E., Secretary to the Government of Bombay, Public Works Department, to the Secretary to the Government of India, No. 93A. – 188A, May 30, 1871", reprinted in: Bombay Chamber of Commerce and Industry, 1871–1872, Annual Report, APA, BL, p. 65.

202 Act no. I of 1873, The Bombay Port Trust Act of 1873, Section LIX, Acts of the Legislative Council of the Governor of Bombay 1871–1874, IOR, BL, p. 21.

203 In 1860, Britain had a regular army of about 300,000 men (more could of course be recruited for specific wars). Two-thirds of the soldiers were stationed in India (and many were Indian). They could be dispatched to other locations in the Empire when conflict arose. See: Darwin, *Unfinished Empire*, 132–147. The port officials in Bombay sought to profit from the service their port provided due to the constant flow of soldiers in and out of the port.

204 An anna is a former currency unit equivalent to one-sixteenth of a rupee. "Letter from R.B. Chapman, Esq., Secretary to the Government of India, Financial Department, to the Secretary to the Government of Bombay, Public Works Department, No. 3372, September 8, 1871", in Bombay Chamber of Commerce and Industry, 1871–1872, Annual Report, APA, BL, p. 78.

the growing size of ships. The Government of India responded that it could not agree on providing additional funds because of the Government of Bombay's delay in implementing the port trust.[205] This stalemate finally ended with the institutionalization of the BPT on 26 June 1873, ending the four-year negotiation.

The conflict regarding the financing of the port trust revolved around the dual nature of the proposed institution as a local body that was to serve an imperial and a local function. The trust was to be managed by the appointment of trustees and through legislation by the Government of Bombay, which ultimately appointed locals, prominent Britons and Indians who made Bombay their home, to the board. Therefore, the trust functioned partially as a local institution in that it had to provide for the needs of the local merchant communities. The trust also had an "imperial character"; it provided facilities "for a commerce in which the whole of India is interested." By paying the capital debt on the estate, "the Imperial Treasury is secured forever at the expense of the local trade."[206]

These conflicts were present in other cases of trusts that were instituted throughout England and Scotland in the prior years, but not to the same degree. For example, in Liverpool, the Mersey Dock and Harbour Board, instituted in 1857, was made up of a board of 28 members, only four of whom were appointed by the government while the rest were elected by the dock ratepayers.[207] In contrast to the Liverpool arrangement where those who paid for services elected the majority of board members, in Bombay, the original organization of the board stipulated that members were chosen by the Government of Bombay. The Government nominated 9 to 13 members to the board, and between one-third and half of these members were to be public servants.[208] The proposed board would be financially independent from the government,

205 See, for example: "Letter from Colonel M.K. Kennedy, R.E., Secretary to the Government of Bombay, Public Works Department, to the Secretary to the Government of India, No. 34 A – 77, February 17, 1872"; "Letter Colonel C.H. Dickens, R.A., Secretary to the Government of India, Public Works Department, to the Secretary to the Government of Bombay, No. 118 B. – C., March 5, 1872"; "Letter from Colonel M.K. Kennedy, R.E., Secretary to the Government of Bombay, Public Works Department, to the Secretary to the Government of India, No. 58 A. – 118, March 16, 1872", in: Bombay Chamber of Commerce and Industry, 1871–1872, Annual Report, APA, BL, pp. 95–101.
206 "Letter from Colonel M.K. Kennedy, R.E., Secretary to the Government of Bombay, Public Works Department, to the Secretary to the Government of India, No. 179 A – 369, October 21, 1871", in: Bombay Chamber of Commerce and Industry, 1871–1872, Annual Report, APA, BL, p. 83.
207 H. G. Gilcriest, "The Mersey Dock and Harbour Board", *Public Administration* 3 (1925) 3, pp. 273–278, at 273.
208 Copy of the Bombay Port Trust Act 1873 in Bombay Chamber of Commerce and Industry, 1872–1873, Annual Report, APA, BL, p. 44; Act no. I of 1873, The Bombay Port Trust Act of 1873, Section 3BL, Acts of the Legislative Council of the Governor of Bombay 1871–1874, IOR, BL.

though the Government of Bombay would be responsible for legislation that would control the board's actions, appointments, and oversee its finances. If the trust had a budget deficit, the trustees were required through legislation to increase revenue by raising port fees, rents, and other charges. If the board did not implement these changes, the Government of Bombay would be able to implement higher fees by government order.[209] The BPT was in that sense more of a subordinate to the presidency government rather than an independent body. Though the port trust was modelled after such trusts "at home", it did not come to fully resemble them in its structure or in practice.

Arguments about instituting a port trust and docking fees in Bombay were characterized by the dual function of the port as both imperial and local, and thus Indian. That is, the Government of India involved itself more in directing the nature of port development in Bombay. This dual function can be further divided into commercial and naval purposes. The naval function was not the only port function that was vital to the empire. This tension may not have been unique to imperial ports, but the situation in Bombay appears more contentious than in the "model cases" in Britain that government officials and British merchants looked to for a solution.

Port Competition within Bombay Harbour

The BPT was created in 1873 and was partially based on the Liverpool and Glasgow model of harbour boards run by a trust. Like the formation of the BPT, the Mersey Dock and Harbour Board (Liverpool) was formed as a public trust resulting from a half-century of disagreements over town dues paid by merchants at the docks going towards town rather than port improvements. Furthermore, the proliferation of steamships required the deepening of the waterway and harbour facilities if they were to dock at the port.[210] The situation was similar to what had been facing the mercantile community in Bombay.

Unlike the trusts established in Britain, the BPT faced competition for traffic *within* its own harbour. Other private docking facilities were still in operation along Bombay's foreshore. These were for-profit docks operated by local companies and businessmen that could undercut the fees charged by the port trust.

209 Act no. I of 1873, The Bombay Port Trust Act of 1873, Section LX, Acts of the Legislative Council of the Governor of Bombay 1871–1874, IOR, BL, pp. 21–22.
210 S. Mountfield, *Western Gateway: A History of the Mersey Docks and Harbour Board*, Liverpool: Liverpool University Press, 1965, pp. 3–14.

The trust in Liverpool was also instituted partly out of the turmoil of port competition between Liverpool and Birkenhead. Negotiations in the years prior to the formation of the trust involved combining the competing Birkenhead and Liverpool facilities under one authority. In contrast, Bombay's port trust was formed without considering this aspect. Competing properties were not immediately acquired for the new trust. Correspondence between the Government of India and the Government of Bombay only briefly mentions the effects of possible competition in Bombay's harbour as a non-issue. The Bombay Chamber of Commerce's recommendation to create a trust also failed to mention private competition. This key difference between the port trust models in Britain and in Bombay is crucial to understanding the early problems faced by the new trust.

Colonel Alexander Fraser, a royal engineer influential in the construction of railways and lighthouses for the Government of India, visited Bombay in 1872 to analyse the state of the BPT negotiations and potential works at the government docks. He questioned Thomas Ormiston extensively on the possible success of the port trust in contrast to other facilities along the foreshore. Like the correspondence between the Government of India and the Government of Bombay, he assumed that the port trust, as a consolidated property, formed from the Elphinstone Estate and the Fort Customs Bunder would remain indispensable to trade in Bombay because its main bunders bordered the native town:

> I believe fully half the cotton trade is done on the Colaba Company's Wharf, a good deal of timber and some coals at the Mazagon, and a small quantity of coals at the Frere Company's Bunder. Otherwise, the greater part of the general trade of Bombay is done at the Elphinstone and Town Custom House Bunders, the former doing about ¾ths and the latter ¼th of the whole; that which goes to the Custom House is principally piece-goods, copper, opium, wines and spirits, simply because at present none of these are allowed by the Custom House authorities to be landed on the Elphinstone Bunder; arrangements are however in progress to enable this to be done, and when these are carried out, I believe the trade will be done almost entirely at the Elphinstone Bunder, even if no basins or piers are made. The fact is, the commercial quarter of Bombay is and always has been in the native town, in rear of the Bunders. I do not think there is much chance of this trade being shifted, even if a pier was made off the Wellington Bunder.[211]

He assessed that competition would not undercut the centrality of the port trust, but also that this centrality relied on Indian merchants. The Elphinstone Estate, as it continued to be called even after its purchase by the government, was the closest bunder to the native town. Indian merchants relied on these properties for their trade.

211 Bombay Chamber of Commerce and Industry, 1871–1872, Annual Report, APA, BL, p. 122.

Despite Ormiston's positive prognosis, the new port trust faced private competition. The first administration report analysed causes for the decreased revenue of the government docks:

> Until the passing of the Bunder Fees Act of 1870, no wharfage fees were charged at the Customs Bunder; and this fact, coupled with its central position, prevented the Colaba Bunders from competing with it for foreign imports. But since the passing of the Act in question, English goods have been gradually transferred to Arthur Bunder, partly owing to the lower rate of wharfage fees charged by the Colaba Company, and partly to the excellent warehouse accommodation, which they provide. To meet this competition, the Trustees have reduced the wharfage fees on wines and spirits and on cotton by one-half, but as yet with little effect.[212]

As mentioned by Sandip Hazareesingh and indicated in BPT administrative reports, the new trust's main source of revenue was the import of grain.[213] A famine in the Deccan was the result of the displacement of grain in order to grow cotton, and as a result, grain was imported through Bombay and distributed through its hinterland.[214] Additional warehouse space was built to accommodate grain, including private godowns on BPT property. However, the port trust's Ryan Market for grain did not receive nearly enough business at to make up for lost traffic in other commodities.[215]

The trust also turned to other avenues for revenue. The port trust leased parts of the Elphinstone property bordering the native town, mainly to Indians who sought commercial space between the Masjid Bunder and the native town. The port trust benefited from its land through rents, and this profit was the core of the trust's scheme to pay off the capital debt imposed on it by the Government of India. However, the basic principle established by the Elphinstone Company to separate the Dock Estate from the Land Estate remained intact. The port trust needed to pay off its debt to the Government of India by finding a way to cater to the needs of local merchants.

In order to compete with private docks within the harbour, the port trust began considering dock improvement schemes. Certain port facilities such as wet docks were a continuous point of contention with Ormiston, who first advocated them in his 1866 engineer's report to the Elphinstone Company.[216] A wet

212 Bombay Port Trust, "Administration Report to 31st March 1874", Bombay Port Trust Records (BPTR), IOR, BL, p. 2.

213 Ibid.; Bombay Port Trust, "Administration Report to 31st March 1879", BPTR, IOR, BL, pp. 51–55; Hazareesingh, "Interconnected Synchronicities", p. 26.

214 Hazareesingh, "Chasing Commodities", p. 16.

215 Bombay Port Trust, "Administration Report to 31st March 1879", BPTR, IOR, BL, pp. 55–66.

216 Elphinstone Land & Press Company Limited, "Report of the Directors to the Shareholders at the Seventh Annual General Meeting", 1866, APA, BL, pp. 12–13.

dock is a type of dock that is enclosed through a lock system so that the water remains level during high and low tide. This system allows ships to unload during all hours, not only during certain tides, thus reducing the amount of time it takes dock workers to load and unload ships, and thereby also reducing the time a ship spends in port, allowing for greater turnover at the docks.

Ormiston detailed the benefits of wet docks in addition to the open basins already in use on the Elphinstone Estate:

> I have shown on the accompanying plan how the Musjid and Clare Basins may be made into Wet Docks with entrances 60 feet wide; they are each shown to be 1,050 feet long and 300 feet wide, which gives an aggregate area of 15 acres, and a length of wharfage of 1,760 yards, or one mile. It will give some idea of the size of these to compare them with some well-known docks at home. The Liverpool is 1,050 feet long and 360 feet wide, and the Prince's Dock at the port is 1,485 feet long and 360 feet wide, with an area of 11 acres, and a length of wharfage of 1,187 yards. The Old Bute Dock at Cardiff is 20 acres in extent, and have worded in one year 788,960 register tons of sailing ships, or 255 tons per lineal yard of wharf. The Liverpool Docks work 185 register tons per lineal yard of wharf, at which ration the Musjid and Clare Docks would accommodate 325,600 register tons per annum.[217]

He mentioned the Prince's Dock in Liverpool as a starting point for comparison for what could be done in Bombay. The Elphinstone Company never agreed to the wet dock he advocated in this report. Fear of stagnant water, especially in the "unsanitary" foreshore, was the main problem of constructing such a dock in Bombay.[218]

In 1867, the Government of Bombay set up a committee to decide on the necessity of such a dock in Bombay. It based its decision on health issues (related to stagnant water), the dock's necessity for trade, and the scheme's profitability. The Wet Dock Committee failed to reach an official conclusion, but the majority of members were in favour of wet docks in order to accommodate both steamships and sailing vessels, while the minority was in favour of the system that was already in use at the time of ships lying in stream. The Government of Bombay favoured the minority opinion and argued that the potential sanitary problem posed by wet docks should not be lightly discarded in favour of commerce.[219] The resulting consensus was that there was no need for wet docks in Bombay, but that open deep tidal basins be constructed. In Bombay's harbour, a lock system would actually have only been beneficial during the monsoon

217 Ibid., pp. 12–13.

218 Elphinstone Land & Press Company Limited, "Report of the Directors to the Shareholders at the Seventh Annual General Meeting", 1867, IOR, BL, p. 4.

219 Bombay Chamber of Commerce and Industry, 1867–1868, Annual Report, APA, BL, p. 129.

season. Unlike in many British ports, the harbour in Bombay during the rest of the year allowed ships to remain generally productive regardless of tide.

The Wet Dock Committee remarked that either Mody Bay or the Elphinstone basin could be possible sites for such a dock in the future, but concluded that Mody Bay should be chosen for two reasons. First, in terms of engineering, it would be a preferable location as only 1,000 feet would need to be dredged compared to the half a mile channel that would be necessary were the Elphinstone basins made into deep water basins.[220] Second, Mody Bay was government property while the Elphinstone Estate was still in the hands of a private firm in 1867. Proponents of the plan acknowledged that the government should carry out this work as the Elphinstone Company had previously rejected the profitability and feasibility of wet docks for steamships the previous year.

By the 1870s, the number of steamships in use was increasing in Bombay, but sail remained important. The transition from sail to steam was slow since its introduction in commercial and naval use in the early 1800s. On a single day in Bombay, 7 April 1872 (unattested date), the number and types of merchant vessels docked anywhere in the harbour at private or government bunders were recorded to analyse the need for a deep-water basin. In total, there were only 32 steamers to 109 sailing ships. Of these sailing ships, nearly 70 per cent were large "native craft", presumably involved in intra-Asia/Indian Ocean trade. The gross tonnage of these vessels was recorded at 72,891 tons by the Commissioner of Customs.[221] In short, various types of ships frequented the harbour, and this analysis only extended to merchant vessels, excluding naval and fishing craft.

Ormiston met with Colonel Alexander Fraser of the Royal Engineers in April 1872. One of the main topics they discussed was the feasibility of deep-water basins in Bombay to accommodate the increase in the size of ships. Wet docks were one possibility, but the focus of the discussion was on the decision between deep-water basins at either Mody Bay or the Elphinstone bunders, or the construction of a pier proposed by the Government of India. Enclosed wet docks filled with stagnant water were still considered unsuitable for Bombay's climate. Ormiston was generally against the construction of a pier for various reasons, namely that they were suited for small ports and for transit, "but they are utterly unsustainable for a depot trade of the magnitude we have to deal

220 "Memorandum by Colonel Alex. Fraser, R.E., C.B., on Mr. Ormiston's Scheme for Deep Water Berthage for Ships and Steamers in Bombay", in: Bombay Chamber of Commerce and Industry, 1871–1872, Annual Report, APA, BL, pp. 132a–132m, at 132a–132b.

221 "Questions by Colonel Fraser, R.E., C.B., as to Deep Water Berthage for Ships and Steamers in Bombay and Answers thereto by Mr. Ormiston, C.E.", in: Bombay Chamber of Commerce and Industry, 1871–1872, Annual Report, APA, BL, pp. 109–126, at 122.

with here."[222] One wonders if he is referring to the port's actual situation or rather the image such a pier would convey.

Ormiston detailed the various ways in which Mody Bay or one of the Elphinstone bunders could be transformed into deep-water basins, but also took commercial aspects of the locations into account: "Mody Bay is nearer the Fort, certainly, but though the Fort is where European merchants' offices are situated, and will probably be so wherever the Docks are constructed, the great bulk of the trade is in the hands of natives, and is located in the native town, to the year of the Musjid Bridge."[223] At this time, Mody Bay was still the property of the Government of Bombay while the Elphinstone Estate had been purchased by the Government of India for the formation of the BPT. He concluded: "I cannot see how it is possible to avoid coming to the conclusion that the Elphinstone works ought to be made as soon as possible, and take precedence of the others."[224] This conclusion was unusual in that the deep-sea basins were to be constructed with the purpose of expanding accommodation for deep-sea vessels, mainly steamships. Yet, the bulk of native trade, the backbone of the estate, was carried out by sailing vessels.

The above quotes can be interpreted in three ways. First, the idea of deepening the bunder can be seen as either a scheme to displace native trade with British traffic and as a way to profit from native trade by taking over its location and taxing it (Sandip Hazareesingh argues for both in various dock schemes).[225] Second, it can be seen as a plan to improve the bunders that were most often frequented by merchants and most needed in the presidency for its general economy and trade. The deep-sea basins were not intended to be used exclusively for steamers, but were also meant to accommodate steam and sail vessels side by side. Third, when reading Ormiston's reports to the trust, one gets the sense that he was guided by personal ambition to build Bombay's first wet dock. He was a respected advocate of Bombay's port projects since his time with the Elphinstone Land and Press Company and later with the port trust, but he also used his position to further his career goals. He suggested that Bombay's infrastructure should project its (and his) desired image for the city: modern, advanced, and central to the empire. This image applied not only to the port city's centrality in Indian trade but to his own ambition and reputation. The port's success was tied to his reputation.

222 Ibid., p. 122.
223 Ibid., pp. 109–127, at 124.
224 Ibid.
225 Hazareesingh, "Interconnected Synchronicities."

Once the BPT was formed in 1873, the idea of building a wet dock on the property resurfaced. The question of a deep-water basin was substituted with a proposal to construct a wet dock at either the Elphinstone Bunders or Mody Bay. The Bombay Chamber of Commerce held a special meeting on 14 September 1874 to put forward a proposal to the port trust and to the government on the issue. The trust's previous report, dated 29 September 1873, preferred the Elphinstone bunders as the future site for the location of such facilities, advocated by Ormiston as its chief engineer. The Government of India had already agreed to advance the funds necessary for the project, but the Government of Bombay still refused to sanction the work. Contrary to the port trust's findings, members of the chamber felt that wet docks built on the Elphinstone property would be unsuitable to the needs of the mercantile community.

The chamber decreed the following resolution:

> While the Members of the Chamber avoid expressing any decided opinion as to the engineering difficulties, and relative cost of either scheme, they would point out the many commercial advantages offered by Mody Bay over the Elphinstone Estate, the former being much more central and convenient for that portion of the sea-borne trade for which docks are specially wanted, consequently much less likely to suffer from the competition with the present cargo boat system, and would not in any way interfere with the extensive and important country trade carried in native craft. That this Chamber, whilst aware that the Government of India naturally feels anxious to try to improve the value of the Elphinstone property, trusts that, in any decision arrived at, such a consideration will not be allowed to weigh against what is best for the mercantile interests of the port.[226]

However, this resolution was voted down, 17 to 14, and was not passed on to the Government of India. Instead, the chamber's official suggestion was that it agreed that either Mody Bay or the Elphinstone basins would be suitable for a wet dock, thereby ignoring a plan that was considered by nearly half of the chamber's committee to be potentially harmful to Indian trade.

By 1875, the type and location for the deep-water dock was finalized: a wet dock rather than open tidal basins that would be built on the Elphinstone Estate rather than at Mody Bay. The first wet dock in Bombay opened in 1875, though not at the port trust: the Sassoon Dock of Sassoon & Co. The establishment of this private facility seemed to have quelled any fears about the sanitary problems that might accompany wet docks. The only open issue for the port trust was "what price the trading community are willing to pay for the accommodation afforded."[227] The problem of competitive wharfage fees at private

226 Bombay Chamber of Commerce and Industry, 1873–1874, Annual Report, APA, BL, pp. 5–6.
227 Bombay Port Trust, "Administration Report to 31st March 1876", BPTR, IOR, BL, p. 2.

bunders continued to haunt the port trust. The Sassoon Dock and the Arthur Bunder, another private bunder, "ran the Trust Bunders very hard as usual, and secured the greater part of the English dry goods trade."[228]

By 1880, four years after construction on the dock began, the Prince's Dock was open for traffic. The dock, rather than catering to both sailing vessels and steamers, ultimately served the steam trade of major British shipping companies like Peninsular and Oriental Steam Navigation Company, Clan Lines, and William Mackinnon's BISN.[229] In the early 1880s, the number of sailing vessels entering the dock reflected the actual percentage of sailing vessels active in the harbour, about 23 per cent (800–1,000 vessels). It was also frequented by Indian troops who were dispatched to other parts of the empire.[230] By 1886, only 9 per cent of vessels that used the Prince's Dock were sail (generally native craft).[231] The result was a displacement of native trade, carried out under the guise of modernization, improvement, and necessity.

Ormiston was central to the decision to build a wet dock in Bombay. He reached beyond his position as a technical expert and engineer to achieve his personal goal of designing the first wet dock in Bombay and India. In fact, a private company got to it first, but the Prince's Dock was more ambitious in size, and would serve an imperial purpose. Instead of reporting to the chairmen of the port trust, he went beyond them to speak directly to one of the foremost royal engineers for the Government of India, Colonel Alexander Fraser, and the increasingly influential Bombay Chamber of Commerce, thus bypassing the wavering Government of Bombay and the port trust (his own employers). Ormiston is credited with designing the docks, but George Ormiston (perhaps a close relation) carried out the project. Thomas Ormiston, a Glasgow native, eventually retired in Bombay as the Dean of the Faculty of Engineering at Bombay University.[232] His professional ambition projected Bombay with the image and infrastructure of a great imperial port city.

In the next decades, the BPT continued to expand, thus repositioning itself within the harbour's trade. The Victoria Dock (1888) and the Merewether Dry Dock (1891) followed the construction of the Prince's Dock. The Alexandra Dock opened in 1914. These docks are still in operation today, though the Alexandra Dock has since been renamed the Indira Dock.

---

228 Bombay Port Trust, "Administration Report to 31st March 1879", BPTR, IOR, BL, p. 64.
229 Hazareesingh, "Interconnected Synchronicities", p. 28.
230 Bombay Port Trust, "Administration Report to 31st March 1881", BPTR, IOR, BL, p. 85.
231 Hazareesingh, "Interconnected Synchronicities", p. 28.
232 Ibid., p. 29.

Restructuring and Institutionalizing the Port

By 1879, the future of the BPT was in jeopardy. It faced a choice of either returning the land estate (and therefore much of the debt) to the government and resuming the previous practice of free trade at the port, or of retaining the land estate and maintaining docking fees, leases, and fees for godowns to pay off the debt. In 1867, the Elphinstone company had considered a similar solution to its financial woes: separating the land estate from the docks. The land estate might remain with the company and the docks could be sold to government. Instead, the negotiations led to the sale of the entire Elphinstone Estate. In 1874, a year after the port trust was formed, the trustees asked the Government of India to take back the land to reduce their debt, which was refused. In 1879, a memorandum on the suggestion of separating the land estate from the dock estate read as follows:

> To reduce them [fees], and ultimately to make Bombay a nearly free port, the Trustees must make a profit, where it is most legitimate to make it, namely on the land. By covering this land with buildings and markets, for which good rent is readily obtainable and paid without murmur, the Trustees will in time be able to pay the whole of their interest out of the ground rent. And in time, too, the land will sell at a profitable rate, and the capital debt of the Trust will be liquidated, without any burden being placed on commerce. But without the land the capital cost of the docks and bunders can only be paid off by levying excessive dock dues and wharfage rates.[233]

The trustees eventually agreed that such a policy was necessary and that the trust's operations could continue. The Bombay Chamber of Commerce concurred. Perhaps part of this agreement was derived from self-preservation; the board observed that without a land estate to manage, a port trust would hardly be necessary.

The BPT held on to its land estate and expanded its holdings along Bombay's foreshore. By 1879, the port trust began negotiations to acquire the entire foreshore to control the import and export trade in Bombay "so as to save the necessity of having to compete with any private parties at all."[234] The move to acquire the foreshore was a significant shift for the city's trade and for the government's ability to control it. No longer would individual private ports compete with one another. Competition was rescaled from the harbour level to the city and its trade networks.

---

233 Bombay Port Trust, "Administration Report to 31st March 1879", BPTR, IOR, BL, p. 135.
234 Ibid., p. 64.

Through the original Port Trust Act of 1873, the Government of Bombay negotiated the acquisition of land for "public purpose" through agreement either with the private landowners or by force through compensation.[235] In 1880, the port trust acquired the Sassoon Dock, the competitor to Prince's Dock; the Colaba Company's bunders, the main location for the cotton trade; the Jamsetjee Bunder; and the Mazagon and the Frere Land Companies' properties, in addition to property at Sewree.[236] With competition eliminated, the trust increased the wharfage fees on opium from only 2 annas to 1 rupee per chest, increasing its revenue from opium by 11,467 rupees in the first year.[237] The location of the opium trade shifted as well, from Sassoon Dock to the Customs Bunder. Trade overall shifted within the harbour, and the dock takeover allowed the BPT to oversee most trade in and out of Bombay and to charge higher fees, thus increasing its revenue on multiple fronts.

Until 1880, John Ryan, the traffic manager for the port trust and previously the Elphinstone Land & Press Company, had been integral to the trust's information about general traffic within the harbour and at its own facilities. He recommended that the trust apply the fees on certain goods to remain competitive. He died shortly after the takeover of additional private docks. He was replaced by two men; after his death, the trust separated the management of the Prince's Dock from the rest of the estate. The trustees noted that it was impossible "to procure any one who could carry on all the duties, as he has done."[238] Ryan's extensive knowledge of Bombay's traffic patterns; its main commodities and their specific needs; and a comparative view of practices elsewhere in India and Britain were not easily replaceable qualities.

Before his death, Ryan had also actively investigated the practices of other ports, particularly within India, not only private foreshore properties. He called several times over the years for housing employees on the dock estate.[239] In his last report, he wrote: "I am given to understand that the Port Trust at Calcutta has lately undertaken to supply some of the jetty employees with free quarters adjacent to where work is carries on, so as to have the advantage of always having trained men close at hand in cases of emergency."[240] He appealed to the trustees that the men worked 12-hour days, received low wages, and often had

235 Act no. I of 1873, The Bombay Port Trust Act of 1873, Section XXXII, Acts of the Legislative Council of the Governor of Bombay 1871–1874, IOR, BL, p. 13.
236 Bombay Port Trust, "Administration Report to 31st March 1880", BPTR, IOR, BL, p. 1.
237 Ibid., pp. 4–5.
238 Bombay Port Trust, "Administration Report to 31st March 1881", BPTR, IOR, BL, p. 5.
239 Bombay Port Trust, "Administration Report to 31st March 1879", BPTR, IOR, BL, p. 64.
240 Bombay Port Trust, "Administration Report to 31st March 1880", BPTR, IOR, BL, p. 78.

far to commute to work. These facilities were built. A port hospital had already existed on the property, which catered especially to British crewmen.[241] The Mumbai Port Trust continues to provide some of these facilities for port employees today, and it owns roughly the same property today as it did by the 1880s, about 1,800 acres of the foreshore, one-eighth of Bombay's land. Land management was increasingly tied to the practices of the port. For example, by 1880, the port trust sold rights to graze cattle and gather mangoes on the property, earning 1,045 rupees in the first year.

The administration of the port trust changed with the Port Trust Act of 1879. This act was proposed concurrent to the negotiations to acquire the private foreshore properties. The original proposal for a new board of trustees was based on one-third representation by bond holders, one-third elected by the merchant community, and one-third nominated by the Government of Bombay.[242] The Chamber of Commerce protested the inclusion of bond holders, who would only be interested in the profit but not the trade of the port, as well as several proposals during the negotiation phase of the act, namely that the land estates of the private docks should not be acquired by the port trust.[243] The land estates were included in the final acquisition, but the Chamber of Commerce gained influence over the board of trustees as the voice for the local mercantile community in Bombay, though its members were mostly British, especially Scottish, and prominent Indians. The chamber elected five members to the board and the Government of Bombay nominated seven members. Three of the total board members were required to be Indians who lived in Bombay (and spoke English).[244] The right to acquire, sell, and lease land was extended in this act.[245]

This final negotiation shaped how the port trust was managed since the 1880s; it remains the basis for how ports are managed in Mumbai and in India today. The board is still based on the elected model, but other interests gained a voice after 1947, namely the Indian Merchants' Chamber. The Bombay Chamber of Commerce and Industry is no longer the only institution that elects

241 Bombay Chamber of Commerce and Industry, 1873–1874, Annual Report, APA, BL, p. 348.
242 Bombay Chamber of Commerce and Industry, 1875–1876, Annual Report, APA, BL, p. 29.
243 Ibid., pp. 30–32.
244 Act No. VI, 1879. An Act to consolidate the immoveable and other property vesting in the Trustees of the Port of Bombay, and certain other property on, or connected with, the foreshore of the Island of Bombay into one estate, and to vest the control and management of the same in one Public Trust; and for other purposes, Acts passed by the Governor of Bombay in Council in the years 1878–1879–1880, IOR, BL, p. 4.
245 Ibid., p. 14.

members to the board, but these types of trade organizations continue to play a key role in steering the city's largest landowner.[246]

Conclusion

This chapter described how the port became a single government agency through land possession and institutionalization. In order to manage the port, actors involved in decision-making looked to institutions around India and Britain for management models. The port came to represent multiple scales of interest while overlooking the needs of less prominent Indian merchants.

Negotiations over the port began anew as India became more territorial, that is, as the Government of India sought to better control trade within its territory, build institutions, and manage populations, land, and resources. The port had never been a port of natural trade that could be captured by the colonial government. Instead, centuries of policies had fostered trade in Bombay. Actions by the commercial elite, some of whom were also closely associated with the Government of Bombay, worked to make Bombay an important place in imperial trading networks in order to foster local agendas. As Bombay became increasingly incorporated into the Indian state, the Government of India and the Government of Bombay oversaw this trade for their own purposes. The port transitioned from a space of relatively local or translocal significance to a space of national or imperial importance that it had prior to that time not acquired. The controls put on trade were less about fostering specific external connectedness, which had already been achieved by merchants in the previous decades, than about internally restructuring the city's harbour space along imperial lines.

Personal ambitions also played an important role in remaking the harbour. Thomas Ormiston advocated specific types of projects that would divert native trade out of certain port facilities. This trade was not marginal. On the contrary, it was significant and profitable. In his reports, Ormiston appears captivated by projects that foster a certain type of trade, not in specific commodities per se but trade that would require modern infrastructure for modern steamships. His professional goals and ideas of grandeur for the city played a role in shaping its foreshore.

246 A major port is the current classification of a port run independently as a trust but managed by the central government.

Various levels of government that administered Bombay were dealing with doling out competencies. In the end, the port trust was an institution that resulted in a compromise. It involved governments of both levels in the process, the Bombay Presidency and the Government of India. It also allowed for the participation of local commercial interests. The institution that remained was a multiscalar government body that has lasted through the present day.

4 An Export Processing Zone in the Making, 1940s–1980s

As colonies like India gained independence by the mid-twentieth century, UN agencies, international foundations, and foreign governments sought to steer the paths taken by these emerging states in a new international order. Many of these newly independent countries, especially in South and East Asia, began implementing manufacturing and transhipment enclaves from the 1960s through the 1980s called EPZs. Scholars have tended to focus on the role of these agencies and organizations in the spread of zones around the world. However, some zones in both post-colonial and Western contexts preceded these interventions, and these agencies appear to have also standardized a wider phenomenon.[247] During the formation of an independent Indian state in 1947 and, therefore, at a moment when "territorializing India" was of the highest importance, the Indian government began researching the implementation of zones, preceding the involvement of these foreign agencies in spreading EPZs by over a decade.

This chapter outlines the zone model construct by policy experts and academics, which sought to enable the spread of new zones and to standardize the processes enabled by these zones. While these agencies were key in spreading zone policies, this chapter argues that they also standardized a practice that had already existed. The chapter recounts the history of zone implementation in India, which shows a more complicated trajectory.[248] India's first zone was implemented at Kandla in 1965, a project under discussion since 1948. While United Nations Industrial Development Organization (UNIDO) policy models did influence India's zones, these zones only began to conform to this policy model in the 1980s. This chapter thus shows how the implementation of zones in India was part of state processes of territorialization. Therefore, unlike much of the zone literature that pits zones against the nation state as a symbol of the loss of state sovereignty under globalization, this chapter shows how the zone enjoyed a more complicated relationship with the state in India. This observation may be valuable for a critical analysis of the emergence of zones along with the nation state in other contexts. The history of the zone as a broader practice

247 For various agencies, see: Neveling, "Export Processing Zones, Special Economic Zones."
248 Much of this chapter and parts of the following chapter have been previously published in: M. Maruschke, "Zones of Reterritorialization: India's Free Trade Zones in Comparative Perspective, 1947 to the 1980s", *Journal of Global History* 12 (2017) 3, pp. 410–432, published by Cambridge University Press and reproduced with permission.

https://doi.org/10.1515/9783110615135-004

may reveal changes in state territoriality and territory's relation to other spatial formats such as zone enclaves.[249]

Zone Models in Policy and Academia

The institutional involvement of UNIDO is key to understanding the spread of these EPZs around the world.[250] Patrick Neveling traces the UNIDO policy origins back to the earliest plans to relocate American companies from the mainland US to Puerto Rico to save costs on labour and taxes. Since Puerto Rico's residents do not have the right to vote at the federal level in the US, under the principal of "no taxation without representation", federal taxes do not apply to the island.[251] Arthur D. Little, an American consulting firm, established EPZ-like practices in Puerto Rico in the late 1940s, which later became a model for export-led development promoted by the US through Point Four and the Alliance for Progress during the Cold War.[252] Richard Bolin, an Arthur D. Little employee in the Puerto Rico office, applied a version of the policy in Mexico in the 1960s, establishing what are known as maquiladoras.[253]

UNIDO was formed in 1966 and supported implementing zone policies in developing countries early on. Its role in the proliferation of zones around the world is well established. In 1965, with assistance from the United States Agency for International Development (USAID), a zone was set up in Taiwan's Kaoshiung Port. UNIDO, instituted the next year, sought to position Kaoshiung as a model zone in which it could offer training facilities to promote the zone to other industrializing countries. The US supported a zone policy in the region to open markets in East Asia to Japan, as both countries sought to instigate the regionalization of East Asian markets to combat the spread of communism.[254] When China entered the UN system in 1971, the training facilities in Taiwan, before they even opened, were moved under the "one China logic" out of

---

249 Agnew, "The Territorial Trap"; Brenner, "Between Fixity and Motion"; Brenner, "Beyond State-Centrism?"; Maier, "Consigning the 20th Century to History"; Brenner, *New State Spaces*; Agnew, *Globalization*; Middell and Naumann, "Global History."

250 P. Neveling, "Export Processing Zones and Global Class Formation", in: J. G. Carrier and D. Kalb (eds.), *Anthropologies of Class: Power, Practice and Inequality*, Cambridge: Cambridge University Press, 2015, pp. 164–182.

251 Palan, *Offshore World*, p. 119.

252 Neveling, "Export Processing Zones, Special Economic Zones."

253 Neveling, "Free Trade Zones", p. 1011.

254 The Pacific-Asia Resources Center, *AMPO: Japan-Asia Quarterly Review* 8 and 9 (Special Issue: Free Trade Zones and Industrialization of Asia, 1977) 4, 1–2.

Taiwan to Shannon, Ireland. Shannon's zone had emerged out of a different context than the aforementioned Point Four and UNIDO policies. Since 1947, Shannon had been a customs-free airport, an early version of the now ubiquitous airport duty-free shop. In trying to reposition the airport in relation to transatlantic air traffic that had begun to bypass Shannon, a refuelling stop, after the development of the jet engine, planners proposed extending this "customs-free" programme under an umbrella of three features: warehousing and freight handling, an industrial estate, and tourist facilities.[255] Through UNIDO, Shannon's zone extended its business into consulting and promoting its own scheme as a model. Delegations from around the world were invited to tour the facilities and receive training. UNIDO promoted a standardized zone. It eventually published a manual written by Shannon representatives thereby establishing the zone's international best practice.[256] Therefore, while UNIDO certainly promoted the proliferation of their model EPZ, a spatial-juridical practice resembling these zones had already existed in other contexts and was thereby categorized and systematized by this international agency.

By the mid-1980s, UNIDO had reduced its support for EPZ development. This change in tone followed the growing criticism of EPZs in the late 1970s by academics in various fields.[257] Previously, economic geographers studied zones in local and later countrywide contexts. In contrast, the new international division of labour (NIDL) thesis positioned the zone globally as a key component of what would soon be called neoliberalization, or even what others understand as globalization. As Western and Japanese corporations shifted production to developing countries, the rights of workers in both developed and developing countries were undermined. This thesis and the UNIDO handbook both describe the zone as a space that facilitates deregulation within this delimited space, including features such as the relaxation of labour laws (elimination of the minimum wage, no right to strike), the tax holiday, and other concessions to corporations.[258] Additional standard features included publicly funded warehouse and factory space that corporations could rent, thus reducing their start-

255 J. A. Soulsby, "Shannon Free Airport Scheme: A New Approach to Industrial Development", *Scottish Geographical Magazine* 81 (1965) 2, pp. 104–114, at 108.

256 T. Kelleher, "Handbook on Export Free Zones", United Nations Industrial Development Organization, 1976. For analysis of the handbook, see: Neveling, "Free Trade Zones", p. 1012; Neveling, "Export Processing Zones, Special Economic Zones", p. 76.

257 Takeo, "Free Trade Zones in Southeast Asia", p. 35; *AMPO: Japan-Asia Quarterly Review*; Frank, "Third World Manufacturing"; Fröbel, Heinrichs and Kreye, *New International Division of Labour*.

258 Kelleher, "Handbook."

up costs, and the elimination of customs duties. Of course, UNIDO and zone critics focused on the different outcomes that these features enabled. On the one hand, these policies would encourage Western and Japanese firms to move their production to developing countries, helping to offset the balance of payments problems faced by developing countries, create jobs, and transfer technology and technical expertise. On the other hand, according to the NIDL thesis, these policies enabled worker exploitation and increased unemployment in developed countries as manufacturing jobs moved overseas. All the while, developing countries lost tax revenues.

From the perspectives of both policy and academia, the zone was identified as a single policy present in the developing world, from Latin America, to Asia, to Africa. Both UNIDO and the NIDL authors statistically abstracted zones to compare their features with one another. This chapter shows India's use of zones prior and parallel to UNIDO's activities, elucidating the various concerns of Indian officials in creating India's first zone. These issues are not easy to capture in statistics and policy lists abstracted for international comparison. Rather, these impulses for implementing India's first FTZ speak to the very foundation of India's independent territorializing state. These findings indicate that scholars' overreliance on seeing through the lens of formats – from what the nation state should entail to what a zone enables – needs re-evaluation in light of the intertwined process of territorialization and globalization and the role enclaves have played in managing these processes in India.

A Free Port for India

India became an independent state in 1947. During the British Raj, India was part of the sterling currency area. The Reserve Bank of India had reserves of approximately GBP 1,280 million on 14 June 1946.[259] However, within just the first 11 months of the 1948–1949 fiscal year, India's balance of payments deficit reached 101.34 crore rupees (1.0134 billion), comprising "the entire amount of the Purchase Authority from the International Monetary Fund and also the amount of released spendable sterling."[260] In other words, India's foreign

259 P. B. "The Sterling Balances: Britain's Debts to the Sterling Area Countries", *The World Today* 2 (1946) 8, pp. 353–362, at 359.

260 Letter No. 9–FTA (4)/48 dated 29 June 1949 from the Ministry of Commerce, Government of India to Chamber, in Indian Merchants' Chamber, 1949, Annual Report, Indian Merchants' Chamber Library (F. E. Dinshaw Commercial and Financial Reference Library, hereafter IMC), p. 415.

currency reserves were rapidly depleting on account of increasing imports and decreasing exports. Soon after independence, India's Ministry of Commerce and Industry began to worry about India's foreign exchange earnings.

In the 1950s, like many other newly independent countries, the Government of India pursued import substitution policies that prioritized self-sufficient manufacturing for the Indian market in order to decrease India's reliance on foreign imports. In order to manufacture within India, machinery and manufacturing inputs were often needed from hard currency countries, which further depleted India's foreign exchange reserves. State planners began to regulate foreign trade through licences and permits.[261] Along with import restrictions, the Ministry of Commerce appointed the Export Promotion Committee to increase the quantity and quality of India's exports. This committee was vital in pushing FTZs as a possible solution.

The Export Promotion Committee considered Bombay, Madras, and Calcutta as possible locations for free ports or free zones.[262] On 29 June 1949, the Ministry of Commerce addressed various business chambers in India to solicit opinions on the relatively new US foreign trade zones (FTZs). The purpose of such an enquiry was twofold. On the one hand, the ministry argued that such a system may be useful at Indian ports to increase exports of Indian products through reexport trade. On the other hand, zones in the US could also be used by Indian exporters. The Ministry of Commerce had received complaints about the quality of Indian exports; such spaces could serve as entry points to the US market where Indian products could be reassembled to meet US or international product standards.

The US FTZ was implemented at certain US ports starting in the 1930s, allowing a portion of the port to be sectioned off for custom's-free import and export of goods and their "manipulation."[263] Dara Orenstein notes that the foreign trade zone board promoted the zone abroad, and official delegations from around the world came to tour FTZ 1 at Staten Island. The American zone policy was, at least in rhetoric, based on a practice that began at European ports as early as the 1880s. Free ports in Europe at this time were not the free cities of the Hanseatic League. Rather, as European fragmented economic spaces entered customs unions and were incorporated into nation states, certain ports such as Hamburg were able to negotiate their tax status to allow a

261 I. Milbert, "Building the Economy: 1947–1980", in: C. Jeffrelot (ed.), *India since 1950: Society, Politics, Economy and Culture*, New Delhi: Yatra Books, 2012, pp. 84–104.
262 Ministry of Commerce and Industry, Government of India, Resolution No. 64–LW (34)/49, "Report of the Export Promotion Committee", 1949, IMC, pp. 126–127.
263 Orenstein, "Foreign-Trade Zones."

designated zone at the port site that would enable customs-free transhipment.[264] Such a space became common practice and when American engineers went to study the free port model in the 1920s, they saw such sites throughout the European continent.[265]

While the proposal for a free port zone was inspired by the US system, Indian planners were willing to expand this system to manufacturing, stating that it was not necessary to strictly follow the American model.[266] Manipulation versus manufacturing is not clearly defined, but manipulation might include, for example, dyeing textiles or assembling already manufactured products, while manufacturing involves more extensive activities, such as creating entirely new products from various components. The report suggested that planners rename the policy "free trade zone", to distinguish it from the American "foreign trade zone." Indian reports during this period used these two terms interchangeably.

Allowing manufacturing in such a zone conformed to the existing practice in India's system of bonded warehouses at that time. The government's policy had been to freely permit manufacture in bond, so an FTZ or customs-free zone at certain ports would only be an additional measure to promote exports.[267] This scheme included the drawback of duties paid on imported items, which were then reexported. It also allowed manufacturing and reexport in bond.[268] The proposal to create a zone overlapped considerably with this system, which the Ministry of Finance highlighted much later in its 1958 report. The Ministry of Commerce largely ignored the bonded warehouse system in the debate on the zone policy. Though the practice of manufacturing in bond was not new, it needed rebranding. In contrast to India, the US FTZ system emerged out of debates on the inadequacy of the bonded warehouse.[269] It is not clear how widespread the use of bonded warehouses was in India prior to 1947. By the mid-1960s, these bonded zones were only located at India's largest ports: Calcutta, Madras, Cochin, and Bombay. By 1965, only Bombay's custom zone was

264 W. Delius, *Die Rechtsentwicklung zum heutigen Freihafen Hamburg*, Hamburg: Hans Christians Druckerei und Verlag, 1933, p. 43.
265 Board of Engineers for Rivers and Harbors, War Department and the Bureau of Operations, United States Shipping Board, *Foreign Trade Zones (or Free Ports), Analyzed with Special Reference to the Advisability of their Establishment in the United States*, Washington, DC, 1929.
266 Letter No. 9–FTA (4)/48 dated 29 June 1949, p. 414.
267 Ministry of Finance, Department of Revenue, Government of India, "Report of the Customs Reorganisation Committee", 1958, p. 69, Annual Reports (AR), India Official Department (IOD), Central Secretariat Library (CSL).
268 Ibid.
269 Orenstein, "Foreign-Trade Zones."

actively importing and reexporting, although the imported goods vastly exceeded the value of goods exported or reexported. By 1967–1968, as the first FTZ at Kandla opened, the use of Bombay's bonded zones declined significantly.[270] The fact that such a system already existed in India, but was not widely cited by the Ministry of Commerce raises the question whether the American FTZ was more attractive as a marketing label for such a policy rather than an actual policy model. Research suggests that international economic planning consultants in India during the 1950s and 1960s tended to lend legitimacy to plans pursued by Indian bureaucrats and politicians rather than conclusively influencing Indian planning.[271]

Once the first zone was approved, it was marketed as "Indian" without further reference to the American zone system. An exception is a 1964 report by the Maharashtra Economic Development Council, which sought to create its own zone near Bombay, a plan that was never implemented. This report details the items and "manipulations" carried out at various "free trade zones" in the US, and suggests setting up a free trade zone board based on the American system to oversee numerous zones.[272] The council, an association of business chambers in Maharashtra, referenced annual reports written by the foreign trade zone board to the US congress. Rather than seeking to overcome problems in bonded warehouses, the fact that bonded warehouses functioned so well in Bombay were a sign that the policy could be expanded to FTZs at Indian ports.[273]

In the drive to increase India's exports, the Ministry of Commerce was also interested in the other side of the coin: how Indian exporters could use US FTZs to their advantage. The Indian Standards Institute had already attempted to improve standards on certain Indian export products, but still regularly received complaints about the poor quality of Indian exports, which did not meet Western European and North American import standards. In order to increase India's hard currency exports, it was important to increase manufacturing directly for the US market rather than for foreign markets that would reexport the goods to the US, thereby shifting India's rightful hard currency earnings to

270 Transport Research Division, Ministry of Shipping and Transport, Government of India, "India Ports and Shipping Statistics 1970", AR, IOD, CSL, p. 50.

271 D. C. Engerman, "The Political Power of Economic Ideas? Foreign Economic Advisors and Indian Planning in the 1950s and 1960s", in: A. Hilger and C. R. Unger (eds.), *India in the World since 1947: National and Transnational Perspectives*, Frankfurt am Main: Peter Lang, 2012, pp. 120–135.

272 Maharashtra Economic Development Council, "Report on Free-Trade Zone in Maharashtra", 1964, reprinted 1970, GRC, BL, pp. 13–16.

273 Ibid., p. 11.

a third party. There is no further indication in later documentation whether Indian exports were exported from India to US FTZs for manipulation and then imported to either the US or another market.

Indian officials may have become aware of the American FTZ policy, which began in the 1930s, through numerous channels. As Dara Orenstein writes, the American foreign trade zone board was eager to promote the scheme and used the first FTZ at Staten Island to market it. The zone board hosted tours for foreign officials and published reports on the workings of FTZs. Indian officials may have approached the foreign trade zone board; in any case, the board became aware that the Indian Ministry of Commerce was contemplating a similar scheme. On 2 July 1949, US congressman Emanuel Celler, proponent of the FTZs, wrote a letter to Vitaya Lekahmi Pandit regarding the zones.[274] Pandit, the Indian ambassador to the US and Mexico between 1949 and 1951, was the sister of India's first prime minister, Jawaharlal Nehru. Celler wrote her that he understood India was considering FTZs and enclosed a brochure for her consideration. Beyond the scope of that exchange, there is no indication that an Indian delegation visited the Staten Island FTZ.

The Ministry of Commerce discussed the American recommendations with business chambers. American recommendations specified that zones must be located at the "crossroads of traffic" of international trade; located at a place with access to ample banking facilities; and located where businessmen would be able to establish markets. The report noted that while the second two options could be developed along with the zone, the first element, shipping, needed to be already established. The zone should be sited at a busy port. For that reason, the three major ports of India, Bombay, Madras, and Calcutta, were considered prime locations for such a scheme. The zone required connection to foreign markets.

To the minds of Indian planners, the zone also necessitated isolation. Their goal was not to open up the entire Indian market, but to protect the national economy from the connectedness enabled by the zone. The Ministry of Commerce rejected the 1949 proposal to convert a major port, a government-run port trust, into a free port zone because it could not ensure control over the zone. Extreme congestion and shipping delays, especially in Bombay, became a hassle not only to the Ministry of Transport but also to the Ministry of Commerce. These delays contributed to higher prices on Indian exports.[275] The second reason for not implementing the FTZ policy was that the export promotion

274 Dara Orenstein, email message to author, 31 May 2015.
275 "Report of the Export Promotion Committee", 1949, IMC, p. 22.

committee had difficulty identifying reexport commodities that might benefit from such a scheme apart from the diamond and cashew trade. The diamond trade, they surmised, would be too susceptible to smuggling in this congested port. In the end, the committee recommended the introduction of a drawback duty on the import of foreign goods that would later be reexported.[276] From that position, the committee might be able to identify emerging reexport manufactures and reconsider an FTZ proposal at a later date.

Indian planners debated the merits of having free port cities compared to zones near ports in which taxes would be eased. Indian planners saw the free trade zones or foreign trade zones (the terms were used interchangeably) as possible modified free ports or entrepôt ports. They provided example entrepôt ports in their plans: Singapore and Hong Kong. The planners discussed these as free port cities rather than more restricted free port zones. The American-style zones were seen as preferable to a free port city because it was deemed impossible to open import and export duties in dense cities such as Bombay and Calcutta, whose residents consumed many foreign imports and produced many of the country's exports.[277] Manufacturing in bond, the policy the American FTZs followed, was considered a better solution due to the congestion of India's cities and their ports. A free port zone would offer the state more control over the activities undertaken there and the ability to prevent these goods from entering Indian economic territory. However, early in the debate, the FTZ was discussed as a possible intermediate step towards a complete free port rather than an alternative to such a system.

Although the planners at the Ministry of Commerce initially entertained the zone plan for the traditional economic remedies UNIDO later prescribed it for – increasing foreign exchange earnings – they also saw the potential in using this policy to address other problems associated with territorializing India. This uneven spatial development policy was ironically seen as a way to increase uniform economic growth of India's fragmented territory.

A National Tabula Rasa

At the same time as the Ministry of Commerce sought to deal with India's issues with foreign exchange, Indian planners in various ministries were also dealing

276 Ibid., pp. 26–27.
277 Ibid.; Ministry of Commerce and Industry, Government of India, "Report of the Export Promotion Committee", 31 August 1957, IMC, pp. 47–49.

with territorializing India. The effects of these strategies informed the location of India's first FTZ, substantially shifting the aforementioned policy considerations.

Itty Abraham describes the process of how India became territorial. Abraham claims that Indian politicians sought to turn India into a state recognizable to the West to gain external sovereignty; as a result, India was construed as a territorial nation state.[278] Following independence, planners restructured the state into a federal entity to deal with the plurality of India's states and ethnic groups as well as the princely states (more than 500) that left India's territory fragmented.[279] A post-independence map of India would show "holes" totalling approximately 40 per cent of India's new territory that needed to be integrated into the federal system. While borders were constantly in flux during the colonial period, they continued to fluctuate after India gained independence as they simultaneously came to align with cultural and linguistic lines.[280] India's internal state borders were modified as late as 2015, and Indian official policy continues to censor maps depicting India's internationally recognized external borders.[281] India's federal system emerged as a reaction to and rejection of the highly centralized, but territorially fragmented colonial state.[282]

The shift from an imperial understanding of India's territory towards shaping India as a nation state meant that different territorialization strategies needed to be deployed. Abraham argues that internal territorialization strategies by the British reinforced the image of the Hindu Indian subject at the expense of a minority Muslim subject, many of whom later became Pakistani.[283] The effects of these nation-state territorialization strategies, namely the partition of India and Pakistan, formed part of the motivation for creating a zone in India as well as the choice for the location of such a zone. Indian planners sought to deal with India's newly articulated internal and external space. Rather than focusing exclusively on using the zone to increase foreign exchange reserves, two other key issues emerged: resettling permanent refugees from Pakistan and developing an alternative to Karachi's port, which had previously serviced northern India, including the capital, New Delhi. A future site of

---

278 Abraham, *How India Became Territorial.*

279 L. Kennedy, "Indian Federalism: Moving Towards a More Balanced System", in: Jaffrelot (ed.), *India since 1950*, pp. 249–270, at 251.

280 Ibid., p. 258; Louise Tillin highlights "post-linguistic" state formation in India as a new dynamic in India's internal reorganization: L. Tillin *Remapping India: New States and Their Political Origins*, London: C. Hurst and Co., 2013.

281 "Blacked Out", *Economist*, 21 September 2010, http://www.economist.com/node/17082677.

282 Kennedy, *Politics of Economic Restructuring*, p. 18.

283 Abraham, *How India Became Territorial*, pp. 31–33.

resettlement and a replacement port for Karachi were later combined through the implementation of the Kandla Free Trade Zone (KFTZ).

The small port of Kandla, previously developed in the 1930s by the princely state of Kutch (Kachchh), part of northern Gujarat, was redeveloped as a major port in 1949 in order to offset the loss of Karachi. As a former princely state, it had previously been a semi-sovereign territory. India focused its development efforts on integrating these gaps in territory as quickly as possible. During this period, Gujarat and Maharashtra were both regions part of Bombay State before splitting into two states in 1960. Kutch was its own state until it merged with Gujarat (then Bombay State) in 1956. A secondary but important motivational factor for siting a major port at Kandla was to decongest Bombay, India's busiest major port on the west coast. A major port refers to a port that, for reasons of national importance, is owned by the central government and operated as a financially independent port trust. Kandla Port was not connected by railway and had almost no trade, but "its geographical position is best suited to replace the port of Karachi in its service to the hinterland", despite these drawbacks.[284] In sum, an insignificant remote port gained national significance for planners in numerous government agencies.

As there was no significant trade at Kandla, it was considered essential that a town should be developed near the port in order for one to support the other. Following partition, the Government of India began to develop Gandhidham, comprising 4,337 acres within the port trust estate, to rehabilitate displaced people through the "Kandla Port Organisation" and the Sidhu Resettlement Corporation Limited.[285] In 1949, the township's master plan was "prepared by an American Firm of Town-Planning Consultant's whose services were obtained from the U.S.A. under President Truman's Point Four Programme."[286] The firm Adams Howard & Greenley replaced an Italian firm that had initially been hired for the job.[287]

Though the Ministry of Commerce had ruled out FTZs as an option in 1949, the development commissioner for Kandla Port, K. K. Mitter, proposed Kandla

---

284 Ministry of Transport, Government of India, "Report of the West Coast Major Port Development Committee regarding the possibility of siting a major port on the coast covered by Kathiawar and Cutch", 1949, AR, IOD, CSL, p. 11.

285 Ministry of Transport, Government of India, 1955–1956, Annual Report, AR, IOD, CSL, p. 10.

286 Kandla Port Trust, 1958–1959, Administration Report, annexure II, AR, IOD, CSL.

287 S. Batra, *Port of Kandla: The Gateway of Northwest India*, Adipur, Kutch: The Kandla Commercial, 1964, p. 48.

as the site for such a zone in 1951.[288] The Indian Merchants' Chamber, Bombay's primary business chamber after independence, received communication to the effect from Kandla's development commissioner. The chamber recommended that such a scheme, while full of possibilities, should be considered as a system of zones rather than as a single zone at Kandla. This suggestion mirrored the idea of a zone system as found in the US FTZ policy. This advice was not heeded and the government continued to consider a single zone to be a priority.

The topic was reintroduced in 1957s export promotion committee. The Ministry of Commerce identified Kandla Port as a promising location for a zone. This was not because traffic at Kandla was booming. On the contrary, planners wanted to increase the port's trade. The ministry did not officially approve the final scheme until 1964, although it was advertised abroad as early as 1960. The FTZ could both supply the port with traffic for foreign trade and provide the township with industry. In all cases, these considerations were national rather than local. The question was how to balance the national development space for the newly arrived refugees as well as how to balance India's nodes of external articulation, that is, how to shift trade from Bombay to Kandla to decongest Bombay Port. The zone was an attempt by Indian planners to create a mediated transfer point between the internal and the external.[289] Many of the reasons why Kandla was chosen related to its isolation; the potential connectedness such a policy would generate could be better managed there than at an existing place of transit like Bombay. Isolation became a key selling point in the creation of a space warranting control over external articulation.

The FTZ fell under the purview of the central government. The administration of the zone was carried out from Gandhidham under the direction of the KPT on behalf of the Ministry of Commerce.[290] By 1972, the KPT completed the works on the FTZ, the administration of which was completely turned over to the Ministry of Commerce, and further works were entrusted to the central government's Public Works Department.[291] In addition to an administrator appointed by the Ministry of Commerce to run KFTZ, the ministry also instituted a committee of subnational state government officials and other central government ministries to advise on setting up export-oriented industries within the zone, matters of taxation, and

288 Letter No. 1257 dated 2 April 1952 from Chamber to the Government of India and Letter No. 6–TP(P)(2)/50 dated 9 May 1951 from the Ministry of Commerce and Industry to Chamber. Printed Indian Merchants' Chamber, 1952, Annual Report, pp. 469–471.
289 Geyer, "Portals of Globalization."
290 Kandla Port Trust, 1964–1965, Administration Report, AR, IOD, CSL, p. 13.
291 Ibid., p. 17.

procuring resources for these industries such as electricity, water, and mineral resources.[292] Therefore, multi-scalar involvement in the FTZ policy entailed a multi-scalar logic, but in compliance with central government mandates.

Along with the FTZ, another manufacturing policy was promoted in India at that time: the industrial estate. An industrial estate was developed at Kandla prior to the FTZ to promote industry and trade in the township and at the port. There is some evidence that industrial estates were a precursor to EPZs and some of the earliest FTZs emerged out of modified industrial estates. Shannon FTZ was first developed as an industrial estate that added tax incentives based on duty-free airport schemes.[293] Anthropologist Jamie Cross included an extensive discussion of the industrial estate in India as a precursor to the lived experiences in India's current SEZs.[294] In India, however, industrial estates and FTZs were separate policies controlled by separate levels of government for different purposes. Industrial estates, launched in 1954, were typically planned by subnational states and local governments to promote small-scale industry for national production, while FTZs were planned by the central government to balance the current account. In other words, one policy formed a key part of India's import substitution drive; the other was its antidote.[295] India's federal system further contributed to the separation of these policies.

Distinctions between spatial scales often break down at ports, as actors' strategies from global, regional, national, subnational, and local levels meet and are rearticulated. Gandhidham township was included in Kandla's Port Trust estate, which meant that the entire area theoretically fell under the purview of the central government, but in fact all administrative levels were involved in administering and planning this township, from the national to the municipal.[296] Though the industrial estate at Gandhidham was separate from the FTZ policy, the industrial estate did not strictly conform to the federal division of the two policies elsewhere in India. Kandla's industrial estate was developed and financed by both the KPT and the state Government of Bombay.[297] Work on the township began

292 Ministry of Commerce, Ministry of International Trade, Government of India, 1964, Administrative Report, AR, IOR, CSL, p. 17.
293 Soulsby, "Shannon Free Airport Scheme."
294 Cross, *Dream Zones*, pp. 30–35.
295 D. Nagaiya, *Industrial Estates Programme: The Indian Experience*, Yousufguda, Hyderabad: Small Industry Extension Training Institute, 1971.
296 Ministry of Transport and Communications, Department of Transport, Government of India, 1958–1959, Annual Report, AR, IOD, CSL, p. 11.
297 Kandla Port Trust, 1958–1959, Administration Report, AR, IOD, CSL, annexure II.

in 1955. The port trust and state government developed seven residential sectors, two industrial sectors, one warehousing sector, along with business and office areas and schools. When Bombay State was dissolved and separated into Maharashtra and Gujarat in 1960, the industrial estate was developed by the KPT in cooperation with Gujarat state. The Government of India continued to support the development of the township.[298]

The industrial estate and the FTZ were considered separate projects at Kandla. By 1964, the industrial estate was completed and comprised 52 sheds, although only 15 industries had begun their operations there and 29 sheds had been allotted.[299] These sheds were constructed and managed by the port trust, a central government authority, on behalf of the Gujarat State Government. Unlike this multi-scalar policy, the FTZ fell completely under the purview of the central government. The administration of the zone was carried out from Gandhidham under the direction of the KPT on behalf of the Ministry of Commerce.[300] KFTZ opened in 1965.

During the 1960s and 1970s, UNIDO promoted both zones and industrial estates to countries of the non-aligned movement, of which India was a prominent member. UNIDO developed a management training programme for industrial estate managers.[301] Yet again, zones were considered a separate policy. They enabled legal and spatial features that the estate did not. As with the industrial estate, UNIDO sought to implement an international best practice of the zone. By 1976, UNIDO published a handbook on setting up EPZs and trained government employees from around the world how to establish a zone policy, offering sample legislation and describing detailed features of the zone.[302] As shown here, India's first zone preceded these activities.

Shifting policy concerns, from economic challenges to territorialization strategies, changed the idea of the FTZ in India. Once it was instituted, it still operated to some degree as a modified free port based on the US FTZ policy, although the unofficial goals for the policy had shifted considerably.

---

298 Kandla Port Trust, 1962–1963, Administration Report, AR, IOD, CSL, p. 13.
299 Kandla Port Trust, 1963–1964, Administration Report, AR, IOD, CSL, p. 9.
300 Kandla Port Trust, 1964–1965, Administration Report, AR, IOD, CSL, p. 13.
301 UNIDO, "Guidelines for the Establishment of Industrial Estates in Developing Countries", Vienna: United Nations, 1978, pp. 73–74.
302 Kelleher, "Handbook."

From Free Trade Zones to Export Processing Zones

KFTZ is frequently discussed as India's first EPZ and, as such, India's first zone that can be linked with India's current SEZs.[303] However, KFTZ did not take on the features most commonly associated with EPZs in other countries, including restrictions of workers' rights and corporate tax breaks until the 1980s. KFTZ is an EPZ that grew out of shifting state territorialization policies, becoming the zone it is now over time, not through a single intervention by an international organization.

Despite the unofficial motivations for KFTZ discussed earlier, KFTZ was still officially envisioned for the same purpose that drove many import substitution-based developing countries to institute zones: to increase foreign exchange earnings. By April 1960, the Lok Sabha, the directly elected lower house of India's parliament, decided to establish an FTZ at Kandla with the purpose of increasing foreign exchange earnings by increasing exports through the reduction or elimination of import and export duties within a delimited space.[304]

At that time, although the Kandla zone was no longer publicly linked to the American FTZ model, the proposed plan more or less adhered to this formula. A zone within the port would be enclosed by a barbed wire fence (KFTZ was near the port property, not within it), and customs personnel would control the entry and exit of all goods. Within this enclosed space, unfinished goods and raw materials would be imported, manufactured, and exported without a customs duty. Exclusive warehouses for transshipment were also considered at first, making this a proposal for an entrepôt free port. Manufacturing, therefore, was not the sole purpose of the zone. Though the lapidary industry had previously been considered one to benefit from a space designated for transshipment, imports of diamonds, gold, and other gems were prohibited, mainly due to fear of smuggling.[305]

KFTZ was a space of central government oversight, not free trade or deregulation:

> The industries to be established in the Zone will be licensed, where necessary, in accordance with the rules for the licensing of industries elsewhere in India and be subject to suitable supervision and control. The intention is that a party wishing to start a particular industry will be allowed to do so unless the establishment of such an industry is likely to set up unfair competition with a similar existing industry elsewhere in India.[306]

---

303 Aggarwal, *Social and Economic Impact*, pp. 64–65.
304 M. Dattatreyulu, *Export Processing Zones in India: A Case Study of Kandla Free Trade Zone*, New Delhi: Indian Institute of Foreign Trade, 1990, pp. 2–3.
305 Ministry of Transport and Communication, Government of India, 1960–1961, Annual Report, AR, IOD, CSL, p. 20.
306 Ibid.

The zone was not a haven for foreign corporations to operate within an Indian enclave without restriction. Rather, foreign or Indian companies operated there under the control of the Ministry of Commerce. Exports were encouraged and imports into India's domestic tariff area from the zone were subject to all customs duties and requirements. Indian officials were willing to forego revenue from customs duties for the sake of foreign exchange earnings. The zone was part of the so-called Licence Raj – in which private companies could only operate under extensive licensing and oversight – not an exception to it.

KFTZ was fully operational by 1967. The zone was located just 9 km north of Kandla Port and 6 km from Kandla's township, Gandhidham. The site was originally 640 acres in size and later increased by 320 acres. This multiproduct zone had 23 units (firms operating inside the zone) in operation and generated 70 jobs in its initial year.[307] Although multiple sectors were allowed, manufactures were mostly in engineering (e.g. stainless steel, hand-knitting machines, and electrical), chemicals, and textile products.[308] The number of units operating within the zone remained steady for the next decade, although employment rose to 650 employees by 1976. Several reports discuss that the numbers generated by the zone authority were not always accurate. In some cases, units were approved, but were not operational or employees were "employed", but not working. The numbers of units and employees are mere estimates.

The Government of India established India's second zone in Bombay in 1973. In the early 1960s, various electronics committees were convened by noted scientists to review the state of the entire field of electronics in India from production to research. By 1970, the Government of India created a separate department of electronics under the direct supervision of the prime minister.[309] Professor Menon was appointed secretary of the department. Since 1971, many of the initiatives to bolster the electronics industry were undertaken at the subnational state level and supported by the central government. Santacruz Electronics Export Processing Zone (SEEPZ) was one such initiative, established together with the cooperation of the central government department of electronics and the Government of Maharashtra.

SEEPZ is located in one of Bombay's northern suburbs of the city only 6 km from the international and domestic airport. In contrast to KFTZ's vicinity to Kandla Port, SEEPZ is approximately 30 km from Bombay Port. Based on its

307 Dattatreyulu, *Export Processing Zones in India*, p. 19.

308 N. Vittal, "Free Trade Zones and Export Strategy", *Foreign Trade Review* 12 (1977) 3, pp. 396–414, at 406–410.

309 S. M. Agarwal, "Electronics in India: Past Strategies and Future Possibilities", *World Development* 13 (1985) 3, pp. 237–292, at 284.

name, SEEPZ was envisioned as an EPZ rather than a modified free port. This change in name can be attributed to the fact that SEEPZ was not made in Kandla's image alone, but the Government of India's Trade Development Authority, in cooperation with the Department of Electronics, visited several EPZs abroad and reported on the possibilities such zones would offer India in terms of electronics manufacturing and export. Despite the foreign tours, SEEPZs operated along a similar incentive structure to KFTZ. The tax holidays and limited rights of workers found in other EPZs abroad were not included in its initial structure.

SEEPZ was a uniproduct zone focused on computer manufacturing and assembly, other electronics, and computer software. In addition to increasing exports and earning foreign exchange, it was also a part of India's national policy of specializing in electronics and computing. Like KFTZ, SEEPZ focused fully on export-oriented production. By 1977, only 5 per cent of total production in India was export based, and, in 1974, out of a total of 4,500 industrial enterprises in India, only 125 enterprises contributed significantly to India's manufacturing exports.[310] Although just small drops in the ocean, SEEPZ and KFTZ were spaces in which the Indian government could focus on export-oriented industries, sometimes industries of its choosing like electronics. These zones became strategic sites for state-driven economic engagement between India and the global economy.

In March 1988, SEEPZ expanded its expertise beyond electronics to set up a special section for gems and jewellery. The zone expanded in this industry though, from the earliest years of KFTZ's development, imports of gems and gold, along with pharmaceuticals, were prohibited in the zone for fear of smuggling.[311] Diamond cutting was a long-established industry on India's west coast. Although Kandla had originally prohibited diamond and gem processing, in 1949 the very first mention of a FTZ in India proposed precious gem processing as one profitable transshipment industry that could benefit from such a zone.[312] A 1953 public notice allowed for uncut diamonds to enter India under bond for cutting and reexport, but the import licences were restrictive, and the lapidary industry was not considered part of India's national export promotion scheme.[313] By 1979, Bombay had been identified by zone planners as a nodal

310 Vittal, "Free Trade Zones", p. 413.

311 Batra, *Port of Kandla*, p. 13.

312 Letter No. 9–FTA (4)/48 dated 29 June 1949 from the Ministry of Commerce, Government of India to Chamber, in Indian Merchants' Chamber, 1949, Annual Report, IMC, p. 413.

313 Letter No. O–729–Exp./53 dated 25 February 1953 from the Government of India to Chamber, enclosed, Public Notice No. 18–ITC(PN)/53, in: Indian Merchants' Chamber, 1954, Annual Report, IMC, pp. 256–257.

point in the global gem, jewellery, and diamond trade.[314] Instead of creating a new zone to facilitate this trade, SEEPZ accommodated this addition, expanding to its current 111 acres.

An International and Regional Assessment of KFTZ and SEEPZ

By the late 1970s, UNIDO's reports assessed KFTZ and SEEPZ in a broader international context. In a regional context, the success of East Asian zones in Taiwan and South Korea gained publicity as did their state-led, export-oriented development models. The establishment of a zone near India's southern coastal boarder in Sri Lanka in 1978 solidified the view that KFTZ and SEEPZ were not isolated, nationally-bound spaces. They were competing with zones in other countries. The motivations for SEEPZ and KFTZ had never been exclusively focused on gaining foreign investors. Rather, the majority of zone units were smaller, Indian firms. However, these comparisons to other zones led Indian planners to reassess the facilities and incentives offered in both zones.

Until the 1980s, SEEPZ and KFTZ offered firms a number of incentives, including no import duties on goods, materials, or equipment used for export processing; access to raw materials from the domestic tariff area; no municipal tax or octroi tax (town dues on goods entering or exiting a municipal area); income tax concessions of 20 per cent of the profits for ten years; exemption from Gujarat state sales tax (after 1974, KFTZ) on items purchased for use in zone such as machinery; reimbursement of central sales tax paid by zone units (after 1978); foreign investment was permitted, but not automatically; non-resident Indian (NRI) investment was permitted in any form; and profits by foreign firms could be repatriated after the payment of a tax to the extent of half the year's net export earnings.[315] NRI refers to Indian citizens who reside abroad and maintain tax status outside of India. These incentives provide a relatively extensive picture of the incentives provided by these zones. These incentives changed over time, as can be seen by the elimination of sales taxes in the zones in the 1970s. These incentives cross all tiers of central, state, and local government concessions to zone units. There are two incentives generally attributed by international policy models to EPZs conspicuously missing from this list: the tax holiday and the loss of workers' rights.

314 "Committee on Export Strategy 1980s", New Delhi: Ministry of Commerce, Government of India, 1980, in: V. Kumar (ed.), *Committees and Commissions in India 1979*, vol. 17, part B. New Delhi: Concept Publishing Company, 1994, pp. 437–473.
315 Dattatreyulu, *Export Processing Zones in India*, pp. 14–17.

In order to assess whether SEEPZ and KFTZ were successful, that is, whether they contributed to India's exports and thereby increased India's foreign exchange reserves, Indian ministries studied both zones in the late 1970s. On 11 November 1977, the free trade zone advisory committee visited Kandla Port. This committee was headed by P.K. Kaul, the additional secretary to the Ministry of Commerce and president of the SEEPZ board.[316] This committee later issued the Kaul report on the workings of KFTZ.[317] Likewise, in 1978 the Ministry of Steel, Mines and Coal's Review Committee on Electronics assessed SEEPZ's activities in detail in what is known as the Sondhi report, after the name of the committee chairman, Mantosh Sondhi.[318] Finally, the Tandon report, based on the advice of the previous two reports, was a more comprehensive report on India's export strategy led by Chairman Prakash Tandon, the director general of the National Council of Applied Economic Research.[319] Mantosh Sondhi was also a member of the 1979 Tandon committee.

These reports shifted the discussion on India's zones. The initial comparisons had mainly been of the incentives offered within the zones as opposed to export incentives in the domestic tariff area. The Sondhi and the Tandon reports began to highlight the deficiencies of KFTZ and SEEPZ in relation to other zones operating abroad. The Sondhi report emphasized the problems faced by Indian and foreign investors:

> The interest of Indian investors in the Zone has declined because the incentives available to the units in the Zone are not significantly better than what is available to the hinterland units; nor have the foreign investors found in the Zone a red-tape free climate as in free trade zones established in countries like Taiwan, Ireland, Korea, Singapore, Puertorico, Philippines, Panama and more recently Sri Lanka.[320]

The report continues: these foreign zones offer "far greater attractions and inducements" in contrast to SEEPZ. The 1979 Tandon report repeats this view: SEEPZ's facilities are not on par with international standards. This report explicitly proposes a tax holiday at Indian zones in addition to other exceptions

316 Kandla Port Trust, 1977–1978, Administration Report, AR, IOR, CSL, p. 22.
317 Ministry of Commerce and Industry, Government of India, "Problems Hindering the Growth of KFTZ", in: "Report of the Committee Appointed under the Chairmanship of Shri P.K. Kaul", 1978, IOR, CSL.
318 Ministry of Steel, Mines & Coal, Government of India, "Report of the Review Committee on Electronics", 30 September 1979, IOR, CSL.
319 Kumar, "Committee on Export Strategy 1980s."
320 "Report of the Review Committee on Electronics", p. 45.

from levies and dues.[321] As planners began to shift their focus towards increasing investment from foreign firms, they feared that if facilities and incentives were not on par with competing zones in other countries throughout South and Southeast Asia, SEEPZ and KFTZ would never attract these companies.

An official visit by Indian business communities to zones in Asia generated knowledge about their functioning. The Federation of Indian Chambers of Commerce and Industry, a non-government but nationally oriented business chamber, sent a study team to South Korea, Taiwan, Hong Kong, and Singapore to ask a single question: do we have this at our FTZs?[322] This delegation's report was sent to the Ministry of Commerce in the early 1980s, leading public office holders to quote the document to advocate *new* zones that would be "completely free from normal rules and regulations", including eliminating labour laws, licensing, and offering offshore banking facilities. Notably, the zones visited also included Hong Kong and Singapore, which became integrated into government reports and visions of successful zones despite being (semi)independent port cities. This visit was regionally focused on East Asia and addressed zones within the context of the larger questions Indian planners were grappling with at that time: how shifting from import substitution to an export-based economy appeared to stimulate growth, employment, and alleviate poverty in India's East Asian neighbours.

The Government of India established a Committee on Trade Polices under the auspices of the Ministry of Commerce in the early 1980s to reassess India's export strategy. The secretary of the committee, Abid Hussain, answered an extensive memorandum on India's export policy, describing the hindrances to both FTZs in relation to international standards for logistics infrastructure and zone incentive packages. He referenced South Korea, Taiwan, Malaysia, and notably Sri Lanka, India's southern neighbour that established a zone in the late 1970s.[323] His knowledge of these facilities came from the aforementioned report by the delegation from the Federation of Indian Chambers of Commerce and Industry. When KFTZ had first opened in 1965, analysis of the zone was independent of regional or international comparisons. By the early 1980s, so many zones existed throughout the region that these comparisons formed the basis for shifting standards.

While India's KFTZ developed out of the US model of the FTZ, the international zones these committees referenced include those zones known to have

321 Kumar, "Committee on Export Strategy 1980s", pp. 449–451.
322 Indian Merchants' Chamber, 1984, Annual Report, IMC, p. 155.
323 Ibid.

developed under UNIDO advisement. Only once SEEPZ and KFTZ were assessed in international rankings did Indian planners consider enhancing the scope of their investment incentives. These comparisons went beyond zones and included the port cities Singapore and Hong Kong, which provided special incentives for reexport trade. By comparing Indian zones on an international level, the Sondhi report found that unlike many of the other zones, SEEPZ, like KFTZ, did not offer a five-year tax holiday or the reduction of red tape in the form of quick decision-making (analysing time to approval). It did not permit 100 per cent foreign equity participation without assessment of merits and it did not grant more exemptions on the personal income of foreign zone staff in comparison to policies in the domestic tariff area.[324] Based on this comparison with EPZs abroad and the export incentives given to firms in India's domestic tariff area, Indian planners began to reassess what they offered within these enclaved spaces to make them nationally, regionally, and internationally competitive.

Towards a UNIDO Model Zone in India

The UNIDO handbook published by Shannon Free Airport Development Company in 1976 highlights the incentives offered by zones around the world:

> *The most important incentive offered in EFZ's* [export free zones] *is total relief from income tax on export profits.* Over 80% of EFZ's offer this form of incentive [...]. The Arab Republic of Egypt offers the longest tax relied – it lasts forever. There is however a 1% tax on exports. Senegal offers tax relief for 25 years [...]. A large number of zones have tax reliefs for periods from 5 to 10 years. *There is no relief in the Bataan Zone or in Santa Cruz in Bombay.* At Bataan there is, however, accelerated depreciation, and operating losses in the first five years can be set against profits in the succeeding 5 years.[325]

The tax holiday was an essential part of the incentive package offered to firms. As outlined by UNIDO, SEEPZ did not fit with the other 80 per cent of zones that offered these tax breaks. Likewise, KFTZ was barely included in the handbook. In fact, only SEEPZ is named as India's export-free zone, although KFTZ later shows up in the appendix charts.[326] This is remarkable considering that Kaoshiung, the original UNIDO model in Taiwan, and KFTZ were instituted in the same year. The lack of congruity with other zones supported by UNIDO may account for UNIDO's oversight. Based on the recommendations by the Sondhi

324 "Report of the Review Committee on Electronics", pp. 156–159.
325 Kelleher, "Handbook", p. 42 (emphasis added).
326 Ibid., pp. 16, 18, 70.

and Tandon committees, on 1 April 1981, the Ministry of Commerce implemented a tax holiday of five years within five consecutive years in the first eight-year period. This particular aspect, which was considered a crucial element of the zone – both in UNIDO's model and in critical studies of zones – was not implemented in Indian zones until the 1980s.

Like the tax holiday, SEEPZ and KFTZ had differed from UNIDO recommendations in another essential manner: labour. The UNIDO handbook reiterates: "In most EFZ's [economic free zones] the incentive package is built around tax reliefs on export profits and low cost land or buildings for sale or rent [. . .]. [L] ow cost labour and freedom from industrial unrest are also stressed."[327] In short, minimum wages in zones were not enforced and strikes were also prohibited. SEEPZ and KFTZ did not adhere to this aspect present in the other zones referenced by UNIDO. Along with the additional tax holiday, labour laws also changed for these Indian zones in 1981. Zones were no longer assigned an employment or industrial sector.[328] The central government Minimum Wages Act of 1948 did not represent a blanket minimum wage, but a variegated one across subnational states, employment sectors, and worker-skill level, allowing local wage boards to dictate the minimum levels across industries. As zone units were no longer recognized as part of an industrial sector, minimum wages no longer applied to their workers.

Zone authorities requested a minimum wage throughout the 1980s, but units within zones were legally free to set their own standards, which were often lower than those requested by the zone authorities. Wages in SEEPZ and KFTZ were lower than wages in zones in other countries, but not necessarily lower than employment in comparable sectors in India. Few federal laws applied to small business (such as those that operated in KFTZ) with the exception of child labour laws (age 14 was the legal minimum age), minimum wages, and hygiene standards.[329] The zone wages were also lower than in other zones in the region. In SEEPZ, for example, the average wage per hour in electronics manufacturing was 0.17 US dollar (USD) (in 1983) compared 0.30 USD per hour in Philippines zones (in 1978) and 0.42 USD per hour in Malaysian zones (in 1980).[330] In comparison, American workers in this sector earned 6.96 USD per hour (in 1980).[331]

327 Kelleher, "Handbook", p. 41.
328 R. Kumar, *India's Export Processing Zones*, New Delhi: Oxford University Press, 1989, p. 116.
329 G. Heuzé, "Labour Movements and Organisations in India", Jeffrelot (ed.), *India since 1950*, pp. 425–444, at 434.
330 Fröbel, Heinrichs and Kreye, *New International Division of Labour*, p. 351.
331 Kumar, *India's Export Processing Zones*, p. 113.

In addition to abolishing minimum wages, zone units were declared public utility services under the Industrial Disputes Act of 1981. This policy change made striking without notice illegal and required a reconciliation process through the Labour Commissioner's Office prior to striking. However, strikes and union membership were not entirely forbidden. Between 1978 and 1983, SEEPZ faced 7 strikes involving 720 workers in 5 units. In KFTZ, on the other hand, there were 15 closures over the same time period, involving 8 units and 2,339 workers.[332] Yet, the policy changes did not completely prevent zone workers from resorting to strikes, even flash strikes, over labour disputes.[333] These labour disputes often began because zone authorities were unable to compel the firms operating in the zone to pay their workers minimum wage and overtime pay as the policy was left to the discretion of the zone units. Labour in Bombay's manufacturing industry tended to be casualized, despite the important role unions played in the city's social fabric.[334] Although wages had always been low when compared internationally, restricting strikes as much as possible was an important step in shifting SEEPZ and KFTZ from the past free port zones they resembled to the EPZs they became.

Finally, the changes at SEEPZ and KFTZ allowed fully owned foreign corporations to invest in the zone. With regard to Kandla, after announcing the tax holiday in 1981, the number of units inside the zone increased drastically, from a stagnant 47 in 1980 to 108 by 1989, increasing employment from approximately 3,000 to 8,000 people.[335] These three changes, in addition to numerous others, signalled a shift within the zones' operations, which finally began to conform to UNIDO recommendations and an international standard zone. This shift in policy, however, should not be viewed as unique to KFTZ and SEEPZ. In 1985, a United Nations Conference on Trade and Development (UNCTAD) report stressed that due to the extreme mobility of firms operating in zones, a growing competition between zones in various countries led to ever expanding incentive packages as each zone authority sought to outdo the others. The report closed with a word of caution: "In view of the existing competition among EPZs, it

332 Ibid., pp. 116–117.

333 K. N. Ghorude, "Labour in Export Processing Zones: The Case of SEEPZ, Mumbai", *The Indian Journal of Labour Economics* 47 (2004) 4, pp. 1093–1100, at 1099.

334 R. Chandavarkar, *The Origins of Industrial Capitalism in India: Business Strategies and the Working Classes in Bombay, 1900–1940*, Cambridge: Cambridge University Press, 1994, pp. 239–277.

335 Dattatreyulu, *Export Processing Zones in India*, p. 19.

seems particularly important that developing countries should assess carefully the costs and benefits of the operation of free zones for their economies."[336]

As UNIDO compiled information about the international standards set in seemingly similar spaces around the world, especially in Asia, planners in India became more aware of the practices in KFTZ and SEEPZ as part of an international model. The rationale for the zone shifted from the construction of KFTZ as a place to enhance growth in an impoverished region to SEEPZ as an experimental space to enhance India's capabilities in electronics. With the increasing awareness of these zones as only two of many, the focus shifted from internal concerns towards an international and regional understanding of these zones as spaces of global competition. Planning for zones shifted from an understanding of the zone as an internal spatial strategy within India's geography to an externalizing spatial strategy oriented to the global scale.

Conclusion

While foreign and international agencies, particularly UN institutions, had pressured host countries to implement zones, in the Indian case, Indian policy makers had considered a zone/free port very early, almost simultaneously to independence. It appears that Indian policy makers looked outwards to find policy models that would justify their practice of creating Licence Raj "loopholes" in several locations near ports in order to legitimize their own practices. As a result of ongoing debates and policy inspirations, India's first two zones developed out of multiple policy transfers over many decades. Similar zones (bonded warehouses) for manufacturing had already existed at several ports in India, but foreign policies helped legitimize the new practice.

Though zones are today often associated with neoliberalism and corporate exploitation, zones in India were part of India's state planning space, as scholars later argued for India's current SEZ.[337] These findings suggest that a comparative study may reveal a much larger story of the zone beyond the Indian context: that the zone was not a singular model but perhaps a ubiquitous spatial economic and political practice that became increasingly portrayed as a single model by UNIDO. The spread of such a model informed current historical zone research that traces back aspects of this model to the past rather than

336 United Nations Conference on Trade and Development (UNCTD), "Export Processing Free Zones in Developing Countries: Implications for Trade and Industrialization Policies", New York: United Nations, 1983.

337 Kennedy, *Politics of Economic Restructuring*, pp. 78–111.

looking for the emergence of individual zones in both developed and developing countries. Studies that focus on neoliberalism as an analytical lens for studying the EPZ in other places might similarly fail to capture the larger context of the zone's emergence.[338] By expecting to see a particular model, UNIDO as well as scholars working on the NIDL thesis failed to capture the dynamism and complexity of zones in various contexts, including at KFTZ and SEEPZ.

What appears to be of historical interest – beyond the spread of the policy and the role of agencies in spreading it – is the interplay between state territoriality and the zoned enclave. That is, at the moment of independence the nation state faced issues that required a spatial solution. The zone allowed the state some leeway in dealing with its territorialization and globalization projects, as the following chapter demonstrates in more detail.

338 Ong, *Neoliberalism as Exception*; B. G. Park, "Spatially Selective Liberalization and Graduated Sovereignty: Politics of Neo-Liberalism and 'Special Economic Zones' in South Korea", *Political Geography* 24 (2005) 7, pp. 850–873; P. Neveling, "Structural Contingencies and Untimely Coincidences in the Making of Neoliberal India: The Kandla Free Trade Zone, 1965–91", *Contributions to Indian Sociology* 48 (2014) 1, pp. 17–43.

5 Managing World Orders, 1960s–1980s

The New International Economic Order emerged as a set of proposals put forward in 1973 to UNCTAD by the Non-Aligned Movement (NAM), a group of states not aligned with either the Eastern or the Western power bloc. It aspired to be an international economic order system that would be favourable to the Third World: an economic order that would assure developing states to have more control over their natural resources, increase their market access, and expand their access for development, aid, and assistance.[339] By 1979, such a powerful statement was reduced by Bombay's business chamber to a marketing slogan to entice US investors to Bombay.

In a speech to welcome an American delegation to a conference at Bombay's business chamber in 1979, the Indian Merchants' Chamber, Ramkrishna Bajaj, president of the chamber, stated: "[b]oth India and the USA could join together in setting up export-oriented projects in India. India could be of use as a spring-board to manufacture a host of items not only for exporting to the USA, but also to other countries in the West and South-East Asia."[340]

This conference, "Trade and Investment in the New International Economic Order", brought together American and Indian business leaders, who discussed the extent to which multinational corporations could be benevolent tools for growth in developing countries like India. American or other foreign firms could hire Indian subsidiaries to produce products for export to the US market, and India's geographical position in the Indian Ocean would allow US firms to tap markets in West and East Asia alike. That same year, the Indian Merchants' Chamber met a Soviet delegation to discuss how exports to the USSR from India could be increased. The extent to which India could function as a springboard for US corporations to ship American products to the USSR was overlooked at the American meeting.

This chapter shows how KFTZ and SEEPZ, India's first zones, functioned as portals of globalization to manage a variety of spatial orders.[341] Both spaces were envisioned by the Government of India as nodal points that would

339 J. Bockman, "Socialist Globalization against Capitalist Neocolonialism: The Economic Ideas behind the New International Economic Order", *Humanity* 6 (2015) 1, pp. 109–128.

340 Indian Merchants' Chamber, 1979, Annual Report, IMC, p. 291.

341 Middell and Naumann, "Global History", p. 162; a section of this chapter appears in Maruschke, "Zones of Reterritorialization", and is reproduced with permission by Cambridge University Press.

https://doi.org/10.1515/9783110615135-005

connect India to new markets and investment opportunities. They served as enclosed spaces of connectedness that were part of the Ministry of Commerce's de- and reterritorializing strategy: to open certain spaces to investment and imports/exports that would continue to serve a national purpose of increasing foreign exchange earnings, while simultaneously shielding the rest of the Indian economy from such openness.[342] To that end, physical barriers seemed necessary as did isolation. This reterritorialization project also extended to Indian citizenship. The Government of India specifically targeted Indian citizens residing abroad to become zone investors while allowing them to remain tax resident outside of India. The goal was to connect Indian manufactures to the Western markets where Indians abroad resided.

Though zones as planned portals of globalization are state-based strategies, as this chapter discusses, the state relied on the actors within these portals to articulate its desired connections. Zone units made up of Indian family members who are residents in the West and in India drove these connections. These families used India's preferential access to the Soviet market to channel their goods there by connecting through Kandla Port and forging new connections and economic spaces not envisioned by the Government of India. Although planned portals of globalization as spaces designed to manage internal and external connections have been state-based strategies, the connections facilitated by these spaces allow for the articulation of other, non-state–based strategies to deal with global connectedness.

World Orders and Zones

The Cold War was typically thought of as a bipolar world order, but reactions to and rejections of this bipolarity by much of the developing world and "peripheral" states suggest a more complicated story.[343] Rather than seeing the Cold War political divisions and their competing ideologies as imposed, others have discussed how states in the developing world helped shape the fundamental

342 Brenner, "Beyond state-centrism?"

343 I use "world order" to indicate hegemonic political projects that are never quite complete and academic attempts to explain them. It has been suggested that world order should be replaced by world ordering: S. Chaturvedi and J. Painter, "Whose World, Whose Order? Spatiality, Geopolitics and the Limits of the World Order Concept", *Cooperation and Conflict* 42 (2007) 4, pp. 375–395; See also: U. Engel and M. Middell, *World Orders Revisited*, Leipzig: Leipziger Universitätsverlag, 2010.

features of the Cold War.[344] The NAM was one such reaction against Cold War bipolarity based on the ambitions of developing countries that did not have a stake in Cold War rivalries, but rather sought an alternative path. Indian politicians were active leaders at the forefront of that movement.[345] The US and USSR engaged with non-aligned developing countries, vying for influence over their development paths.[346] India in particular sought to utilize this rivalry to increase the amount of aid it could receive from both parties. South Asia became a key region for US and Soviet Cold War rivalries.[347] The Cold War did not emerge out of a vacuum, and therefore, historical discussions on the Cold War and developing countries led to wider debates on development and decolonization.[348] In some cases, the so-called Third World in the Cold War has been studied within a larger temporal and spatial framework of not only decolonization, but also South-South cooperation and structural adjustment programmes as well as the history of cities and states in the developing world.[349]

During this period, researchers identified the EPZ as a relatively ubiquitous policy found around the world, but mainly in developing countries.[350] Such a space, in their view, facilitated a shift in the location of manufacturing in the world economy: the NIDL. Based on this economic order, these researchers viewed the world as divided into two types of national economies: (1)

344 T. Smith, "New Bottles for New Wine: A Pericentric Framework for the Study of the Cold War", *Diplomatic History* 24 (2000) 4, pp. 551–565. Smith argues that peripheral states were more than mere pawns in the Cold War but also contributed to its central dynamics, using the Cold War to meet their own ends. See also, S. D. Krasner, *Structural Conflict: The Third World against Global Liberalism*, Berkeley: University of California Press, 1985; O. Sanchez-Sibony, *Red Globalization: The Political Economy of the Soviet Cold War from Stalin to Khrushchev*, Cambridge: Cambridge University Press, 2014.
345 M. A. Lawrence, "The Rise and Fall of Nonalignment", in: R. J. McMahon (ed.), *The Cold War in the Third World*, Oxford: Oxford University Press, 2013, pp. 139–155.
346 See: McMahon, *Cold War in the Third World.*
347 See different perspectives: A. J. Rotter, *Comrades at Odds: The United States and India, 1947–1964*, Ithaca, NY: Cornell University Press, 2000; R. J. McMahon, *The Cold War on the Periphery: The United States, India, and Pakistan*, New York: Columbia University Press, 1994.
348 Sanchez-Sibony makes a similar statement regarding Soviet aid to former colonies in: *Red Globalization*, p. 125. He argues that the relations between Third World countries, the US and the USSR were in fact shaped more by previous experiences with colonialism and the domination of Western economies rather than Cold War politics. He argues that it appears that India used Soviet aid as a way to leverage an increase in the amount of US aid, meaning that India's relationship with the USSR was generally guided by its relations with the West. See: pp. 157–169.
349 V. Prashad, *The Darker Nations: A People's History of the Third World*, New York: New Press, 2007; J. Dinkel, *Die Bewegung Bündnisfreier Staaten: Genese, Organisation und Politik, 1927–1992*, Berlin: De Gruyter Oldenbourg, 2015.
350 Fröbel, Heinrichs and Kreye, *New International Division of Labour.*

developed or industrialized and (2) developing or industrializing countries.[351] While this vision divided the world into two categories of development, all countries were seen as united in a single capitalist world system, regardless of Cold War political ideologies.[352] While the authors of the NIDL saw the EPZ as only one tool that shifted manufacturing from developed countries to developing countries (including Second World socialist countries among developing nations),[353] others saw an association with the EPZ and US Cold War policies towards the Third World as key to understanding zone proliferation and the shift towards an NIDL.[354] These US policies encouraged export promotion rather than import substitution.

Import substitution as a path towards development gained currency among many developing countries, including many NAM members, as they sought to undo the colonial pattern of international trade. Developing countries (colonies) exported raw materials to developed countries (colonizers), where they would be manufactured and then returned as finished products for sale to the developing countries that had supplied the raw materials, including minerals and agricultural products. This pattern of international trade was identified by both Raúl Prebisch, known as the first secretary-general of the UNCTAD (1964–1969), and Hans Singer in the late 1940s and early 1950s as harmful to low-income countries as the terms of trade declined against primary products over time, leading to the support of import substitution measures in many developing countries following colonial independence.[355] Such a policy was not without its downsides. Industrialization and self-sufficient production still often relied on imports for manufacturing from developed countries. While

351 I focus on the above-mentioned perspectives because the authors specifically discuss the zone as a key feature enabling this shift. For other similar perspectives, see: I. Wallerstein, "The Rise and Future Demise of the World Capitalist System: Concepts for Comparative Analysis", *Comparative Studies in Society and History* 16 (1974) 4, pp. 387–415; G. Arrighi and J. Drangel "The Stratification of the World-Economy", *Review* 10 (1986) 1, pp. 9–74.

352 The authors of the new international division of labour along with, for example, Immanuel Wallerstein, saw the world as a single capitalist world economy: Fröbel, Heinrichs, Kreye, *New International Division of Labour*, p. 10.

353 There were also attempts to change the terms of trade and create a Soviet division of labour: Viktor Rymalov, *Economic Co-Operation between the U.S.S.R. and Underdeveloped Countries*, Moscow: Foreign Languages Publishing House, 1962.

354 The Pacific-Asia Resources Center, *AMPO: Japan-Asia Quarterly Review* 8 and 9 (1977) 4, 1–2; Takeo, "Free Trade Zones"; Rosen, *Making Sweatshops*; J. F. Taffet, *Foreign Aid as Foreign Policy: The Alliance for Progress in Latin America*, New York: Routledge, 2007.

355 J. Toye and R. Toye, "The Origins and Interpretation of the Prebisch-Singer Thesis", *History of Political Economy* 35 (2003) 3, pp. 437–467.

manufacturing within the developing country focused on domestic consumption, many countries pursuing import substation faced imbalanced trade and declining foreign exchange reserves.

The NIDL describes the shift in the developing world from import substitution that stressed production for the domestic economy towards export-based development models. The zone was associated with US foreign policy towards developing countries during the Cold War. The evidence for such a thesis appears stronger in Latin America and East Asia, where American-led development policies (and Japanese-assisted in East Asia) were particularly prominent.[356] In contrast, by the 1960s and 1970s, countries like India that continued to stress import substitution also focused on export production to earn the reserve currencies necessary for the imports needed for domestic production/consumption. They continued to strive for self-sufficient production but needed to increase exports in order to achieve it.

While the thesis that the EPZ was a product of US Cold War policies appears to apply in other contexts, the previous chapter demonstrated that India's first EPZ was not a product of Cold War rivalries. That is, it was not a clear result of US foreign policy – even if it was discursively connected to a similar policy in the US – nor was it a direct product of UN development agencies. On the contrary, it only conformed to a UNIDO zone model from the 1980s onwards. This chapter explores this perspective by looking at how the Indian government used the zones and how actors within those spaces sought to forge their own business connections. Government reports suggest that the EPZ was also not seen by Indian bureaucrats as connected ideologically with any development model other than India's own state planning. Rather, the zone enabled a spatial flexibility to articulate the state of India beyond India; in other words, to enhance the diaspora's contribution to India's balance of payments problem through an export drive to NRIs' new homelands. The zone in India was an extension of India's changing domestic policies abroad.

The sources for this chapter are limited due to how the KFTZ and SEEPZ were managed by the Ministry of Commerce. During the 1970s and 1980s, the timespan this chapter covers, there was no overarching zone authority or legislation governing the zones. Furthermore, as the zones did not permanently employ statisticians, data was collected by zone authorities for the Ministry of Commerce on request. As a result, data generated by the zones are not recorded in the same manner and, in some cases, certain export statistics or numbers of units are thought to be overestimated. There are two main publications written

356 Taffet, *Foreign Aid as Foreign Policy*; Rosen, *Making Sweatshops*, pp. 27–54.

in the late 1980s that offer a fuller picture of operations within SEEPZ and KFTZ, both of which I rely on heavily in some sections of this study. The first publication is a policy analysis by the Indian Institute of Foreign Trade, a professional training institute established in 1963 by the Government of India to train professionals for foreign trade, especially for the purpose of increasing India's exports.[357] The second is a monograph published by the University of Oxford Press in India by a researcher at the Indian Council for Research on International Economic Relations, an independent think tank established in 1981 dedicated to economic policy analysis.[358] Both sources are intended for policy purposes and can be read as reports for government on the economic aspects of the zones and their functioning.[359] Patrick Neveling has also used these two publications as the main sources in his 2014 article on KFTZ.[360] Apart from the aforementioned sources, very little has been written about India's early zones. This chapter highlights certain aspects of these two reports, along with Indian Merchants' Chamber annual reports and several contemporary secondary sources, to understand how the state and zone units used these spaces of exception to create connections and, as a result, produce new spatial realities within and beyond India.

These sources present other limitations. Though the aforementioned world order of the time involved significant cooperation between private corporations, state-directed development policies, and technical cooperation from international organizations, both regions and states appear to be the dominant spatial references. It is difficult to specify with much accuracy the individual actors within the zone, as most statistics available list regions or countries rather than individual importing and exporting firms. Notable here is that trade between India and the USSR was mainly listed as Eastern European trade. For these reasons, states are often discussed here as exporters and importers. In reality, though bilateral agreements between states or regional blocs allowed

357 "About IIFT", Indian Institute for Foreign Trade website, http://edu.iift.ac.in/iift/landing/index.html (accessed 17 September 2015).

358 "About ICRIER", Indian Council for Research on International Economic Relations website, http://icrier.org/abouticrier/about-icrier/ (accessed 17 September 2015).

359 Dattatreyulu, *Export Processing Zones in India;* Kumar, *India's Export Processing Zones.*

360 His article seeks to establish a periodization of neoliberalism in India, arguing that the debates between 1991 or 1980s as starting dates for neoliberal policies in India should be extended further back, using Kandla's founding in 1965 as evidence of a longer history of neoliberalism: Neveling, "Structural Contingencies." His article, however, overlooks the fact that several zone incentives were introduced in KFTZ only in 1980, such as a rollback on workers' rights and a tax holiday, as shown in the previous chapter.

India protect its export markets for state-based motivations, private firms were the main actors taking advantage of these state-based agreements.

KFTZ, a Zone Like Any Other?

KFTZ was operational by 1967. It was developed at the same time that many other zones were established throughout Asia, namely Kaoshiung in Taiwan in the mid-1960s, followed by zones in Malaysia, Philippines, and South Korea, all of which were established in the early 1970s.[361] Though on the surface these zones appear to be similar – they all focused on export production, operated outside the domestic tariff area of their respective states, and shared *zone* in their names – they differed from KFTZ in several significant ways. The previous chapter discussed how KFTZ and SEEPZ did not start out with the same incentive packages as other zones and rather conformed to international zone standards over time. This chapter addresses the foreign investment and export profiles of the two Indian zones. While the function of East Asian FTZs was an important part of the discussion on the changing international division of labour, on the contrary, this argument could not fully account for either the emergence of or the activities within India's FTZs.

The Masan zone in South Korea was based on Taiwan's experience with Kaoshiung, formerly UNIDO's top choice for zone training. Though Kaoshiung no longer featured in UNIDO reports on EPZs once China joined the UN system, Masan became a staple in these reports. Masan differed from KFTZ in many ways, but two particular aspects stand out. In South Korea, foreign investment required 50 per cent South Korean firm investment, but this standard was not enforced inside the zone. Masan units were entirely foreign or involved joint ventures with Korean firms. By August 1975, 100 enterprises were operating inside the zone out of 105 total enterprises approved. Out of these 105 enterprises, 95 were Japanese owned (including 22 joint ventures with Korean firms), 8 were US owned (including 3 joint ventures with Korean firms). The remaining two firms were from West Germany and Italy.[362] The total foreign investment in the zone amounted to 88.5 million USD, of which almost 88 per cent came from Japan. Masan's export destinations were not specified by country, but the reports generally note that production was oriented for export to Japan and the

361 Kelleher, "Handbook", p. 2.

362 Ibid., p. 76; T. Takeo, "Masan: An Epitome of the Japan-ROK Relationship", *AMPO: Japan-Asia Quarterly Review* 8 and 9 (1977) 4, 1–2, pp. 53–66, at 56.

US. For example, Tsuchiya Takeo summarizes the zone's functions as follows: "Small- and medium-sized Japanese firms, drawn by the special favors held out by the south Korean government, take raw materials from Japan, process them by exploiting the low-wage labor of young south Korean women, and then sell the finished product in the U.S. and Japan."[363] This description understands the zone's functionality based on the origin of imports, destination of exports, and the origins of firms undertaking this process. Since Japan had been a colonial power in Korea and Masan's site was chosen specifically to cater to Japanese production, this zone was viewed through a neo-imperialist lens as part of an American and Japanese effort to foster a NIDL in the region.

In contrast to Masan, the Bataan zone in the Philippines did involve significant Filipino investment. Out of the 19 firms operating there in 1976, 6 were Filipino, and 10 were joint ventures between Filipino and Japanese, UK, or "other" firms.[364] The joint ventures include a Filipino-Danish-American-Canadian firm (Jade International); a footwear firm involving Austrian and Filipino investment (Fitschuh); a Japanese-Canadian-Filipino producer of women's sweaters (Pasig Textile Industries); a Filipino-British (Hong Kong) golf club manufacturer; and a Filipino-Chinese (Hong Kong) textile company. Foreign investors included firms from Japan, Australia, and a joint venture from Hong Kong, "China" (Taiwan), and Cambodia.[365] Export production was, like in Masan, likely oriented towards Western countries and Japan. The authors of these reports assume that export production was oriented towards those markets.

Based on this assumption, assessments of KFTZ by international agencies like UNIDO and UNCTAD did not specify the export destinations of KFTZ's goods in their analyses of KFTZ because, in other contexts that adhered to UNIDO's model zones – Kaoshiung, Shannon, Masan, and Bataan – exports were mainly destined for Western Europe, North America, and Japan.[366] In most cases, these zone exports earned the countries' foreign exchange, so knowing the exact destination of particular products was irrelevant to any thorough analysis of the zone's operations. Instead, the focus was on the nationality of the firm/investor and the amount of exports generated. The foreign investors were generally an important indicator of the manufactures' final destination. In a 1985 UNCTAD report with a list of zones in 12 countries, India's SEEPZ and KFTZ are ranked among the others based on the country of origin of the main

363 Takeo, "Masan", p. 56.
364 Kelleher, "Handbook", p. 72.
365 O. Ken, "Bataan Export Processing Zone: Its Development and Social Implications", *AMPO: Japan-Asia Quarterly Review* 8 and 9 (1977) 4, 1–2, pp. 93–120, at 95.
366 Kelleher, "Handbook."

foreign investors, production sectors, and labour cost.[367] These zones appear to conform to other zones since the main foreign investors are from the US, Canada, and West Germany. The report declines to specify the number or percentage of foreign investors in comparison to other zones or the destination of these products. The authors of the UN reports allowed the "zone model" to influence the way in which they compiled zone statistics. They assumed that the zone was a singular policy that had been replicated in various contexts. The authors of the NIDL thesis appear to have made the same assumption.

Until the tax holiday and other tax incentives were enhanced in 1981, the units operating in KFTZ were owned by small-scale Indian firms. During the 1980s, more units opened, including non-Indian firms. Still, there were only 8 large-scale firms, 24 medium-scale, and 88 small-scale firms by 1987.[368] In 1987, of the 120 operating units in KFTZ, 6 were owned by multi-national firms, 8 were NRI units, and 9 units involved partial equity participation by either foreign or NRI partners from the UK, USA, France, Canada, Brazil, and Hong Kong.[369] By 1989, KFTZ's exports were destined for 50 countries around the world. Though prior to 1981 KFTZ did not resemble zones in other countries in the region because KFTZ's investment was Indian in origin, by the mid- to late 1980s, KFTZ began to resemble those zones in terms of foreign equity participation, even though the percentage of foreign firms out of total units was low: only 17 per cent were foreign firms (including NRI firms) and 11 per cent were joint ventures between Indian and foreign firms.[370] Because of KFTZ's increase in foreign investors during the 1980s, it appeared to conform to UNIDO's standard zone.

Planning for SEEPZ began in 1970. By this time all units operating in KFTZ were still Indian owned.[371] In contrast to KFTZ, Indian planners in the Department of Electronics envisioned SEEPZ from the start as an electronics-manufacturing zone based mainly on foreign investment rather than domestic investment. In order to structure the zone, a commission from India visited zones in Taiwan and South Korea that also focused on electronics exports. One of the main purposes of the visit was to understand how to entice foreign

367 UNCTD, "Export Processing Free Zones in Developing Countries", p. 13.

368 These terms are not defined in the policy report. The categories demonstrate that most units were not large Indian business houses or multinationals.

369 Dattatreyulu, *Export Processing Zones in India*, p. 21.

370 These percentages were calculated based on the number of operating units (80) rather than the total number of units in the zone (120), 40 of which apparently received no export orders for the year. The numbers of foreign operations specify them as "working units." Ibid., p. 21.

371 D. Wall, "Export Processing Zones", *Journal of World Trade Law* 10 (1976) 5, pp. 478–489, at 488.

investors to the zone. However, like in KFTZ, SEEPZ did not offer foreign investors any extra incentives to invest inside the zone in comparison to the domestic tariff area. Following the zones' restructuring in 1981, by 1983 only 8 of KFTZ's 53 operating units involved any foreign collaboration (including marketing or foreign equity). In contrast, 21 of SEEPZ's 38 units did so, 14 of which came from the US, 2 from Europe (1 from the UK), 2 from the "far East", and 4 from Africa (numbers include joint ventures).[372] However, as in KFTZ, much of the foreign equity participation was only partially "foreign" in that the Indian citizens (NRIs) who invested were tax resident in another state, namely the US, the UK, or other countries where Indians had immigrated.

Although both SEEPZ and KFTZ were and continue to be zones, neither was originally designed to cater to foreign investors. As a result, their investor profiles and, as will be described later, their export markets did not conform to the model of zones found in East Asia or those promoted by UNIDO. Although foreign investment began to increase in the zones in the 1980s, the zones approved fully foreign owned companies' applications to operate as units only on a case-by-case basis. In contrast, blanket permission on foreign investment did exist for one category of foreign investment: NRI investment. Any proposed investment in the zone by an NRI would be automatically approved. The NRI status would allow these investors to maintain their tax residency abroad rather than in India. Both zones were designed to cater to "foreign Indian investment" rather than foreign investment.

Extending India

Prior to independence, Indians lived across the globe, inside and outside the British Empire. "Theirs was a globally dispersed nonterritorially defined national formation."[373] Though others might have recognized them based on language, religion, and physical features, as "Indian", they had varying degrees of connection to and identification with "India." In 1947, as India became a politically sovereign state, it became territorial in the sense that citizenship was strictly confined to those Indians found within India's territorial borders while those outside might still identify as Indian, but were not offered Indian citizenship. Ironically, though the fight for independence had been a global struggle

372 Kumar, *India's Export Processing Zones*, p. 129.
373 Abraham, *How India Became Territorial*, p. 74.

about the treatment of Indians overseas as well as in India, overseas Indians were excluded from politically sovereign India.[374]

Independence leaders had sought to form India as a nation state in an image recognizable to the international community to legitimize their cause. Clearly delimiting territorial borders and differences between people – Pakistanis, Indians, and Bangladeshis – was an important step towards this formation of the Indian citizen. When during independence India's borders were still fraught, "turning away from the diaspora [. . .] was part of a larger process by which India's borders were 'hardened' to conform to the norm of a territorially bound nation-state."[375] Part of this exclusion of the Indian diaspora was linked to international negotiations between other former colonies that feared losing large populations of "Indians" upon independence such as in Myanmar and Malaysia. This stance was based on an ideology that prevented India from interfering in the internal affairs of other countries.

India's approach to its diaspora after independence focused more on bilateral engagement with states that hosted many "cultural Indians" without Indian citizenship.[376] In many cases, the migrants who had left India before independence were poor and indentured labourers.[377] While their treatment had been the driving force of the independence movement, Indians living in the changing definition of "abroad" represented an undesirable legacy of poor migrant workers. However, as more Indians moved abroad after independence, a new "global Indian" emerged. This diaspora's profile represented a high-caste, middle-class, educated Hindu who took advantage of new skills-based immigration laws to relocate to the US, Canada, Australia, and the UK in the late 1960s.[378] Unlike the working-class Indians who left before independence,

374 Ibid., pp. 74–75.

375 Ibid., p. 75.

376 Ibid., p. 98.

377 Many, but not all. One of the largest sub-groups of Indians abroad were also Indian students studying abroad, namely in the UK.

378 The US changed its immigration law in 1965 to abolish national quotas and preferences for northern European migrants but added a provision that those with family members in the US could apply for US green cards. For a recent discussion, see: Tom Gjelten, "In 1965, A Conservative Tried to Keep America White. His Plan Backfired", *National Public Radio*, 3 October 2015, http://www.npr.org/2015/10/03/445339838/the-unintended-consequences-of-the-1965-immigration-act.
A report by the US Census Bureau discusses the successes of Asian Americans in terms of higher earnings and higher qualifications that the median US household for all racial groups. By 2004, there were 1.6 million "Indian Asians" in the US: Terrence J. Reeves and Claudette E. Bennett, "We the People: Asians in the United States", Census 2000 Special Reports, US Census Bureau, December 2004, http://www.census.gov/prod/2004pubs/censr-17.pdf.

the Government of India sought to engage with these Indians who represented a different kind of diaspora. This type of engagement rang true for India's reliance on NRI investment in the zone.

The Government of India created the category "non-resident Indian" in the Foreign Exchange Act of 1973, which facilitated remittance payments of Indians working abroad. This law reworked the NRI category that was established in 1961 through the Income Tax Act. The NRI category, along with that of "overseas Indians" (indicating Indian heritage without Indian citizenship), were further developed during the 1990s and 2000s. Through KFTZ and SEEPZ, investment from NRIs was targeted in the 1980s and earlier, specifically those residing in Western countries who could bring transfers of technologies and financial capital with them, along with knowledge about the desirable export markets in which they resided. Though NRI investment had not been specifically mentioned in the discussions leading to the implementation of KFTZ, a planning proposal from the Maharashtra Economic Development Council (MEDC) from 1964 for a proposed FTZ just outside of Bombay (which was never implemented) describes the desire to establish the zone to attract the capital of Indian nationals settled abroad.[379] The zone was envisioned as a tool to connect with the diaspora. Policies actually implemented in KFTZ and SEEPZ suggest that this motivation played a central part in the zones' design. While there was no blanket approval for foreign investment in either zone, there was blanket approval for investments from NRIs. Therefore, foreign companies would only be considered on a case-by-case basis, but companies registered in foreign countries like the US or UK that were run by NRIs were automatically approved to operate inside the zones.[380] The hope was that, through engaging with Indians abroad, the state of India would be able to accrue foreign exchange earnings from the countries in which these Indians resided. As individuals aware of both market situations in India and the target export markets like the US, they were particularly selected to steer India's export drive.

There were two types of foreign collaboration recorded in the zones. In one case, the foreign collaboration was labelled "marketing." Marketing meant that a foreign firm would supply an Indian unit inside the zone with the materials and instructions to manufacture an item, at which point the item could be bought back by the foreign firm, which marketed it as its own product. This investment pattern basically relied on outsourcing. The second type of foreign

379 MEDC, "Report on Free-Trade Zone in Maharashtra", p. 10. This council is a private association of business chambers that played a role in shaping the economic and industrial development of Maharashtra and Bombay.
380 Kumar, *India's Export Processing Zones*, p. 42.

collaboration involved foreign investment in a zone unit in different forms, either 100 per cent foreign ownership or percentage foreign equity participation in the zone unit. In some cases, the Indian partner might have more than a 50 per cent stake and therefore greater control over the unit.

While KFTZ was designed to cater to Indian investors to develop more exports, by the time SEEPZ was established in 1973, the need to generate investment from NRIs was part of the plan. In the case of KFTZ, foreign collaboration was very low, and all foreign partners represented outsourcing ("marketing") of production. Out of 11 total units with foreign collaboration, 7 began after 1980 and were likely drawn to the increased tax incentives. Another important feature of both zones was the role that family ties between the diaspora and India played in this investment pattern: 9 out of these 11 foreign collaborators in KFTZ were relatives with the Indian unit owner.[381] Family ties were an important investment incentive that drew NRIs to invest in India's export drive.

In contrast, SEEPZ had more foreign collaboration, which might be related to the strong industrial base in Bombay and its diaspora in particular in contrast to the relative isolation of KFTZ. For example, while Bombay was a bustling city, KFTZ was extremely isolated. For this reason, government officers appointed to run the zone left at the earliest possible opportunity, which led to excessive turnover of personnel.[382] Within KFTZ, nearly all Indian firms were headquartered elsewhere in India. Since such issues were never discussed in regard to SEEPZ, it can be assumed that Bombay's position as India's business centre was favourable for the zone, or at least did not hinder it. Between 1973 and 1989, 22 of SEEPZ's 63 approved units involved foreign equity participation while only 3 units involved "buy-back marketing" or outsourcing production. Furthermore, 15 out of these 22 foreign equity ventures were majority owned by the foreign firm. In total, about 40 per cent of investment in the zone involved foreign collaboration, and, like KFTZ, "nearly all these investments were made by non-resident Indians with members of the family managing both the foreign and Indian ends of the business."[383] Thus, an Indian citizen resident in the US could connect with family still in India and jointly operate a family business inside the zone.

Data for SEEPZ between 1988 and 1989 indicate that investment and collaboration with SEEPZ involved both foreign nationals and NRIs. Numerically, however, the two categories are not separated except in terms of units.[384] By 1989,

381 Ibid., p. 125.

382 "Meeting with Shri Niranjan Singh, Development Commissioner, Kandla Free Trade Zone on 27th February, 1980", in Indian Merchants' Chamber, 1980, Annual Report, IMC, p. 95.

383 Kumar, *India's Export Processing Zones*, p. 125.

384 Dattatreyulu, *Export Processing Zones in India*, p. 5.

six of the units were multinational units while ten units were run by NRIs. However, in relation to Rajiv Kumar's assertion that nearly all foreign firms or subsidiaries were run by family members, it very well could be that these multinationals, too, were run by "Indians" without Indian citizenship. The total number of units at this time was 80. A total of 35 units involved "foreign/NRI equity participation", representing nearly 45 per cent of all units, and almost one-third of these units were run by Indian citizens (NRIs), meaning that this was not a completely international space of corporate investment, but involved significant investment from Indian firms inside and outside of India's domestic economy. The fact that these investments are labelled as NRI investment demonstrates the extent to which KFTZ and SEEPZ were envisioned to increase NRI participation in the Indian economy while allowing these investors to remain exempt from tax residency in India. These features were not captured through UNIDO or UNCTAD documentation because this type of investment was not a standardized feature of their model zone.

The investment profile of foreign collaborators also differed between zones. In KFTZ, foreign collaborators were diverse, but investment from the UK represented the largest group (three out of eight foreign collaborators).[385] These investors were identified as very likely Gujarati in origin who had left East Africa for the UK. Gujarat as a place to invest represented a return but also a strategy to integrate a company's production transregionally through linguistic and cultural channels. In SEEPZ, the vast majority of foreign collaborators, mainly investors, were from the US, representing 67 per cent of foreign collaboration and 37 per cent of total zone units, both foreign and domestic.[386] Due to the fact that Indian residents in the US had mainly taken advantage of changing US immigration laws in the 1960s that based immigration on skills, these investors were likely of a different diaspora group: middle-class, upper-caste Indian citizens who left India after independence, the kind sought by the zone authorities. These investors used their connections with their new homeland, the US, and their family ties in India to internationalize their firms' production. Some of this production was based on exports to the US, where these families would be familiar with demand, product standards, and import conditions.

This type of foreign investment in SEEPZ can be understood as part of the NIDL, though of course with a diaspora driving the process. For example, in some cases the zones were used as typical offshore assembly lines that looked similar to the activities in Taiwanese and South Korean zones, the type that SEEPZ was

385 Kumar, *India's Export Processing Zones*, p. 129.
386 Ibid., pp. 128–129.

modeled after. One of the most important export generating firms for SEEPZ in the 1980s produced disc drives for a parent company in California. This parent company subcontracted from four units in SEEPZ, which were all run by family members. The firm's labour intensive production was shifted to SEEPZ, which received all inputs as imports from the parent company, and the product was assembled and exported through a buy back to the parent company "for final assembly and packaging in California."[387] This particular group of firms under the parent company accounted for 43 per cent of all of SEEPZ's exports, 54 per cent of its employment, and 19 per cent of its investment in 1982–1983.[388] Although SEEPZ's activities resembled the trend towards the NIDL identified by German researchers in the 1970s, family ties rather than multinational corporations or US Cold War policies mainly drove these connections.

There were other foreign investors in the zones who based their exports on the Indian diaspora as a type of niche within a foreign market. For example, a story recorded about one investor in SEEPZ, labelled a "typical case", describes the relation between the NRI and his export strategy: "In one typical case, the foreign partner, a non-resident Indian, had a retail agency for audio equipment in one of the West Asian countries. He contracted with his principals to start a video recording unit at SEEPZ. This records Hindi films on video cassettes for sale in West Asian markets which are handled by the non-resident Indian who has 100 percent equity."[389] Hindi films are popular in the Gulf States, but many Indians also work there as migrant labourers. While these were the types of Indians abroad not desired by the Indian state for Indian citizenship or engagement once they moved outside of India, they represented key markets for Indians shifting to export production.

Ironically, these migrant workers in the Gulf likely made more gains to India's foreign exchange than KFTZ did:

> In spite of the relatively low wages, racial and religious discrimination, and harsh working conditions, the sheer number of Indians workers [sic.] working in the Gulf led to substantial financial remittances returning to India from the 1980s onwards. No serious economic policy maker could deny that India's historically weak balance of payments calculus was now eased in no small measure because of the contribution of Indians coming from the lower end of the economic and social scales [. . .]. It would take the government of India decades to appreciate the economic value of these working-class migrants and to begin targeted diplomatic activities directed at protecting their rights.[390]

387 Ibid., p. 130.
388 Ibid., p. 86.
389 Ibid., pp. 125–128.
390 Abraham, *How India Became Territorial*, p. 100.

Different Indian diasporas were targeted in separate ways. Opening SEEPZ and KFTZ to the investment of certain types of diaspora groups was an effort to articulate the state of India beyond India; in other words, to enhance the diaspora's contribution to India's balance of payments problem through an export drive to their new homelands. These zones allowed NRIs to invest and operate their businesses within India but maintain tax residency outside of India. The Indian diaspora in the Gulf, as the quote above illustrates, made a significant contribution to this effort without such targeted articulation, described as the "mainstay" of India's foreign exchange reserves by the 1980s.[391] In some cases, like the exporter of Hindi films, private interests also targeted various diaspora groups, meaning that using the zone to articulate global connections was layered: there was the way in which planners envisioned the zone, designing it for particular types of desired connections, and the ways that the firms and investors inside the zones actually used the zone to pursue their own interests and connections for profit.

A Soviet-American Zone

During the course of the Cold War, the USSR became an important export market for Indian products. Even though bilateral agreements between the two countries allowed for Indian exports to the USSR, this was not a planned feature of the zone. Rather, the Ministry of Commerce specifically had intended these zones to be portals for exports to Western countries, as outlined in the previous section, based on engagement with Indian diasporas there. However, the businesses within the zones used them for their own purposes and utilized India's preferential access to Soviet markets to export to the USSR, creating new connections beyond India and new spatial realties within India, namely the division of Bombay and Kandla ports into Western and Soviet ports respectively.

In the late 1950s, the Government of India sought to increase India's import capacity by increasing its imports from Eastern European socialist countries. India's sterling balances in London were nearly completely exhausted by 1957 by imbalanced imports and exports to and from hard currency countries. As early as 1956, Eastern European countries had adopted the Indian national rupee as the currency unit for trade with India. Until 1959, any imbalances in the trade between Eastern Europe and India, though accounted for in rupees, would be

391 "Memorandum on Export Strategy during 1980's – Submitted to Tandon Committee", in: Indian Merchants' Chamber, 1979, Annual Report, appendix 65, IMC, p. 311.

settled in pounds sterling. Imports from most industrial countries were carried out in USD or pounds sterling. In contrast, by 1959 trade between India and socialist countries was expanded through agreements known as rupee payment agreements that allowed for all transactions to be accounted for in inconvertible rupees, with trade imbalances settled through exports or imports of certain products.[392] Furthermore, aid flows and debts could be converted to trade. This plan to engage more with Eastern Europe was only one-half of a bifurcated strategy to deal with India's balance of payments and foreign exchange crisis. The other half of the strategy involved increasing exports to hard currency countries and pursuing the Aid-India Consortium, a multilateral aid scheme organized by India through the International Bank for Reconstruction and Development, today known as the World Bank (WB), in 1958.[393] Therefore, the political division of the world provided India with the opportunity to engage in different ways with both camps.

The documents referenced in this chapter demonstrate the Cold War shift and the changing economic relations by the spatial references they catalogue. During the early 1950s, trade to Europe was mainly labelled "continental" to indicate Europe without the UK, whereby the UK was a separate category. By the late 1950s, Europe was divided into two categories: (1) Western Europe (including the UK) and (2) Eastern Europe, indicating socialist countries behind the Iron Curtain, including the USSR. Though trade was mainly conducted with the USSR, it was often described as Eastern European trade. The reason for this label stems from this spatial reference as indicative of the rupee payment area. Indian planners responded to changing world orders and political alliances by changing the ways in which they categorized India's external space, which sometimes differed slightly from other interpretations. For example, outside of India "Eastern Europe" was not always used as shorthand for the USSR and socialist countries in Europe, but Eastern Europe as a category became incredibly important because it indicated a fixed space for India in which trade could be accounted for in rupees. Everything outside this particular category in zone documents (e.g. whether trade should be labelled by country or region) could shift while Eastern Europe remained a solid classification. Therefore, on the one hand, the categories used to describe India's external space reflected changing world orders of political alliances. On the other hand, however, the

392 D. Nayyar, "India's Trade with the Socialist Countries", *World Development* 3 (1975) 5, pp. 273–298, at 274.

393 Original donor countries included the UK, the US, West Germany, Canada, and Japan. See: Shigeru Akita, "The Aid-India Consortium, the World Bank, and the International Order of Asia, 1958–1968", *Asian Review of World Histories* 2 (2014) 2, pp. 217–248.

spatial references used by Indian planners to divide the world economy into Eastern Europe and everything else (mutable combinations of regions and states) also had real-world applications that affected India's economy in general and how zone units used KFTZ in particular.

Before the 1956 agreement, very little of India's foreign trade was carried out with Eastern European countries, which made up less than 1 per cent of India's foreign trade between 1955 and 1956. In contrast, during that same fiscal year over 60 per cent of India's trade was carried out with Western Europe (28 per cent of which was with the UK) and 15 per cent with the US.[394] This trade was a drain on India's foreign exchange reserves if India that could not export more to these regions, so new trading partners willing to pay in rupees were targeted, leading to the 1959 agreement. Trade between Eastern Europe (mostly the USSR) and India grew substantially over the course of the 1960s. By 1970/1971, 22.9 per cent of India's exports were destined for Eastern Europe while 14 per cent of its imports arrived from this region.[395]

While at first there were few economic incentives for the USSR to pursue such an agreement, there were mutual geopolitical considerations on both sides. From 1955 onwards, the USSR sought additional engagement with developing countries to persuade them to develop their economies based on Soviet ideals as well as to garner international support. However, over the course of time, additional common interests developed between India and the USSR, namely India's position towards China, which was at first positive. India recognized the People's Republic and supported the country's admission into the UN, but later this relationship deteriorated due to border conflicts and war, which coincided with the so-called Sino-Soviet split.[396] It would be too simplistic to characterize India's geopolitical ambitions as a product of the Cold War. Most of India's ambitions had little to do with the Cold War and namely involved conflicts with neighbours like China, Pakistan, and Sri Lanka, though these conflicts and interests were externally framed by the Cold War.[397] As the

394 S. Chishti, *India's Trade with East Europe*, New Delhi: Indian Institute of Foreign Trade, 1973, pp. 13–17.

395 The statistics regarding India's imports from the USSR are often incomplete as defence imports were not included in official statistics.

396 R. J. McMahon, "On the Periphery of a Global Conflict: India and the Cold War, 1947–1991", in: Hilger and Unger (eds.), *India in the World since 1947*, pp. 276–299, at 287–288. This author argues that the Sino-Soviet split was deepened by the preceding Sino-Indian split.

397 McMahon, "On the Periphery of a Global Conflict."

Sino-Soviet split coincided with the Sino-Indian conflict,[398] by 1960 India and the USSR signed the first of many military aid agreements that allowed the USSR to supply India with weapons. This support later culminated in the Treaty of Peace, Friendship, and Cooperation between the two countries signed on 9 August 1971.[399]

The resulting rupee payment area allowed for Indian imports from Eastern European countries to be accounted for in rupees; imports from all other countries would continue to be accounted for in USD or pounds sterling. India was, therefore, able to import from certain socialist countries without depleting reserve currencies. This development was at first advantageous, resulting in the spatial division of the world into two payment areas for Indian planners: (1) the rupee payment area represented by socialist Eastern Europe and (2) the convertible currency area represented by other countries outside of Eastern Europe. Trade with Eastern Europe through these agreements was planned in advance with a trade target for certain commodities in an annual trade plan involving collaboration between various Indian ministries, namely the Ministry of Commerce and the Ministry of Finance.[400] The USSR was India's largest trading partner in terms of imports and exports. Czechoslovakia, Poland, East Germany, and Yugoslavia (until 1973) were also significant trading partners under this arrangement. Any imbalances would be adjusted for in the next annual trade plan.

Under this agreement, aid flows and trade flows overlapped so that aid required repayment in trade: "The trade target is calculated in such a way that after taking the credit inflows from the socialist countries to India and the debt servicing outflows from India to the socialist countries into account, the trade is bilaterally balanced each year."[401] The USSR was not India's most significant aid donor, representing only 10 per cent of aid to India until 1971, trailing behind both the US (41 per cent) and UN agencies (combined to 14.2 per cent). In fact,

---

398 For the Sino-Soviet split, see: L. Lüthi, *The Sino-Soviet Split: Cold War in the Communist World*, Princeton, NJ: Princeton University Press, 2008.

399 P. I. Mathew, "India's Economic Relations with the Soviet Union during 1951–1976: A Study in Political Economy", PhD diss., University of Connecticut, 1979, pp. 57–60. See also: S. Raghavan, "Between Regional and Global Interests: The Indo-Soviet Treaty of 1971", in: Hilger and Unger (eds.), *India in the World since 1947*, pp. 326–345. The author does not see the 1971 treaty as an abandonment of non-alignment but rather as complementary to this strategy.

400 S. K. Rao, and R. Jaikumar, "Trade Plans and Production Cooperation", in: *Emerging Opportunities for India's Trade and Economic Cooperation with East Europe*, New Delhi: Indian Institute of Foreign Trade, 1977, pp. 103–114, at 106.

401 Nayyar, "India's Trade", pp. 274–275.

India only utilized just over 60 per cent of its Soviet aid until 1971 compared to over 90 per cent of its aid from the US. What made loan agreements from the USSR and other Eastern European countries significant for the development of India's zones was that the loans could be repaid through the export of goods to those countries rather than in rupees or foreign currency.[402] The rupee payment agreements stipulated that aid received from rupee payment countries such as the USSR would be repaid in rupees tied to a gold standard, which could be used for the exports of Indian goods and services to the USSR.[403]

This clause led to the disadvantageous aspect of this agreement. As India accrued debts to the USSR over the course of the 1950s and the 1960s, it also devalued the Indian rupee by 57 per cent in 1966, meaning that debts accrued prior to this period needed to be repaid at the pre-1966 value rather than the post-1966 value.[404] For every rupee of debt accrued prior to 1966, multiple rupees needed to be repaid to the USSR through exports. This debt was not the only driver of exports from India to the USSR, as India also procured weapons, aircraft, and other military imports throughout the 1970s and 1980s. In addition to the foreign aid used to fund specific projects (Soviet aid was often tied to projects), India amassed additional debt for these defence imports. Throughout the 1970s, 85 per cent of imported military procurements originated from the USSR, driven largely by the Indo-Pakistan conflict of 1971.[405] By the late 1970s, India's oil imports from the USSR rose, and, as a result, exports from India to the USSR needed to be increased.[406] During the 1970s, the burden of servicing Soviet debt through trade was significant. Additionally, while it seems that India had an export surplus in relation to USSR imports, defence imports were excluded from official statistics in order to hide the extent of India's actual military procurement.

While the USSR was a significant trading partner for India by the 1970s, India was less significant for the USSR. In 1975, India's exports made up just 1.38 per cent of the USSR's imports. Exports from the USSR to India, likewise, account for only 1.15 per cent of the USSR's total exports.[407] In contrast, in

402 Mathew, "India's Economic Relations", pp. 74–76.

403 S. Chishti, "India's Trade with East Europe: An Overall View", in: *Emerging Opportunities for India's Trade*, pp. 1–29, at 3.

404 Aid inflows from the USSR to India were halted from 1966 to 1971.

405 J. M. Conley, *Indo-Russian Military and Nuclear Cooperation: Lessons and Options for U.S. Policy in South Asia*, Lanham, MD: Lexington Books, 2001, p. 34.

406 Kumar, *India's Export Processing Zones*, p. 75.

407 V. Vithal Babu, "Foreign Trade Outlook of East Economies", in: *Emerging Opportunities for India's Trade*, pp. 195–243, at 212–213.

1975/1976, 10.5 per cent of India's exports were destined for the USSR, indicating that while India was a significant trading partner with the USSR – along with the US and Japan – the USSR as an import and export market was more important for India relative to India's importance to the USSR.[408]

At first, from 1959 through the 1970s, much of India's trade to the USSR consisted of so-called traditional exports from India, that is, raw materials and commodities like tea and tobacco along with textiles. For example, in 1953–1954, 93.31 per cent of India's exports to Eastern Europe consisted of primary commodities. By 1970–1971, this was reduced to 45.2 per cent of exports by sector as manufactured items increased.[409] India signed an agreement with the USSR to increase the export of manufactured items from India to the USSR to 60 per cent of total exports by the year 1976.[410] Therefore, zones like KFTZ and SEEPZ where items were manufactured exclusively for export could become significant locations for channelling India's debt repayments through trade flows.[411] The extent to which this was planned by the Government of India remains unclear.

On the contrary, it appears that planners specifically wanted these zones to export to convertible currency countries like the US, not rupee payment countries like the USSR. Though there were structural reasons why India needed to increase exports to rupee payment area countries, the zone had been designed to facilitate trade to general payment area countries, though safeguards to guarantee these export destinations were never put in place. Whether or not this focus on rupee payment area exports was a feature of the zone policy or simply an outcome of lack of controls is unclear. However, given the Ministry of Commerce's concern with the overreliance of exports from the zone to the rupee payment area, it seems that the linkage between KFTZ and Eastern European countries was a bottom-up process pursued by private exporters rather than a feature managed by the central government. Likewise, the fact that KFTZ was used as a nodal point for trade between the capitalist and socialist blocs appears unintentional.

KFTZ and SEEPZ had originally been designed for trading with the general payment area rather than the rupee payment area. In both SEEPZ and KFTZ the "exclusive criterion" for a unit application was based on value addition.[412]

408 O. P. Sharma, "India's Exports to the East European Countries: Issues and Prospects", in: *Emerging Opportunities for India's Trade*, pp. 30–102, at 64.
409 Chishti, *India's Trade with East Europe*, p. 19.
410 Ibid., p. xii.
411 These zones were meant to be export driven, but trade to the domestic tariff area was allowed if customs duties were paid.
412 Kumar, *India's Export Processing Zones*, p. 62.

Thus, any material imported to the zone from a hard currency (general payment area) country would be processed, through which value would be added to the manufacture that could be reexported to the same or another hard currency country. Through such a process, the Government of India would earn foreign exchange to fund imports from hard currency countries. While this specification was followed in SEEPZ, units in KFTZ followed a different logic. KFTZ was used by units to import from the general payment area and then items processed there were exported to the rupee payment area, thereby contributing to India's bilateral trade obligations with Soviet bloc countries without earning foreign exchange. In fact, KFTZ would be losing foreign exchange by this logic since imports to the zone would be paid for in USD from India's foreign exchange reserves but exports from the zone would not earn any foreign exchange, whether or not value was added to the manufacture.

Though KFTZ finally included foreign investment in the zone, KFTZ did not resemble other zones due to this trend. By 1989, 86.29 per cent of KFTZ's exports in terms of value in rupees were destined for the USSR.[413] Total exports in this year were 2,71,59.38 in rupees lakhs; trade to the USSR accounted for 2,34,36.78 rupees lakhs.[414] Goods from KFTZ were shipped to dozens of countries, but the USSR's share in KFTZ's exports sometimes exceeded 90 per cent of KFTZ's total exports, thereby dominating the zone's rationale.[415] If exports for all rupee payment countries are included, their share of KFTZ's exports was 96 per cent. Over the course of the 1980s, as more units opened in KFTZ following the announcement of the tax holiday, total exports from KFTZ rose and fell in line with Soviet demand.

In comparison to the zones in East Asia, the production for export to the USSR was unusual, though as Masan's high levels of Japanese investment shows, dependence on a single market was not uncommon for all EPZs.[416] KFTZ's export profile was so reliant on the USSR that a decline in demand could bring units within the zone to a standstill, resulting in gaps between units in operation and the number of exporting units. In 1983–1984, there were 15 such units out of 95 total units that were active but did not export during the

---

413 Compare, for example, with the earlier discussion in this chapter on the export profiles of Masan, South Korea, and Bataan, Philippines.

414 One lakh is 100,000.

415 Dattatreyulu, *Export Processing Zones in India*, pp. 29–34; Kumar, *India's Export Processing Zones*, p. 91.

416 For that matter, during this time nearly all EPZs in South and Central America, as well as *maquiladoras* in Mexico, were dominated by US investment and manufactures were exported to the US.

year. By 1986–1987, the number of non-exporting units reached 38 out of a total of 120 units.[417] Due to near complete reliance on USSR orders, more than 20 units inside the zone closed between 1981 and 1983 when orders were curtailed due to the fall in oil prices, the USSR's trade deficit with India, and the reduction of defence purchases by India from the USSR.[418] The USSR's dominance was present in most sectors of the zone's production. In terms of the three largest sectors, by the late 1980s, 87 per cent of engineering products, 87 per cent of chemical products, and 80.2 per cent of textiles were exported to the rupee payment area rather than the convertible currency area.[419] KFTZ alone contributed approximately 10 to 11 per cent of India's total exports to the USSR.[420] In fact, one policy report found the Soviet market so central that the author of it did not bother to detail the other export market shares, though other export markets for the 1988–1989 fiscal year included, in descending order: Dubai, Japan, UK, Switzerland, Italy, Saudi Arabia, and Malaysia.[421]

In contrast to KFTZ, SEEPZ mainly exported to convertible currency markets like the US, Canada, Western Europe (including the UK), and the "Far East." Exports to Eastern Europe fluctuated from only 3 per cent in 1980–1981, to 15 per cent of zone exports for 1982–1983 before dropping down again to 4 per cent the next year.[422] By 1988–1989, exports from SEEPZ to Eastern Europe peaked at 35 per cent. In contrast to the electronics part of the zone, the jewellery section of SEEPZ, which opened in 1988, did not export to any Eastern European markets. Gem and jewellery exports were sent to the US (58 per cent), Western Europe and the UK (24 per cent), and Southeast Asia and Japan (18 per cent).[423] These exports from the gem and jewellery section may or may not be included in the summary of total zone exports noted above for the year 1988–1989. The records for the electronics and jewellery section were frequently calculated separately and do not specify the graphs. SEEPZ's export markets were diversified in comparison to KFTZ's reliance on the USSR.[424]

Because of its export profile, Indian planners viewed SEEPZ as relatively successful in comparison to KFTZ in that most exports did earn foreign

417 Dattatreyulu, *Export Processing Zones in India*, p. 20.
418 Ibid., p. 92.
419 Ibid., pp. 29–34.
420 Ibid., p. 63.
421 Dattatreyulu, *Export Processing Zones in India*, p. 20. The data from Dattatreyulu does not completely match that of Kumar, though the results are similar.
422 Kumar, *India's Export Processing Zones*, p. 91.
423 Dattatreyulu, *Export Processing Zones in India*, p. 16.
424 Ibid., p. 7; Kumar, *India's Export Processing Zones*, p. 91.

exchange, the Ministry of Commerce's goal for the zone policy. By the early 1980s, zones as a policy concept beyond SEEPZ and KFTZ finally emerged as a more coherent strategy that, using SEEPZ and KFTZ as the testing ground, proposed the establishment of additional EPZs around India, resulting in the Cochin, Noida, Falta, and Chennai zones in the 1980s. Additionally, single enterprises could establish themselves as export-oriented units and operate with EPZ-like tax and customs regulations without operating physically inside a zone, though they would fall under the administrative control of a neighbouring EPZ's development commissioner, the zone's manager appointed by the Ministry of Commerce. In modelling these new zones, SEEPZ's export profile was seen as more desirable as the ministry's concern over KFTZ grew.

Directing Global Flows

Rajiv Kumar and Patrick Neveling identified the balance of payments with the USSR as a central issue driving KFTZ's exports to the USSR.[425] They argue that because of the excessive reliance on rupee payment countries for exports from KFTZ, KFTZ was not perceived by planners as successful in achieving Indian planners' main goal: increasing foreign exchange by accumulating hard currency, which could only be achieved through exports to the convertible currency area (general payment area). Consequently, even though KFTZ was booming, it was discussed as a failure rather than a success.

Relieving India's debt to the USSR through KFTZ leads to two additional observations: the collapse of the division between the capitalist and socialist world markets within one space, KFTZ; and conversely the reinforced division of trade between these blocs, which was divided between Kandla and Bombay ports. Based on the view that the world was unified in a single capitalist economy divided by political blocs, it was in fact Indian planners' reactions to these political divisions that separated Eastern European economies from other economies through the creation of the rupee payment area. KFTZ operated as a geopolitical springboard between the socialist East and the capitalist West. Subsidiaries of Western firms, often run by NRIs or family members, could import their wares to KFTZ and transfer goods between KFTZ Indian units and the USSR. For many of the products, there was direct trade between the USSR and the United States. The separation of the rupee payment area from the general payment area, however, made India, KFTZ in particular, an advantageous

425 Kumar, *India's Export Processing Zones*; Neveling, "Structural Contingencies."

springboard for companies since Eastern Europe served as a protected export market for Indian goods. KFTZ was not merely embedded in a particular economic system. Indian planners also played an active role in defining India's external economic space in a way that affected how zones like KFTZ could be used to engage with that space.

A report by a professor at Sogang University in South Korea and a consultant to the Asia Productivity Organization, a regional organization supported by Japan and the US that championed the EPZ throughout Asia, assessed EPZ operations in five member countries, including India. The report notes that one of the selection criteria for zone unit applications was to export specifically to the convertible currency area in order to maximize foreign exchange generation from exports.[426] The main selection criterion for zone applicants was 30 per cent value-added to imported products that would be reexported, which was the basis for calculating the extent to which a unit would contribute to India's foreign exchange earnings. However, things did not go according to plan for the Ministry of Commerce. Once inside the zone, units operated with relative freedom and entry decisions were sometimes lax or arbitrary. The Indian Institute of Foreign Trade report of 1990 sums up KFTZ's achievements: "The freedom given to every entrepreneur to get into the zone had also its own share in adding to the woes."[427]

One feature of zones in India that has been enduring is their focus on Indian companies rather than exclusively foreign participation. For example, a 1984 trade policy report on which P.K. Kaul of the Kaul Committee also served noted that Indian FTZs put Indian firms "at complete par with other competitors in the world market."[428] The zone was intended to flatten and ease the entry of Indian businesses into international markets by levelling the playing field, allowing them to compete with international firms. Most zone units were small and medium-sized enterprises rather than major Indian companies, which did not begin to participate in the zones until the late 1980s since most of their production focused on the protected Indian market rather than the globally competitive market. Just like domestic market production, the USSR served as a protected export market (i.e. not globally competitive) for Indian manufacturers that units operating in KFTZ sought to access.

The heightened distinction between the general currency area and protected access to the rupee payment area by Indian planners broke down within

426 B. G. Van, "Survey on Duty-Free Export Processing Zones in Asian Region", *The Seoul National University Economic Review* 9 (1975) 1, pp. 126–244, at 169.
427 Dattatreyulu, *Export Processing Zones in India*, p. 59.
428 Indian Merchants' Chamber, 1984, Annual Report, IMC, p. 33.

KFTZ, which was used by units as a nodal point to facilitate trade from the general currency area to the rupee payment area. India's preferential access to the Soviet market was used to the advantage of these smaller Indian firms. Part of KFTZ's success during the 1980s is attributed to the implementation of tax holidays and the subsequent increase of foreign participation within the zone. While these tax holidays were helpful in attracting foreign investors, a major incentive for NRIs and foreign firms was the protected access to trade with the USSR. As subsidiaries of foreign firms began to produce in KFTZ in the 1980s, they used the zone as a channel to the Soviet market: "Some of the multi-national companies joined the zone with the explicit purpose of exporting to Russian market, which was otherwise not easily accessible. In that way the Zone is used as a conduit for tapping mainly the Russian market."[429] Further sections of this policy report highlight the role that these multinational companies and particularly the units run by NRIs played in this foreign trade connection. Some of these investors were interested in the quick access that KFTZ provided them to such markets: they could rent ready-made facilities that the zone provided and use it to produce Indian goods from Western inputs for the Eastern European market. In some cases, goods were not manufactured but simply imported from the US and reexported to the USSR without value added.[430] This meant that KFTZ also facilitated entrepôt trade in addition to manufacturing. India's combination of zone incentives and bilateral trade agreements facilitated unidirectional trade flows between the capitalist and socialist blocs that in other circumstances would have been more difficult.

It was not only NRIs living in the West who used KFTZ to their benefit. Soviet importers also identified KFTZ as a useful space that could be utilized to ease the USSR's foreign exchange burden. Instead of procuring items directly from a hard currency country like the US, through a subsidiary in KFTZ, the USSR could acquire the same Western items without spending foreign exchange reserves. Kumar writes that,

> the principal firm in an OECD [Organisation for Economic Co-operation and Development] country is directed by the Soviet importer to an Indian firm, which will be willing to enter into an agreement with the principal firm. The Indian firm then establishes a unit in an EPZ (or uses an existing unit) and imports the goods from the principal seller. With some value addition, these are then exported to the USSR with barely any manufacturing or processing.[431]

429 Dattatreyulu, *Export Processing Zones in India*, p. 37.
430 Kumar, *India's Export Processing Zones*, p. 99.
431 Ibid., pp. 98–99.

This diversion would save the USSR foreign exchange by procuring the necessary items through KFTZ or SEEPZ rather than paying for the imports through convertible currency. KFTZ was, therefore, advantageous as a nodal point for both Soviet importers and Western exporters.

The effect of this trade policy was a bifurcation of services between Kandla and Bombay ports. Kandla Port had been developed to decongest Bombay Port, and KFTZ was envisioned as a source of traffic. Yet, even through the end of the 1980s, international ships continued to bypass the port, and the facilities were not capable of handling larger ships. Its facilities were subpar, and there was such little trade in its hinterland that Kandla could not attract international shipping lines to call there. In effect, nearly all imports for both SEEPZ in Bombay and KFTZ in Kandla arrived through Bombay Port as they originated in convertible currency countries. Until the 1980s, KFTZ's exports were also routed through Bombay Port. By the 1980s, KFTZ's trade with Eastern European countries grew to such an extent that Eastern European shipping lines began to run regular services to the port. However, other international shipping lines bypassed the port, not necessarily due to Soviet presence, but rather because there was simply no economic reason to be there as trade destined for other markets besides the rupee payment area was negligible.[432]

This uneven logic led to a division between Bombay and Kandla ports. In the early 1950s through the 1960s, Eastern Europe did not at all factor into spatial references present in Ministry of Transport shipping statistics. Eastern European vessels would simply be labelled "continental" and placed in a general category equivalent to greater Europe (without the UK). In 1955 India signed a shipping agreement with the USSR, Poland, and the German Democratic Republic that stipulated that, when possible, trade between India and each country respectively would be carried out in vessels owned by the importing or exporting country. Upon independence in 1947, the Government of India set a goal of carrying 50 per cent of India's foreign trade in Indian vessels, but, by the mid-1950s, still less than 6 per cent of India's trade was shipped in Indian vessels.[433] Increasing Indian shipping became a government priority. The parties in the bilateral shipping agreement negotiated fixed shipping schedules, though by 1969, this fixed schedule represented only 36 sailings between India and the USSR.[434] However, Kandla Port factored into the 1960s schedule

432 Dattatreyulu, *Export Processing Zones in India*, p. 56.

433 Indian Merchants' Chamber, 1959, Annual Report, IMC, p. 149.

434 Ministry of Shipping and Transport, Government of India, 1968–1969, Annual Report, AR, IOD, CSL, p. 8.

negotiation as a future destination for routing Indo-Soviet cargo once the port was linked to its hinterlands by rail.

As trade with the USSR increased substantially over the course of the 1970s, in 1976, India renegotiated this shipping agreement with the USSR, again maintaining that goods should be shipped in ships of their two national flags and third-country ships would only be used if necessary. A similar agreement was again extended to Poland and the German Democratic Republic.[435] While KFTZ was located adjacent to Kandla Port, the port was inadequate for certain types of trade. Namely, larger ships were not able to call at the port as the harbour's draft was not deep enough to accommodate them.[436] Until the late 1980s, units within KFTZ received subsidies of 2 per cent of the value of the shipment in order to offset the extra costs accrued to the unit to ship their wares through Bombay Port, 791 kilometres away, because Kandla Port lacked the facilities to cater to their needs.

By the early 1970s, the imbalance in Kandla's imports and exports was already drawing attention from planners. For example, in 1970, Kandla imported 1,300,000 tons of cargo but only exported 173,000 tons (in foreign trade).[437] The imbalance between Kandla's imports and exports affected the selection and use of port equipment, like trains, as they required more wagons for cargo exiting the port after import, but fewer wagons for cargo were delivered to the port for export. This meant that empty wagons had to be frequently mobilized by the port to facilitate the import trade.[438] During the 1960s and 1970s, most of India's major ports regularly imported more cargo than they exported, with the exception of Mormugao, Paradip, and Visakhapatnam.[439] Even Bombay Port's imports greatly exceeded exports on an annual basis.[440] Yet, Kandla had been envisioned as a national, strategic port that would fix many woes; its problems may have been interpreted with deeper regret than Bombay's decades-long

435 Chishti, "India's Trade with East Europe", p. 3.

436 Dattatreyulu, *Export Processing Zones in India*, p. 38.

437 "India Ports and Shipping Statistics 1970", pp. 21–22.

438 Indian Merchants' Chamber, 1972, Annual Report, IMC, p. 140.

439 The term "major port" signifies a port owned by the central government. It is not clear why these three ports exported more, but their export profiles in petroleum, oil, and other liquids suggest they may have key nodal points for these exports and additionally these three ports were the only three significant transshipment ports among India's major ports. See: Ministry of Shipping and Transport, Government of India, 1984–1985, Annual Report, AR, IOD, CSL, p. 58.

440 This trend is supported by annual reports of the Ministry of Shipping and Transport for these decades. The statistics in the annual reports include foreign and domestic trade, so traffic reports simply recorded total goods entering the ports and total goods leaving.

struggle with congestion. By 1981, Kandla Port finally reached its full operating capacity, exceeding its annual capacity for handling cargo for the first time, as traffic handled India-wide increased by several million tons in comparison to 1980.[441]

By the end of the 1980s, rather than relying on Bombay exclusively for shipping, KFTZ's trade was divided between Bombay and Kandla ports along general payment area and rupee payment area lines. The subsidy for KFTZ units was reduced to 1 per cent of the value of the consignment when Eastern European shipping lines, including container vessels, began to call more frequently at Kandla Port.[442] However, nearly all of KFTZ's imports arrived from general payment area countries. These ships continued to call at Bombay Port. The exports generated from KFTZ became significant enough that Eastern European and Soviet ships began to frequent the port while, on the other hand, the zone played a negligible role in convertible currency area, that is, capitalist bloc, trade. These ships continued to exclusively frequent Bombay on India's west coast and were not enticed to call at Kandla. From Bombay, the imports to KFTZ were routed northwards, processed in KFTZ, and exported through Kandla Port to Eastern Europe.

KFTZ units' "misuse" of access to world markets became particularly worrying for the Ministry of Commerce during the 1980s. The imbalance in the zone and in the port was such a concern that the Ministry of Commerce attempted to stipulate that 50 per cent of KFTZ's exports should be destined for countries trading in convertible currency. Within the context of the late 1980s, the Indo–Soviet bilateral trade agreements were reaffirmed in 1987 with even more vigor, envisioning more than doubling trade between the countries in the early 1990s. Though KFTZ had been widely criticized, the 1990 Indian Institute of Foreign Trade report on the zone's operations recommended that KFTZ finally be encouraged in this effort rather than stigmatized for not fulfilling its official purpose of increasing India's foreign exchange reserves.[443] It seems that what was in fact an informal practice of zone units to import from the general payment area and export to the rupee payment area through KFTZ was on its way to being formalized by the Government of India as a practice useful to the state under its new commitment to increase Soviet trade. The report's author concludes that the former socialist states in Eastern Europe will potentially join the European Community; the long and positive history of India's trade relations with these countries could be vital for entering a future expanded European common market as an exporter.

441 Ministry of Shipping and Transport, Government of India, 1981–1982, Annual Report, AR, IOD, CSL, p. 46.

442 Kumar, *India's Export Processing Zones*, p. 46.

443 Dattatreyulu, *Export Processing Zones in India*, pp. 60–64.

Likewise, Kumar's study, which was also originally a semi-official report, recommended turning the activities pursued in KFTZ by the zone units, multinationals, and NRIs into an official government policy. Why not utilize India's bilateral trade agreements and "Western" NRIs to form India officially as an "Austria" or a "Finland", both transshipment locations between capitalist and socialist markets?[444] KFTZ could become an official conduit for such trade rather than the unofficial victim of its geopolitical position. Of course, none of these recommendations were sustainable after the collapse of the USSR in 1991. Though in the late 1980s trade was planned to double between the USSR and India during the 1990s, in fact, the volume of trade more than halved, dropping from 4.2 billion USD in 1990 to 2.2 billion USD in 1995 and even lower to 1.6 billion USD for the 1997–1998 fiscal year.[445]

At the conclusion of the Cold War, Indo-Russian relations were strained over currency, exchange rates, and India's debt. Though KFTZ had dedicated its exports almost entirely to the USSR, there had been little demand there for Indian products, meaning that over half of the rupee-based debt had not been collected. Once the USSR collapsed, negotiations began with Russia on how to proceed. A repayment schedule was established in 1993 that allowed India to repay Russia 1 billion USD annually in Indian exports through 2005, after which time the rest of the debt would be repaid without interest over 45 years. Russia provided Indian producers with a 180-day forecast of the amounts of various products required.[446]

Whether any of these exports were sent through KFTZ is not clear. The Ministry of Commerce in the 1990s created standardized charts to display data for all six of India's EPZs. Russia was not a country specified as an export destination, likely indicating that it was not an important destination for zone products. It is clear that KFTZ suffered for a number of years after 1991, while other zones like SEEPZ grew. For that reason, growth at KFTZ likely stalled for several years because of the collapse of its export market, the USSR, rather than the restructuring of the Indian economy in 1991. The number of units in KFTZ decreased from 141 operating units in 1991–1992 to 91 units in 1994–1995 before finally increasing in 1998.[447] Likewise, KFTZ's exports dropped from 4,271.80 million rupees in 1991–1992 to the lowest in nearly a decade by the next fiscal

444 Kumar, *India's Export Processing Zones*, pp. 99–100.

445 L. Lee, "Russia's Engagement of India: Securing the Longevity of a 'Special and Privileged' Strategic Partnership", in: I. Hall (ed.), *The Engagement of India: Strategies and Reponses*, Washington, DC: Georgetown University Press, 2014, pp. 61–87, at 64.

446 Conley, *Indo-Russian Military*, pp. 61–62.

447 A. Kundra, *The Performance of India's Export Zones: A Comparison with the Chinese Approach*, New Delhi: Sage Publications, 2000, p. 88.

year: 1,672.10 million rupees.[448] In contrast, SEEPZ added more units by 1992–1993 and increased exports by about 3 billion rupees. Over the course of the 1990s, both SEEPZ and KFTZ increased the percentage of their exports to the US. In 1990–1991, only 1 per cent of KFTZ's exports were destined for the US, 1 per cent to the UK, and 1 per cent to the United Arab Emirates. By 1997–1998, these shares increased to respectively 20 per cent, 10 per cent, and 10 per cent of the zone's exports.[449] SEEPZ units, meanwhile, concentrated their exports more heavily on the US even as they expanded to other markets like Singapore, Germany, and the United Arab Emirates. Exports to the UK, formerly nearly one-quarter of the zone's exports in 1990–1991, shrank to just 6 per cent by 1997–1998 while the US increased from 28 per cent to 52 per cent of the zone's exports over the same period.[450]

Although foreign investment increased among some typical zone investors like the US, the UK, and Japan, NRI investment as well as domestic investment continued to play a dominant role in India's EPZs. However, KFTZ was the only zone that by 1998 still had more NRI investors than foreign investors, and total investment in the zone was low in comparison to India's other zones.[451] Both KFTZ and SEEPZ, along with the others established in the 1980s (Noida, Falta, Cochin, and Chennai), formed the basis for the expansion of these isolated zones into a formalized SEZ policy in the 2000s. By this time, India's strategic goals and geopolitical position had altered quite substantially, leaving Cold War logics behind.

Conclusion

India's first FTZs were an outcome of India's state-driven efforts to offset the economic imbalances India faced in establishing its post-colonial economy during the Cold War. Scholars have often understood zones to be a standardized international policy. Yet, analyzing zones as a single international policy has hindered a full understanding of their functions, which may surpass their prescribed purpose. In their studies and surveys, international and government agencies as well as scholars expected an international model, and in their statistics, therefore, highlighted certain characteristics of India's zones while obscuring other non-conforming features from intense scrutiny. This standardization during the formation of the EPZ model may have similarly

448 Ibid., p. 89.
449 Ibid., p. 97.
450 Ibid., p. 96.
451 Ibid., pp. 103–104.

concealed the functions of zones in other contexts. The EPZ model statistics fail to account for the complex interplay between state and private practices inside India's zones.

In particular, these statistics did not account for the fact that foreign firms operating inside Indian zones were run by NRIs. Furthermore, they were often joint enterprises with a family member who is resident in India. The strong presence of NRI investment was not coincidental; the Government of India targeted them in their investment drive. This strategic targeting is similar to the Chinese SEZ drive in the 1980s, which sought to reconnect its Southeast Asian diaspora to mainland China through zone investments and trade.[452] India's diaspora is so geographically dispersed and economically and culturally diverse (in terms of religion and language) that it is difficult for the Government of India to strategically connect to its many diasporas of 25 million (in 2012).[453] Nevertheless, the NRI policy was expanded by the Government of India in the 2000s, officially recognizing a policy of layered citizenship and rights depending on claims to Indian heritage and status. These NRIs were important in shaping how the zones functioned through the 1970s and the 1980s.

KFTZ and SEEPZ both emerged from India's reterritorialization strategy: an attempt to carve out small enclaves in India's state at strategic entry and exit points – Kandla and Bombay – to create, enhance, and regulate flows, that is, imports into and exports out of India. This attempt was a state-based desire to create a planned portal of globalization, where the internal and external are regulated and negotiated by the state.[454] However, in doing so, the private actors within these spaces pursued their own interests, thus creating a different kind of portal: one where different types of actors – NRIs, Indians, family members, and foreign investors – sought to negotiate world orders by forging trade connections not envisioned for this space by the state.[455] Although the visions and planning for KFTZ and SEEPZ are state-based, the resulting articulations can be attributed to individuals and firms and represent private globalization strategies to deal with the global condition. On the one hand, these private globalization strategies were personal attempts to deal with the actors' own global mobility and profit from it by connecting business networks to family members within and outside of India through the zones. On the other hand,

452 Ong, *Neoliberalism as Exception*, pp. 75–118.
453 Kundra, *Performance of India's Export Zones*, p. 199; "India and its Diaspora", The Ministry of Overseas Indian Affairs website, http://moia.gov.in/accessories.aspx?aid=10 (accessed 15 December 2015).
454 Geyer, "Portals of Globalization."
455 Middell and Naumann, "Global History", pp. 162–163.

however, these connections also took advantage of existing economic agreements between India and Eastern Europe to turn KFTZ into a springboard between the US and the USSR. Through the zones, these actors contributed to producing global connections within the framework of various entanglements like the rupee payment agreements, which also allowed new connections to emerge between general payment countries and rupee payment countries routed through Bombay and Kandla ports, facilitated by KFTZ and the investors inside the zone. In short, these actors were not only embedded within but also involved in the production of spatial orders. Eventually, these private practices were again subjected to scrutiny by the state, which ultimately recommended formalizing these practices to foster connections to the USSR. KFTZ's Cold War story, therefore, ends with a proposal to formalize the informal practices pursued by zone units.

6 Strategizing Global India and Transregional Mumbai, 1990s–2014

In 2000, India's existing EPZs including KFTZ and SEEPZ were converted to SEZs. This new policy has a similar tax incentive structure to the EPZ. However, the zone-land itself can also be purchased and run ("developed") by a private corporation. Additionally, only part of the zone area must be set aside for manufacturing or processing. SEZs may include residential and other facilities. Since India's implementation of the new SEZ policy, extended through the 2005 SEZ Act, the zone is once again connected not only to urban spaces, as discussed frequently in the literature on SEZs in India, but also to port infrastructure. This chapter highlights port-zone connections. For those studying SEZs from the zone perspective, this connection may not be evident. From the viewpoint of India's port sector, the connection between the policies shows how India's ports are being strategically linked to manufacturing, freight corridors, and trade routes inside and outside of India as part of India's strategy to position itself centrally in Indian Ocean and Asian trade. As economic geographers have noted, port-zone complexes, as they are often located near one another, represent a policy bundle: an intersection of "spaces of production and spaces of circulation", which serve as an interface "between global and local spaces." In short, the port-zone bundle is a planned space of "global articulation."[456]

This chapter analyses these port-zone bundles within the context of India's post-2000 SEZ policy and port reform. It does so by discussing economic liberalization and decentralization pursued by the central government since the 1990s, the specific changes these new plans fostered in the municipality, the zone, and the port sectors, and the specific trade and transit connections the Government of India is pursuing through these port-zone complexes. These port-zone policies are not just about creating isolated nodes of articulation like KFTZ that connect to existing trade agreements; the Government of India is attempting to use the zone and port-zone bundle within and beyond India, particularly through Mumbai, to generate, capture, and manage national and foreign investment and trade flows.

Loraine Kennedy has noted the connection between India's 2005 SEZ policy and its strategy to create specific places within India that can connect to global capital and trade flows.[457] Her research shows that India's new policies, such

---

456 Wang and Olivier, "Port-FEZ Bundles", p. 1487.
457 Kennedy, *Politics of Economic Restructuring*, pp. 78–111.

https://doi.org/10.1515/9783110615135-006

as the SEZ policy, are not a product of global economic flows or foreign intervention but are based on India's political and economic strategy to engage with these flows selectively. Her work, however, does not articulate the specific flows the SEZ policy seeks to capture. In conjunction with an analysis of India's port sector, this chapter builds on her argument and outlines these transregional connections. Other countries such as the US, China, and Japan have used the EPZ or SEZ as part of their foreign policy. This chapter finds that India is now also using the port-zone as a foreign policy tool. The SEZ may function as a portal of globalization that strategically seeks to negotiate the "internal" and the "external" through specific de- and reterritorialization features. The use of this tool in India's foreign policy has intermeshed the internal and the external, so that the distinction between foreign policy and domestic policy becomes blurred.[458]

Rather than discussing the markets tapped by India's zones as global, this chapter describes India's port-zone policy bundle as facilitating transregional connections. "Global" and "transnational" are incomplete descriptions of the linkages fostered through these portals of globalization. The port-zone dynamic is rather an attempt to rearticulate India's connections with transregional spaces thorough Greater Mumbai's newest port, Jawaharlal Nehru Port Trust (JNPT).[459] The term "transregional" applies to economic and political spaces that may in fact be regional, meaning that they do not attempt to connect Mumbai or India to the whole globe. However, the articulation of these spaces challenges ideas in area studies and international relations of India's given region, South Asia.[460] The term "transregional" is also a product of Eurocentric concerns. In the context of this chapter, regions referred to in Indian documents do not always correspond with Western imaginations of regions. Furthermore, the connectedness formed through the projects discussed here do not seek to connect the whole Indian market with foreign markets but concentrate on certain

458 John Agnew discusses the false opposition between foreign and domestic policy, which he argues are under constant renegotiation: Agnew, "Territorial Trap", pp. 65–68.

459 For a comparative view on this topic with China's SEZs, see: M. Maruschke, "Special Economic Zones and Transregional State Spatiality", in: M. Middell (ed.), *The Routledge Handbook of Transregional Studies*, London: Routledge, 2019, pp. 197–203.

460 Middell, *Handbook of Transregional Studies*. The term comes out of a growing concern within Area Studies that prescribed regions are not natural containers that can be separated by social scientists, and the boundaries of regions are shifting; on the other hand, not all connections that go beyond these regions are global. See also J. H. Bentley, R. Bridenthal and A. A. Yang (eds.), *Interactions: Transregional Perspectives on World History*, Honolulu: University of Hawai'i Press, 2005.

subnational spaces designated for this purpose through transport corridors and zone projects within India and abroad.

Unlike the previous chapters of this book approached with the clarity of hindsight, this chapter deals with post-1990s reforms until Prime Minister Narendra Modi's (in office since 2014) early plans for India's zones and ports.[461] The various projects under discussion have been changing rapidly in the last several years. This chapter demonstrates how port and zone projects are being used to link domestic and foreign transregional agendas, which helps to contextualize global capital inflows or global trade. Instead, the Indian government targets specific places and routes for investment both within and beyond India.

Economic Liberalization and State Decentralization

There has been considerable debate about the impetus behind economic liberalization in India. The year 1991 symbolizes what appears to be a juncture, though most scholars acknowledge that the process was gradual and began as early as the 1970s.[462] Indian leaders preempted structural adjustment programmes by implementing reforms in 1981 before approaching the International Monetary Fund (IMF) for a loan.[463] In 1991, India sought another loan from the IMF due to a balance of payments crisis and debt, which were compounded by international instability. The Iraqi invasion of Kuwait added to India's balance of payment problems, as Gulf workers, who contributed substantially to India's foreign currency reserves, were unable to send remittances home.[464]

---

461 Other Indian political parties and prime ministers have not been dealt with in this book (let alone British political parties pre-1947). Yet, there appears to be a larger break with previous practices and widespread overhaul enfolding post-2014. A conclusion on that subject is for future historians to decide.

462 DeLong, for example, determines 1980 as the beginning of the first wave of liberalization based on GNP: J. B. DeLong, "India since Independence: An Analytic Growth Narrative", in: D. Rodrik (ed.), *In Search of Prosperity: Analytic Narratives on Economic Growth*, Princeton, NJ: Princeton University Press, 2003, pp. 184–204; Nayar suggests that liberalization began in 1975: B. R. Nayar, "When did the 'Hindu' Rate of Growth End?", *Economic and Political Weekly* 41 (2006) 19, pp. 1885–1990; Panagariya writes that the first of three pre-1991 liberalization phases began in 1975: A. Panagariya, *India: The Emerging Giant*, Oxford: Oxford University Press, 2008, p. 80.

463 B. R. Nayar, *The Geopolitics of Globalization: The Consequences for Development*, Oxford: Oxford University Press, 2007, p. 233. Oxford Scholarship Online Edition.

464 Kennedy, *Politics of Economic Restructuring*, pp. 37, 50; C. Hurtig, "The Restructuring of India's External Relations: 1971–1998", in Jaffrelot (ed.), *India since 1950*, pp. 183–193, at 190.

Loraine Kennedy argues that though the immediate economic restructuring in 1991 may be viewed through the lens of the prescribed structural adjustment programme, the reforms continued and intensified long after the "crisis" was resolved.[465] This meant that the reforms were a calculated political strategy pursued by India's policy makers, and that they were shaped by certain internal and external constraints rather than externally imposed reforms.[466] This view has also been shared by others.[467] Indeed, port sector restructuring and the SEZ policy, discussed subsequently in this chapter, both gained traction since the 2000s and are under continuous reform. Although these reforms are viewed by scholars within the framework of 1991 restructuring, which did correspond with significant new legislation, the year 1991 appears to also be a symbolic indicator of change that rhetorically sets India's internal economic restructuring within the worldwide framework of post-1989–1991 political shifts. Situating economic restructuring within the "global moment" of 1989 legitimizes potentially democratically unpopular changes that Indian politicians and bureaucrats sought for India's economy for over a decade. At the same time, academic acceptance of this "global moment" removes agency from Indian planners by suggesting that only "external impulses" affect India's internal changes.[468]

Subnational States have been empowered through India's state restructuring,[469] leading to what Kennedy describes as the dual impact of simultaneous economic liberalization with state decentralization policies:

> In effect, until the nineties, the central state maintained strict control over private investment decisions, including the geographical location of firms, through a complex system of licenses and permits [...]. With the dismantling of the "licence-permit raj" in the 1990s, there has been a twofold decentralisation: investment decisions to private firms, and economic development initiatives to State governments. To clarify, macro-economic

465 For a discussion on structural adjustment programmes in general and their impacts, see: W. Easterly, "What did Structural Adjustment Adjust?: The Association of Policies and Growth with Repeated IMF and World Bank Adjustment Loans", *Journal of Development Economics* 76 (2005) 1, pp. 1–22.

466 Kennedy, *Politics of Economic Restructuring*, p. 38.

467 Nayar, *Geopolitics of Globalization*, p. 233. Cf. P. Choudhury and T. Khanna, "Charting Dynamic Trajectories: Multinational Enterprises in India", *Business History Review* 88 (2014) 1, pp. 133–169.

468 M. Mann, "India 1989: Overcoming the Post-Colonial State", in U. Engel, F. Hadler and M. Middell (eds.), *1989 in a Global Perspective*, Leipzig: Leipziger Universitätsverlag, 2015, pp. 259–295, at 259–260.

469 "State" is capitalized to clarify that it refers to a subnational state in India. L. Sáez, *Federalism without a Center: The Impact of Political and Economic Reform on India's Federal System*, New Delhi and Thousand Oaks, CA: Sage Publications, 2002.

> and monetary policies continue to be made by central ministries and national institutions like the Reserve Bank of India, but States have more manoeuvring space than in the past and can adopt measures that influence the investment climate within their boundaries.[470]

Investment decisions are based on commercial decisions rather than government mandates, so that India's subnational States compete with one another, and presumably other states (nation states), in order to attract investments.[471] Likewise, restrictions preventing industry from being located in metropolitan areas were relaxed.[472] While the previous industrial and economic policies were intended to lessen differences between lagging rural areas and cities, the current policy intends to heighten these differences in order to connect metropolitan areas to what Saskia Sassen calls "global circuits."[473]

Although Kennedy starts her research on state rescaling in India by repeating the perspectives of Neil Brenner, she departs from a different vantage point. Rather than suggesting that state rescaling is occurring in reaction to crisis or economic stagnation (as was the view of US and Western European cities since the 1970s), she finds that India's state rescaling strategies are now pursued as active articulations of India's policy goals to create spaces of capital accumulation.[474] State rescaling is not occurring in reaction to structural adjustment programmes imposed by the IMF; rather, Indian planners look for strategies to carefully connect certain spaces with global markets and investments.

Articulating State Rescaling

The Government of India's state rescaling strategies in the port and zone sectors can be broadly described as outcomes of economic liberalization and state

470 L. Kennedy, "Large-Scale Economic and Infrastructure Projects in India's Metropolitan Cities: New Policies and Practices Among Competing Subnational States", paper presented at the Fourth International Conference of the International Forum on Urbanism (IFoU), Amsterdam/Delft, 2009, pp. 1055–1065, at 1056, http://newurbanquestion.ifou.org/proceedings/.
471 J. Dehejia, "Economic Reforms: Birth of an 'Asian Tiger'", in: P. Oldenburg (ed.), *India Briefing: 1993*, Boulder, CO: Westview Press, 1993, pp. 75–102.
472 S. Chakravorty and S. V. Lall, *Made in India: The Economic Geography and Political Economy of Industrialization*, Oxford: Oxford University Press, 2007, p. 35.
473 S. Sassen, "Locating Cities on Global Circuits", *Environment & Urbanization* 14 (2002) 1, pp. 13–30.
474 Kennedy, *Politics of Economic Restructuring*, p. 148.

decentralization policies. However, Kennedy identified the tension between what appears to be state decentralization and the simultaneous reinsertion of the central government in policies at the subnational level, particularly within the context of the new SEZ policy that came into effect in 2005.[475] It is for this reason that state rescaling is at the centre of discussion and not exclusively state decentralization.

The 2005 SEZ policy was one of the more controversial policies connected to India's decentralization and economic liberalization. The Indian SEZ myth, like many other zone "origin stories" today, began with a trip to China. In 2000, Commerce and Industry Minister Murasoli Maran visited China and reportedly Shenzhen SEZ.[476] Following this visit, the Ministry of Commerce converted India's existing EPZs to the SEZ label as part of a restructuring of India's export-import policy. The Ministry of Commerce then took steps to establish a comprehensive SEZ policy that would enable new SEZs to be not only spaces for manufacturing for export, but also to include other facilities such as housing, schools, recreational facilities, hospitals, and commercial spaces. This comprehensive shift towards city building resembles China's SEZs, some of which formed booming metropolises. In 1997, the Indian Council for Research on International Economic Relations, a think tank devoted to "informing India's policy makers" and "improving the interface with the global economy", published a book that analysed the relevance of China's SEZs to India.[477] An associate of this think tank also published a book in 2000, in which he compared India's EPZs to China's SEZs.[478] The purpose of both books was to understand China's experience with zones in order to augment India's zone policy, or lack thereof.

According to Kennedy, the most significant feature of India's new SEZs is the provision for infrastructure development, which coincides with a non-processing area within the zone. The SEZ policy allowed for zones with up to 65 per cent non-processing areas, though that has since been reduced to 50 per cent. Kennedy notes that the major shift seems to be the privatization of city-building.[479] These features deviate significantly from the EPZ of the past that was an exclusive processing area and adds a degree of central government oversight to urban planning, which has typically been a prerogative of

475 Ibid., p. 85.
476 Ibid., p. 79.
477 S. P. Gupta (ed.), *China's Economic Reforms: Role of Special Economic Zones and Economic and Technological Development Zones*, New Delhi: Allied Publishers Limited, 1996.
478 Kundra, *Performance of India's Export Zones.*
479 Kennedy, *Politics of Economic Restructuring*, p. 80.

the State. In this respect, India's SEZs do resemble China's in that they go beyond export processing to include urban features.[480] Though rhetorically China has been the origin of the policy, scholars also discuss the policy origins as emerging out of India's past EPZs,[481] or compared SEZs to India's industrial estate programme.[482] For example, Aradhna Aggarwal discusses the "evolution" of India's zone policy. However, some aspects of the new policy resemble Chinese SEZs, many aspects are either new or deviate from the Chinese example, while other aspects of the policy appear very similar to how India's past EPZs operated.[483] The 2005 SEZ Act, though surely motivated by the rising numbers of SEZs around the world, was not a "cookie-cutter" implementation of any specific SEZ policy from another context, nor was it imposed by a UN agency. As one sociologist writes, "unlike many economic policies in India, the role of the World Bank is notable by its absence."[484]

The SEZ Act was passed in 2005 and went into effect in 2006 with very little parliamentary discussion.[485] Between 2000 and 2006, 12 additional SEZs were established out of 133 approved SEZs, which were all, apart from 13 private projects, sponsored by State governments.[486] By 2011, 133 of the formally approved 585 SEZs were already operational.[487] The latest numbers from December 2017 provided by the Ministry of Commerce state that 222 zones are operational and 423 zones have been approved.[488] The policy allows State governments or private companies (or joint partnerships) to establish SEZs. The notable difference between past EPZs is that private developers may set up the zones and become zone developers, which may then rent processing space to other firms, the zone units. Developers and units receive numerous tax incentives (some of which have been scaled back over time, as India's "regular" tax regime has undergone

480 Bach, "Urban Imagination"; Easterling, *Extrastatecraft*.

481 Kennedy, *Politics of Economic Restructuring*; Jamie Cross also discusses townships and industrial estates prior to the SEZ Act: Cross, *Dream Zones*, pp. 28–35.

482 All the while concluding that they are very different: M. Levien, "Regimes of Dispossession: From Steel Towns to Special Economic Zones", *Development and Change* 44 (2013) 2, pp. 381–407.

483 Aggarwal, *Social and Economic Impact of SEZs*, pp. 63–87.

484 Levien, "Regimes of Dispossession", p. 396.

485 Kennedy, *Politics of Economic Restructuring*, pp. 78–80.

486 Aggarwal, *Social and Economic Impact*, p. 67.

487 Jenkins, Kennedy, Mukhodpadhyay, *Power, Policy and Protest*, p. 4.

488 "Operational SEZs in India", Special Economic Zones in India website, http://sezindia.nic.in/cms/operational-sezs-in-india.php (accessed 2 July 2018).

extensive changes in the last two decades)[489] such as 100 per cent exemption from tax in export income over five years, which is scaled back to 50 per cent for the following five years, as well as tax exemptions on inputs from the domestic economy and imports.[490] States, too, have been encouraged to offer incentives through removing State taxes. Thus, States may compete with one another to offer better incentives for developers and units.

As aforementioned, these rescaling reforms do not aim at state decentralization only, but are accompanied by a range of features that empower India's subnational States while enhancing central government oversight. Kennedy sees the SEZ policy as a continuation of certain Licence-Raj practices.[491] The Ministry of Commerce approves all zone projects through the board of approvals and also appoints zone development commissioners to head selected SEZs, which manage other zones in their area[492] For example, the development commissioner of SEEPZ in Mumbai is the commissioner appointed to all SEZs in Maharashtra as well as the State's export oriented units, that is, zone status granted to single firms' operations. The board therefore controls SEZ project selection, though it manages this in cooperation with the State since any project must also be approved by the State government in which the project is located. Once SEZs are in operation with exporting units, the Ministry of Commerce continues to have direct oversight of SEZ activities through the development commissioners. For this reason, Kennedy claims the SEZ policy represents state-based development planning rather than privatization and neoliberalism.[493]

State rescaling has also affected the port sector. These strategies to connect India to global and regional trade flows are articulated through India's ports. As India's economy liberalized, foreign trade increased substantially in the early 1990s. Exports alone grew to 32 billion USD in 1995, a 30 per cent increase from the previous three years.[494] The Ministry of Shipping boasts that 68 per cent of India's foreign trade by value is exported through India's ports, which is

489 Aggarwal, *Social and Economic Impact*, p. 80.
490 "Facilities and Incentives", Special Economic Zones in India website, http://www.sezindia.nic.in/about-fi.asp (accessed 19 December 2015).
491 Kennedy, *Politics of Economic Restructuring*, p. 85.
492 The selected SEZs appear to be mainly the earlier EPZs such as Kandla, SEEPZ, Falta, Cochin, etc. See: "List of State-wise Exporting SEZs", Special Economic Zones in India website, dated 31 March 2015, http://www.sezindia.nic.in/writereaddata/pdf/ListofoperationalSEZs.pdf (accessed 19 December 2015).
493 Cf. S. Banerjee-Guha, "Space Relations of Capital and Significance of New Economic Enclaves: SEZs in India", *Economic and Political Weekly* 43 (2008) 47, pp. 51–59.
494 N. Shashikumar, "The Indian Port Privatization Model: A Critique", *Transportation Journal* 37 (1998) 3, pp. 35–48, at 35.

95 per cent of trade by volume.[495] As a result of the importance of India's ports to the economic liberalization drive, state decentralization and liberalization policies have also focused on India's port sector.

New policies have encouraged State governments to set up their own ministries of shipping to generate individual port policies regarding "minor" and "intermediate" ports, while the central government, through the Ministry of Shipping, would continue to administer "major" ports like JNPT, the newest large container port in Mumbai's harbour.[496] However, corporations can also privately run minor ports and private investment is also allowed in major ports according to multiple investment models such as landlord ports (where terminals are rented to private terminal operators and the port trust acts as a landlord), as well as a variety of public private partnership models. Not only were States encouraged to set up their own ministries, but the central government's Ministry of Shipping and Road Transport and Highways (the name of this ministry has often shifted) split into two ministries, so that the Ministry of Shipping became an independent ministry in 2009.[497] Put together, nearly half of all 200 minor and intermediate ports in India are located in Maharashtra (48) and Gujarat (41).[498] More than any other State, Gujarat has the most private ports with a large operating capacity, which serve as feeder ports to the major ports in Mumbai area, Mumbai Port Trust (MPT) and JNPT, but also add competition to these ports.[499] All ports, both major and minor, located in Gujarat handled more than 40 per cent of India's total cargo from 2014 to 2015.[500] In comparison, Mumbai's two major ports, MPT and JNPT, handled 21.6 per cent.[501] Despite these numerous

495 Ministry of Shipping, 2014–2015, Annual Report, http://shipping.nic.in/showfile.php?lid=2016, p. 7.

496 In India, ports are divided into two basic categories: major ports which are run as port trusts, with the exception of Ennore, which is run as a company, and minor/intermediate ports. The terms "major" and "minor" not only relate to the volume of traffic handled at the ports but also denote the administrative authority of the ports. Major ports operate independently but are owned by the central government under the jurisdiction of the Ministry of Shipping while minor and intermediate ports may be private ports that fall under the jurisdiction of States' departments for transport.

497 Ministry of Shipping, 2014–2015, Annual Report, p. 5.

498 Ministry of Shipping, Government of India, "Update on Indian Port Sector", p. 26, http://shipping.nic.in/showfile.php?lid=2020 (accessed 31 March 2015).

499 Ministry of Shipping, 2014–2015, Annual Report, p. 9. Gujarat's minor ports accounted for three-fourths of the total traffic of minor ports in India.

500 "Update on Indian Port Sector", pp. 27–29.

501 Ibid., p. 9.

small ports in Gujarat and Maharashtra, the Government of India is now focusing its attention on the creation of what it has called "mega ports."

In 2010, the Ministry of Shipping instituted a Maritime Agenda for 2010 through 2020, which aims to increase India's share of world trade by competing globally with other ports.[502] This agenda is set within the specific framework of enabling India's economic liberalization by facilitating the physical connectedness between India and the outside world, which also implies restructuring the port sector to meet these demands through privatization. It is set within a framework of globalization and global competition: India, the "I" in BRICs (Brazil, Russia, India, China), should become the global nation it is projected to be by economists at Goldman Sachs. The "globalization" of the port sector, which entails competition among carriers as well as networks of terminal operators, is one way of becoming "global."[503] According to the Indian Maritime Agenda, globalization is not merely something facing ports around the world; globalization is an active strategy that the Ministry of Shipping hopes to utilize. It appears that the path towards globalization, however, entails the nationalization of global trade flows, that is, Indian ships should handle more cargo (and especially Indian cargo should be carried on Indian ships), and India's ports should increase their capacity and efficiency to handle global traffic. The "global traffic" terminology is not clear: most of India's foreign trade is shipped first to Dubai, Colombo, or Singapore. Does handling global traffic mean India should become a direct shipper of its own goods to reduce transshipment? Or should Indian ports become transshipment ports in their own right? In either case, it implies that Indian ports or shipping, private or public, should control a greater portion of foreign trade.

Various privatization schemes at major and minor ports have coincided with the reassertion of control by the central government, at least regarding the operations of major ports. Several major ports including JNPT have pursued the landlord port model, which allows for private Indian and foreign firms to operate terminals. Other schemes include public-private partnerships and build-operate-transfer. Up to 100 per cent foreign direct investment (FDI) is permitted for projects, including the construction of ports and their maintenance.[504] Though private investment and foreign terminal operators are now allowed at major ports, deregulation was actually accompanied by new regulations. Ports' tariffs are controlled by the Tariff Authority for Major Ports (TAMP), which was

502 Ministry of Shipping, Government of India, "Maritime Agenda: 2010–2020", 2011, http://shipping.nic.in/showfile.php?lid=261.

503 Ibid., pp. 12–14.

504 Department of Shipping, Ministry of Shipping, Road Transport and Highways, Government of India, 2005–2006, Annual Report, AR, IOD, CSL, p. 15.

instituted in 1997 through altering the Port Trust Act of 1963.[505] This rule controls the maximum tariffs that can be charged at major ports with the exception of Ennore, the first corporate port, while minor ports' tariffs are not regulated.[506] Though decentralization has meant that subnational States may compete with one another, TAMP essentially limits the extent to which major ports may compete with other ports within India and abroad for traffic, though the trusts are always able to offer fees below those scheduled by the TAMP. Meanwhile, the corporatization of major ports has been on the agenda since 2001, though has yet to be implemented.[507] Corporatization, however, is not synonymous with privatization. Corporatization would give India's major ports more leeway to make investment decisions and, like Ennore, would no longer be held to the port trust regulations but to the Company Act. In short, scrapping TAMP and converting major ports from trusts to corporations or authorities has been on the agenda for many years.

Since the SEZ Act of 2005, major and minor ports have been able to set up their own SEZs. The basic model involves the elimination of import and export duties for export-oriented manufacturing on port property. A private developer can acquire land, receiving certain tax benefits, and lease units for manufacturing to other private companies that would also benefit from tax reductions. Different types of zones, singled out by sector, have different requirements. There are two types of zones that are likely to be located at ports: (1) port-based multiproduct zones and (2) free trade and warehousing zones.[508] Some private ports in Gujarat include Adani Ports SEZ (formerly Mundra port), a port-based multiproduct zone, and a free trade and warehousing zone at Haldia, which is also promoted by Adani. Among the major ports, KPT also approved a privately developed port-based multiproduct SEZ as has Cochin Port Trust.[509] Likewise, Mumbai's JNPT has been planning a multiproduct SEZ on its property, which has been notified since 2014 and since then formally approved.[510]

---

505 Resham Nagpal, "Tariff Guidelines for Major Ports", *Indian Infrastructure* 15 (2013) 10, pp. 60–61.

506 Department of Shipping 2005–2006, Annual Report, pp. 15–17; P. Manoj, "A turf war could potentially spoil India's port tariff de-regulation plan", *Live Mint*, 26 July 2013, http://www.livemint.com/Opinion/FgtczAsa08XXlkH7DKo4tO/A-turf-war-could-potentially-spoil-Indias-port-tariff-dere.html.

507 Department of Shipping 2005–2006, Annual Report, p. 116.

508 Any type of zone could be located at a port, though usually these two types are singled out.

509 "Update on Indian Port Sector", p. 49.

510 Operational SEZ means exporting; formally approved indicates that the SEZ developer has the land and may go ahead; notified signifies that the developer may begin acquiring land and permissions.

Though these numbers are small in comparison to the total 202 operational SEZs, the 412 formally approved SEZs, and the 329 notified SEZs around India, there are only 12 major ports in India, 3 of which will soon have SEZs directly on port property.[511] SEZs have become a key part of the privatization of the port sector as Indian ports compete with one another for traffic. These plans have intensified and are connected to the construction of industrial and urban spaces along transport corridors within India, which will eventually link to certain foreign investors, ports, and transport corridors abroad.

Integrating the Port-Zone Corridor

Since 2014, under the government of Narendra Modi, reforms have yet again intensified in the port and SEZ sectors.[512] The Make in India campaign entails overhauling the economy by opening most sectors to 100 per cent FDI while also implementing de-licensing and de-regulation reforms through a number of new initiatives.[513] The focus on foreign investment is not only sought directly for manufacturing as the slogan Make in India would suggest, but also for construction, ports and shipping, IT, entertainment, and leisure.[514] This makes the 100 per cent FDI allowed in India's SEZs less relevant. The Make in India promotions are also not exclusively export oriented but advertise India as an important market destination with a rising middle-class that can afford electronic items, automobiles, entertainment, and so on.[515] The Make in India project is probably the most visible of the new reform projects because, first, it is the

511 For all statistics, see the numerous factsheets at: "About SEZs", Special Economic Zones in India website, last updated 31 March 2015, http://www.sezindia.nic.in/index.asp (accessed 9 January 2016).

512 Prime Minister Narendra Modi of the Bharatiya Janata party has gained considerable momentum in reforming India's economy. His economic reform record in Gujarat was the basis of his political campaign. Gujarat has been at the forefront of these areas, with successful SEZs and the largest number of private ports in India.

513 Sectors of national importance like defence are excepted, though defence manufacturing allows less than 50 per cent foreign investment.

514 "Sectors", Make in India website, http://www.makeinindia.com/sectors (accessed 31 December 2015).

515 This promotion states that India has 168 million television households and nearly 300 million internet users, second only to China: "Media and Entertainment", Make in India website, http://www.makeinindia.com/sector/media-and-entertainment (accessed 31 December 2015). Furthermore, it claims that there is significant local demand for electronics, 65 per cent is being met by imports: "Electronic Systems", Make in India website, http://www.makeinindia.com/sector/electronic-systems, (accessed 31 December 2015).

umbrella under which other initiatives fall, and second, the tangible economic reforms are also accompanied by a marketing campaign, complete with a Twitter emoji of "India's brand", a black lion on an orange background, when the brand's hashtag is used (#MakeInIndia).[516] The logo is now found on numerous government sites, labelling it the umbrella project of India's current economic strategy, although many initiatives began before 2014.

The brand Make in India has accompanied the remaking of the government's online presence and how projects are marketed. The Make in India website accompanies several other new government sites that are based on design, logos, and current user experience, in contrast to the websites of many Indian ministries that are cluttered and likely made in the 1990s or the early 2000s.[517] In short, it is clean, colourful, and built for tablet use; this is important since the Indian national brand constructed by the Make in India campaign seeks to make India a hub for design, innovation, and IT. The Indian national brand can not only offer its citizens as manual labourers who are paid lower wages than currently offered in China, but also those who are educated, English-speaking members of the so-called global knowledge economy. In essence, the Make in India brand highlights economic inequality in India as an opportunity for foreign investors.

Under the umbrella of the Make in India campaign, various government ministries have initiated a series of other projects that deal with urban and transport infrastructure. Some of these projects had been previously advocated by government and have been given new life, like the SEZ policy and a series of five transport corridors that will construct and link industrial corridors to India's major ports. The Make in India webpage highlights that the five industrial corridors were identified and planned within the 2014–2015 budget "to provide an impetus to industrialisation and planned urbanisation."[518] These corridors, the only projects listed in the "live projects" section of the webpage, were planned as early as 2006 with the Delhi Mumbai Industrial Corridor (DMIC)

---

516 "Make in India", Twitter, https://twitter.com/makeinindia?lang=en (accessed 31 December 2015); "Twitter Launches Make in India Emoji", *Economic Times*, 4 November 2015, http://economictimes.indiatimes.com/tech/internet/twitter-launches-make-in-india-emoji/articleshow/49659333.cms.

517 See, for example, the Make in India website and the official website of the Prime Minister: http://www.makeinindia.com/home (accessed 8 November 2018); http://pmindia.gov.in/en/ (accessed 8 November 2018).

518 "Industrial Corridor", Make in India website, http://www.makeinindia.com/live-projects-industrial-corridor (accessed 31 December 2015).

project, which was launched jointly by the Government of India and the Government of Japan through India's Ministry of Commerce and Japan's Ministry of Economy, Trade, and Industry. The purpose of the project was to reduce freight travel time between Delhi and Mumbai's JNPT.[519] This project has now expanded to five such areas and will entail freight rail networks, highways, and industrial areas. As the quote illustrates, this project also supports planned urbanization, which is taking place under another programme launched by the Ministry of Urban Development, the Smart City project. This project identifies 100 cities in India for refurbishment through central government funds based on planned infrastructure.

A more recent development in terms of SEZs is that the policy has also shifted in line with the Make in India campaign, the Smart Cities project, and the planned transport corridors. The DMIC is to be developed with planned cities (including eight smart cities), industrial townships, and SEZs. Additionally, a new type of zone has recently been named by the Government of India through the industrial corridor projects: national manufacturing investment zones (NMIZs).[520] These new zones will include SEZs within them, meaning these zones will be much larger than current SEZs. The minimum space required by establishing a NMIZ is 50 square kilometres, wherein the processing area must reach at least 30 per cent.[521] These spaces envision bringing together multiple clusters of SEZs, export-oriented units, and other manufacturing spaces along with townships to form a much larger area that, like an SEZ, can be developed by a private developer. Overall, 16 such NMIZs have been announced, 8 of which will be situated along the DMIC, which is being jointly developed by Japan and India.[522] In fact, the 16 NMIZs were simply labelled on the Make in India webpage as the DMIC NMIZs and the non-DMIC NMIZs.[523] This is the first instance in which zones are being layered within India to create

519 S. Tripathy, "Master plan for Delhi-Mumbai Industrial Corridor First Zone Notified", *Times of India*, 28 May 2013, http://timesofindia.indiatimes.com/city/jaipur/Master-plan-for-Delhi-Mumbai-Industrial-Corridor-first-zone-notified/articleshow/20302230.cms?referral=PM.

520 A. Palit, "NMIZs in India: Haunted by SEZs?", ISAS Brief 203, 17 June 2011, http://www.isn.ethz.ch/Digital-Library/Publications/Detail/?lang=en&id=130416.

521 "National Manufacturing", Make in India website, http://www.makeinindia.com/policy/national-manufacturing (accessed 30 December 2015).

522 "16 National Investment and Manufacturing Zones (NIMZs) to Boost Manufacturing Sector", *Business Standard*, 9 July 2014, http://www.business-standard.com/article/news-cm/16-national-investment-and-manufacturing-zones-nimzs-to-boost-manufacturing-sector-114070900694_1.html.

523 "National Manufacturing."

a range of exceptions in much larger spaces than EPZs or SEZs, but that may also concentrate SEZ features within these areas.

Since the announcement of the Make in India campaign, new momentum in India's port sector, which has already been changing over the last two decades, is now tasked with facilitating the external connections of the aforementioned industrial corridors. In 2015, the Government of India announced a new scheme for selective ports, the Sagarmala Project.[524] The Sagarmala Project will focus on linking investment in ports to these revitalized urban spaces and industrial corridors, thereby launching the "blue revolution"; this nickname is evocative of the post-independence "green revolution", a period in which the Government of India focused on increasing agricultural yields through technological advances in the industry.[525] The blue revolution project is meant to increase investment in Indian ports, both public and private, while identifying specific spaces through which ports can be linked to other transport systems, manufacturing spaces, and urban areas, thereby making India's vast coastline the main impetus of the state's connectivity and growth.[526] This project appears to be the culmination of multiple projects meant to encourage investment in infrastructure and links back to the umbrella Make in India campaign.

The Sagarmala Project focuses on coordinating the effects of various liberalization schemes in the aforementioned sectors: ports, urban spaces, and zones. The prime minister's website states the following:

> For a comprehensive and integrated planning for "Sagarmala", a National Perspective Plan (NPP) for the entire coastline shall be prepared within six months, which will identify potential geographical regions to be called Coastal Economic Zones (CEZs). While preparing the NPP, synergy and integration with planned Industrial Corridors, Dedicated Freight Corridors, National Highway Development Programme, Industrial Clusters and SEZs would be ensured.[527]

The project's funding period began in 2015. According to a government press release, the funding for the project is set at 692 crore rupees, and also foresees

524 The project had been announced in the early 2000s but has only begun to materialize in 2015.

525 See, for example: C. R. Unger, *Entwicklungspfade in Indien: Eine internationale Geschichte, 1947–1980*, Göttingen: Wallstein Verlag, 2015, pp. 74–148.

526 Ministry of Shipping, 2014–2015, Annual Report, p. 11.

527 "Sagarmala: Concept and Implementation towards Blue Revolution", Prime Minister of India website, http://pmindia.gov.in/en/news_updates/sagarmala-concept-and-implementation-towards-blue-revolution/ (accessed 29 December 2015).

substantial private investment in the project.[528] These coastal economic zones will be comparable to a coastal equivalent to the incentives given to the aforementioned NMIZs that will also encompass SEZs, freight corridors, and industrial clusters, including what the Ministry of Shipping is calling coastal economic units with tax incentives.[529] Fourteen coastal economic zones have so far been identified, including the Maharashtra region with Mumbai and JNPT as the two main transit ports.

JNPT was built in the 1980s and was operational in 1989. By the late 1990s, it was put at the forefront of India's efforts to use privatization schemes to increase investment in the port sector such as the landlord port model, which allows private terminal operators to operate terminals while the port trust handles the day-to-day management.[530] JNPT is now a mixed landlord port with four container terminals as well as a liquid cargo berth. It allows private participation at two of these terminals,[531] operated by APM terminals, a Dutch firm that operates 75 ports and terminals around the world; and DP World, a firm from Dubai with a similar profile of 78 marine and inland terminals in 40 countries.[532]

As India's largest container port, JNPT has been the focus of other efforts to connect India's interior to foreign trade, in particular to the capital region. The aforementioned Delhi Mumbai Industrial Corridor project will start in Delhi and connect various nodes across 1,483 kilometres, over six States, to an end terminal at JNPT.[533] As previously mentioned, the project entails the construction of a railway-based freight corridor and industrial areas. The DMIC is, however, now only one in a string of corridors that will encircle India. The other five

---

528 One crore equals ten million. "Sagarmala: Concept and Implementation Towards Blue Revolution", *Business Standard*, 25 March 2015, http://www.business-standard.com/article/government-press-release/sagarmala-concept-and-implementation-towards-blue-revolution-115032501253_1.html.

529 "Port Led Industrialization", Ministry of Shipping website, http://sagarmala.gov.in/project/port-led-industrialization (accessed 28 June 2018).

530 U. R. Patel and S. Bhattacharya, "Infrastructure in India: The Economics of Transition from Public to Private Provision", *Journal of Comparative Economics* 38 (2010) 1, pp. 52–70, at 64.

531 "Terminals", Jawaharlal Nehru Port Trust website, http://www.jnport.gov.in/container.aspx (accessed 2 June 2018).

532 "About Us" APM Terminals website, http://www.apmterminals.com/about-us (accessed 28 June 2018); "About DP World", DP World website, http://web.dpworld.com/about-dp-world/ (accessed 28 June 2018).

533 Department of Industrial Policy and Promotion, Ministry of Commerce and Industry, "Concept Paper: Delhi-Mumbai Industrial Corridor", August 2007, available on the Delhi Mumbai Industrial Corridor website, http://www.dmicdc.com/frmDownloads.aspx?pgid=43.

industrial corridors seek to promote manufacturing in India by connecting dedicated manufacturing space to transport infrastructure and to specific smart city nodes along the corridor.[534] It is not clear how these projects and the eight NMIZs along the DMIC will fit in with the coastal economic zone schemes in the Sagarmala project. However, it is clear that there is a strong focus on integrating port and zone development with intermodal transport corridors, that is, container shipment, which can explain why JNPT is often at the forefront of these initiatives.

The purpose of the Sagarmala project, like the industrial corridors and Smart City project, is to set guidelines and give financial incentives for subnational States to implement reforms. Projects will be chosen based on the willingness and ability of States to comply with and carry out the reforms sought by the central government. The central government will set up a committee to oversee all projects as well as a development company to assist State companies and the special purpose vehicles that will be established by the selected ports. The three administrative levels will work together on the development plans. It is not clear if private minor ports or central government major ports will be selected. This project, like the many others mentioned in this section, involves motivating States to compete with one another for investment by liberalizing certain sectors and providing financial support to State agencies. These projects involve extensive central government oversight.

This coordinated effort between ports and the "industrialization" of India is being called, within the confines of the Sagarmala project, a "port led development model", which is based on Gujarat's experience.[535] A government press release states that Gujarat's focus on privatization and liberalization of the port sector in the 1990s led to the State's higher rate of growth compared to the rest of the country.[536] The broadening zone policies also begin to resemble China's open coastal cities, special economic zones, free trade zones, and high-tech industrial development zones. These different types of zones are of various sizes and purposes and allow the government of China to implement a policy of spatial differentiation, whereby some spaces within China become linked to global capital flows while others are not. In India, the various layers

---

534 Department of Industrial Policy and Promotion, Ministry of Commerce and Industry, Government of India, "India and Japan: A Winning Partnership", 2014, p. 18, https://www.jetro.go.jp/ext_images/jetro/topics/pdf/1409_topics1_1.pdf.

535 "Sagarmala: Concept and Implementation."

536 Ibid. The press release states that in the 1990s Gujarat grew at about 8.15 to 10 per cent annually while India averaged at 6.98 per cent annually.

of zones also represent various sizes and degrees of incentives, so that now an SEZ may be located within an NMIZ, just as an EPZ may be located within Shenzhen SEZ in China. The "Chinese case" has been considered unique by the WB because of its layered zone policies that integrate inland regions and corridors to coastal areas, and its policies that specifically connect outwards to its diaspora.[537] India may be changing its zone policies to a more comprehensive model that integrates multiple types of zones. These zones also connect outwards to specific international transport corridors and target foreign investors.

Look East, Look West

International relations scholars have discussed the use of the EPZ and SEZ as an important tool in regionalization.[538] Zones, along with transport corridors, pipelines, and rivers, contribute to forms of formal regionalisms that are not clearly distinguished from informal regionalization processes.[539] In Asia especially, many of these projects form hybrid "formal regionalization" strategies.[540] Investments in transport infrastructure have been especially important in Asia, so that states seek to complement formal trade agreements with infrastructure, which in turn assist private and state-owned business networks.[541] Rather than focusing solely on the regional, India's zone and port projects are facilitating transregional connections that challenge the formal political construction and the academic construction of a South Asia region.

The term transregional is useful in the Asian context because Asia as a category opens up multiple formal and informal regional entanglements without

537 J. Wang, "The Economic Impact of Special Economic Zones: Evidence from Chinese Municipalities", *Journal of Development Economics* 101 (2013) C, pp. 133–147, at 136.
538 T. M. Shaw, J. A. Grant and S. Cornelissen, "Introduction and Overview: The Study of New Regionalism(s) at the Start of the Second Decade of the Twenty-First Century", in: Shaw, Grant and Cornelissen (eds.), *The Ashgate Research Companion to Regionalisms*, Surrey: Ashgate, 2011, pp. 3–30, at 13.
539 F. Söderbaum, "Formal and Informal Regionalism", in: Shaw, Grant and Cornelissen (eds.), *Ashgate Research Companion to Regionalisms*, pp. 51–68.
540 F. Söderbaum, "Theories of Regionalism", in: M. Beeson and R. Stubbs (eds.), *Routledge Handbook of Asian Regionalism*, Abingdon: Routledge, 2012, pp. 11–21.
541 See: D. H. Brooks and J. Menon (eds.), *Infrastructure and Trade in Asia*, Cheltenham: Edward Elgar Publishing and Asian Development Bank Institute, 2008; D. H. Brooks and D. Hummels, *Infrastructure's Role in Lowering Asia's Trade Costs: Building for Trade*, Cheltenham: Edward Elgar Publishing and Asian Development Bank Institute, 2009.

clear boundaries.[542] Asia is also a question for historians and political scientists alike who try to understand why the idea of Asia as a category has remained constant, but also how the region itself is continuously being remade through the interactions of so many formal and informal regionalisms as well as state-based, sometimes nationalist, agendas.[543] Its cultural diversity is also a challenge in the Area Studies context that is split across many studies: Sinology, Indology, Central Asian Studies, Middle Eastern Studies, not to mention the Indian Ocean as a field of research. Not only do India's zone projects purposefully seek to cross formal regions within Asia, the zone projects overlap foreign and domestic policy, so that it becomes difficult to distinguish between the two.[544]

As early as the 1990s, India initiated a new economic and foreign policy called Look East, a slogan indicating India's purposeful efforts to engage with East Asian neighbours. From 1992 onwards, India participated in discussions at the ASEAN (Association of Southeast Asian Nations) level and met bilaterally with nearly every ASEAN member state throughout the 1990s.[545] The Look East policy has also been complemented by the westward expansion of ASEAN, which eventually culminated in the bilateral trade agreement between ASEAN and India (in effect since 2010).[546] India is pursuing "connectivity diplomacy" with ASEAN by focusing on the complementarity between trade agreements and the construction of transport infrastructure.[547] India has sanctioned transport corridors from India's east coast that link to ASEAN member states in order to complement their trade. India's Look East policy has also focused on the so-called tiger economies – Singapore, Hong Kong, and Taiwan – as well as Japan and South Korea. For example, bilateral trade grew between South Korea and

542 One development here is Sogang University's *TRaNS: Trans-Regional and -National Studies of Southeast Asia* journal, published by Cambridge University Press since 2013. The journal focuses on Southeast Asia, which it claims can only be understood as a region through its transregional connections (usually within Asia). See the introductory article: James C. Scott, "Introduction to the Launch Issue", *TRaNS: Trans-Regional and -National Studies of Southeast Asia* 1 (2013) 1, pp. 1–4.

543 A. Acharya, "Asia Is Not One", *The Journal of Asian Studies* 69 (2010) 4, pp. 1001–1013; W. Hui, "The Idea of Asia and Its Ambiguities", *The Journal of Asian Studies* 69 (2010) 4, pp. 985–989.

544 Agnew, "Territorial Trap", pp. 65–68.

545 A. M. Thomas, "India and Southeast Asia: The Look East Policy in Perspective", in: R. Harshe and K. M. Seethi (eds.), *Engaging with the World: Critical Reflections on India's Foreign Policy*, New Delhi: Orient Longman, 2005, pp. 297–316; D. Brewster, "India's Engagements with Southeast Asia: Singapore, Vietnam, and Indonesia", in: Hall (ed.), *Engagement of India*, pp. 147–167.

546 Prior to this agreement, India signed a bilateral trade agreement with Singapore in 2005.

547 A. B. Chakraborty, "Fostering Physical Connectivity in India's Look East Policy", *Journal of Infrastructure Development* 1 (2009) 1, pp. 45–65, at 45.

India from around 600 million USD in 1993 to 15.6 billion USD in 2008.[548] A Comprehensive Economic Partnership Agreement between South Korea and India came into effect in 2010.

One of the focal relationships in the Look East policy is that with Japan. India and Japan have enjoyed positive political and economic ties since Indian independence, though formal meetings between the two countries intensified only since the early 2000s.[549] The relationship was strategic and focused on maintaining safe trade routes in the Indian Ocean.[550] Negotiations soon turned towards economic partnerships. Both countries view China's growth cautiously and see each other as potential regional counterweights while keeping engagement with China open since the largest share of each country's imports come from China, and China remains an important export market.[551] Even as Japan has been officially supportive of the so-called rise of China, Japan's government seeks to remedy its reliance on China for its export and import trade. In 2007, 20.5 per cent of Japan's imports arrived from China, and 14.3 per cent of Japan's exports were destined for China.[552] In contrast, imports from India to Japan stood at 0.7 per cent of Japan's imports and exports to India were also only 0.7 per cent of Japan's total exports.[553] Japan is not one of India's top ten trading

548 D. Brewster, "India's Developing Relationship with South Korea: A Useful Friend in East Asia", *Asian Survey* 50 (2010) 2, pp. 402–425, at 410.

549 P. Jain, "Japan-India Relations: Peaks and Troughs", *The Round Table: The Commonwealth Journal of International Affairs* 99 (2010) 409, pp. 403–412.

550 M. Ghosh, "India and Japan's Growing Synergy: From a Political to a Strategic Focus", *Asian Survey* 48 (2008) 2, pp. 282–302.

551 D. Brewster, "Indian Strategic Thinking about East Asia", *Journal of Strategic Studies* 34 (2011) 6, pp. 825–852; Brewster, "India's Engagements"; I. Rehman, "Keeping the Dragon at Bay: India's Counter-Containment of China in Asia", *Asian Security* 5 (2009) 2, pp. 114–143; I. Saint-Mézard, "A Quest for Power: India's Foreign Policy after the Nuclear Tests of 1998", in Jaffrelot (ed.), *India since 1950*, pp. 194–211. Another view is that the US relationship with both Japan and India has changed substantially in the last decade, which also facilitates closer cooperation between all three as a balance to China: H. D. P. Envall, "Japan's India Engagement: From Different Worlds to Strategic Partners", in: Hall (ed.), *Engagement of India*, pp. 39–59; H. V. Pant, "India in the Asia-Pacific: Rising Ambitions with an Eye on China", *Asia-Pacific Review* 14 (2007) 1, pp. 54–71; H. V. Pant, "China's Half-Hearted Engagement and India's Proactive Balancing", in: Hall (ed.), *Engagement of India*, pp. 111–128.

552 Japan's trade with China is generally comparable to its trade with the US. Likewise, most of India's imports, 14 per cent, come from China.

553 H. Laurence, "Japan's Proactive Foreign Policy and the Rise of the BRICs", *Asian Perspective* 31 (2007) 4, pp. 177–203, at 185.

partners.[554] JETRO, the Japan External Trade Organization, has actively advocated diversifying Japan's trade and investments to focus on the other three BRICs (Brazil, Russia, India) as potential counterweights to the fourth (China).[555] To change their current bilateral trade relations, India and Japan signed a Comprehensive Economic Partnership Agreement in 2011 to increase economic cooperation and lower tariffs on approximately 8,000 products ranging from apparel and machinery to services and investments.[556]

Jawaharlal Nehru, India's first prime minister, saw India as a key global player, which manifested in the creation of the non-aligned movement. He also had a vision of India's position in Asia that was not limited to South Asia.[557] Some have argued that India's current foreign policy is a reflection of Nehru's vision.[558] Whether or not Nehru's vision contributes to Indian leaders' vision of India's foreign policy today, policy makers are actively marketing India as a pivot between east and west. The terms "east" and "west" are interpreted by some state agencies differently. India's west is namely West Asia, that is, the Middle East. Government agencies market India as the midpoint within greater Asia. This current form of marketing takes place through the Make in India campaign, which was launched in 2014 to encourage investment and exports in 25 sectors of the Indian economy by allowing 100 per cent FDI.[559] The Make in India campaign has complemented the two-decade-old Look East strategy, as many investors appear to be India's East Asian partners, particularly South Korean and Japanese firms.

The Make in India campaign was launched in the 2014–2015 fiscal year. The extent to which the policy caters to Japan is striking. The Ministry of Commerce's Department of Industrial Policy and Promotion disseminated information on the new campaign to Indian embassies and consulates, but they went above and beyond for one country in particular. The Department of Industrial Policy and Promotion set up an exclusive management team to cater to

---

554 "Top Countries of India's Import and Export in US $ Million", State Trading Corporation of India website, http://www.stc.gov.in/WriteReadData/Countr_ImpExp_US.pdf (accessed 2 January 2016).

555 Laurence, "Japan's Proactive Foreign Policy."

556 These reductions apply to approximately 98 per cent of bilateral trade: G. Nataraj and A. Bhunia, "India and Japan Asia's win-win Partnership", *East Asia Forum*, 26 January 2014, http://www.eastasiaforum.org/2014/01/26/india-and-japan-asias-win-win-partnership.

557 J. K. Ray and S. Chakrabarti, "Institutionalization of the Regional Space in South Asia", in: J. K. Ray (ed.), *Aspects of India's International Relations 1700 to 2000: South Asia and the World*, New Delhi: Peason Longman, 2007, pp. 429–480, at 434.

558 Discussion outlined in: Hurtig, "Restructuring of India's External Relations."

559 "Sectors", Make in India website, http://www.makeinindia.com/sectors/.

Japanese investment, which would fast track investment proposals from Japanese firms.[560] In December 2015, the government of Japan announced a "Japan-India Make-in-India Special Finance Facility" to promote Japanese investment in infrastructure projects in India, totaling approximately 12 billion USD, which is only part of an overall 35 billion USD allocated for Japanese public and private investments in India.[561] The 35 billion USD had been pledged in 2014 and was to be implemented over the next five years, though reportedly nearly all of the investment has already been committed to projects.[562] Japan's financing of certain projects correlates with JETRO's push to move Japanese firms westward to India.

Japanese manufacturers have increasingly viewed India as a promising location for medium-term business operations, overtaking China as a key potential site for location in a 2013 government survey.[563] As of 2012, however, only 410 Japanese overseas affiliates were located in India (1.8 per cent of Japanese firms overseas), out of 23,351 around the world of which 15,234 (65.2 per cent) were concentrated in (East and South) Asia.[564] In contrast, a 2014 report compiled by the Indian Ministry of Commerce and Industry lists 1,072 Japanese companies operating in India with 2,542 business bases.[565] Though it appears unlikely that the number of Japanese firms in India has more than doubled in two years, a third source also confirms this sharp increase: 248 Japanese firms as of April 2005 to 926 in November 2012.[566] Whether 410 or 926 Japanese firms were operating in India in 2012 is an open question, and it is likely the Indian government and Japanese government defined Japanese affiliates differently. The Ministry of Commerce report discusses the increase in bilateral trade between India and Japan

560 The management team is known as "Japan Plus": "About Us", Make in India website, http://www.makeinindia.com/about (accessed 30 December 2015).

561 D. R. Chaudhury, "Japan's $12 Billion 'Make in India' Fund to Push Investments", *Economic Times*, 13 December 2015, http://articles.economictimes.indiatimes.com/2015-12-13/news/69006246_1_pm-shinzo-abe-india-fund-oda.

562 "Japan to Set up Financial Facility for 'Make in India' Initiative", *Business Standard*, 12 December 2015, http://www.business-standard.com/article/news-ians/japan-to-set-up-financial-facility-for-make-in-india-initiative-115121200666_1.html.

563 Ministry of Economy, Trade and Industry, "White Paper on International Economy and Trade 2014", 2014, p. 431, www.meti.go.jp/english/report/data/gWT2014fe.html.

564 "White Paper on International Economy", p. 416.

565 "India and Japan: A Winning Partnership", p. 14.

566 N. Bangia, "Japanese Overtures: Increasing Investments in Indian Infrastructure", *Indian Infrastructure* 15 (2013) 11, pp. 14–16, at 14.

since the 2004 trade agreement and notes that Japan is currently India's fourth largest source of FDI.[567]

To cater to the planned additional entry of Japanese firms to India, the Ministry of Commerce has marketed the aforementioned NMIZ's to JETRO as potential spaces for Japanese firms to invest in, particularly along the DMIC.[568] Japanese firms have a history of forming distinctive economic geographies as they internationalize their firms' operations. As they shift their firms' operations abroad, Japanese firms have historically tended to cluster in specific geographic areas.[569] Japan first used an EPZ abroad in South Korea, which was dominated almost completely by Japanese firms.[570] Rajasthan has become one of several subnational States, in which Japanese firms have focused their investments. Approximately 40 per cent of the 1,483-kilometre-long freight corridor will pass through Rajasthan.[571] The project envisions development within 150 kilometres along both sides of the corridor. Subnational States rather than the central government are marketing these areas to foreign firms and foreign trade agencies like JETRO, linking this practice back to India's state decentralization reforms, despite the high degree of central planning involved in the corridor.[572]

Within Rajasthan, an approximately 1,200 acre "Japanese Zone" has opened in Neemrana, in which firms like Nissan, Nippon, and Daikin operate.[573] The Japanese industrial park opened in 2006, in which 44 Japanese firms have invested since 2013.[574] Reportedly, South Korean firms are also seeking an exclusive South Korean zone in Neemrana.[575] A second industrial

---

567 "India and Japan: A Winning Partnership", p. 9.

568 Ibid., p. 24.

569 M. L. Gerlach, *Alliance Capitalism: The Social Organization of Japanese Business*, Berkeley: University of California Press, 1992; A. Delios and P. W. Beamish, "Regional and Global Strategies of Japanese Firms", *Management International Review* 45 (2005) 1, pp. 19–36, at 34.

570 N. Kenji, "Japan's Overseas Investment Patterns and FTZs", *AMPO: Japan-Asia Quarterly Review* 8 and 9 (1977) 4, 1–2, pp. 33–50.

571 Tripathy, "Master Plan."

572 The corridor planning between Japan and India took place in official high-level diplomatic meetings.

573 Mahim Pratap Singh, "The Japanese Connection", *The Hindu*, 6 April 2013, http://www.thehindu.com/business/Industry/the-japanese-connection/article4585093.ece.

574 Japan External Trade Organization, "'Look West,' with the Strategic Partnership between India and Japan", Asia and Oceania Division, Overseas Research Department, September 2013, p. 15, http://www.jetro.go.jp/ext_images/jetro/topics/pdf/1309_topics1_annexion3.pdf.

575 S. Gupta and Sidhartha, "Korea, Japan Seek Industrial Zone in Rajasthan's Neemrana", *Times of India*, 21 July 2014, http://timesofindia.indiatimes.com/india/Korea-Japan-seek-industrial-zone-in-Rajasthans-Neemrana/articleshow/38772143.cms.

zone in the area for Japanese firms has been confirmed.[576] These zones do not appear to be SEZs exactly, but part of "industrial townships" that have been guaranteed central sales tax decreases and at least the first Japanese zone has been considered a "public utility", which is meant to prevent labour strikes by workers in the zone's factories.[577] This Japanese zone is only one of many SEZs, industrial estates, and other industrial areas set up for Japanese firms throughout the world, 34 of which are in Asia (East and South).[578] Within the context of the DMIC, Japanese officials stated that Japan has agreed to further implement the Japanese industrial township concept within India.[579]

JETRO sees India as a manufacturing base that can help Japanese firms to "Look West." The concepts of Asia and West appear to differ between JETRO and the Make in India campaign. JETRO promotes India as an important new base for Japanese firms based on the idea of expanding Japanese trade to the west market, a category that JETRO applies mainly to Africa and the Middle East. For that reason, the concept of Asia here is not universally applied by the Japanese ministries that demark Asia as mainly North Asia, Southeast Asia, and South Asia (Central Asia remains ambiguous). The various policies that India employs to enable Japanese firms to operate in India such as the SEZs and NMIZs are seen as useful springboards to the west market,[580] which complements and expands India's self-promotion as a nodal point between east and west to include Africa. Though the SEZs are the tool to enable this trade from within India, investing in India, not only in its zones, offers Japan several advantages, notably its geographic position and long history of trade ties to certain countries in the Middle East and Africa, which are particularly enhanced by India's diaspora. From the perspective of the Indian government, Indian diasporas in African and the Gulf States are not homogenous, but reflect different periods of removal from India, which is not articulated in JETRO's west market

---

576 "Rajasthan to Have Second Japanese Industrial Zone", *Business Standard*, 8 April 2015, http://www.business-standard.com/article/news-ians/rajasthan-to-have-second-japanese-industrial-zone-115040800931_1.html.

577 Ibid.

578 Wakana Sato brought this text to the author's attention; it is written in Japanese by Ernst & Young for Japan's Ministry of Economy, Trade and Industry (MITI). The report explores the ways in which the government could support small and medium sized Japanese firms abroad, and industrial parks are considered one of the key ways to do that: Ernst & Young ShinNihon LLC, "Kaigai Kogyo Danchi Jigyo Tyosa Houkokusho" [Overseas Industrial Parks and Research Report], 2014, http://www.meti.go.jp/meti_lib/report/2014fy/001018.pdf.

579 "Japan to Set up Financial Facility."

580 JETRO "'Look West' with the Strategic Partnership", p. 10.

promotion.[581] Nevertheless, some of India's top ten import and export markets include these western market countries that Japan seeks to increase trade with United Arab Emirates, Saudi Arabia, Qatar, Iraq, and Nigeria.[582]

JETRO extensively outlines the size and location of India's diaspora, which it writes is second in size only to China's. Unlike the Chinese diaspora, which is particularly concentrated in Southeast Asia, not a new market for Japanese firms, the Indian diaspora is both global *and* concentrated in the Gulf States and Africa: "Approximately 5 million Indians reside in the Middle East and approximately 4 million reside in Africa. They form the most promising business network as local bases for business originating from India."[583] To complement the diaspora statistics, in 2012, 21.6 per cent of India's foreign trade by volume was destined for the Middle East and 9.4 per cent went to Africa.[584] In JETRO's view of the two regions as a single west market, that market accounts for approximately one-third of India's foreign trade, the largest regional category. That many Indian firms are family-based is viewed as positive due to the transnational networks these families potentially have. Not only are the transnational family ties important, JETRO notes that English is the chief international business language of companies in the Middle East and Africa. Partnering with Indian firms ensures a high degree of English proficiency among staff, an important advantage to Japanese firms as they seek to tap the west market through India.[585]

Japan's strategy to increase investment in India and trade between India and Japan coincides with India's motives for keeping China at bay in the region. Part of this approach has been to market the new zone, the NMIZs along the DMIC as specific sites for Japanese firms to invest in. Whether this practice will continue to be seen as "balancing China" is an open question as the Government of India has also since granted rights to Chinese firms to operate in Chinese industrial parks that will receive the same benefits given to SEZs and

581 The diaspora in the Gulf States is made up of both professionals and guest workers/manual labourers. This group is likely to be made up of Indians with Indian citizenship residing abroad (NRIs). In Southern and Eastern Africa, for example, people with Indian heritage left in the colonial period are now considered Persons of Indian Origin. A Person of Indian Origin does not have Indian citizenship but may enter India without a visa. This category applies to those with Indian heritage outside of South Asia.

582 "Top Countries of India's Import and Export in US $ Million."

583 JETRO "'Look West' with the Strategic Partnership", p. 8.

584 Ibid., p. 9.

585 Ibid., p. 8.

NMIZs.[586] Like the South Korean and Japanese parks, many projects are likely to be located along the DMIC, as the Chinese government has been coordinating with these subnational States. The DMIC is connected to India's premier container port in Mumbai, JNPT, which is situated on India's west coast and therefore closer to the west market.

Though "transnational" might be the usual adjective to describe the investment of Japanese firms in specific corridors in India, these transnational connections are supported, on the one hand, by official international agreements between Japan and India, and on the other hand, by formal policies that seek to link businesses and investments with imagined regions. India's Look East policy, for example, often does not refer to China, though China is arguably in East Asia. Japan's west market combines Africa and the Middle East as a single regional market. Furthermore, the basis for growing this bilateral economic partnership is based on a security discourse of balancing China, which India uses for its domestic development drive. "Transregionalism" becomes a meaningful way to describe the various entanglements between regionally focused formal policies and their informal outcomes that connect subnational settings to transnational networks.

Transregional Mumbai

Along with enhancing economic partnerships and trade between India and East Asian countries and firms, India has also continued to develop its relations with Russia and has forged new connections with Central Asian republics.[587] The Government of India uses SEZs and transport corridor projects, beyond India, to complement these new economic connections. Some of these economic connections challenge the academic construction of South Asia as a region in Area Studies based on the political pursuit of the South Asian Association for Regional Cooperation (SAARC), the resulting Agreement on South Asian Free Trade Area (SAFTA) as well as the SAARC Agreement on Trade in Services. Tensions in South Asia make it necessary for India to pursue extra-regional connections to pursue economic partnerships with its regional member state partners.

---

586 N. Basu, "Chinese industrial parks to have same incentives as SEZs, NMIZs", *Business Standard*, 1 July 2014, http://www.business-standard.com/article/economy-policy/chinese-industrial-parks-to-have-same-incentives-as-sezs-nmizs-114063001072_1.html.
587 Hurtig, "Restructuring of India's External Relations", p. 191.

Indian policy makers' pursuit of connections beyond India's official regional agreement appears to be part of a larger strategy:

> With a new-found confidence in its economic dynamism, in the resilience of its democratic institutions and in its growing military weight, India saw itself more as the strategic pivot in a vast region stretching from the Persian Gulf to South East Asia, and from Central Asia to the Northern part of the Indian Ocean. This vision, which was articulated by Nehru and the nationalist leaders of the 1950s, before weakening in the 1960s and the 1970s, was reminiscent of a prestigious past, which had seen the Indian civilization influence the entire Asian continent for centuries.[588]

Not only has India pursued formal agreements with Japan, South Korea, and ASEAN, India is utilizing its current SEZ and NMIZ policies along with the Make in India campaign as part of India's Look East strategy to position itself as a pivot between east and west. India's maritime strategy in the Indian Ocean is vital to this plan.[589]

The idea of South Asia as a region emerged out of the region's connectedness under the British Empire; just as under the British, India today sees some of its surrounding states as buffers to other regions or states such as China.[590] India sits geographically in the middle of the region. India's own diverse cultural and linguistic groups tend to overlap with those of the surrounding states, not only challenging ideas of nation states, but also reinforcing India's role at the centre of the region. While states surround and mould with India, they share few geographic or cultural connections with each other.[591] The geographic position of states have also hindered trading relationships as most states trade bilaterally with India rather than with each other. This trade tends to be both one sided and, from India's perspective, marginal. For example, India's total trade to the region accounted for only 4.6 per cent of India's exports in 2008–2009 and just 0.6 per cent of imports.[592] In contrast, Nepal carries out 60 per cent of its international trade with India and almost all of its exports must travel through Indian territory. India's market and investments are important to other states in the region, but India's dominance is also a threat to economic self-sufficiency and autonomy. Increasingly, China has strengthened its bilateral relations with India's South Asian neighbours, which some have seen

588 Saint-Mézard, "A Quest for Power", p. 195.
589 D. Brewster, *India's Ocean: The Story of India's Bid for Regional Leadership*, Abingdon: Routledge, 2014.
590 G. Boquérat, "India in South Asia", in Jaffrelot (ed.), *India since 1950*, pp. 212–231.
591 For example, Tamil in South India and Sri Lanka and the connections between Bangladesh and India's West Bengal.
592 Boquérat, "India in South Asia", p. 224.

as part of a purposeful effort to weaken India's influence in the region.[593] South Asia has therefore been and is currently characterized by extra-regional foreign policy and trade linkages rather than mainly intraregional agreements.[594]

The concept of an institutional region for South Asia bases its legitimacy on the cultural overlaps and historical connections of the region under colonial rule. Formal South Asia regionalism developed out of security concerns like many other forms of formal regionalism in the post-1945 period. SAARC was established in 1985. Member states include India, Maldives, Sri Lanka, Pakistan, Bangladesh, Nepal, and Bhutan. Since 2007, Afghanistan has also become a member of SAARC at India's insistence.[595] Although scholars of regionalism, referring to the European Union model, assume that regionalism eventually "upgrades" from security communities to political and economic integration, South Asia has not taken these steps.[596] SAFTA was adopted in 1995, but it applied tariff reductions item by item and did not address non-tariff barriers. Countries within the region have only made marginal efforts to improve the region's weak cross-border infrastructural connectivity, although this trend is currently changing between India and Bangladesh.[597] Finally, despite the membership of both India and Pakistan in the regional organization, their relationship is still contentious.[598]

In September 2014, Prime Minister Narendra Modi announced the Make in India campaign. In the same speech, he reinforced India's long-standing Look East policy but also added the slogan "Link West."[599] West does not refer to Western countries, but rather to India's immediate neighbours to the west, what India calls West Asia. This vision exceeds the construction of specific

593 Rehman, "Keeping the Dragon at Bay."

594 B. C. Upreti, "India's Policy towards its South Asian Neighbours: Constraints, Impediments and Perspectives", in Harshe and Seethi (ed.), *Engaging with the World*, pp. 203–223, at 207.

595 India had been the main advocate for including Afghanistan within SAARC. The two countries have a history of positive bilateral relations, and both have taken issue with Pakistan.

596 Ray and Chakrabarti, "Institutionalization of the Regional Space."

597 Boquérat, "India in South Asia", p. 227.

598 K. Raman Pillai, "Rethinking India-Pakistan Relations: Challenges Ahead", in Harshe and Seethi (ed.), *Engaging with the World*, pp. 224–242.

599 "PM launches 'Make in India' global initiative", Narendra Modi website, 25 September 2014, http://www.narendramodi.in/pm-launches-make-in-india-global-initiative-6644 (accessed 8 January 2016).

microregions along development corridors within India such as the DMIC by purposefully forging connections beyond South Asia.[600] This is evident in the transport sector, as the Indian Ministry of Shipping carried out joint task forces with representatives from South Korea, Russia, ASEAN, and Iran to locate transport bottlenecks.[601] At the same time, some of these extra-regional connections are in fact meant to connect India to Afghanistan, another SAARC member state.

India has typically relied on oil imports from the Gulf States, but is seeking to diversify its access to oil, gas, and minerals by setting up trade routes with Central Asian states.[602] Cooperation with Russia, an old ally, has been key to gaining access to the region's resources. The distinction between foreign and domestic affairs is particularly precarious in the energy sector, since access to gas and oil imports is important to national security and to the national economy. India's various campaigns and transport corridors are linked to international transport corridors that will connect India to Central Asia through Iran and Afghanistan. Both states in that sense are more like transit spaces on the edge of regions with which India hopes to increase trade. Navi Mumbai's JNPT is the nodal point between the Indian and the international side of these transport corridors thats extend through Iran to Afghanistan, West Asia, and Central Asia.

Motivating these new projects abroad is the particular problem of land access to the region, which cannot be reliably gained through Pakistan – a longtime rival. Port access to Iran was an alternative.[603] India's ties with Iran have deepened especially since the 2000s. India and Iran share cultural ties as these states host the two largest Shia Muslim populations.[604] Though against the wishes of the US, increasing cooperation and bilateral agreements with Iran is important from the Indian perspective for a variety of reasons including access

---

600 Cf. I. C. Taylor, "Spatial Development Initiatives: Two Case Studies from Southern Africa", in Shaw, Grant and Cornelissen (ed.), *Ashgate Research Companion to Regionalisms*, pp. 325–338.

601 Ministry of Shipping, Government of India, 2006–2007, Annual Report, AR, IOD, CSL, pp. 69–71.

602 Lee, "Russia's Engagement of India."

603 I. Bagchi, "India to spread tentacles into Central Asia via Iran", *Times of India*, 13 March 2012, http://timesofindia.indiatimes.com/india/India-to-spread-tentacles-into-Central-Asia-via-Iran/articleshow/12239197.cms.

604 H. V. Pant, "India and Iran: An 'Axis' in the Making?", *Asian Survey* 44 (2004) 3, pp. 369–383, at 373.

to trade, oil, gas, minerals, and natural resources.[605] Approximately 12 per cent of India's oil imports, as of 2012, come from Iran, although they had been steadily decreasing under US diplomatic pressure.[606] As sanctions tightened around Iran due to international condemnation of its nuclear programme, the Society for Worldwide Interbank Financial Telecommunications (SWIFT) expelled Iran from its network in 2012. As other methods of payment rapidly decreased,[607] the Indian and Iranian governments agreed on a rupee payment mechanism that would allow Indian firms to continue purchasing oil from Iran.[608] Iran's excess of rupees, held in a Kolkata bank, allowed Iran to purchase Indian goods, which it has done readily in a number of sectors, including manufactured items, agricultural products, and pharmaceuticals. Thus, Iran has become a growing export market for Indian products.

Iran is the key node for India's regional access to Central Asia, in particular Afghanistan.[609] Through Iran, India may access the region while bypassing the land route over Pakistan.[610] In 2000, India, Iran, and Russia signed an agreement for the International North-South Transport Corridor (INSTC), which plans to link India through Iran to Central Asia and eventually northern Europe.[611] Other signatories of the agreement now include Kazakhstan, Armenia, Turkey, Ukraine, and Syria. What the recent military conflicts in the former two states mean for the project is uncertain. The main route will link Mumbai's JNPT to Bandar Abbas in Iran, from Bandar Abbas over Iran to the Caspian Sea, and from Astrakhan the route ends in Moscow and Saint Petersburg. Additionally, a number of

---

605 Japan and India have shared interests in Iran, which has strengthened both countries' lenient approach to Iran, despite also fostering strong US partnerships: Ghosh, "India and Iran's Growing Synergy", pp. 289–290; H. V. Pant, "India and US-Iran Imbroglio: Difficult Choices Ahead", *Indian Journal of Asian Affairs* 19 (2006) 1, pp. 25–38.

606 V. Prashad, "India's Iran Policy: Between US Primacy and Regionalism", Working Paper Series 19, Assam Fares Institute for Public Policy and International Affairs, American University of Beirut (2013), p. 5, https://www.aub.edu.lb/ifi/international_affairs/Documents/working_paper_series/20131118_AI_WP_Indian_Iran_Policy.pdf.

607 Before 2010, Indian firms paid for Iranian oil through the Asian Clearing Union mechanism, and subsequently used other banks (Turkish and German-based) between 2010 and 2012.

608 Prashad, "India's Iran Policy", p. 14.

609 J. K. Patnaik, "Indo-Iranian Relations", in A. K. Pasha and R. Punjabi (eds.), *India and the Islamic World*, New Delhi: Radiant Publishers, 1998, pp. 84–94; A. K. Pasha, "India and the Gulf States: Challenges and Opportunities", in Harshe and Seethi, *Engaging with the World*, pp. 389–424; Pant, "India and Iran."

610 Pakistan allows goods from Afghanistan to pass into India but not the other way around.

611 Ministry of Shipping and Surface Transport, Government of India, 2007–2008, Annual Report, AR, IO, CSL, p. 73.

road and rail networks are in various stages of development around Iran, which will link outwards and expand Iran's existing overland connections to Central Asia. These connections presumably tie in some of the newer signatories to the agreement. In comparison to the current Red Sea–Suez Canal–Mediterranean Sea route for trade between India and Russia, the INSTC is estimated to be 40 per cent shorter, cutting shipping costs along this route by 30 per cent.[612] Although the INSTC project had mostly deteriorated since the 2000 agreement, it was kick-started again through India's initiative in 2012 as trade with Iran increased.[613]

Along with the INSTC, India agreed in 2003 to expand Iran's Chabahar Port to meet the capacity of the transport agreement and offset congestion in Iran's other ports, particularly Bandar Abbas.[614] Iran has no deep-water port, which hinders the INSTC since larger container ships or tankers have to dock elsewhere (usually in the United Arab Emirates) before shifting cargo to smaller vessels that continue on to Iranian ports. In 1992, the Government of Iran created an SEZ near Chabahar Port, the purpose of which was to increase investment from Southeast Asia.[615] By 2003, the idea for this port-zone shifted to remaking this port into Iran's key port in the INSTC. The Government of India agreed to expand Chabahar, but along with the INSTC, seeks to link the port to a land route through Iran to Afghanistan (to the cities of Zaranj and Delarm), a country not signatory to the INSTC. Both Afghanistan and India receive reduced or eliminated customs fees at Chabahar Port. Meanwhile, Iran agreed to develop the highway system from Chabahar to the border with Afghanistan, while India agreed to build a motorway on the Afghan side of the border. Chabahar Port serves a dual purpose as a main nodal port within two transport corridors.

India has many interests in Afghanistan, again, mainly in accessing its Central Asian neighbours' energy resources. Another key interest is better access to the several mines to which a consortium of six Indian firms have been granted mining rights.[616] Over the last decade, India has provided approximately 2 billion

---

612 S. Ramachandran, "India to Invest in Iran's Chabahar Port", *Central Asia-Caucasus Analyst*, 26 November 2014, http://cacianalyst.org/publications/analytical-articles/item/13099-india-to-invest-in-irans-chabahar-port.html.

613 Lee, "Russia's Engagement of India."

614 M. Balooch, "Iran and India's Cooperation in Central Asia", *China and Eurasia Forum Quarterly* 7 (2009) 1, pp. 25–29, at 27.

615 Prashad, "India's Iran Policy."

616 R. Borah, "India's Challenges in Afghanistan Post-2014", *East Asia Forum*, 5 August 2013, http://www.eastasiaforum.org/2013/08/06/indias-challenges-in-afghanistan-post-2014/; D. R. Chaudhury, "PM Narendra Modi Returns to Regional Diplomacy; Afghanistan-Pakistan Visit Drives Home Need for Cooperation", *Economic Times*, 26 December 2015,

USD in developmental aid to Afghanistan through the construction of roads, telecommunications, and other infrastructure, making India Afghanistan's fourth largest donor.[617] Linked to India's aid, the 218 kilometre Zaranj-Delaram motorway that eventually connects to Chabahar Port was completed in 2009 and transferred to the government of Afghanistan. While the road section has been completed, the Chabahar project has only begun to move forward since 2014. News reports often indicate that project delay is due to US pressure. Chabahar has much more visibility in the media than other infrastructure projects related to the trade corridor and other areas of Indo-Iranian cooperation. It seems that the participants in this agreement have been satisfied with a slow-moving project that looks to the long-term, beyond short-term difficulties and regional instability.

Chabahar Port and the INSTC are seen in the media and by scholars as a counterpoint to the growing regional influence of China, and therefore part of the Sino-Indian rivalry in both the Indian Ocean and in Central Asia.[618] China is pursuing the one belt one road initiative to link western China to Central Asia by freight over the "silk road economic belt" as well as the "maritime silk road."[619] The latter, otherwise known as the "string of pearls", is characterized by Chinese investment and construction of ports throughout the Indian Ocean, including India's immediate neighbours in Sri Lanka and Pakistan.[620] This policy appears connected to Chinese SEZs in Africa, evident in Chinese investment in the Suez Canal zone and port.[621] However, the port often compared with India's Chabahar port in Iran is Gwadar, a port in Pakistan.[622] It was built in 2007 with Chinese financial and technical assistance and it links with the China-

---

http://articles.economictimes.indiatimes.com/2015-12-26/news/69317162_1_indian-pm-regional-cooperation-india-and-pakistan.

617 S. Ashraf, "India and Pakistan Compete for Influence in Afghanistan", *East Asia Forum*, 25 April 2013, http://www.eastasiaforum.org/2013/04/25/india-and-pakistan-compete-for-influence-in-afghanistan/.

618 D. Brewster, "Beyond the 'String of Pearls': Is There Really a Sino-Indian Security Dilemma in the Indian Ocean?", *Journal of the Indian Ocean Region* 10 (2014) 2, pp. 133–149.

619 H. H. Karrar, *The New Silk Road Diplomacy: China's Central Asian Foreign Policy since the Cold War*, Vancouver: UBC Press, 2010.

620 R. Anthony, "Infrastructure and Influence: China's Presence on the Coast of East Africa", *Journal of the Indian Ocean Region* 9 (2013) 2, pp. 134–149.

621 D. Bräutigam and X. Tang, "African Shenzhen: China's Special Economic Zones in Africa", *Journal of Modern African Studies* 49 (2011) 1, pp. 27–54; D. Bräutigam and X. Tang, "'Going Global in Groups': Structural Transformation and China's Special Economic Zones Overseas", *World Development* 63 (2014), pp. 78–91.

622 M. R. Djalili and C. Therme, "Le flanc Est de l'Iran: opportunités et vulnérabilités", *Politique étrangère* 73 (2008) 3, p. 601–612, at 611.

Pakistan Economic Corridor that connects western China to the Arabian Sea.[623] It was originally operated and owned (60 per cent) by Port of Singapore Authority (PSA), but PSA pulled out of the project in 2012 after Pakistan's navy refused to provide land designated for the project.[624] Their share was sold to China Harbour Engineering Co Ltd. In 2015, the government of Pakistan declared the 2,281 acres of port land a free trade zone and handed it over to the Chinese Oversees Ports Holding Company Ltd to manage.[625] The recent push to develop Chabahar is often connected to Chinese investment in Gwadar, and India's wary approach to China's maritime silk road.[626]

Since the restart of the Chabahar project in 2014, the Government of India has set up a special purpose vehicle, a firm created specifically for this project, named India Ports Global, headquartered in Mumbai.[627] India Ports Global is 60 per cent owned by JNPT and 40 per cent owned by Deendayal Port Trust (formerly Kandla Port Trust), two west coast ports that will be able to link their services with Chabahar.[628] The company's board of directors includes the chairmen of both port trusts as well as a nominee from the Indian Ministry of Shipping. The company could potentially invest in other ports abroad that are strategic for Indian firms' shipping needs, along the lines of other state-owned terminal operators such as Singapore's PSA International or Dubai's DP World, which operate globally. For now, however, the firm is focusing on Chabahar.

Chabahar, as previously mentioned, has an SEZ in which Indian firms are likely to invest. Space is allocated for Afghan firms to also operate in the SEZ. India Ports Global has agreed to equip and run one container terminal and one general cargo terminal at the port for the next ten years, at which point the ownership of the terminals will be transferred to Iran's ports and Maritime Organisation, and the two parties may enter into subsequent agreements regarding whether

623 "Chinese Company to Get Lease of Gwadar Port's Free Trade Zone", *Economic Times*, 10 November 2015, http://economictimes.indiatimes.com/news/international/business/chinese-company-to-get-lease-of-gwadar-ports-free-trade-zone/articleshow/49740104.cms.

624 S. Fazl-e-Haider, "China Set to Run Gwadar Port as Singapore Quits", *Asia Times*, 5 September 2012, http://www.atimes.com/atimes/China_Business/NI05Cb01.html.

625 "Chinese Company to Get Lease of Gwadar Port's Free Trade Zone."

626 G. Nataraj, "India should get on board China's Maritime Silk Road", *East Asia Forum*, 27 June 2015, http://www.eastasiaforum.org/2015/06/27/india-should-get-on-board-chinas-maritime-silk-road/.

627 A. Paladhi, "JNPT to take 60% equity in Iran port project", *Business Standard*, 15 December 2014, http://www.business-standard.com/article/economy-policy/jnpt-to-take-60-equity-in-iran-port-project-114121500048_1.html.

628 Kandla Port Trust was renamed to Deendayal Port Trust in 2017.

India Ports Global may continue as the terminal operator.[629] This agreement also hinges on provisions available within the FTZ. Indian officials in the Ministry of Shipping stated that they hope to invest in the zone at a later stage to encourage Indian firms to operate there, and perhaps eventually expand to Oman, which is also building a new port-SEZ and enjoys friendly relations with Iran.[630]

Since at least 2008, JNPT has allocated space within port trust property for an SEZ of its own.[631] By 2010, JNPT hired the consulting firm IL&FS to prepare a feasibility report for the SEZ.[632] The project has been shifted to various consultants, including Ernst and Young; the latest consultant is L&T Infra Engineering, an Indian engineering consulting firm. The Ministry of Commerce's board of approval notified the SEZ project in 2014.[633] The L&T Infra Engineering report was reportedly accepted in May 2015, and the project has been approved as a multi-purpose SEZ that spans 277 hectares and will include assembling, packaging facilities, and warehousing.[634] Like JNPT, Deendayal Port Trust, the other equity partner in India Ports Global, is opening an SEZ on its property, which will be more than double the size of JNPT's at 640 hectares.[635]

Following Narendra Modi's first speech as India's prime minister (in which he announced the Make in India campaign), JNPT was his "first port of call." He laid the foundation stone at a ceremony for the start of construction for JNPT's fourth container terminal, which also commemorated the formal acceptance of the SEZ project.[636] JNPT handles 56 per cent of India's container traffic, and the bid for its fourth container terminal has gone to Singapore's PSA, which will increase JNPT's capacity to handle additional containers,

---

629 P. Manoj, "Chabahar port could shape global strategy of India's state-run ports", *Live Mint*, 23 October 2014, http://www.livemint.com/Opinion/zcC4jzurlSBCFdgrisEa1L/Chabahar-port-could-shape-global-strategy-of-Indias-stater.html.

630 D. R. Chaudhury, "India and Iran trying to seal Chabahar port deal by January", *Economic Times*, 17 December 2015, http://economictimes.indiatimes.com/news/politics-and-nation/india-and-iran-trying-to-seal-chabahar-port-deal-by-january/articleshow/50212231.cms.

631 Jawaharlal Nehru Port Trust, 2008–2009, Administration Report, AR, IOD, CSL, p. 23.

632 Jawaharlal Nehru Port Trust, 2010–2011, Administration Report, AR, IOD, CSL, p. 19.

633 "Approved SEZs in India", Special Economic Zones in India website, updated 31 March 2015, http://www.sezindia.nic.in/about-asi.asp (accessed 9 January 2016).

634 "Work on JNPT SEZ to begin in four months", *Times of India*, 20 August 2015, http://timesofindia.indiatimes.com/city/mumbai/Work-on-JNPT-SEZ-to-begin-in-four-months/articleshow/48562148.cms.

635 "Approved SEZs in India", Special Economic Zones in India website.

636 S. Banerjee, "Major infrastructure boost for Navi Mumbai's JNPT project", *Times of India*, 4 March 2015, http://timesofindia.indiatimes.com/city/navi-mumbai/Major-infrastructure-boost-for-Navi-Mumbais-JNPT-project/articleshow/46447679.cms.

supposedly more than doubling its current capacity.[637] The SEZ is meant to complement the port's expansion. DP World is one bidder for the port's SEZ. JNPT and its zone are national priorities within the Make in India campaign and India's regional strategy.

Some have seen India's cooperation with Afghanistan as a form of subregionalism that increases ties between members of SAARC and SAFTA.[638] Subregionalism, however, neither captures the intricacies of this case nor the role that SEZs and transport corridors play in these connections. While the trade between Afghanistan and India directly over Pakistan would benefit from the tariff reductions under SAFTA, the fact that Indian goods cannot pass through Pakistan necessitates some other agreement. Afghanistan and India both receive duty-free access to Chabahar, India Ports Global controls the terminal, and the SEZ will cater to Indian and Afghan investors. These projects offer India and Afghanistan a loophole to pursue their bilateral relations within a regional trade agreement to which Iran is not party. The future SEZ and fourth terminal at JNPT are also meant to strengthen this connection.[639] These cooperation agreements and infrastructure projects have led Iran and India to express interest in negotiating a preferential trade agreement of their own.[640] The port-zone within India's relations with Iran indicates a complicated layering of regional relationships. The port-zone projects have, in sum, facilitated a transregional route to subregional cooperation.

Conclusion

This chapter demonstrated the close connection between the port policies and the zone policies as they are unfolding in India under current state rescaling processes. Economic geographers have argued that understanding port-zone

637 "PM lays the foundation stone for 4th container terminal of Jawaharlal Nehru Port Trust", *Business Standard*, 11 October 2015, http://www.business-standard.com/article/current-affairs/pm-lays-foundation-stone-for-4th-container-terminal-of-jawaharlal-nehru-port-trust-115101100613_1.html.

638 Chaudhury, "PM Narendra Mode Returns to Regional Diplomacy."

639 This author argues, for example, that the Chabahar project is part of India's SAARC cooperation: R. Jain, "India and SAARC: An Analysis", *Indian Journal of Asian Affairs* 18 (2005) 2, pp. 55–74, at 65.

640 K. Suneja, "India expresses interest in preferential trade agreement with Iran once sanctions are lifted", *Economic Times*, 1 December 2015, http://economictimes.indiatimes.com/news/economy/foreign-trade/india-expresses-interest-in-preferential-trade-agreement-with-iran-once-sanctions-are-lifted/articleshow/49989768.cms.

dynamics and their joint global "diffusion" can lead us to a better understanding of state and corporate internationalization strategies.[641] In the Indian context, these projects are connected to domestic and international transport corridors that stem out of Mumbai's JNPT. These port-zone and corridor projects are being implemented in India under the auspices of state decentralization and economic liberalization policies that seek to draw foreign firms to India. However, these projects, far from being completely global, are part of strategies to target India's external articulation. India's foreign and domestic policy towards Japan uses various types of zones to offer Japanese firms spaces of exception within India, which is also unfolding at a subnational level as States like Rajasthan enter into agreements with JETRO. Not only have zones been used to draw in foreign investors, the Government of India is now also using port-zone complexes to attract Indian firms to set up abroad to increase connections with Iran and ultimately Afghanistan along a specific trade corridor routed through JNPT and the Indian-developed Chabahar Port. The Government of India, therefore, uses port and zone projects to link domestic and foreign transregional agendas.

This chapter elucidates the role of the zone in domestic development strategies and in international agreements. Historically, critical literature on zones has demonstrated that international agencies and consulting firms have advocated the proliferation of zones in developing countries, which were then used mainly by Western firms to exploit wage differences between countries, US and Japanese firms having been the largest players. Recent research has looked carefully at the expansion of Chinese zones in Africa.[642] This chapter outlines how India's Ministry of Shipping and Ministry of Commerce have promoted the zone within India and abroad in ways that correspond to the government's domestic and foreign policy initiatives as connected to an expanded port policy. A comparative look at how China uses zones, associated with its multiple Indian Ocean port projects and its diaspora networks, is useful for contextualizing India's port-zone programme. One important change in the shift from the EPZ policy to the SEZ policy has been the use of the Indian diaspora. Instead of trying to attract NRIs to invest in the Indian export drive as discussed in relation to pre-1989 KFTZ and SEEPZ, the government is now marketing the Indian diaspora as a potential export market for foreign firms that seek to export from India. The use of the diaspora as a source of national economic growth could be contrasted with China's use of its own diaspora through its SEZs.[643] In addition to China's Southeast Asian

641 Wang and Olivier, "Port-FEZ Bundles"; McCalla, "Geographical Spread of Free Zones."
642 Bräutigam and Tang, "African Shenzhen"; Bräutigam and Tang, "Going Global in Groups."
643 Ong, *Neoliberalism as Exception*, pp. 97–120.

diaspora, the research has mainly looked at Chinese integration with Taiwan and Hong Kong.[644] The "regional" adjective becomes less convincing in this context where "nationalization" or "territorialization" may be more appropriate. David Shambaugh's observation that "the common denominator to most of China's global activities and foreign policy is China's *own economic development*" seems applicable in the Indian context, thus reflecting India's simultaneous engagement with East Asian and West Asian neighbours through the domestically oriented Make in India investment campaign.[645]

Transregionalism is a useful lens for analysing the aforementioned projects, which do not fit readily into categories such as national, international, and transnational, nor do their results correlate precisely with distinctions between global/globalization and regional/regionalization. In India, the port-zone, the SEZ, and the NMIZ policies are not based on indiscriminately global connections but rather specific plans to connect certain spaces within India transregionally. India's use of the port-zone in a transregional context uses it as a "backdoor" to facilitate regional cooperation under SAFTA with Afghanistan, offering a new perspective on the zone within the context of regional trade agreements that does not conflict with regional integration but complements and possibly expands it.[646]

644 K. Sasuga, "Microregionalization across Southern China, Hong Kong and Taiwan", in: S. Breslin and G. D. Hook (eds.), *Microregionalism and World Order*, Basingstoke: Palgrave Macmillan, 2002, pp. 66–94.
645 D. Shambaugh, *China Goes Global: The Partial Power*, Oxford: Oxford University Press, 2013, p. 7.
646 Cf. N. Koyoma, "SEZs in the Context of Regional Integration: Creating Synergies for Trade and Investment", in: T. Farole and G. Akinci (eds.), *Special Economic Zones: Progress, Emerging Challenges, and Future Directions*, Washington, DC: The World Bank, 2011, pp. 127–156.

7 Globalizing Mumbai, 1940s–2014

Several texts on the urban dynamics of the zone from a global perspective have called Navi Mumbai, a city on the mainland side of Mumbai's harbour, an SEZ. Jonathan Bach names Navi Mumbai an example of an ex-city, that is, a zone that has copied the city template, becoming Mumbai's simulacrum.[647] The ex-city, that is, zone as city, contrasts with modular production-based zones like EPZs. Likewise, Keller Easterling writes, "now major cities and even national capitals, supposedly the centres of law, have created their own zone doppelgängers, like Navi Mumbai."[648] In addition to noting these zone/cities' function as simulacra, she also discusses how building new zone/cities represents a "clean slate" for reproducible models she calls "city in a box." What both she and Bach agree on is that the zone today has become a standardized spatial format that mimics a city yet has no distinguishing characteristics of place (except those that might be superficially Western), meaning it is viewed as a format that can be reproduced in just about any setting.[649] She adds later in her chapter: "CIDCO, the City and Industrial Development Company of Maharashtra, operating under the motto, 'We make cities,' is making Navi Mumbai the double of Mumbai."[650] It appears to be common knowledge that Navi Mumbai is a zone, but anyone travelling there expecting an Indian Shenzhen is in for a surprise. Navi Mumbai is nothing more than a planned city, though nothing less than India's largest urban infrastructure project to date. Since the 1960s, it was planned in connection to a new port and an FTZ. The new city was implemented piecemeal over the next decades by a parastatal agency set up for that explicit purpose, the aforementioned CIDCO (City and Industrial Development Corporation of Maharashtra). The port project took off while the FTZ did not. Yet, numerous SEZs were later planned in the same area. Recently, several key zone projects have been denotified and will seek a special status under new central government initiatives enacted since 2014.

This chapter examines the delicate interplay between central government plans, global standards and discourses, as well as local city and subnational State proposals to "globalize" Mumbai. Much of this effort to globalize Mumbai

647 Bach, "Urban Imagination", p. 106.
648 Easterling, *Extrastatecraft*, p. 26.
649 M. Augé, *Non-lieux: Introduction à une anthropologie de la supermodernité* [Non-Places: Introduction to an Anthropology of Supermodernity], J. Howe (trans.), London, New York: Verso, 1995.
650 Easterling, *Extrastatecraft*, p. 48.

https://doi.org/10.1515/9783110615135-007

is only discursive. This rhetoric is legitimized through its reference to foreign models as well as through the tabula rasa, or blank slate, that each plan seeks to project. Some of these ideas to globalize Mumbai refer to zone and port projects. While the central government effort to create portals of globalization generates specific connections inside and outside India, as discussed in the previous chapter, local goals seek instead to reposition Mumbai – the city, the ports, and its zones – in global rankings with the hope that visibility brings about local change. This chapter takes a long-term look at the shifting plans and how they have been implemented since the period of independence, albeit with a stronger focus on current plans. These projects for a future global Mumbai must deal with the legacies of having once been a central port for British India. They seek to reassert that centrality while also dealing with the tangible consequences of having once been "global."[651]

Plans to use zones to rework the city to achieve these goals are not new but are part of a longer history of business participation in city planning in Mumbai. This chapter provides an overview of the zone and port at the city level from the 1940s until today. The first section discusses the State-business nexus' plan to create an FTZ in conjunction with a new port and new city that would become Mumbai's satellite town (1940s–1980s). A longer history of the use of the zone and the port in a local context is included, which serves to qualify the standard perspective that the SEZ policy is completely new, ushering in a wave of neoliberalism in India, though claims of "accumulation by dispossession" may be warranted.[652] The next section addresses the way in which the city is currently being planned by a number of institutions in light of ideas of state rescaling. The final two sections focus on how ports and SEZs are tightly, if tacitly, connected to official State plans in Mumbai.

A longer perspective shows how the zone appeals to city planners for different reasons than it appeals to the central government. Since independence, local planners have sought to manage the port's and industry's negative impacts on the city space while simultaneously profiting from the opportunities generated by its connectivity. Zones allow the city to be rewritten and made legible to planners as well as to national and international indices. The SEZ is implicitly involved in official and unofficial plans to globalize Mumbai, referring to rankings rather than trade connections or mobility. Mumbai's planned SEZs

---

651 For global legacies of imperial port cities, see: Mah, *Port Cities and Global Legacies*.
652 In reference to David Harvey, see: Bannerjee-Guha, "Space Relations of Capital and Significance of New Economic Enclaves: SEZs in India", *Political and Economic Weekly* 43 (2008) 47, pp. 51–59; S. Bannerjee-Guha (ed.), *Accumulation by Dispossession: Transformative Cities in the New Global Order*, New Delhi, Thousand Oaks, CA: Sage Publications, 2010.

and its ports are connected to current urban planning projects to remake the city in a new, global image while also overcoming the inconveniences that emerge from being India's primary business capital for world trade since the nineteenth century.

New Bombay: Nationally Framing a Local Project

As early as the interwar period,[653] international organizations identified population growth as a potential cause for concern in what would soon be known as "third world" countries.[654] For planners in India, this demographic trend was seen as a challenge that had to be nationally overcome.[655] Urban planning was a related challenge, yet many Indians did not live in large cities. Following independence, the central government did not focus on urban planning as only 16.8 per cent of India's population lived in urban areas in 1951. Rather, industrialization informed urbanization planning.[656] New urban developments were planned based on the location of new industries, or industries were lured away from urban centres to balance population growth and decongest urban centres. By the 1960s and the 1970s, populations in major cities like New Delhi, Bombay, Calcutta, and Madras were growing at an annual rate of 3.3 per cent, meaning that city planning slowly became a central government priority as part of its demographic policy but was largely driven by the subnational States in which these cities were located.[657] By 1961, 17.8 per cent of Indians and 28.2 per cent of Maharashtrians lived in urban spaces. These numbers grew steadily; by 2001, while 27.8 per cent of Indians lived in urban areas, 42.4 per cent of Maharashtra's population was urban.[658] There was, therefore, significant pressure on the State of Maharashtra to create a plan to deal with urbanization before it became a national priority.

Parallel to the shifting focus on city planning, the Bombay Plan was written in 1944 by leading Indian industrialists. This plan outlined the corporate

---

653 Parts of this section appear in: Maruschke, "Managing Shifting Spatial Orders", pp. 29–39.

654 A. Bashford, "Population, Geopolitics and International Organizations in the Mid Twentieth Century", *Journal of World History* 19 (2008) 3, pp. 327–347.

655 C. R. Unger, "Towards Global Equilibrium: American Foundations and Indian Modernization, 1950s to 1970s", *Journal of Global History* 6 (2011) 1, pp. 121–142, at 137–140.

656 Unger, *Entwicklungspfade in Indien*, p. 211. See especially section three, "Industrialization and Urbanization", pp. 152–274.

657 Ibid., p. 211.

658 Planning Commission, Government of India, *Maharashtra Development Report*, New Delhi: Academic Foundation, 2007, p. 321.

sector's vision of independent India's development. It was an unsuccessful attempt to create a strategic partnership between the state and Indian business houses.[659] However, Bombay's business elite, including the authors of the report, influenced later developments in Bombay and the State of Maharashtra, despite not having won over the central government. The State of Maharashtra was the first State in India to establish its own agencies and legislation to deal with urbanization and to increase industrialization.[660] Bombay State, comprising today's Gujarat and Maharashtra, held a Maharashtra Commercial and Industrial Conference in 1956 to solicit views from business interests on the State's economic problems. This conference later became a regular event. In 1957 it formed the Maharashtra Economic Development Council (MEDC), which was a forum for business chambers throughout the State, including the Bombay Chamber of Commerce and Industry as well as the Indian Merchants' Chamber, one of the key institutions behind the Bombay Plan.[661] By 1978, MEDC comprised 33 constituent members, including national associations for specific sectors, and over 300 associate members representing national and local businesses, some of which were subsidiaries of foreign firms.[662] Shortly after founding MEDC, the State set up a Board of Industrial Development in 1960, which eventually became the Maharashtra Industrial Development Corporation (MIDC) in 1962 through the Maharashtra Industrial Act.[663] These agencies promoted business interests and industrialization in Maharashtra.

While urbanization and industrialization became political priorities of the State, the central government also looked for ways to ease congestion at Bombay's port, which was and continues to be owned by the central government. The port trust operates independently and is financed by its own services, but it falls under the authority of the Ministry of Transport (Shipping) and is subject to the Port Trust Act. Bombay Port was and is currently both a commercial port and a naval port. In 1946, the Grace Committee was appointed to reorganize the navy's dockyard at Bombay Port and discuss the future direction of the Indian navy after independence. In 1947, the committee's report concluded that expansion of the naval facilities at the current site was not

659 M. Kudaisya, "'The Promise of Partnership': Indian Business, the State, and the Bombay Plan of 1944", *Business History Review* 88 (2014) 1, pp. 97–131.

660 A. Shaw, *The Making of Navi Mumbai*, New Delhi: Orient Longman, 2004, p. 61.

661 Maharashtra Economic Development Council (MEDC), *MEDC: 1957–1977*, Bombay: The Council, 1978, GRC, BL, p. 1.

662 MEDC, *MEDC: 1957–1977*, pp. 10–18.

663 "About Us – History", Maharashtra Industrial Development Corporation website, http://www.midcindia.org/Pages/AboutUs.aspx (accessed 5 November 2015).

possible since it was restricted by a built-up city and commercial traffic at the port. The committee suggested shifting the navy out of Bombay Port to the mainland side of Bombay's harbour (Thana Creek) at Nhava Sheva.[664] This recommendation was not followed because the site selected, though ideal for a deep-water port, was completely undeveloped. There was no electricity, no running water, no railroad, and no road connected to the site. The navy stayed at its location and sought to reclaim land instead, but the idea of shifting port facilities to Nhava Sheva remained in the minds of BPT planners, who ran the commercial side of the port. Nhava Sheva and the surrounding area of Bombay's eastern mainland side of the harbour became the focus of the State of Maharashtra's efforts to decongest Bombay's population, industry, and port.

Following several expansions of Bombay Port in the early 1950s, the Government of India believed that the present site of the port had been exhausted. There were draft limitations, not to mention congestion facing the port within the harbour and on the mainland rail and road connections to the port.[665] In the 1960s, the BPT proposed extending its current facilities to Nhava Sheva on the mainland side of the harbour across Thane Creek.[666] This extension to the mainland coincided with the identification of the mainland as a site for a future satellite city for Bombay. The planned port at Nhava Sheva set the terms of the agreement for the location of the new satellite city.[667]

By the 1940s, city planners in Bombay were concerned about overcrowding in the city and sought solutions to create a counterpoint that would attract new arrivals away from Bombay and potentially also serve as a new home for many already living in the city. Because of Bombay's geography and historical development based on the colonial city centre adjacent to the port, the southernmost part of the island served as the business centre. Every workday, people travelled from the northern part of the city to the southern part, and then returned to the northern part, leading to severe congestion (this is still the case). Many of the State's industrial areas were located within the city, causing further congestion.

---

664 G. M. Hiranandani, *Transition to Eminence: The Indian Navy 1976–1990*, New Delhi: Ministry of Defence (Navy) in association with Lancer Publishers, 2005, p. 135.

665 "Chronology", Mumbai Port Trust.

666 Ministry of Shipping and Transport, Government of India, 1969–1970, Annual Report, AR, IOD, CSL, pp. 42–43.

667 R. Mehrotra, "Twin City: Navi Mumbai Thirty Years Later", in: *Mumbai Reader '07*, Mumbai: Urban Design Research Institute, 2008, pp. 118–129, at 119.

In 1945, a post-war development committee recommended that areas on the mainland across Bombay's harbour be developed to curb the city's growth. Just two years later, an unofficial report by N.V. Modak and Albert Meyer urged for a policy of "industrial dispersal" out of Bombay that would be supported by housing.[668] Both reports influenced subsequent reports and legislation that sought to restrict industrial sites through land use zoning (districting) policies. A 1965 publication by Bombay's leading architects, Charles Correa and Pravina Mehta, as well as engineer Shirish Patel, advocated a single urban area to be developed on the mainland connected across the harbour to Bombay.[669] Their article in *Modern Architects Research Group* was influenced by the garden city concept developed by Ebenezer Howard. The article secured the idea of a twin city for Bombay as a solution to Bombay's congestion and overcrowding.[670] This publication was endorsed by MEDC, which formed a study council for the development of the mainland across the harbour the following year and invited the authors of this plan to participate. Along with academics and industry representatives, the BPT also sent representatives to the meeting to consider the development of a town that elaborated on the Modern Architects Research Group publication and referred directly to the English New Towns Act of 1946.[671]

A year earlier at the 1964 meeting of the MEDC, an FTZ to be developed by the Government of Maharashtra was proposed for Nhava Sheva to complement the new city and the port expansion scheme.[672] The fact that this zone was proposed by a business lobby for a State government is significant. While major ports like BPT and FTZs fell under the authority of the central government through the Ministry of Transport and the Ministry of Commerce and Industry, the State government in Maharashtra along with private business interests there sought to play a larger role in these policy areas by linking them to a State plan: the creation of New Bombay satellite town on the other side of Bombay's harbour. At first, this zone proposal was rather vague: "The Govt. [of Maharashtra] should implement the proposals for formation of State ports and shipping committee [... and] should investigate the potentialities of creating a free trade zone round one of the ports."[673] Minor and intermediate ports were under the authority of the State rather than the central government's Ministry of Transport. However, congestion was so severe at Bombay Port (a major port)

668 Shaw, *Making of Navi Mumbai*, p. 63.
669 C. Correa, P. Mehta and S. Patel, "Planning for Bombay", *MARG* 18 (1965) 3, pp. 30–56.
670 Shaw, *Making of Navi Mumbai*, pp. 66–67.
671 Ibid., pp. 74–75.
672 MEDC, *MEDC: 1957–1977*, p. 46.
673 Ibid.

that the State played an active role in pushing for the selection of a new site for port expansion at Nhava Sheva.

When the central government intimated that it had no additional plans for zones past Kandla (and later Santacruz), the MEDC changed its strategy: "The Government [of Maharashtra] should establish an *industrial estate* in Maharashtra where goods could be imported under bonded warehouses, processed and reexported so as to avoid the usual formalities of import duties, excise duties, etc."[674] Describing such a policy as a "bonded" industrial estate in the above quote was strategic. The central government sanctioned State governments to implement industrial estates,[675] though in fact bonded warehouses were generally located on central government port trust land and were reviewed by the central government's Ministry of Finance.[676] The proposed space could be a zone without officially being labelled an FTZ. The central or State government could set up an industrial estate on port trust land (Nhava Sheva) and also label it a bonded warehouse, thus creating a zone-estate hybrid that would be equivalent to an FTZ and would likely cater to exporting Indian businesses rather than foreign firms. These industrialists were hoping to create and exploit such a loophole.

Unlike the EPZ, industrial estates were widely pursued by States within India, starting with a first industrial estate in 1955 in Rajkot, Gujarat. In contrast, few publications on EPZs/FTZs within India until at least the 2000s correspond with the very limited implementation of the EPZ, which was not a comprehensive policy like the industrial estate. Many industrial estates set up in the 1950s and early 1960s were joint projects and included Indo-American, Indo-German, Indo-Japanese, and Indo-French centres.[677] By the 1960s, 52 such extension training centres had been set up in connection with industrial estates to develop manufacturing prototypes for small industries in India. The industrial estate model continued to be implemented well into the 1970s. There were already 572 industrial estates approved by 1973, 427 of which had been built, and as many as 366 were already in operation all over India.[678] These estates could be sponsored by either the central government or subnational States, and a small percentage (2 per cent by 1970)

674 Ibid., p. 68. Found in: "Summary of Reports of the Sectional Committees as Finally Adopted at the Maharashtra Commercial and Industrial Conference", 1964 (emphasis added).
675 P. C. Alexander, *Industrial Estates in India*, Small Industry Extension Training Institute, New York and Bombay: Asia Publishing House, 1963, p. 17.
676 Ministry of Finance, Department of Revenue, Government of India, "Report of the Customs Reorganisation Committee", 1958, AR, IOD, CSL, p. 69.
677 A. S. E. Iyer, "Co-operation Between and Assistance to Small-Scale units in Industrial Estates in India", in: *Industrial Estates in Asia and the Far East*, New York: United Nations, 1962.
678 "Report of the Working Group on Financing of Industrial Estate", Bombay: Reserve Bank of India, 1972.

were private.[679] In contrast to the numerous estates, by the same year only KFTZ was in operation and SEEPZ had been approved.

Within India, the industrial estate programme was widely used to encourage small businesses to manufacture for the domestic market.[680] The industrial estate programme, though carried out namely by States, was a national strategy with the explicit purpose of enabling industries to move out of Bombay and Calcutta in order to remove the imbalanced concentration of industries in these cities that developed out of colonial trade relations.[681] In 1963, P.C. Alexander, the Ministry of Commerce and Industry development commissioner for the Small Scale Industry department, published a monograph in which he stated that industrial estates enabled a "dispersed pattern of industrial development", which he followed immediately by asking the following question: "Is it going to prove feasible to develop industry closer to where the people now are, in semi-urban and rural areas, instead of attracting ever larger populations into huge urban agglomerations like Calcutta?"[682] Thus, the industrial estate was a tool to disperse industry in order to decongest major cities.

Both Indian and UNIDO reports reference a seminal work on the industrial estate model by the Stanford Research Institute in California.[683] The industrial estate model promoted by William Bredo connected estates to ideas about city planning, particularly urban districting, that emerged in the US and the UK in the 1920s and sought to develop cities and suburbs through planned districts for industry, services, and residences. The report states that though industrial estates existed since the late 1800s in the US and the UK, the modern industrial estates differ in that they are comprehensive, zoned, and suburban.[684] This work was written after industrial estates had already gained traction in the post-war era. Apart from the US (including Puerto Rico) and the UK, India had the highest number of industrial estates by 1958: 58. The report highlighted the features of estates in Puerto Rico, the US mainland, and India through descriptions of the facilities accompanied by aerial photographs of square warehouses

---

679 UNIDO, "Guidelines for the Establishment of Industrial Estates", p. 21.

680 S. Deva, "Establishment of Industrial Estates in India", *Journal of Administration Overseas* 15 (1976) 3, pp. 150–159.

681 UNIDO, "The Effectiveness of Industrial Estates in Developing Countries", Vienna: United Nations, 1978, p. 57.

682 Alexander, *Industrial Estates in India*, p. vii.

683 W. Bredo, *Industrial Estates: Tools for Industrialization, International Industrial Development Center*, Stanford Research Institute, Glencoe, IL: The Free Press, 1960.

684 Ibid., p. 11.

and other buildings, lumped together in a triangular shape. This triangle was connected by arterial roads to a city, indicated by skyscrapers in the horizon. Such a design was especially advocated as a tool for "urban industrial deurbanization."[685]

UNIDO was also an advocate of industrial estates, which it studied in order to, like the formation of the zone model, institute guidelines for a standardized industrial estate model based on international "best practice."[686] While India's EPZ development was characterized by the absence of foreign technical training, Indian officials in charge of the industrial estates such as P.C. Alexander received funding from the Ford Foundation to travel to California and train at the Stanford Research Institute with William Bredo, the author of the seminal industrial estate manual.[687] The UNIDO and Indian publications on industrial estates do not overlap with those of FTZs; they were seen by these policy makers as separate policies that did not, for example, reference the US FTZ or, later, the UNIDO "Handbook on Export Free Zones."[688]

However, the policies were not completely dissimilar. One social scientist in 1966 described the failure of India's industrial estates and suggested they should invite foreign investors and be based on Puerto Rico's "operation bootstrap", a programme anthropologist Patrick Neveling credits as an early model zone used by the US and later UN agencies.[689] Likewise, State and business elite in Bombay proposed hybridizing different policies to create something like an FTZ, which suggests that the FTZ in Bombay was not seen as a fixed spatial format, but rather was a fluid concept that could be augmented to fit local needs. It could very well be that within the Indian context, ideas of FTZs were also shaped by experiences with industrial estates. Jamie Cross, for instance, claims that current "economic zone" planning in India is shaped by past experiences with a variety of state planning techniques ranging from steel towns to industrial townships, as well as the foreign models circulated by international agencies. These experiences, he writes, are all part of a larger manifestation of state planning techniques to create spaces of experimentation related to a

---

685 Ibid., pp. 66–69.

686 UNIDO, "Effectiveness of Industrial Estates"; UNIDO, "Guidelines for the Establishment of Industrial Estates." The 1978 guidelines were redone in 1995: UNIDO, "Industrial Estates: Principles and Practices", Vienna: United Nations, 1995, https://www.unido.org/fileadmin/user_media/Publications/Pub_free/Industrial_estates_principles_and_practice.ppd.

687 Alexander, *Industrial Estates in India*, p. ix.

688 Kelleher, "Handbook."

689 N. Somasekhara, "Industrial Estates in India", *Artha Vijnana: Journal of the Gokhale Institute of Politics and Economics* 8 (1966) 3, pp. 279–297; Neveling, "Free Trade Zones"; Neveling, "Export Processing Zones, Special Economic Zones."

development imaginary.[690] These state-based experiences were reshaped in a local context as subnational States articulated their own visions of development by utilizing a variety of models.

Through the planning of New Bombay and the Nhava Sheva port, New Bombay was extensively connected to districting development concepts in terms of decentralized residential nodes with accompanying industrial districts. Several industrial belts had been developed in the area by MIDC as early as 1962, before development on the twin city began.[691] These areas were purchased by the parastatal, developed into plots with industrial sheds that were connected to power grids and water supply, and were then leased to small-scale industries. These spaces served a local purpose of decongesting Mumbai while also creating jobs and promoting small-scale industrial production for the domestic market. They were, therefore, outlets for import substitution that simultaneously served as vehicles for local development.

Although the manufacturing and land aspects were similar, these estates lacked the specific de- and reterritorialization features of FTZs. They still operated within the domestic economy, not apart from it, and were oriented towards the even spatial distribution of domestic industrial growth. They were the impetus of the Indian import substitution drive. In contrast, the zone was externally oriented in that it provided an outlet for private firms to compete in the global market place to enable the import substitution drive by generating foreign exchange earnings from exports. The FTZ was thereby meant to enable industrial estates and other initiatives to produce for the domestic economy.

Although the FTZ was meant to facilitate the import substitution drive and thereby the activities of industrial estates through the generation of foreign exchange earnings, India would be shielded from the externally oriented connections generated through these enclaved spaces while simultaneously profiting from them. The FTZ proposed that Nhava Sheva serve a national purpose of generating foreign exchange through exports needed for domestic production to continue. Rather than focusing on internal connections, such a space needed external articulation and a remote location, which served the purpose of shielding the new city from the externally oriented activities of the zone:

> A Free-Trade Zone should be created near a major port where ample facilities for ocean-going ships are available or can be created [...]. It would be advantageous to the Free-

690 Cross, *Dream Zones*, pp. 24–52.
691 Shaw, *Making of Navi Mumbai*, p. 117.

> Trade Zone to have such a natural boundary as would facilitate customs supervision, and thereby discourage the smuggling of goods into the country.[692]

The idea of creating a new space that would shield the area around the zone in order to prevent smuggling had already been fulfilled by Kandla Port and KFTZ. As mentioned, Bombay had been one of the first considerations for India's first zone, but the Free-Trade Zone Committee of the Board of Trade (Ministry of Commerce) found the idea of isolating any portion of Bombay Port "impossible", which is why the plan was shifted to Kandla's remote location.[693]

MEDC planned to turn Bombay Port's congestion into a sign of its strength and importance to the Indian state. The fact that the port was so busy indicated that it should be expanded, and Bombay's population and industries should, along with the port, expand and relocate across the harbour. The zone-port complex was considered an essential component of this strategy:

> All these views and ideas suggest the conclusion that the best remedy for relieving congestion in Bombay and accelerating industrialisation around Bombay is to explore the possibilities of creating a large new port near Bombay and establishing a Free-Trade Zone around such a new port. The satellite towns to be formed for relieving the congestion in Bombay should be, as the Industrial Location Panel has remarked, within a few hours' distance from the City of Bombay in order to enable industrialists and industries to maintain a close contact with the city. Such a port and Free-Trade Zone, in our view, can be created at Shewa-Neva (Sheva-Nhava) located only seven miles to the East of Bombay Harbour and situated on the Kolaba coast line of Thana Creek. This port could serve as a big import and export centre and would thereby reduce appreciably the pressure on Bombay harbor. Moreover, by virtue of its being a new port it would be free from the serious population and industrial concentration and, therefore, it would be ideal for creating a Free-Trade Zone.[694]

This report, while emphasizing the official policy of urban decongestion, acknowledged that connections to dynamic places like Bombay were still central to business interests. Bombay, more so than any other location within India, had the necessary skilled technicians, labourers, and entrepreneurs needed for a national export drive.[695]

Like the portals of globalization that Michael Geyer describes as metaphors for the places that facilitate the articulation of the external and internal on behalf of the nation state, MEDC planners situated Bombay as a port city of national importance. The report continues with references to other US port cities: "Highly industrialised port-cities like New York, San Francisco, New Orleans,

692 MEDC, "Report on Free-Trade Zone in Maharashtra", p. 3.
693 Ibid., p. 4.
694 Ibid.
695 Ibid., p. 5.

etc. have Free-Trade Zones which clearly suggests that it is always convenient to establish Free Trade-Zones near industrial port towns, and that a Free-Trade Zone at Shewa-Neva which is in the proximity of Bombay City would be the ideal location."[696] While the industrial estates and residential nodes were meant to decongest Bombay's industry and population, the FTZ was meant to speed the decongestion of Bombay Port by providing the newer port with additional traffic that would eventually entice shippers to the new port. The Nhava Sheva port and FTZ project enabled, on the one hand, a natural boundary and isolation, and on the other hand connectedness: access to markets such as West Asia (Middle East), North and East Africa, as well as Australia.[697] The interplay between these two tendencies – isolation and connection – indicates a view that managing this space was a national priority. Both the port and the zone were central government policies that served national purposes. State planners in Maharashtra and Bombay hoped these initiatives could, through some persuasion of the national importance of Bombay, be used to serve their local goals of decongesting the city and reformulating both Bombay and New Bombay as modern and connected port cities that resembled those of the industrialized countries they strove to emulate.

The Indian Council of Foreign Trade concurred that Bombay's mainland contained exactly the locational advantage for a zone. It was at once isolated and could be well connected to port facilities.[698] The site already allowed for the physical requirements of the de- and reterritoialization function that was central to the FTZ model. Furthermore, connections to the airport were essential to articulate the space in the image of American FTZs, many of which were not connected by sea but by air. Eventually the project for creating an FTZ at Nhava Sheva was dropped, but the airport connection could prove key to understanding why SEEPZ, the zone eventually established in Bombay in 1973, was instituted and a Nhava Sheva zone was not.

SEEPZ was located adjacent to Bombay's international airport, which can account for why the Santacruz EPZ took on the name of the former Santacruz Airport (as the zone is not located in the neighbourhood of Santacruz). The Nhava Sheva FTZ document, more than any other planning document for KFTZ, looked extensively at the US FTZ model and found that many zones had been established at US airports. The document states that this trend of locating FTZs at airports is possible in industrialized countries like the US, but industrializing

696 Ibid.
697 Ibid., p. 6.
698 Ibid., p. 5.

countries like India should continue to locate zones at ports. The idea of Bombay as a modern city connected not only by sea but also by air (Bombay became a port city in multiple ways) may have played a role in the eventual site selection near Bombay's airport.[699] As Jamie Cross and James C. Scott demonstrate, dreams of development and modernity can win over practical projects.[700] Visions of these development projects as blank slates separate from the state – in reference to Jean-Fraçois Bayart's double meaning of the term "state" – may influence site selection, architecture style, and management practices.[701]

Although the State government's FTZ project for New Bombay was dropped, the idea of a port-city tabula rasa was pursued further. In 1970, the State accepted that Bombay's growth could be curbed by the proposed twin city and formed CIDCO to develop New Bombay. CIDCO is a limited public company listed under the Indian Company Act and is owned by the State.[702] CIDCO drafted a plan for the new city by 1973, which formed the basis for the city's development from the 1970s onwards. Having been developed mainly by this single parastatal agency, the new city's planning was relatively comprehensive.

A clean break with old institutions influenced the development of the new port. The new site at Nhava Sheva was proposed in 1964 in a BPT master plan, undertaken by a consultant, Bertlin & Partners, UK.[703] The BPT was the main advocate of the plan to construct a satellite port on the mainland to relieve traffic congestion at the present site. In the mid-1970s, it appears that the satellite port was planned as an extension of Bombay Port rather than a separate institution, and the BPT was the body that moved to acquire the land at Nhava Sheva.[704] Although initial plans began as early as the 1960s, by 1980 the Nhava Sheva project had only just started acquiring land, constructing the site, and

699 Cross, *Dream Zones*. He discusses throughout the book the importance of dreams of capitalism and modernity in zone planning projects, which may influence site selection, architecture, and management practices.

700 Cross, *Dream Zones*; J. C. Scott, *Seeing Like a State: How Certain Schemes to Improve the Human Condition Have Failed*, New Haven, CT: Yale University Press, 1998.

701 J. F. Bayart, *The State in Africa: The Politics of the Belly*, London: Longman, 1993.

702 Shaw, *Making of Navi Mumbai*, p. 83.

703 World Bank, "Project Completion Report", India. Nhava Sheva Port Project. Report Number 12189, 14 July 1993, p. 1, http://www-wds.worldbank.org/external/default/WDSContentServer/WDSP/IB/1993/07/14/000009265_3960925200204/Rendered/PDF/multi_page.pdf; Ministry of Shipping and Transport, Government of India, 1968–1969, Annual Report, AR, IOD, CSL, p. 35.

704 Ministry of Shipping and Transport, Government of India, 1971–1972, Annual Report, AR, IOD, CSL, pp. 45–46; Ministry of Shipping and Transport, Government of India, 1974–1975, Annual Report, AR, IOD, CSL, p. 39.

receiving the necessary financing. At this point, congestion was so severe at Bombay Port that the Ministry of Shipping reported times when there were more than 30 ships waiting approximately one and a half months to berth at the port.[705] Though Nhava Sheva had been planned for container traffic, by 1980 BPT moved to acquire additional equipment to facilitate the growth in container traffic, at which point in time Nhava Sheva became a separate port project rather than connected to BPT management.[706] Likewise, New Bombay received its own municipal corporation that was not connected to Bombay's.

Severe problems at BPT in terms of labour and infrastructure could be one reason why the port projects were split into two trusts rather than remaining under BPT management. A satellite port had been planned for Calcutta prior to Bombay's satellite project. In the late 1950s, the Government of India had been granted a loan by the WB for financing development schemes at India's major ports between 1957 and 1958. In 1957, the World Bank Technical Mission consulted on India's ports and suggested that a satellite port be set up for Calcutta's port. In 1958, Mr. Posthuma from the Port of Rotterdam (which continues to consult on India's ports to this day) was hired through the UN Technical Assistance Administration. Haldia, 65 miles downriver, was proposed as the site for the new port. The satellite port never became a separate port but rather remained connected to the Calcutta Port Trust (now the Kolkata Port Trust):

> Just when the scheme was about to be put into effect, the Calcutta dock workers claimed that they should be allowed to handle the ships at Haldia although the Port Commissioners had pointed out several practical difficulties in making such an arrangement, at a place 65 miles away from Calcutta. The first ship which was lightened at Haldia was initially boycotted by labour on arrival at Calcutta.[707]

The two satellite projects were sometimes lumped together as the modern ports that would relive India of the problems facing its colonial ports. In 1973, Nhava Sheva and Haldia were both selected by the Ministry of Transport to focus intensively on container traffic, specifically to overtake Bombay Port's container handling abilities.[708]

705 Ministry of Shipping and Transport, Government of India, 1980–1981, Annual Report, AR, IOD, CSL, p. 23.
706 Ibid., p. 27.
707 Ministry of Shipping and Transport, Government of India, 1959–1960, Annual Report, AR, IOD, CSL, pp. 12–13.
708 Ministry of Shipping and Transport, Government of India, 1972–1973, Annual Report, AR, IOD, CSL, p. 46.

In contrast to Haldia, Nhava Sheva became a completely separate port. It seems that not only did the central government want to avoid the problems of Haldia, but also the idea of a tabula rasa for Bombay on all fronts – a new port-city template – extended to the establishment of the new port. By the 1950s, the BPT was the largest employer in the city and, even today, remains the city's largest landowner.[709] The port's sheer magnitude leads to tensions. It is run by the central government, but clearly plays a key role in the dynamics of public space and employment in Mumbai. There have been significant labour actions over the course of the port's post-1947 history. Dockworkers all over India were active in labour rights movements, resulting in, for example, the all-India dockers' strike in 1958.[710] The MPT currently employs over 30,000 workers, which is unusually high, meaning that about 80 per cent of its revenue is spent on wages.[711] It appears that planners were motivated to split the port projects in two, creating a new port on what was viewed as an entirely blank canvas. Proponents of such a perspective have put this in other words: "JNPT [Nhava Sheva] had a relatively young and educated workforce, and did not have to carry the baggage of huge labour supply [...] like Mumbai [...] or, face problems of militant and unreasonable trade union activities."[712] Of course, JNPT was never a blank canvas; project affected persons were resettled elsewhere and the legal issues surrounding that resettlement are still ongoing, resulting in regular protests blocking trucks entering the facilities – the very issues creating a new port was supposed to avoid. Nhava Sheva had merely been described as an empty space in government documents.

By the 1980s, the funding and construction of Nhava Sheva was underway as a separate port, as it was recorded in Ministry of Shipping annual reports under its own section rather than under the BPT.[713] According to the WB project completion report, Kandla Port and Bombay Port were other financiers of the project, along with the central government.[714] It was also financed by loans from the WB, the Government of the Netherlands, and the Saudi Fund Development Authority.[715] All three provided consulting in relation to the port project.

709 D'Monte, *Ripping the Fabric*, p. 236.

710 Ibid., p. 236.

711 Organisation for Economic Co-operation and Development, *The Competitiveness of Global Port-Cities*, OECD Publishing, 2014, p. 237; D'Monte, *Ripping the Fabric*, p. 241.

712 Patel and Bhattacharya, "Infrastructure in India", p. 64.

713 Ministry of Shipping and Transport, Government of India, 1984–1985, Annual Report, AR, IOD, CSL, p. 33.

714 World Bank, "Project Completion Report", p. 20.

715 Ministry of Surface Transport, Government of India, 1988–1989, Annual Report, AR, IOD, CSL, p. 58.

By the time the port opened in 1989, it was named Jawaharlal Nehru Port Trust after India's first prime minister. The name suits it: the port is nationally important in that currently almost 60 per cent of India's entire container traffic is routed through the port.[716] Despite the new name, it is still colloquially referred to by locals as well as shippers and logistics firms as Nhava Sheva.

Today, the two trusts, JNPT and MPT, are both owned by the central government and were meant to be complementary. MP was meant to focus on break bulk cargo and petroleum, oil, and lubricants, while JNP would cover container traffic. Major foreign shipping companies that had frequented MP switched their services to JNP during the 1990s, including Maersk, American President Lines, Sea-Land, and P&O, costing MPT, according to a prominent local journalist, one crore rupees revenue per day.[717] Instead of dying a "natural death", as many city planners and activists in Mumbai would have liked, Mumbai Port has continued to seek new deals to expand its capacity to challenge JNP.[718] MP is extending its facilities to include an offshore berth to handle container traffic while JNP now has a liquid cargo terminal and is in the process of adding special facilities for chemicals.[719] This complete separation in operations accounts for a significant deal of competition between the ports for carriers, which partly shapes how the ports operate today.

Planning Greater and Global Mumbai

Beyond the Navi Mumbai and JNPT projects, the State of Maharashtra as well as all related groups concerned with city planning in Mumbai, such as nongovernmental organizations, think tanks, and corporations, have utilized the central government policies described in the previous chapter to "revise" the city.[720] This revision builds on past efforts to make Navi Mumbai a

716 Patel and Bhattacharya, "Infrastructure in India", p. 64.
717 D'Monte, *Ripping the Fabric*, p. 239. The author of this book was once an editor of the *Times of India*.
718 "Conflicting Signals", *Financial Express*, 8 February 1998, in: D'Monte, *Ripping the Fabric*, p. 240.
719 "Port Details", JNPT website, http://www.jnport.gov.in/AboutJNPT.aspx?id=3&cid=1 (accessed 22 February 2014).
720 This revision has gone both ways: Bombay was renamed Mumbai in 1995 by the Marathi nationalist party, the Shiv Sena. The revision positioned Mumbai as a Marathi city rather than a multicultural city. While in other Indian contexts renaming cities and streets has been accepted, in Mumbai it remains a point of contention among residents with other ethnic or religious identities.

satellite city, where the port project played a decisive role. While in the past, State and business elite argued for the national importance of Bombay, the current efforts seek to position Mumbai globally to legitimize projects as important to the national effort to "globalize" India. SEZs and ports play an important role in these projects, too, as investment spaces for local business elite. Positioning Mumbai as a "global city" is not a project to actually make Mumbai global in terms of capital, goods, or human mobility.[721] It is part of a discursive and visual effort to reposition the city through the use of image-building mega projects.[722] This type of branding is meant to project the image of the global in order to eventually lead to a global city with a central business district – without an industrial port marring the shoreline. In short, these projects simultaneously deal with the legacy of having been a portal of globalization while also seeking to maintain the city's importance for India's globalization efforts.

Adjectives such as local, glocal, or translocal do not fully fit the context of firms and individuals that/who are situated in Mumbai but have national business interests in the "globalization of India" just as much as in the "global repositioning" of Mumbai.[723] The Tata Group, for example, though operating throughout India and abroad, is synonymous with Bombay's business elite for generations, as their first cotton mill opened there in the 1850s. The "transnational capitalist class" is also not fitting, even if many of these individuals received business degrees in the US. Their interests are to operate in a globally competitive fashion at a local and national level.[724] The scale on which control over the reworking of the city through planning is quite local, despite the global visibility these plans hope to project and the connectivity in "city networks" they might ultimately provide. Glocalization may be the ultimate goal of these projects since "'local' characteristics of cities and regions [are important] in maintaining or asserting their global competitive advantages", especially the locality's global advantage for the

721 Cf. Sassen, *Global City*.

722 R. Marshall, *Emerging Urbanity: Global Urban Projects in the Asia Pacific Rim*, London: Spoon Press, 2003; X. Ren, "Architecture as Branding: Mega Project Developments in Beijing", *Built Environment* 24 (2008) 4, pp. 517–531.

723 Cf. M. P. Smith, *Transnational Urbanism: Locating Globalization*, Malden, MA and Oxford: Blackwell, 2001. For glocal and glocalization, there are many understandings of the term, especially as a business strategy by which firms from other states seek to enter new markets by localizing. For geography, see: E. Swyngedouw, "Neither Global nor Local: 'Glocalisation' and the Politics of Scale", in: K. R. Cox (ed.), *Spaces of Globalization: Reasserting the Power of the Local*, New York: Guilford Press, 1997, pp. 137–166.

724 L. Sklair, *The Transnational Capitalist Class*, Malden, MA and Oxford: Blackwell, 2001.

national scale.[725] Here, comprehensive glocalization, which includes multiple scales between local and global, is the strategy, but not a term that can describe these actors' social spaces.[726]

The federal system in India does not operate like other federal systems. Therefore, city management takes on a different form. Metropolitan governance in Mumbai has been described as "polycentric", involving "public organizations, networked vertically and horizontally, operating at different scales and having diverse – often overlapping – functional scopes."[727] Marie-Hélène Zérah, whose research focuses on the provision of services in Mumbai, discusses the "expansion of territorial scales" to understand the proliferation of overlapping public agencies that administer the city's services and that cooperate with various networks of private groups to guide city planning.[728] Zérah looks towards policies that expand the size of Mumbai (what she would call an expansion of the city scale) as well as strategies to consolidate planning authorities. Loraine Kennedy argues that cities are changing in size, creating larger agglomerations of planning agencies and "territory" as part of a state rescaling drive by subnational States. Nevertheless, these larger units do not have much agency and therefore, "municipal governments in India are *not* major actors of this evolution."[729] This is an important distinction that separates the attempts made to globalize cities in India from other contexts, which is done distinctly by top-down efforts to increase a city's physical size even while it remains administratively weak. However, this argument for difference may also take the idea of scale too literally. Separating the particular scale on which an actor is operating becomes challenging as corporate interests, non-governmental organizations, intergovernmental organizations, global consultancy firms in conjunction with State politicians – who work out of Mumbai, Maharashtra's capital – seek to refashion the city to their own needs, sometimes through central governmental promotions on central government land.

---

725 E. Swyngedouw, "Globalisation or 'glocalisation'? Networks, Territories and Rescaling", *Cambridge Review of International Affairs* 17 (2004) 1, pp. 25–48, at 37.

726 On the challenge of locating transnational actors and their multiple, entangled spaces of action, see: A. Dietze and K. Naumann, "Revisiting Transnational Actors from a Spatial Perspective", *European Review of History: Revue européenne d'histoire* 25 (2018) 3–4, pp. 415–430.

727 A. Pethe, V. Tandel and S. Ghandi, "Understanding Issues Related to Polycentric Governance in the Mumbai Metropolitan Region", in: *Mumbai Reader'13*, Mumbai: Urban Design Research Institute, 2013, pp. 240–261, at 242.

728 M. H. Zérah, "Gouvernance métropolitaine et pilotage de réseaux techniques: le cas de la région métropolitaine de Mumbai (Bombay)", *Revue française d'administration publique* 3 (2003) 107, pp. 395–407.

729 Kennedy, *Politics of Economic Restructuring*, p. 132.

The Brihanmumbai Municipal Corporation is the largest municipal corporation in India in terms of its budget and the extent of its responsibilities in the city, which include a range of services such as electricity supply, sewage and water supply, health, public transport, education, and slum improvement.[730] It does not, however, control urban planning or land use. A number of State agencies coordinate Mumbai's planning. In 1975, the State of Maharashtra created the Mumbai Metropolitan Regional Development Authority (MMRDA) to coordinate the development of Mumbai through the cooperation of multiple municipal corporations that cover the larger city region and to connect these municipal corporations to a few key State-planning agencies for urban development.[731] The MMRDA extends over Navi Mumbai to connect planning of Mumbai's island city to the areas surrounding it, though the twin cities still have separate municipal corporations. Since its inception, the MMRDA has been tasked with creating a regional plan for what has become the Mumbai Metropolitan Region (MMR). The MMDRA is, at the city level, the most important agency in terms of connecting the various smaller municipal corporations under an overarching logic. The MMRDA also works to coordinate nationally and internationally funded infrastructure schemes. For example, the WB funds various transport projects in the metropolitan region and has identified the MMRDA as the key agency to cooperate with to realize these projects.[732] The regional plan, however, is tightly focused on the provision of services for the metropolitan region rather than an articulation of a vision for the city's future.[733]

Zérah illustrates in her work that multiple agencies overlap, and a number of State agencies exist above the municipal level and direct the city's development in ways that might diverge from the goals of the MMDRA.[734] Furthermore, the MMRDA has indicated that regional plans do not always adhere to the central government's goals for urban projects as presented in national five-year plans.[735] It is, therefore, not an institution where national and international

---

730 A. Ghosh et al., "A Comparative Overview of Urban Governance in Delhi, Hyderabad, Kolkata and Mumbai", in: J. Ruet and S. T. Lama-Rewal (eds.), *Governing India's Metropolises*, New Delhi: Routledge, 2009, pp. 24–54, at 33.

731 "Who we are", Mumbai Metropolitan Region Development Authority website, https://mmrda.maharashtra.gov.in/who-we-are (accessed 12 December 2015).

732 M. H. Zérah, "Une 'Vision Mumbai' pour transformer la ville ou la difficulté à (re)penser la gouvernance métropolitaine", *EchoGéo* 10 (2009), http://echogeo.revues.org/11389.

733 "Revision of Development Plan (2014–2034)", in: *Mumbai Reader'13*, Mumbai: Urban Design Research Institute, 2013, pp. 37–135.

734 Zérah, "Une 'Vision Mumbai.'"

735 N. Rao, *Reshaping City Governance: London, Mumbai, Kolkata, Hyderabad*, New York: Routledge, 2015, p. 133.

policies are simply channelled, but it selectively steers its own course using their models and funding. Kennedy and Zérah have argued that the lack of democracy and of a single planning agency at the metropolitan level results in a particular kind of urbanization process directed by an assemblage of State agencies as these agencies attempt to frame major Indian cities like Mumbai as global. The lack of accountability at the metropolitan level can account for the form that restructuring takes and the interest groups that are represented in the restructuring process.[736]

Planners at all administrative levels actively look towards other models and rhetorically use success stories from abroad to legitimize projects planned within India. For example, at the central government level, Indian policy makers became increasingly aware of development narratives that appeared effective such as the rise of the "Asian tigers" and the economic liberalization of China.[737] These models stress strong state intervention as well as government cooperation with business. In the documents of the Ministry of Shipping, central government ports like JNP are compared to Asian ports such as Singapore (ranked as the world's second largest container port), and each statistic is broken down with notes on how JNPT could better resemble Singapore's PSA.[738] Local attempts to develop Mumbai in accordance with narratives of global cities focus strongly on what are perceived to be Asian urban models that might suit the particular Indian context. Singapore, Shanghai, and sometimes Seoul are the "Asian global cities" that State officials, business elites, and consulting firms set as benchmarks for Mumbai to achieve. Shanghai in particular has been a main reference since 2003 when the chief minister of Maharashtra announced that he would "turn Mumbai into Shanghai", which soon translated into a key slogan for the national government's re-election campaign.[739] This 2003 remark was made following the release of a development plan proposed by business elites, the 2003 Vision Mumbai report, to turn Mumbai into a "world-class city."

Mumbai First is a think tank that represents corporate interests in the city. Its supporters include major Indian firms based in Mumbai as well as foreign

---

736 Zérah, "Une 'Vision Mumbai.'" This perspective is shared by K. C. Sivaramakrishnan, former secretary for Urban Development, Government of India, in: K. C. Sivaramakrishnan, "Megacity Governance", *Business Standard*, 8 March 2009, http://www.business-standard.com/article/opinion/k-c-sivaramakrishnan-megacity-governance-109030800019_1.html.

737 Nayar, *Geopolitics of Globalization*, p. 235.

738 "Maritime Agenda: 2010–2020", pp. 98–100.

739 X. Ren and L. Weinstein, "Urban Governance, Mega-Projects and Scalar Transformations in China and India", in: T. R. Samar, S. He and G. Chen (eds.), *Locating Right to the City in the Global South,* Florence: Taylor Francis, 2013, pp. 107–126, at 107.

corporations: Mahindra, Siemens, Blue Star, Philips, HDFC, and various subsidiaries of the Tata Group.[740] This think tank was set up in 1994 by the Bombay Chamber of Commerce and Industry in cooperation with the British Council. It was inspired by London First, a group that pursues London's redevelopment through public-private partnerships.[741] London First actively looks at city indices developed by, for example, Peter Taylor, and measures the city in relation to other global cities or world cities, labels used interchangeably by the group.[742] Rather than focusing on maintaining a certain status in city rankings like London First, Mumbai First focuses on moving Mumbai up in these rankings, creating a Mumbai that can be statistically abstracted and compared to other cities. Mumbai First aims to "canalize international knowledge and expertise" in order to "disseminate knowledge" to government planners to "transform Mumbai into a world-class city, one of the best places in which to live and do business in."[743] Rather than looking to London, the group is particularly focused on cities in Asia, especially Singapore, a city-state with a long history of engagement in India and, as discussed in Chapter 2, Mumbai's oldest muse.[744] Although the Vision Mumbai report was released in 2003, the plans gained momentum after Mumbai was identified by Peter Taylor's World Cities Research Network as an "Alpha" global city in 2008, up from Mumbai's "Alpha minus" ranking in 2000.[745]

Sassen identifies global cities as those that actively engage in competition on a national and a global scale.[746] However, the regional scale also appears important in discursively positioning the city on global indices. Mumbai is "Asian", which gives the city a competitive particularity/identity in global

---

740 "Patron Members", Mumbai First website, http://www.mumbaifirst.org/patrons.php (accessed 15 December 2015).

741 London First homepage, http://londonfirst.co.uk/ (accessed 10 December 2015). The homepage states: "We are a non-profit organisation with the mission to make London the best city in the world in which to do business. We aim to influence national and local government policies and investment decisions to support London's global competitiveness."

742 "London as a World City", London First website, http://londonfirst.co.uk/our-focus/londons-economic-development-strategy/london-as-a-world-city/ (accessed 10 December 2015).

743 "Vision and Mission", Mumbai First website, http://www.mumbaifirst.org/vision.php (accessed 10 December 2015).

744 F. bin Yahya, *Economic Cooperation between Singapore and India: An Alliance in the Making?*, London and New York: Routledge, 2008.

745 "World According to GaWC 2008", World Cities Research Network website, http://www.lboro.ac.uk/gawc/world2008t.html (accessed 8 December 2015); See also: P. Knox and P. J. Taylor (eds.), *World Cities in a World System*, Cambridge: Cambridge University Press, 1995. See discussion on ranking in second footnote: Zérah, "Une 'Vision Mumbai.'"

746 Sassen, *Global City*.

competition. The regional label allows the city to maintain "subpar" features that diverge from the perceived global city model that in effect validate the city's self-image as an authentic Asian version of this template. Another difference, Zérah notes, is that these plans to create a global city stem from the local political situation in which a Marathi nationalist political party, the Shiv Sena, prioritizes Marathis at the expense of others in what is otherwise a diverse city, characterized by multiple languages and religious practices.[747] Therefore, though nationalist parties may rise in reaction to the diversity present in global cities in other contexts, in effect, the idea of intensifying Mumbai's globality is also a reaction of Mumbai's business elites to nationalist identity politics at the local level. On most fronts, rather than being a global city that sociologists could identify through its existing features, Mumbai is in fact the location of various projects that seek to create a global city.

Mumbai First supports a comprehensive development plan for Mumbai, one that goes beyond the MMRDA plan for city services. The 2003 Vision Mumbai report was developed together with McKinsey, a global consultancy firm.[748] The report's preface highlights the "active participation" of city/State institutions in formulating the report, including the Brihanmumbai Municipal Corporation, the MMRDA, and the Government of Maharashtra. The authors of the report state:

> In the course of the study, we conducted interviews with more than 30 key stakeholders of Mumbai; we held more than ten brainstorming workshops with major government institutions, businesses and NGOs; and researched and developed case studies on five international and five domestic city transformations. We also built on the multiple reports already existing on the city. Based on work done by McKinsey in other parts of the world, we developed a framework and database for benchmarking Mumbai with other international cities.[749]

Swapna Bannerjee-Guha argues that this report, which claims to be built on consensus but in fact also draws extensively from McKinsey's other consulting projects, has influenced official city plans at the State level as well as the Jawaharlal Nehru National Urban Renewal Mission (JNNURM) at the central government level.[750]

---

747 Ghosh et al., "A Comparative Overview of Urban Governance", pp. 44–45.
748 McKinsey & Company, Inc., "Vision Mumbai: Transforming Mumbai into a World-Class City", 2003, http://www.visionmumbai.org/aboutusdocs/McKinseyReport.pdf.
749 "Vision Mumbai", p. vii.
750 S. Banerjee-Guha, "Revisiting Accumulation by Dispossession: Neoliberalising Mumbai", in: S. Bannerjee-Guha (ed.), *Accumulation by Dispossession: Transformative Cities in the New Global Order*, New Delhi, Thousand Oaks, CA: Sage Publications, 2010, pp. 198–226, at 210.

In 2005, the central government launched the JNNURM, the first major comprehensive effort by the central government to invest in urban infrastructure.[751] The mission, run by the Ministry of Urban Development between 2005 and 2014, prioritized State and municipal level reforms that would encourage planned urbanization. Through this reform, 50,000 crores rupees were allocated for investment in India's cities. The plan facilitated a shift in how government bodies saw cities as sites of economic growth, evidenced by a change in the central government's promotional rhetoric for urban development from "livable Indian cities" to "world class cities", mirroring the Vision Mumbai language.[752] Though Bannerjee-Guha analyses the implemented changes through the lens of neoliberal reforms and privatization, the renewal mission also represents an extension of central government oversight of local planning rather than a "scaling back" of the state or its "unbundling."[753] At the same time, the State of Maharashtra and local business groups had already sponsored comprehensive planning reports for Mumbai that went beyond JNNURM mandates.[754]

The Vision Mumbai report, which advocates a restructuring of the entire city block by block, looks to US city models with strong mayors and city councils as possible solutions to Mumbai's woes.[755] This McKinsey report suggests that the chief minister of Maharashtra "play the role" of mayor of Mumbai in the sense that this position would begin to combine agencies under more stringent and cooperative oversight. This plan follows Sassen's global city concept, which suggests to policy makers that a strong mayor and a city council system, as found in US cities, can implement tax advantages. These features are a necessary prerequisite in achieving what David Harvey calls "entrepreneurialism" as a strategy to locate cities within "global circuits", rather than entrepreneurialism as an effect of those circuits.[756] Instead, entrepreneurialism – a focus on the economic growth and management of a city – is found in the central and State levels of government rather than at the municipal level.[757] Therefore, various actors within India pursue state rescaling as an offensive strategy to connect particular spaces to global markets. In line with creating

751 Jawaharlal Nehru National Urban Renewal Mission website, http://jnnurm.nic.in (accessed 19 December 2015).

752 Bannerjee-Guha, "Revisiting Accumulation by Dispossession", p. 205.

753 Ibid.; Kennedy, *Politics of Economic Restructuring.*

754 These efforts also went beyond the 2014 central government smart city initiative mandates.

755 "Vision Mumbai", pp. 23, 30.

756 Harvey, "Managerialism to Entrepreneurialism"; Sassen, "Locating Cities on Global Circuits."

757 Kennedy, *Politics of Economic Restructuring*, p. 132.

entrepreneurialism, the report also advocates the creation of an "empowered committee" that would meet regularly to coordinate the multiple State agencies in charge of the city's development while also giving a voice to select business groups associated with Mumbai First.[758] According to the aforementioned comparative views of urban governance within India, urban planning is generally a top-down process directed by the State. In Mumbai, the plans of business elites are endorsed by the State, which allows local business elites to become important actors in directing the city's development.[759]

Following the release of the Vision Mumbai report in 2003, steps were taken by the State of Maharashtra, Mumbai First, the Cities Alliance (a global non-profit dedicated to the development of cities and slum elimination),[760] the WB, and USAID to set up the Mumbai Transformation Support Unit. The aim of this organization was to direct the numerous agencies in charge of the city's development, provide a central place for knowledge distribution about the various projects underway, and identify a long-term development plan for the municipal region.[761] Two years later, under the direction of the Mumbai Transformation Support Unit, the Empowered Committee was constituted, which gave numerous municipal, State, and central government agencies (e.g., port trusts) a place to regularly discuss the city's development plans with business elites and celebrities, giving corporations and select individuals the ability or at least visibility to influence city development plans.[762]

The Mumbai Transformation Support Unit issued a concept plan for the MMR. The city is now a region of 20.75 million people and spans 4,355 km (comprising 40 planning authorities). The Vision Mumbai document, though not explicitly cited by the new comprehensive plan, seems to have been a catalyst as the Mumbai Transformation Support Unit website's domain name is visionmumbai.org. This plan is much more extensive than the MMRDA's plan for 2014–2034, which mainly dealt with the provision of services. It is also more detailed than the Vision Mumbai report; it is a business and growth vision for the city region.

---

758 "Vision Mumbai", pp. 30–32.

759 J. Ruet, "Thinking the Delhi, Hyderabad, Kolkata, and Mumbai Experience: Emerging Modes of Urban Governance and State Intervention", in: Ruet and Lama-Rewal (eds.), *Governing India's Metropolises*, pp. 270–303, at 272.

760 Cities Alliance homepage, http://www.citiesalliance.org/ (accessed 11 December 2015).

761 "About Us", Mumbai Transformation Support Unit website, http://www.visionmumbai.org/aboutus.aspx (accessed 11 December 2015).

762 The minutes of these monthly meetings are published on the Mumbai Transformation Support Unit webpage: "Documents", Mumbai Transformation Support Unit website, http://www.visionmumbai.org/document.aspx (accessed 11 December 2015).

There have been several drafts of the plan, but by 2011, it began to entail a comprehensive restructuring of the city that seeks specifically to frame the MMR as a global city:

> To launch MMR into the global arena, in the short term, the existing financial centres at Nariman Point and BKC [Bandra-Kurla Complex, a business park] would have to be revitalized. This is not enough to position Mumbai as a preferred gateway of South Asia; a step further is to develop a grand new business centre of notable image. New land could be created in the harbor bay east of South Mumbai for the CBD [central business district] to expand. As a result, the consolidated CBD will look even more central in the overall MMR, easily accessible from all directions through an extensive transportation network to the north, south and east.[763]

The report uses extensive benchmarking to position and rank Mumbai among global cities, particularly those in East Asia. The plan proposes a comprehensive restructuring of the entire city as well as the creation of new land in the harbour. As the aforementioned quote illustrates, the concept plan is visual in that the business district at the south end of the city can be visually repositioned as a true city centre that will also be spatially central within a city region connected by bridges and water taxies.

These initiatives by corporate think tanks and the State government, in reference to central government initiatives, envision a larger Mumbai than the immediate city. Not only has the scale of planning expanded to include all tiers of government, but also the city itself has begun to extend beyond its own boundaries.[764] The city alone contributes approximately 40 per cent of the State of Maharashtra's and 4 per cent of India's gross domestic product.[765] Like the Vision Mumbai report, which notes the importance of infrastructure planning like linking SEZ projects to the port trusts, roads, railways, and the hinterlands, the new plan focuses even more heavily on coordinating infrastructure initiatives.[766] What has emerged from these concerted efforts to rethink the city of Mumbai as a single metropolitan region rather than a series of disconnected municipal corporations is a plan that envisions restructuring the entire city as well as its regional and global position.

---

763 Mumbai Metropolitan Region, Final Regional Concept Plan Report, May 2011, p. 10, http://www.visionmumbai.org/images/projects/concept%20plan%20report_06May2011-final.pdf.

764 Zérah, "Gouvernance métropolitaine."

765 Ghosh et al., "A Comparative Overview of Urban Governance", p. 28.

766 "Vision Mumbai", p. 19.

The "notable image" this new Mumbai will take is in fact based on the generic waterfront redevelopment projects that create high-end residences, museums, and entertainment venues along former port and industrial shorelines, found especially in Europe and the US.[767] The development plan focuses on three possible scenarios, the most ambitious of which is "the city of islands" development concept, which the report mentions is the preferred option. This concept envisions not only the redevelopment of the eastern shoreline but also the creation of new islands through land reclamation within the harbour. These islands would connect Mumbai to the mainland and link the entertainment and business centres with additional bridges. This "city of islands" concept aims to "re-create Mumbai's legacy by crafting new islands for the expansion of the inner city area."[768] It is within that context that, like many other infrastructure projects, the Mumbai "city of islands" project seeks to capitalize on the city's legacy as an important port city while also potentially removing the port.

The "city of islands" references the city's unique past as an archipelago. Ironically, filling in the islands had been an important driver of the city's and port's growth during the colonial period. The "city of islands" project is likely supported by the Government of the Netherlands, which has successfully won bids for Dutch companies to undertake similar projects in other parts of the world, for example, Eko Atlantic off the coast of Lagos, Nigeria as well as a land reclamation project in Jakarta.[769] Both projects reassemble the "city of islands" in that they use land reclamation to produce elite spaces of leisure and commerce within otherwise overcrowded cities. Land reclamation that will bridge Mumbai to the mainland is part of a model growth trajectory pursued in other island-city contexts as strategies to "win" land and investment.[770] The Dutch government markets land reclamation as environmentally friendly. A report advocating reclamation for Mumbai prepared by the Dutch consulate describes the technique as "building with nature", that is, the "(re)creation of nature" through the land reclamation process, which can be understood as an

767 See, for example: Mah, *Port Cities and Global Legacies.*

768 "Concept Plan for MMR", p. 4–2.

769 "Eko Atlantic Nigeria", Royal HaskonigDHV website, http://www.royalhaskoningdhv.com/en-gb/projects/eko-atlantic-nigeria/103 (accessed 29 December 2015); "Reclaiming Jakart's Future- Pluit City, Jakarta", Royal HaskonigDHV website, http://www.royalhaskoningdhv.com/en-gb/projects/s-projects-s-pluit-city-land-development-indonesia/2136 (accessed 29 December 2015).

770 M. Sparke et al., "Triangulating the Borderless World: Geographies of Power in the Indonesia-Malaysia-Singapore Growth Triangle", *Transactions of the Institute of British Geographers* 29 (2004) 4, pp. 485–498.

assumption that nature is only what one can see above water.[771] Dutch firms have already been employed to research the possibility of situating Navi Mumbai's planned airport on a reclaimed island instead of land.[772] Creating land may be less of a legal hassle than acquiring land from existing owners, despite strict environmental clearances. The Dutch consulate and subsidiaries of Dutch firms are supporters of Mumbai First.[773] Mumbai First's chairman presented the plan at the 2014 World Cities Summit in Singapore,[774] a biannual event hosted by the think tank, Centre for Livable Cities Singapore.[775]

The attempts in this plan to recreate this island city legacy ironically include the removal of MPT. In contrast to the hopeful high rankings of Mumbai in the global cities index, Mumbai Port ranks poorly in comparison to other "global ports":

> In 1994–1995, Rotterdam alone carried 288 MT [metric tons], Singapore alone 274 MT and Shanghai alone 165 MT. As a matter of fact, during the same period, Mumbai port handled the highest cargo of 32 MT in India which was insignificant compared to other global ports. A comparison of India's port traffic and openness with those of China makes it clear why China won the first round of liberalisation.[776]

Mumbai Port has become a pretext for the issues of the whole city, and getting rid of the port is meant to be the remedy that will push Mumbai onto the global stage. This port may become, like many other former imperial ports, a site of leisure and consumption.[777] In Mumbai, this proposal has been put forward

---

771 Consulate General of the Kingdom of the Netherlands, Mumbai, "Building with Nature: Where Economic Development and Care for the Environment Go Hand in Hand", 8 November 2013. This report was sent to me by the Consul General of the Kingdom of the Netherlands in Mumbai, Geoffrey van Leeuwen, following our meeting at the consulate in January 2014.

772 "Government eyes reclaimed land from the sea for Mumbai's new airport", *Economic Times*, 16 November 2013, http://articles.economictimes.indiatimes.com/2013-11-16/news/44138236_1_navi-mumbai-new-airport-reclaiming-land.

773 The Consulate General of the Kingdom of the Netherlands funded a conference and book project on mutual learning between the Netherlands and Mumbai in 2012, which was presented to Mumbai First: P. Poiesz, G. J. Scholte, S. V. Ghandi, *Learning from Mumbai: Practicing Architecture in Urban India*, Rotterdam, 2013.

774 "Narider Nayar", World Cities Summit website, http://www.worldcitiessummit.com.sg/whos-coming/narinder-nayar (accessed 22 December 2015).

775 This think tank, set up at the behest of the government of Singapore, appears to act as a consultancy for urban planning, which it channels through its biannual conference: Centre for Livable Cities Singapore website, http://www.clc.gov.sg/ (accessed 22 December 2015).

776 B. Ghosh and P. De, "Indian Ports and Globalisation: Grounding Economics in Geography", *Economic and Political Weekly* 36 (2001) 34, pp. 3271–3283, at 3274.

777 Mah, *Port Cities and Global Legacies*.

under the guise of (elite) citizen access to public space and to the waterfront. It includes themes of reconnecting the public to the waterfront and (manmade) nature.[778] City planners hope to shift the port's activities to JNPT as well as to a new port project just south of Mumbai, Rewas. However, since MPT is not owned by the city or the State, these plans cannot be enforced.

Citizen groups and architects advocate the opening up of port trust land, but they remain sceptical that it will be for public benefit. Mumbai's cotton mills, which had been a main driver of the city's economy since the 1860s, closed following a series of strikes in the early 1980s. The mill lands comprised 600 acres, approximately 400 of which were meant to go to the city but instead were used for commercial interests.[779] The port trust lands are much larger, representing approximately 1,860 acres of opportunity for many public and private interest groups.[780] Planners maintain that the port trust is the only possibility to gain access to open space in the city. Furthermore, prominent local architects like Rahul Mehrotra concede that access to the city's waterfront is crucial within the larger project of connecting Mumbai to Navi Mumbai and thereby Navi Mumbai's (future) SEZs.[781]

Ports and Zones: Reworking Mumbai's City Space

Port and zone projects play a crucial role in plans to rank Mumbai globally. Zones can externally connect the city. They can also remove the hindrances to being a part of a state in general or the Indian state in particular. From the subnational State's perspective, zones are useful as vehicles for infrastructure development. Several of the proposed plans seek to re-establish the city region as a great port city, while also transforming the historical port of Mumbai into a space of leisure and consumption. Many of these plans, which connect to zone projects, are used to position Mumbai in terms of global city rankings but are not concerned about where specific connections through zones and ports will

778 H. Burte and M. Krishnankutty, "On the Edge: Planning, Describing and Imagining the Seaside Edge of Mumbai", in: *Mumbai Reader'07*, Mumbai: Urban Design Research Institute, 2008, pp. 356–367.

779 D'Monte, *Ripping the Fabric*; S. Nair, "The Paradox of Mumbai Mills Land Sales", in: *Mumbai Reader'13*, Mumbai: Urban Design Research Institute, 2013, pp. 420–425.

780 D. D'Monte, "Old Port Trust, Lands on the Dock", in: *Mumbai Reader' 08*, Mumbai: Urban Design Research Institute, 2009, pp. 204–209, at 204–205.

781 R. Mehrotra, "Remaking Mumbai", in: *Mumbai Reader' 07*, Mumbai: Urban Design Research Institute, 2008, pp. 392–399, at 397. See also: *A Study of the Eastern Waterfront of Mumbai*, Mumbai: Urban Design Research Institute, 2005.

lead. Unlike the clearer policies developed by the central government for Mumbai's JNPT and the INSTC that envision specific transport and trade connections, these State and city projects are about global appearances rather than global connections. Some of the same corporations that have a role in the empowered committee have designed SEZ projects of their own. These SEZ projects are linked to the official plans in areas around Navi Mumbai, the harbour space, and ultimately to one of the private port projects meant to offset the (proposed) future loss of MPT.

Both the conservative concept plan and the ambitious "city of islands" concept plan for Mumbai's development include a port that, as of yet, only exists in planning: Rewas Port. Rewas Port has been identified in the concept plan as the private port just south of Mumbai that would offset the loss of MPT, which would, according to these plans only, become a site of leisure. The upcoming Rewas Port project is majority owned (55 per cent) by Reliance Logistics and Ports Private Limited, part of the Reliance Group, as well as Jai Corp Limited, which has a 10 per cent stake in the project. Reliance is owned by Mukesh Ambani, known as the wealthiest man in India. Jai Corp, which operates in various sectors including infrastructure development and manufacturing, is run by Ambani's close associate, Anand Jain. Minority partners on the project include the Maharashtra Maritime Board with an 11 per cent stake, and Amma Lines, once the majority shareholder, with a 24 per cent stake.[782]

Rewas Port was originally announced as a 2,850 hectare SEZ in 2001.[783] In 2002, the land surrounding Rewas Port was earmarked for the Reliance sponsored Maha Mumbai SEZ project, a multi-product SEZ of about 10,000 hectares.[784] Just north of this zone was the planned Navi Mumbai SEZ, co-sponsored by the parastatal CIDCO. All three SEZ projects – Rewas SEZ, Maha Mumbai SEZ, and Navi Mumbai SEZ – were sponsored by Reliance or Jai Corp

782 "Promoters", Rewas Ports Limited website, http://www.rewasports.com/promoters.html (accessed 16 December 2015); P. Manoj, "Centre considers redefining Mumbai port's limits to allow Reliance port's right of way, *Live Mint*, 13 January 2015, http://www.livemint.com/Politics/jW5PdLJ7xz09EBE4wEWd5H/Centre-considers-redefining-Mumbai-ports-limits-to-allow-Re.html.

783 K. Ghoge, "Reliance SEZ in Raigad gets one-year extension", *Hindustan Times*, 22 June 2011, http://www.hindustantimes.com/mumbai/reliance-sez-in-raigad-gets-one-year-extension/story-QrNnJmttzo8kiXRlQ2UOpM.html.

784 R. Mujumdar and B. Menezes, "Maharashtra: Institutional Politics and the Framing of Resistance", in: Jenkins, Kennedy and Mukhopadhyay (eds.), *Power, Policy, and Protest*, pp. 239–271, at 247. Another news report states the project was 5,000 hectares. The Ministry of Commerce lowered the ceiling on SEZ size, which could explain the discrepancy. See: Ghoge, "Reliance SEZ in Raigad."

as private SEZs or in conjunction with a State co-developer. They were three separate projects that met the central government's regulations on land ceilings for SEZs (at the time they were announced) as well as rules stipulating that zones must fall within a contiguous space. They differed in name, but were planned simultaneously and were endorsed by the state.

The Rewas Port SEZ and Maha Mumbai SEZ projects were both cancelled when Reliance was unable to acquire the land necessary in the time set by the Ministry of Commerce's board of approvals. The board of approvals is appointed by a State representative and representatives from various central government ministries, including finance, commerce, and urban development.[785] This board has some leeway in deciding which projects will be approved so long as developers follow the ever-shifting SEZ rules. Rohit Mujumdar and Benita Menezes documented the contentious process of land acquisition for the Maha Mumbai SEZ project, finding stark resistance from villagers to give up their land.[786] The project's various opposition groups launched a series of court cases against the project in the early 2000s. By 2009, the cases moved to the supreme court, which ruled that the Maha Mumbai SEZ project did not acquire the land necessary for the project in the time allotted by the SEZ regulations and the board of approvals. As a result, the regulations of the Ministry of Commerce stipulated that the State denotify the project in 2011. As Kennedy claims, the idea of state rescaling is not merely a matter of empowering States to play a larger role in their own economic growth. Their actions are also tightly regulated by the central government.[787]

Rewas Port is still set to be developed after the SEZ title was dropped, but not as originally anticipated. Denotification of the SEZ means the developers needed to obtain permission from the Maharashtra Ministry of Shipping rather than the central government's Ministry of Commerce. The Ministry of Commerce has not been the only hindrance to this project. This port plans to share an approach channel with MPT, which requested large sums to grant Rewas access to the channel.[788] Plans for Rewas are slowly moving forward, but the prognoses and updates on the port's importance for global Mumbai are far from reality. As of yet, the port has not been built and the latest information states that

---

785 Kennedy, *Politics of Economic Restructuring*, p. 86.

786 Mujumdar and Menezes, "Maharashtra."

787 Kennedy, *Politics of Economic Restructuring*.

788 "Reliance Industries Rewas Port: Nitin Gadkari promises to resolve issues in a month", *Economic Times*, 7 June 2015, http://economictimes.indiatimes.com/industry/transportation/shipping-/-transport/reliance-industries-rewas-port-nitin-gadkari-promises-to-resolve-issues-in-a-month/articleshow/47574652.cms.

MPT and JNPT, in combination with the Maharashtra Maritime Board, will likely take over the project from Reliance, thus entirely shifting the significance of this port as a private venture that competes with Mumbai's port trusts.

There are other SEZs already operating in Mumbai. For example, SEEPZ is still in operation. Maharashtra's development commissioner is located there, making SEEPZ the State's main administrative zone. Of the three major zones for MMR, the Navi Mumbai SEZ is, like Rewas Port, being converted after not taking off. This particular project is being carried out by a special purpose vehicle: Jain's Dronagiri Infrastructure Private Limited and Ambani's SKIL Infrastructure Limited have a 74 per cent stake in the project while CIDCO has a 26 per cent stake. This zone is actually a series of nodes rather than a single zone. Its plan resembles the nodal development of Navi Mumbai. Recently, the government has started the SEZ denotification process and announced the zone's conversion to an integrated industrial area. The total area comprises 2,140 hectares along the mainland, neighbouring Navi Mumbai, MIDC industrial estates, JNPT, and the harbour.[789] The number of nodes are increasing as parcelled areas become administratively smaller, while the project remains quite large.[790] These nodes are all strategically situated adjacent to existing infrastructure such as freight routes but also State-planned infrastructure projects: the Mumbai Trans Harbour Link that will connect roughly JNPT to the MPT's Ballard Estate; the future Navi Mumbai Airport; and a coastal road along the mainland side of the harbour.[791] The Navi Mumbai SEZ had faced numerous delays and negative press coverage. Despite these setbacks, the Ministry of Commerce's board of approvals had granted numerous extensions to implement the project. However, like so many other SEZs in India and Maharashtra in particular, the promising project fell through, as its recent denotification and its potential transition to an "industrial integrated area" has made visible.[792]

Part of the problem, according to developers in an extension application to the board of approvals, has been the shifting environment of SEZs in

789 Navi Mumbai Special Economic Zone website, http://www.nmsez.com/index.html (accessed 16 January 2016).

790 K. Ghoge, "CM asks SEZ developers to begin projects in 3 months", *Hindustan Times*, 16 August 2015, http://www.hindustantimes.com/mumbai/cm-asks-sez-developers-to-begin-projects-in-3-months/story-GcmbSbbJXe7gmbZaLeYjTI.html.

791 Navi Mumbai Special Economic Zone website, http://www.nmsez.com/index.html (accessed 16 January 2016).

792 "Investors not keen on SEZs anymore; 57 to surrender zones", *Hindu Business Line*, 10 February 2015, http://www.thehindubusinessline.com/economy/investors-not-keen-on-sezs-anymore-57-to-surrender-zones/article6878327.ece?ref=relatedNews.

India.[793] The SEZ policy has been constantly renegotiated since it was enacted based on developers' experiences and notably the infighting among governmental ministries. The Ministry of Finance and the central bank were against the tax breaks stipulated by the SEZ Act due to fears of lost revenue.[794] Notably, the act caused consternation "even [in] the International Monetary Fund."[795] The minimum alternate tax and dividend distribution tax were then reapplied to SEZs. The maximum size of zones has been reduced from 10,000 to 5,000 hectares; and the minimum processing area within the zone was raised from only 25 to 50 per cent.[796] Neither the central government nor Maharashtra have been uniform in their support for the SEZ policy.

The 2011 concept plan for Mumbai, which proposes replacing MPT by shifting activity to JNPT and eventually to Rewas Port, is complicated by the fact that, unlike in many of the Western contexts this plan resembles, the MPT is owned by the central government and has shown little interest in shutting down its operations. Many ports in Europe and the US have been privatized but, especially in the case of the US, are regulated by subnational State or city port authorities, even if privately run. When a city or subnational State decides to relocate port facilities based on a city-restructuring plan, it has the authority to do so. In Mumbai, the MPT is governed by the central government's Ministry of Shipping. As a trust, this central government body operates independently while subject to Ministry of Shipping regulations. The central government must also have an interest in shifting the port's facilities. It seems this had been the case with the creation of JNPT across the harbour, but the fact that it became a separate facility from MPT meant that it also became a competing port trust rather than an extension of MPT's services, leading to the expansion of both properties rather than the elimination of one.

MPT has been in the process of expanding its services through the construction of offshore container terminals. The State government has opposed the expansion of the port, and it also sought to use some of the trust's land to rehouse slum dwellers displaced by the State's infrastructure projects in the city, namely, a plan to transform Dharavi, Mumbai's famous slum on prime real

793 A. Sen, "One year extension for Navi Mumbai's three IT/ITES SEZs", *Hindu Business Line*, 10 January 2016, http://www.thehindubusinessline.com/companies/one-year-extension-for-navi-mumbais-three-itites-sezs/article8089304.ece.

794 Kennedy, *Politics of Economic Restructuring*, p. 88.

795 J. Johnson, "Attack on India's economic zone plan", *Financial Times*, 24 September 2006, http://www.ft.com/intl/cms/s/0/151b19c0-4bfa-11db-90d2-0000779e2340.html#axzz3xQAYTOzA.

796 The board of approvals, however, may disregard the 5,000-hectare ceiling at its discretion: Kennedy, *Politics of Economic Restructuring*, p. 87.

estate, into a business district.[797] The MPT has no intention of allowing slum dwellers to resettle on its land estate, which it uses to lease out space to firms. Furthermore, not only is MPT unwilling to allow its land to be used to rehouse slum dwellers, it is removing slum "encroachments" on its land to preserve the image that the land estate, a colonial remnant from the Elphinstone Land and Press Company, is still necessary for the port's operations.[798] These evictions have been particularly controversial because those living on central government land are not entitled to the resettlement rights given to slum dwellers on State or city land.[799] The fact that this largest land parcel in the city belongs to a central government institution is contentious.

There is some indication that the State and central government are beginning to move in a similar direction regarding the usefulness of MPT land. MPT, a Singapore planning authority, and the central government's Ministry of Shipping have laid out plans to turn large portions of its land into a tourist attraction while shifting some of the port's activities elsewhere.[800] The State government has plans to utilize the majority of the MPT's 1,800 acres, though at least 680 acres, approximately 36 per cent, have been leased to various private and public entities, all of which would need to be compensated.[801] The MPT redevelopment plan has been with the Ministry of Shipping for approximately one year without being rejected or accepted. The plan may very well be accepted: the latest reports from the Ministry of Shipping indicate that port trusts should shift some of their old facilities such as colonial-era light houses to tourist attractions and redevelop their land estates to encourage tourism. Much of the recommendations are based on the MPT's latest plan to shift towards tourism.[802] Since 2016, the Ballard Estate, the otherwise sleepy neighbourhood near MP, hosts regular festivals during

---

797 D'Monte, "Old Port Trust", p. 206; Xuefei and Weinstein, "Urban Governance, Mega-Projects."

798 The MPT has been demolishing encroachments since November 2015, though it has in the past denied that encroachments existed.

799 A. Sarkar, "MbPT land oustees spend chilly nights in the open", *Indian Express*, 14 December 2015, http://indianexpress.com/article/cities/mumbai/mbpt-land-oustees-spend-chilly-nights-in-the-open/.

800 M. K. Mehta, "Govt to free up Mumbai port land for development", *Times of India*, 4 June 2015, http://timesofindia.indiatimes.com/good-governance/centre/Govt-to-free-up-Mumbai-port-land-for-development/articleshow/47537120.cms.

801 M. Phadke, "A year on, report to develop Port Trust land gathers dust", *Indian Express*, 19 November 2015, http://indianexpress.com/article/cities/mumbai/a-year-on-report-to-develop-port-trust-land-gathers-dust/.

802 Ministry of Shipping, Government of India, "Vision for Coastal Shipping, Tourism and Regional Development", 2015, pp. 57–65, http://shipping.nic.in/showfile.php?lid=1959.

the cooler, dry months to encourage entertainment in an otherwise vacant part of the city during weekends, a first sign of this area's transition.

Satellites for the Satellites?

Plans for Mumbai have shifted frequently over the last two decades. New initiatives have taken hold or given new life to previous policies since 2014. Which plans will become reality – for Mumbai, its ports, and its zones – has not yet been determined. Many plans are ambitious, and some appear to dominate the news cycle before fading away.

Mirroring the famous slogan for China's Shenzhen, "Uran, a fishing-village turned special economic zone, will acquire a new status soon – that of a city."[803] JNPT SEZ and the (cancelled) Navi Mumbai SEZ's Dronagiri node are located on the Uran peninsula. The 2013 plan to create a "third Mumbai", as the project is colloquially referred to, was drafted by the Maharashtra Housing and Area Development Authority (MHADA). According to Maharashtra's minister for housing, "The development of a third city in Uran was being considered in view of the constraints faced by Mumbai and Navi Mumbai. MHADA will put in place the necessary infrastructure along with other government agencies over 10 sq km, but the private sector would have to come into the picture to make the 100-sq km city a reality."[804] In order to link this third city with the first, it would be integrated into the MMR to strengthen its "state-of-the art transport infrastructure" by connecting it with the Navi Mumbai airport and the Mumbai Trans Harbour Link, the proposed bridge linking the island with the mainland.[805] Once the transharbour link is implemented, the harbour area becomes the centre of the Mumbai metropolitan region, which then justifies encorporating Uran (until now, disconnected from Mumbai) into the region.

This project for Uran is part of the aforementioned plans to increase the size of Mumbai in conjunction with business interests. After the 2013 announcement, little has been written about the project, nor are there plans on the MHADA website. Whether or not Uran will become a "third Mumbai", it will likely feature more industry to link up with JNPT's expansion, as more recent city plans indicate. It is, however, not the only initiative to create a satellite. As

803 S. Jog, "Maharashtra plans another city, 50 km off Mumbai", *Business Standard*, 4 October 2013, http://www.business-standard.com/article/economy-policy/maharashtra-plans-another-city-50-km-off-mumbai-113100300844_1.html.
804 Ibid.
805 Ibid.

Mumbai Port possibly shifts to entertainment and leisure, JNPT, MPT's original satellite port, is planning a satellite port of its own beyond Rewas. The tabula rasa idea is extended in both cases – as blank spaces to start fresh, regardless of the fact that both projects will likely cause displacements as well as environmental harm.[806]

JNPT plans to construct a satellite port at Wadhwan along Maharashtra's northern border with Gujarat.[807] The site had originally been earmarked in the late 1990s for a minor port, which would be the forefront of the State of Maharashtra's port privatization scheme.[808] P&O (now DP World), which was awarded the contract to develop the port, was unable to acquire the land for the project due to fierce opposition by local residents and environmental activists.[809] The port is planned as a landlord port where private firms will be invited to operate container terminals. The project will mainly be based on reclaimed land, which is foreseen to ease the burden of acquiring land. Nevertheless, the president of the Anti-Wadhwan Port Project Action Committee has already pledged to protest the project.

The most striking feature of the project is that it is a joint venture by JNPT, which will hold a 74 per cent stake, and the Maharashtra Maritime Board, which is owned by the State. Typically, the Maharashtra Maritime Board has restricted itself to maximum 11 per cent stake in any private minor port project, but in negotiations with the central government's Ministry of Shipping, 26 per cent was the lowest equity option for its participation in the joint venture.[810] It is not clear in this case what type of port it will become. If it remains a pure satellite port of JNPT, how does the partial ownership by a State agency play a role in its administrative structure? Will it remain under JNPT's authority as

---

806 K. N. Thakur, "Project Report on Impact of Special Economic Zone (SEZ) on Birds in Uran, Maharashtra", Report for the Mumbai University and WWF India, 2010, http://awsassets.wwfindia.org/downloads/impact_of_special_economic_zone.pdf; Aamir Khan, "New JNPT terminal may plunge 'delicate' coastline into danger", *Indian Express*, 21 December 2015, http://indianexpress.com/article/cities/mumbai/new-jnpt-terminal-may-plunge-delicate-coastline-into-danger/.

807 M. Gadgil and P. R. Sanjai, "JNPT to build Rs 10,000 crore satellite port at Wadhwan", *Live Mint*, 22 December 2015, http://www.livemint.com/Companies/7K7QoESH7c0VCamaHQIiCL/JNPT-tobuild-Rs10000-crore-satellite-port-at-Wadhwan.html.

808 H.E. Haralambides and R. Behrens, "Port Restructuring in a Global Economy: An Indian Perspective", *International Journal of Transport Economics* 27 (2000) 1, pp. 19–39, at 35.

809 Gadgil and Sanjai, "JNPT."

810 S. Jog, "Maharashtra Maritime Board, JNPT plan all-weather port at Wadhwan", *Business Standard*, 19 May 2015, http://www.business-standard.com/article/companies/headline-maharashtra-maritime-board-jnpt-plan-all-weather-port-at-wadhwan-115051800481_1.html.

part of JNPT, a major port? In any case, the port project would increase Maharashtra's share of India's maritime trade, and the port intends to connect by rail to the Delhi Mumbai Industrial Corridor.[811] Both the central government and the State government have a stake in the project's future. Furthermore, if India's ports "corporatize" as has been discussed for many years, JNPT could own and operate numerous ports within India and abroad, as seen in its first foreign venture in Iran discussed in Chapter 6.[812]

Some of the State's new foreign partners are also looking to set up "satellites" within the State's zones. Though India's SEZ policy has mainly been geared towards Indian investors, the State of Maharashtra has recently begun to cater to foreign firms. It met with a Chinese delegation in 2014 to discuss a Chinese industrial park in Maharashtra. Japanese firms have also looked to establish operations in Maharashtra.[813] Their entry has been carefully directed by the State. The Government of Maharashtra, through its agencies like MIDC, can direct foreign investors to specific locations within Maharashtra. Since the SEZ policy began, about 70 SEZ projects in which the developer had acquired the land withdrew their projects. The failed SEZ projects developed by private firms in Maharashtra that used land obtained by the State through eminent domain policies are required to return the land to the State, creating what is known as a land bank, or a reserve of State-owned land.[814] MIDC now has land at the ready for foreign investors.

The largest deal in recent years with a foreign investor has come not from a Chinese or Japanese firm but from Foxconn, a Taiwanese firm known as the largest electronics manufacturing company, which produces well-known electronics items such as Apple's iPhone and Amazon's Kindle. Foxconn negotiated the deal directly with Maharashtra's chief minister and plans to set up additional facilities in other States.[815] Foxconn is the largest private employer in China and perhaps in the world with over one million employees. It operates all over eastern China

811 Gadgil and Sanjai, "JNPT."

812 J. Mukul and A. Paladhi, "Corporatisation of ports back on track", *Business Standard*, 9 September 2014, http://www.business-standard.com/article/economy-policy/corporatisation-of-ports-back-on-track-114090800978_1.html.

813 "India makes pitch for Chinese investments in Special Economic Zones", *Economic Times*, 15 October 2014, http://articles.economictimes.indiatimes.com/2014-10-15/news/55059512_1_indian-embassy-indian-ambassador-special-economic-zones.

814 "Cancelled SEZs in Maharashtra will have to return government land", *Economic Times*, 22 November 2015, http://articles.economictimes.indiatimes.com/2015-11-22/news/68484435_1_sezs-special-economic-zones-government-land.

815 "Foxconn to 'Make in India', will invest $5bn in Maharashtra", *Hindustan Times*, 8 August 2015, http://www.hindustantimes.com/business/foxconn-to-make-in-india-will-invest-5bn-in-maharashtra/story-8NNM9g8wqF5Nsj7XBgRxxL.html.

but is most known for its Shenzhen SEZ factory, where a series of suicides on its Shenzhen "campus" sparked worldwide attention in 2011.[816]

In 2015, Foxconn signed a memorandum of understanding with Maharashtra regarding investments in the region. Foxconn reportedly will "cooperate" with local Indian firms and Mumbai's Indian Institute for Technology.[817] It plans to establish facilities over 1,500 acres (over 6 km) "somewhere between Mumbai and Pune" in order to take advantage of connections through Mumbai.[818] Just as JETRO intends to make India its hub for the "west market", the head of Foxconn in India announced that "these [West Asia and Africa] are huge markets and are logistically cheaper than supplying from China", and India is meant to sustain the firm's entry to these markets.[819] Foxconn is an intermediary, working under contract for specific electronics firms. Whether or not Foxconn's contractors are behind this shift to India is not clear.

The 1,500-acre zone has not yet been developed, despite the large announcement. The latest reports indicate that Foxconn will instead establish a unit in JNPT's SEZ to better enable their exports to the West Asian and African markets. In so doing, they plan to connect to the numerous other initiatives to reposition India and Mumbai in particular as the gateway to African and Middle Eastern markets for East Asian companies.[820] Bach and Easterling have called Navi Mumbai a zone based on Mumbai's double – implying it functions for Mumbai the way Shenzhen has functioned for Hong Kong. Instead, one of Shenzhen's largest employers is establishing its operations in a Navi Mumbai-based SEZ.

Conclusion

Much of what has been discussed in this chapter is elite talk of forming a "global city." Plenty of plans have failed to materialize, have been postponed,

816 J. Johnson, "1 Million Workers. 90 Million iPhones. 17 Suicides. Who's to Blame?", *Wired Magazine*, 28 February 2011, http://www.wired.com/2011/02/ff_joelinchina/.
817 "Foxconn to set up production unit in Maharashtra for $5 bn", *Business Standard*, 8 August 2015, http://www.business-standard.com/article/companies/foxconn-to-invest-5-billion-to-set-up-facility-in-maharashtra-115080800341_1.html.
818 Ibid.
819 P. Doval, "Foxconn plans to make India hub for Africa, West Asia", *Times of India*, 14 January 2016, http://timesofindia.indiatimes.com/business/india-business/Foxconn-plans-to-make-India-hub-for-Africa-West-Asia/articleshow/50569582.cms.
820 G. Aulakh, "Committed to investing $5 billion in Maharashtra: Foxconn", *Economic Times*, 17 February 2018, https://economictimes.indiatimes.com/news/economy/finance/committed-to-investing-5-billion-in-maharashtra-foxconn/articleshow/62953320.cms.

or changed to accommodate new central government schemes. This talk has not been without controversy. Some citizens' groups point to the problems facing London, New York, and other cities that undertake expensive private projects, costing residents through taxes and environmental degradation.[821]

The aim of this conclusion is not to speculate about where these policies, ideas, and plans are heading, but to look at how these plans are developing in relation to the past. Throughout Mumbai's history, local private firms have played a prominent role in planning, whether for its twin city and proposed FTZ, or even the private ports that once lined the harbour in the 1860s.[822] As in the past, State agencies continue to play the main role in directing the city's infrastructure development. Yet, these agencies are forced to cooperate with the central government, not only for government schemes such as the SEZ policy or urban investment initiatives, but also because some of the city's largest employers and landholders – MPT and JNPT – are owned by the Government of India and operate independent of State control. Likewise, the central government cannot fulfil its transregional agenda to connect India to specific markets without private and State participation in directing local schemes.

Like the past FTZ plans for a "nationally important" New Bombay, the argument for "globalizing" Mumbai is based on local considerations. Though projects reference Shanghai or Singapore, they do so not to imitate these cities nor to foster specific business or trade connections with these places. The purpose of these references is to legitimize business activities in Mumbai. Although many plans are privatized, they are regulated by central and State oversight, including joint equity partnerships. Neoliberalism is not the overriding appeal of the zone, nor does the outcome of this policy's implementation represent "actually existing neoliberalism", especially as these projects reinforce the central government's oversight at the local level.[823] From a local point of view, these plans are not about linking the city to any specific territory, place, or network beyond India. They are about seeking solutions to tangible issues through tools designed for another purpose entirely. This local perspective contrasts with the central government's specific policies to connect certain growth corridors, ports, and zones to particular foreign investors and foreign markets.

821 V. Date, "Mumbai as a World Class City", in: *Mumbai Reader' 07*, Mumbai: Urban Design Research Institute, 2008, pp. 288–295.

822 Compare Bombay's post-independence development plan with Calcutta's, which was influenced by the World Bank and the Ford Foundation: Unger, *Entwicklungspfade in Indien*, pp. 221–274.

823 N. Brenner and N. Theorode, "Cities and the Geographies of 'Actually Existing Neoliberalism'", *Antipode* 34 (2002) 3, pp. 349–379.

The central government has a different motivation for encouraging the use of zone policies than the State government. The previous chapter discussed the importance of features of control and connectedness that enclaves like SEZs enable: their de- and reterritorializing functions. In contrast, at the local level, the binary of connection and isolation the SEZ offers is less lucrative as part of a globalization agenda. Though the planned New Bombay FTZ was marketed to the central government as a space that would be isolated to encourage foreign connections, in reality, the main goal behind these zones today as in the past has been to seamlessly integrate them into urban spaces in order to imagine and plan an ordered city. The purpose for local planners is not to isolate these spaces from local infrastructure but to enhance their connectedness to city spaces. Isolation still plays a role. These plans can remove unwanted, dangerous, or environmentally harmful business activity out of the city, especially from the port. Isolation and connection take on new meanings: these plans are about connecting specific sites through better infrastructure as well as shifting unwanted, dangerous, harmful, or disruptive business and housing concerns out of the city.

These projects, based on visions of a global modernity, are not clean slates as so frequently described but displace the many at the expense of a few.[824] As the central government becomes more interested in specific projects that are selected as vital to the Make in India campaign, compensations for project affected persons have suddenly become a national priority. The rhetoric behind zones that relates to blank slates and global standards while displacing farmers gives credence to work by Jonathan Bach, Jamie Cross, and Aihwa Ong, who argue that the zone is as much about remaking space as it is about remaking citizens.[825] As the prime minister laid the foundation stone for JNPT's fourth terminal, the port's future SEZ was in the foreground. He "promised the sorting out of the almost 25-year-old problem [...] ensuring that protests did not mar the ambitious JNPT SEZ project."[826] Though JNPT was commissioned in 1989, 3,524 families had still not received compensation. Each new project will in turn displace people from their homes with the pretext of creating an ordered space that appears to conform to visual standards, perhaps standards that confuse "visual order" with "experienced order."[827]

824 See especially: Banerjee-Guha, "Space Relations of Capital."
825 Bach, "'They Come in Peasants and Leave Citizens'"; Cross, *Dream Zones*; Ong, *Neoliberalism as Exception.*
826 Banerjee, "Major infrastructure boost."
827 Scott, *Seeing Like a State*, p. 133.

8 Conclusion

> Prime Minister Narendra Modi of India issued a strong call on Tuesday for nations to embrace globalization [. . .]. "Forces of protectionism are raising their heads against globalization," Mr. Modi said during a speech to the World Economic Forum here. "Their intention is not only to avoid globalization, but they also want to reverse its natural flow." Notably missing from the speech was any mention of recent moves by Mr. Modi's own government to restrict imports into India as part of a broad industrial policy meant to force foreign companies to increase manufacturing operations in the country. In essence, he is pursuing a protectionist agenda, at odds with the mantra of globalization[828]

India under current Prime Minister Narendra Modi is "pursuing a protectionist agenda, at odds with the mantra of globalization." Yet, to any specialist on India, the thought of India allowing foreign investment inside India would be considered liberal and unthinkable on its current scale just two decades ago. Notable is the complexity of how India deals and has dealt with global trade flows. Rather than the usual globalization rhetoric of "opening up" to foreign trade and investment and "letting go" of restrictions and regulations, India has sought to manage flows by enacting specific controls. In some cases, this globalization strategy is particularly place-bound. The foreign companies investing in India are not increasing their manufacturing operations just anywhere. They have been channelled into certain locations that often include enticements such as NMIZs and SEZs, which may comprise access to seaports and other transport infrastructure. These sites of connectivity have also tended to necessitate some form of isolation. India's 2000 SEZ policy/2005 SEZ Act represented India's comprehensive plan to enhance and control transregional flows of capital and goods into and out of India through specific sites.

Since 2005, the SEZ media frenzy has died down, and while much academic work exists on the topic, the speed of academic publications, including this one, cannot keep pace with the constant reformulation of the policy and the extension of the zone logic to multiple sectors of the Indian economy. Fortunately, this study is intended as a historical work. While the specifics of the SEZ policy have shifted and will likely continue to do so, the archival research presented herein demonstrates the long, complex history of India's and Mumbai's management of global flows within particular sites. These current policy shifts,

828 K. Bradsher, "Modi, in Davos, Praises Globalization Without Noting India's Trade Barriers", *New York Times*, 23 January 2018, https://www.nytimes.com/2018/01/23/business/modi-in-davos-praises-globalization-without-mentioning-india-trade-barriers.html.

https://doi.org/10.1515/9783110615135-008

therefore, share a much longer history with prior initiatives. With the Make in India campaign launched in 2014, taxes and planning are being streamlined through major revisions that integrate more Indians into the formal economy through banking and currency reform. As investment restrictions are rescinded, zone incentives appear less relevant, and SEZs are expected to decrease in number. In January 2016, the finance minister declared new incentives for start-ups the "final break from the conventional licence raj system."[829] Nevertheless, government ministries are finding new applications for the SEZ. For example, owing to regulations prohibiting the convertibility of the Indian rupee, the Ministry of Finance proposed "finance SEZs" that will create loopholes that "reshore" the derivative trading in rupee movements taking place "offshore."[830] The creation of a deterritorialized space is intended to reterritorialize profits in currency speculation, indicating a new use for a practice with a much longer history.

This book has shown that, while India's current SEZ policy is new, the act of seeking to direct global trade, capital, and human "flows" through particular sites as a strategy to regain control over them is not. SEZs are often associated with enclaves and offshoring – sites and activities linked to deterritorialized corporate profit seeking. Based on global history perspectives on the rise of territoriality since the seventeenth and particularly since the nineteenth century as a strategy to manage global connectivity, this book argues that current SEZs in India as well as India's past zones and ports have long served as sites of reterritorialization in which both territorializing and globalizing strategies have been carried out.[831] For Mumbai, territorialization processes become relevant once this trading outpost became part of a "nationalizing" Indian economy under the British Empire in the early nineteenth century.[832] At times, the zone logic was used to better connect sites to India's territory, not just to global markets. Furthermore, connections abroad were often targeted and sought to rework Mumbai's positionality within a variety of spatial frameworks such as the British Empire, regional trade blocs, or de-colonized terms of trade. Through the lens of one of India's key commercial port cities, this study has

829 Surabhi and A. M. Jigeesh, "Govt to be facilitator for start-ups: Jaitley", *Hindu Business Line*, 16 January 2016, http://www.thehindubusinessline.com/info-tech/govt-rbi-will-help-bankers-lend-more-jaitley/article8113541.ece?homepage=true.

830 M. Shetty, "Finance SEZs can halt rupee trading exodus: Finance Ministry", *Times of India*, 23 February 2015, http://timesofindia.indiatimes.com/business/india-business/Mumbaai-special-economic-zonesfinance-ministry/articleshow/46337112.cms?.

831 See: Elden, *Birth of Territory*; Maier, *Once within Borders*; Mukerji, *Territorial Ambitions*.

832 See: Goswami, *Producing India*.

shown the variety of actors who sought to channel and control connectivity through Mumbai's ports and zones since the 1830s, while focusing on pivotal moments of global and national change. In doing so, this book advanced the analytical perspective of portals of globalization for understanding how these sites are used by actors to manage shifting spatial orders under the global condition.

Chapter 2 began by exploring Bombay's first plan to create a free port in the city in 1833. This plan ultimately failed, but it indicates the interplay between the various scales of colonial authorities and private traders as Bombay became increasingly territorialized over the course of the prior decades. It was a plan to resituate the port-city within the British Empire's trading networks through the creation of tax incentives to dock in Bombay. This plan was part of an attempt to rescale competition under free trade from the firm level to the city level by creating free port incentives. When this plan conceptualized by the city's business elite failed, these actors, together with the local Government of Bombay, later implemented other schemes.

In the 1860s, in order to deal with the cotton boom, private firms were incentivized to build government infrastructure necessary for trade in exchange for rights to develop their own private docking facilities. This chapter detailed the incentives the local government and these firms used in order to build the needed physical infrastructure as well as the institutional expertise to deal with increases in foreign trade and port activity. Chapter 3 discussed the interplay between local actors and the Government of India as all involved tried to form an institution from the multiple private ports to best regulate foreign trade to their own benefit. The Government of India and Government of Bombay eventually took over this private port infrastructure to create a port trust. Out of a compromise, the central government sanctioned a multiscalar institution to manage Bombay's port and the largest tract of land in the city, an institution that has remained in place to this day. These two chapters show the attempt to control foreign trade by various actors and scales of government as Bombay became increasingly drawn in to India's colonial state formation.

The next chapter dealt with the first post-independence plans by the central government's Ministry of Commerce to create a free port in India. In 1949, the first references were made to the perceived benefit of the American foreign-trade zone, a policy that emerged out of the drawbacks of bonded warehouses. However, India's busiest ports like Bombay did not offer the type of isolation the government considered necessary for a free port in order to fully regulate its trade. Eventually, Kandla Port was chosen as the location for a free trade zone to decongest Bombay Port as well as to better integrate Kandla's region, a former princely state, into independent India. The dynamics between isolation and connection were important for Indian planners. Isolation was key in two respects. First, the deterritorialization feature of the zone required isolation in order to protect the Indian market from zone activities. Second, this uneven spatial strategy was ironically used to try to integrate an isolated area into India's new state space, pointing to the relationship between state territorialization strategies and the zone.

Chapter 5 further discussed how Indian officials targeted Indian families living abroad (NRIs) to invest in KFTZ and SEEPZ. At the time, India's designated external trade space related to areas in which the rupee could be used as the unit of transaction instead of hard currencies. These spatial frameworks, formed through trade agreements, allowed firms run through Indian family networks in the US and India to import US products into India's zones and re-export these goods to the USSR. Though the zone had been originally designed to increase Indian exports to the US and other Western countries, KFTZ became a transshipment node that increased India's exports to the USSR. At first, the Ministry of Commerce sought to prevent such a practice, but by 1989, policy experts had discussed formalizing this arrangement. Although the state created a specific space with "built-in" de- and reterritorialization features, it relied on private individuals and firms to forge the connections the state desired.

Chapter 6 unravelled the current SEZ and port plans in India within the context of India's ongoing processes of state rescaling. This chapter focused on the zone as part of India's foreign policy and its domestic growth agenda, arguing that the zone is not only seen as a domestic tool for growth, but it is also being used as a foreign policy tool that allows Indian officials to encourage investment from Japan and South Korea. Furthermore, India uses zone and port projects abroad that link with Mumbai in pursuit of closer relations with Iran and Afghanistan. The use of the zone was not indiscriminately global. Indian planners use the zone in a targeted effort to foster and control specific transregional trade connections.

Chapter 7 explored Mumbai's twin city plans from the 1960s, which involved a satellite port and zone. It also examined current efforts to make Mumbai a "world class city" by potentially developing zones around Mumbai, strengthening JNPT, and remaking MPT's current waterfront. The zone's appeal as a tabula rasa rather than as a de- and reterritorialized space has been the main appeal for planners at the city level. The plans to "globalize" Mumbai do not relate to creating specific trade connections. Instead, these zones, ports, and other renewal projects seek to improve the city by looking to international rankings that quantify the city through identifiable and measurable categories. The de- and reterritorializing function of the zone, key to the Government of India's plans to reposition India regionally, is not the primary motivation of city and State officials keen on achieving local goals: better infrastructure and higher rankings in international indexes.

In short, the zone represents the latest local policy mania that seeks to deal with the legacy of having been an important imperial and national port city.

This study advanced portals of globalization as a research lens through which to understand how a variety of actors sought to reposition their society under changing circumstances, and how they tried to order these changes themselves. Together, the histories presented here of zone and port plans in Mumbai, India, since the 1830s highlight the complex interplay between competing globalization and territorialization projects as they unfolded against the backdrop of shifting spatial orders. That is, both projects – globalization and territorialization – as they came to fruition in the mid-nineteenth century have been channelled through and managed in specific sites. These projects shifted substantially overtime. This *longue durée* empirical study focused on moments of change – the increasing institutionalization of the British Raj, Indian independence, and the liberalization of the Indian economy. Additionally, these moments coincided with global and regional shifts of the spatial order – the advent of free trade in the British Empire and its expanded presence in Asia; decolonization compounded by Cold War rivalries; and the rise of regional trade blocs and neoliberalism in the wake of the Cold War. Individuals, think tanks, institutions, merchants, business chambers, government ministries, port planners, and others used ports and zones in the Mumbai area to channel their own agendas to deal with a world increasingly interconnected. These globalization strategies do not necessarily oppose (nation state) territorialization but may also be part of this process.

Furthermore, these strategies are related to a shifting broader set of spatial categories in two ways. First, rarely have the targets of these projects been global in scope. More often, policy and infrastructure plans have referenced specific trade or diaspora networks, regional markets, or other concrete sites such as ports or cities that function as nodes along trade corridors or supply chains. Mumbai's ports and zones also mange shifting connections to certain locations within India, such as the railway lines built to connect Bombay Port to opium and cotton regions; freight services to Delhi, and the various zone and corridor projects today along which dry ports, factories, and cities can be found. Using portals of globalization as a lens opens up the way in which the shorthand "globalization" has masked references to the shifting connections between concrete spaces. Likewise, a focus on the nation state's "lost sovereignty" under globalization hides the state's complex transformation and participation in generating both "internal" and "external" connections and the complex relationship between both forms.[833]

833 For the nation state's role in governing globalization, see, Löhr and Wenzlhuemer (eds.), *Nation State and Beyond.*

Second, the various attempts to reposition Mumbai over almost two centuries illustrate in what ways the city, its ports, and its zones have a shifting relationship with certain types of space – spatial formats – and these formats' recombination within spatial orders. Bombay Port's positionality in imperial hierarchies – comprising port enclaves; Parsi, Arab, and Scottish trade networks; the Bombay Presidency – gave way to a new hierarchy of rival nation states as well as a federal state system within India. Migration out of independent India produced diaspora networks that had differed from those of the past. Regional trade agreements offered new opportunities for this diaspora to expand their supply chains, routing their American wares over KFTZ and SEEPZ to the USSR. Forms of societal organization shifted overtime so that new logics became dominant. The portals of globalization lens demonstrates how actors and places are situated in a variety of shifting and overlapping spatial formats, which adds complexity to customary local/global perspectives in global studies and global history. Instead, empires, regions, states, diasporas, cooperation agreements, transport corridors, and supply chains continue to shape the global age with waxing and waning levels of significance. Within the context of such formats, the portals of globalization concept is an analytical lens through which one can observe these shifting logics and, therefore, begin to periodize the shifting combinations of relevant spatial formats. Yet, the quality of the concept portal of globalization also changed overtime.

The empirical observations collected in this study allow for several points of reflection. Much of the writings on the original concept have focused on how portals of globalization, these places of intense transnational connectedness, are sites of trade, migration, or culture and develop institutional capacities to deal with shifting spatial orders under the global condition. In short, previous works have focused extensively on the functionality of portals of globalization as places that enable connectivity. In depictions of portals of globalization as places of cultural and economic connectivity, one thinks of financial centres such as London, port cities such as Hong Kong, or metropoles and cultural centres like Paris. This functionality of connectivity extends to institutions such as museums, the headquarters of regional organizations, ports, and universities as places that also manage connectivity through their networks and embeddedness in a variety of systems such as states and regions. These vibrant economic and cultural centres clash with imaginations of export processing zones, special economic zones, and other enclaved places secluded from view by fences and security guards. Sometimes militaries demarcate them. These guards control entry and exits of employees and goods. The zone enforces strict regulations while allowing relaxed labour laws, and these spaces facilitate tax reductions and incentives. The zone appears to be at odds with places that encourage intercultural transfer, knowledge exchange, mobility, and the institutionalization of strategies to deal with growing interconnections.

Yet, to think about what formats a space is to think of the actors and groups of actors who give that space relevance and the processes of spatialization resulting from their interactions. Chapters 2 and 3 show the Parsi and Scottish business and familial networks that turned Bombay city and port into a central trading hub in British Indian Ocean trade, not to mention the Gujarati merchants who dominated trade between Bombay and the East African coast. The establishment of institutions in Bombay, including the implementation of the port trust, facilitated the goal of advancing these trading networks, to the detriment of certain country craft traders. A century later, Indians who had family ties to the US and other Western countries used KFTZ and SEEPZ along with their corresponding ports to widen their families' transregional businesses, eventually expanding their reach to the USSR. Both the port of the late-nineteenth century and the port zone of the twentieth century are planned and enabled by the state. The state relies on non-state actors to make this space meaningful and to pursue its goals of furthering particular trades, adding a degree of contingency to the processes of spatialization that ensue. The types of actors as well as the processes of spatialization enabled – in this case, transregional trade enabled by diaspora networks – are similar.

Today, portals of globalization encompass more than connectivity. Aspects of isolation and enclaving became integral to its functionality under nation state territoriality. This study has shown that zone logics were part of but not key to understanding Bombay's rise during the nineteenth century. Indeed, a free port that would separate the port from the empire's tariffs and trade restrictions was proposed. However, it is only by forming a territorial nation state and dealing with the legacy of colonialism, the legacy of having once been a globally important port, and the repercussions of that centrality, that zones became increasingly important to India's and Mumbai's repositioning since 1947. This new quality of portals of globalization represents the complex interactions between spaces of connection and spaces of isolation and their recombination under a new spatial order. Portals of globalization gained something by writing in forms of isolation when combined with the decolonized nation state in the mid-twentieth century.

Bibliography

Literature

I. Abraham, *How India Became Territorial: Foreign Policy, Diaspora, Geopolitics*, Stanford, CA: Stanford University Press, 2014.
A. Acharya, "Asia Is Not One", *The Journal of Asian Studies* 69 (2010) 4, pp. 1001–1013.
T. Adam, *Intercultural Transfers and the Making of the Modern World, 1800–2000: Sources and Context*, Basingstoke: Palgrave Macmillan, 2012.
N. Adarkar and V. K. Phatak, "Recycling Mill Lands: Tumultuous Experience of Mumbai", *Economic and Political Weekly* 40 (2005) 51, http://www.epw.in/journal/2005/51/commentary/recycling-mill-land.html.
S. M. Agarwal, "Electronics in India: Past Strategies and Future Possibilities", *World Development* 13 (1985) 3, pp. 237–292.
A. Aggarwal, *Social and Economic Impact of SEZs in India*, New Delhi: Oxford University Press, 2012.
J. Agnew, "The Territorial Trap: The Geographical Assumptions of International Relations Theory", *Review of International Political Economy* 1 (1994) 1, pp. 53–80.
—, *Globalization and Sovereignty*, Lanham, MD: Rowman & Littlefield Publishers, 2009.
S. Akita, "The Aid-India Consortium, the World Bank, and the International Order of Asia, 1958–1968", *Asian Review of World Histories* 2 (2014) 2, pp. 217–248.
P. C. Alexander, *Industrial Estates in India*. Small Industry Extension Training Institute, New York and Bombay: Asia Publishing House, 1963.
P. Amitendu and S. Bhattacharjee, *Special Economic Zones in India: Myths and Realities*, New Delhi: Anthem Press India, 2008.
S. Ananthanarayanan, "New Mechanisms of Imperialism in India: The Special Economic Zones", *Socialism and Democracy* 22 (2008) 1, pp. 35–60.
R. Anthony, "Infrastructure and Influence: China's Presence on the Coast of East Africa", *Journal of the Indian Ocean Region* 9 (2013) 2, pp. 134–149.
A. Appadurai, *Modernity at Large: Cultural Dimensions of Globalization*, Minneapolis, MN: University of Minnesota Press, 1996.
—, "Sovereignty Without Territoriality: Notes for a Post-National Geography", in: P. Yaeger (ed.), *The Geography of Identity: Notes for a Postnational Geography*, Ann Arbor, MI: University of Michigan Press, 1996, pp. 40–58
—, "Grassroots Globalization and the Research Imagination", in: A. Appadurai (ed.), *Globalization*, Durham: Duke University Press, 2001, pp. 1–21.
G. Arrighi and D. Jessica, "The Stratification of the World-Economy", *Review* 10 (1986) 1, pp. 9–74.
A Study of the Eastern Waterfront of Mumbai, Mumbai: Urban Design Research Institute, 2005.
M. Augé, *Non-lieux: Introduction à une anthropologie de la supermodernité* [Non-Places: Introduction to an Anthropology of Supermodernity], J. Howe (trans.), London, New York: Verso, 1995.
P. B. "The Sterling Balances: Britain's Debts to the Sterling Area Countries", *The World Today* 2 (1946) 8, pp. 353–362.

https://doi.org/10.1515/9783110615135-009

V. V. Babu, "Foreign Trade Outlook of East Economies", in: *Emerging Opportunities for India's Trade and Economic Cooperation with East Europe*, New Delhi: Indian Institute of Foreign Trade, 1977, pp. 195–243.

J. Bach, "'They Come in Peasants and Leave Citizens': Urban Villages and the Making of Shenzhen, China", *Cultural Anthropology* 25 (2010) 3, pp. 421–458.

–, "Modernity and the Urban Imagination in Economic Zones", *Theory, Culture & Society* 28 (2011) 5, pp. 98–122.

M. Balooch, "Iran and India's Cooperation in Central Asia", *China and Eurasia Forum Quarterly* 7 (2009) 1, pp. 25–29.

N. Bangia, "Japanese Overtures: Increasing Investments in Indian Infrastructure", *Indian Infrastructure* 15 (2013) 11, pp. 14–16.

S. Bannerjee-Guha, "Space Relations of Capital and Significance of New Economic Enclaves: SEZs in India", *Political and Economic Weekly* 43 (2008) 47, pp. 51–59.

– (ed.), *Accumulation by Dispossession: Transformative Cities in the New Global Order*, New Delhi, Thousand Oaks, CA: Sage Publications, 2010.

–, "Revisiting Accumulation by Dispossession: Neoliberalising Mumbai", in: S. Bannerjee-Guha (ed.), *Accumulation by Dispossession: Transformative Cities in the New Global Order*, New Delhi, Thousand Oaks, CA: Sage Publications, 2010, pp. 198–226.

A. Bashford, "Population, Geopolitics and International Organizations in the Mid-Twentieth Century", *Journal of World History* 19 (2008) 3, pp. 327–347.

– (ed.), *Quarantine: Local and Global Histories*, Basingstoke: Palgrave Macmillan, 2016.

S. Batra, *Port of Kandla: The Gateway of Northwest India*, Adipur, Kutch: The Kandla Commercial, 1964.

C. Baumann (ed.), *Universities as Portals of Globalization: Crossroads of Internationalization and Area Studies*, Leipzig: Leipziger Universitätsverlag, 2014.

C. Baumman, A. Dietze, and M. Maruschke, "Portals of Globalization – An Introduction", *Comparativ: Zeitschrift für Globalgeschichte und vergleichende Gesellschaftsforschung* 27 (2017) 3–4, pp. 7–20.

J. F. Bayart, *The State in Africa: The Politics of the Belly*, London: Longman, 1993.

C. A. Bayly, *The Birth of the Modern World 1780–1914: Global Connections and Comparisons*, Malden, MA: Blackwell Publishing, 2004.

S. Beckert, "Emancipation and Empire: Reconstructing the Worldwide Web of Cotton Production in the Age of the American Civil War", *American Historical Review* 109 (2004) 5, pp. 1405–1438.

–, "Das Reich der Baumwolle: eine globale Geschichte", in: S. Conrad and J. Osterhammel, *Das Kaiserreich transnational: Deutschland in der Welt 1871–1914*, Göttingen: Vandenhoeck & Ruprecht, 2006, pp. 280–301.

J. H. Bentley, R. Bridenthal, and A. A. Yang (eds.), *Interactions: Transregional Perspectives on World History*, Honolulu, HI: University of Hawai'i Press, 2005.

F. B. Yahya, *Economic Cooperation Between Singapore and India: An Alliance in the Making?*, London, New York: Routledge, 2008.

J. Bockman, "Socialist Globalization against Capitalist Neocolonialism: The Economic Ideas behind the New International Economic Order", *Humanity* 6 (2015) 1, pp. 109–128.

G. Boquérat, "India in South Asia", in: C. Jaffrelot (ed.), *India Since 1950: Society, Politics, Economy and Culture*, New Delhi: Yatra Books, 2012, pp. 212–231.

D. Bräutigam, and X. Tang, "African Shenzhen: China's Special Economic Zones in Africa", *Journal of Modern African Studies* 49 (2011) 1, pp. 27–54.

—, "'Going Global in Groups': Structural Transformation and China's Special Economic Zones Overseas", *World Development* 63 (2014), pp. 78–91.

W. Bredo, *Industrial Estates: Tools for Industrialization*, International Industrial Development Center, Stanford Research Institute. Glencoe, IL: The Free Press, 1960.

N. Brenner, "Globalisierung und Reterritorialisierung: Städte, Staaten und die Politik der räumlichen Redemensionierung im heutigen Europa", *WeltTrends* 17 (Winter 1997), pp. 7–30.

—, "Between Fixity and Motion: Accumulation, Territorial Organization and the Historical Geography of Spatial Scales", *Environment and Planning D. Society and Space* 16 (1998) 4, pp. 459–481.

—, "Global Cities, Glocal States: Global City Formation and State Territorial Restructuring in Contemporary Europe", *Review of International Political Economy* 5 (1998) 1, pp. 1–37.

—, "Beyond State-Centrism? Space, Territoriality, and Geographical Scale in Globalization Studies", *Theory and Society* 28 (1999) 1, pp. 39–78.

N. Brenner and N. Theorode, "Cities and the Geographies of 'Actually Existing Neoliberalism'", *Antipode* 34 (2002) 3, pp. 349–379.

N. Brenner, et al., *State/Space: A Reader*, Malden, MA and Oxford: Blackwell, 2003.

N. Brenner, *New State Spaces: Urban Governance and the Rescaling of Statehood*, Oxford: Oxford University Press, 2004.

D. Brewster, "India's Developing Relationship with South Korea: A Useful Friend in East Asia", *Asian Survey* 50 (2010) 2, pp. 402–425.

—, "Indian Strategic Thinking About East Asia", *Journal of Strategic Studies* 34 (2011) 6, pp. 825–852.

—, "Beyond the 'String of Pearls': Is There Really a Sino-Indian Security Dilemma in the Indian Ocean?", *Journal of the Indian Ocean Region* 10 (2014) 2, pp. 133–149.

—, "India's Engagements with Southeast Asia: Singapore, Vietnam, and Indonesia", in: I. Hall (ed.), *The Engagement of India: Strategies and Responses*, Washington, DC: Georgetown University Press, 2014, pp. 147–167.

—, *India's Ocean: The Story of India's Bid for Regional Leadership*, Abingdon: Routledge, 2014.

F. Broeze, "The External Dynamics of Port City Morphology: Bombay 1815–1914", in: I. Banga (ed.), *Ports and Their Hinterlands in India (1700–1950)*, New Delhi: Manohar Publications, 1992, pp. 247–272.

D. H. Brooks and D. Hummels, *Infrastructure's Role in Lowering Asia's Trade Costs: Building for Trade*, Cheltenham: Edward Elgar Publishing and Asian Development Bank Institute, 2009.

D. H. Brooks and J. Menon (eds.), *Infrastructure and Trade in Asia*, Cheltenham: Edward Elgar Publishing and Asian Development Bank Institute, 2008.

J. Burbank and F. Cooper, *Empires in World History: Power and the Politics of Difference*, Princeton, NJ: Princeton University Press, 2010.

H. Burte and M. Krishnankutty, "On the Edge: Planning, Describing and Imagining the Seaside Edge of Mumbai", in: *Mumbai Reader '07*, Mumbai: Urban Design Research Institute, 2008, pp. 356–367.

Y. Cassis, *Capitals of Capital: A History of International Financial Centres, 1780–2005*, Cambridge, Cambridge University Press, 2006.

G. Castryck, "Introduction: From Railway Juncture to Portal of Globalization: Making Globalization Work in African and South Asian Railway Towns", *Comparativ: Zeitschrift für Globalgeschichte und vergleichende Gesellschaftsforschung* 25 (2015) 4, pp. 7–16.

A. B. Chakraborty, "Fostering Physical Connectivity in India's Look East Policy", *Journal of Infrastructure Development* 1 (2009) 1, pp. 45–65.

S. Chakravorty and S. V. Lall, *Made in India: The Economic Geography and Political Economy of Industrialization*, Oxford: Oxford University Press, 2007.

R. Chandavarkar, *The Origins of Industrial Capitalism in India: Business Strategies and the Working Classes in Bombay, 1900–1940*, Cambridge: Cambridge University Press, 1994.

S. Chaturvedi and J. Painter, "Whose World, Whose Order? Spatiality, Geopolitics and the Limits of the World Order Concept", *Cooperation and Conflict* 42 (2007) 4, pp. 375–395.

K. N. Chaudhuri, *The English East India Company: The Study of an Early Joint-Stock Company 1600–1640*, London: Routledge/Thoemmes Press, 1999 [1965].

–, *The Trading World of Asia and the English East India Company, 1660–1760*, Cambridge: Cambridge University Press, 2006 [1978].

S. Chishti, *India's Trade with East Europe*, New Delhi: Indian Institute of Foreign Trade, 1973.

–, "India's Trade with East Europe: An Overall View", in: *Emerging Opportunities for India's Trade and Economic Cooperation with East Europe*, New Delhi: Indian Institute of Foreign Trade, 1977, pp. 1–29.

P. Chopra, "A Joint Enterprise: The Creation of New Landscape in British Bombay (1839–1918)", in: *Mumbai Reader'10*, Mumbai: Urban Design Research Institute, 2010, pp. 320–347.

P. Choudhury and T. Khanna, "Charting Dynamic Trajectories: Multinational Enterprises in India", *Business History Review* 88 (2014) 1, pp. 133–169.

J. M. Conley, *Indo-Russian Military and Nuclear Cooperation: Lessons and Options for U.S. Policy in South Asia*, Lanham, MD: Lexington Books, 2001.

C. Correa, P. Mehta and S. Patel, "Planning for Bombay", *MARG* 18 (1965) 3, pp. 30–56.

J. Cowie, *Capital Moves: RCA's Seventy-Year Quest for Cheap Labor*, Ithaca, NY: Cornell University Press, 1999.

J. Cross, *Dream Zones: Anticipating Capitalism and Development in India*, London: Pluto Press, 2014.

D. D'Monte, *Ripping the Fabric: The Decline of Mumbai and Its Mills*, New Delhi: Oxford University Press, 2002.

–, "Old Port Trust, Lands on the Dock", in: *Mumbai Reader'08*, Mumbai: Urban Design Research Institute, 2009, pp. 204–209.

J. Darwin, *After Tamerlane: The Rise and Fall of Global Empires, 1400–2000*, New York: Bloomsbury Press, 2007.

–, *Unfinished Empire: The Global Expansion of Britain*, London: Penguin Books, 2012.

V. Date, "Mumbai as a World Class City", in: *Mumbai Reader'07*, Mumbai: Urban Design Research Institute, 2008, pp. 288–295.

M. Dattatreyulu, *Export Processing Zones in India: A Case Study of Kandla Free Trade Zone*, New Delhi: Indian Institute of Foreign Trade, 1990.

J. Dehejia, "Economic Reforms: Birth of an 'Asian Tiger'", in: P. Oldenburg (ed.), *India Briefing: 1993*, Boulder, CO: Westview Press, 1993, pp. 75–102.

A. Delios and P. W. Beamish, "Regional and Global Strategies of Japanese Firms", *Management International Review* 45 (2005) 1, pp. 19–36.

W. Delius, *Die Rechtsentwicklung zum heutigen Freihafen Hamburg*, Hamburg: Hans Christians Druckerei und Verlag, 1933.

J. B. DeLong, "India since Independence: An Analytic Growth Narrative", in: D. Rodrik (ed.), *In Search of Prosperity: Analytic Narratives on Economic Growth*, Princeton, NJ: Princeton University Press, 2003, pp. 184–204.

S. Deva, "Establishment of Industrial Estates in India", *Journal of Administration Overseas* 15 (1976) 3, pp. 150–159.
A. Dietze and K. Naumann, "Revisiting Transnational Actors from a Spatial Perspective", *European Review of History: Revue européenne d'histoire* 25 (2018) 3–4, pp. 415–430.
J. Dinkel, *Die Bewegung Bündnisfreier Staaten: Genese, Organisation und Politik, 1927–1992*, Berlin: De Gruyter Oldenbourg, 2015.
M. R. Djalili and C. Therme, "Le flanc Est de l'Iran: opportunités et vulnérabilités", *Politique étrangère* 73 (2008) 3, pp. 601–612.
M. Dossal, *Imperial Designs and Indian Realities: The Planning of Bombay City, 1845–1875*, New Delhi: Oxford University Press, 1991.
K. Easterling, *Extrastatecraft: The Power of Infrastructure Space*, London: Verso, 2014.
W. Easterly, "What did Structural Adjustment Adjust?: The Association of Policies and Growth with Repeated IMF and World Bank Adjustment Loans", *Journal of Development Economics* 76 (2005) 1, pp. 1–22.
S. Elden, *The Birth of Territory*, Chicago: The University of Chicago Press, 2013.
Encyclopaedia Britannica, "Sir Bartle Frere 1st Baronet", http://www.britannica.com/EBchecked/topic/219678/Sir-Bartle-Frere-1st-Baronet (accessed 2 December 2014).
U. Engel and M. Middell, "Bruchzonen der Globalisierung, globale Krisen und Territorialitätsregimes – Kategorien einer Globalgeschichtsschreibung", *Comparativ: Zeitschrift für Globalgeschichte und vergleichende Gesellschaftsforschung* 15 (2005) 5–6, pp. 5–38.
—, *World Orders Revisited*, Leipzig: Leipziger Universitätsverlag, 2010.
D. C. Engerman, "The Political Power of Economic Ideas? Foreign Economic Advisors and Indian Planning in the 1950s and 1960s", in: A. Hilger and C. R. Unger (eds.), *India in the World since 1947: National and Transnational Perspectives*, Frankfurt am Main: Peter Lang, 2012, pp. 120–135.
H.D.P. Envall, "Japan's India Engagement: From Different Worlds to Strategic Partners", in: I. Hall (ed.), *The Engagement of India: Strategies and Responses*, Washington, DC: Georgetown University Press, 2014, pp. 39–59.
M. Espagne, "Comparison and Transfer", in: M. Middell and L. Roura (eds.), *Transnational Challenges to National History Writing*, Basingstoke: Palgrave Macmillan, 2013, pp. 36–53.
N. Fernandes, *City Adrift: A Short Biography of Bombay*, New Delhi: Aleph, 2013.
A. G. Frank, "Third World Manufacturing Export Production", *The South East Asian Economic Review* 1 (1980) 2, pp. 83–105.
F. Fröbel, J. Heinrichs and O. Kreye, *Die neue internationale Arbeitsteilung: Strukturelle Arbeitslosigkeit in den Industrieländern und die Industrialisierung der Entwicklungsländer*, Reinbek bei Hamburg: Rowohlt, 1977.
—, *The New International Division of Labour: Structural Unemployment in Industrialised Countries and Industrialisation in Developing Countries*, Cambridge: Cambridge University Press, 1981.
S. Gänger, "Circulation: Reflections on Circularity, Entity, and Liquidity in the Language of Global History", *Journal of Global History* 12 (2017) 3, pp. 303–318.
M. L. Gerlach, *Alliance Capitalism: The Social Organization of Japanese Business*, Berkeley, CA: University of California Press, 1992.
M. Geyer, "Portals of Globalization", in: W. Eberhard and C. Lübke (eds.), *The Plurality of Europe: Identities and Spaces*, Leipzig: Leipziger Universitätsverlag, 2010, pp. 509–520.

K. N. Ghorude, "Labour in Export Processing Zones: The Case of SEEPZ, Mumbai", *The Indian Journal of Labour Economics* 47 (2004) 4, pp. 1093–1100.

A. Ghosh et al., "A Comparative Overview of Urban Governance in Delhi, Hyderabad, Kolkata and Mumbai", in: J. Ruet and S. T. Lama-Rewal (eds.), *Governing India's Metropolises*, New Delhi: Routledge, 2009, pp. 24–54.

B. Ghosh and P. De, "Indian Ports and Globalisation: Grounding Economics in Geography", *Economic and Political Weekly* 36 (2001) 34, pp. 3271–3283.

M. Ghosh, "India and Japan's Growing Synergy: From a Political to a Strategic Focus", *Asian Survey* 48 (2008) 2, pp. 282–302.

H. G. Gilcriest, "The Mersey Dock and Harbour Board", *Public Administration* 3 (1925) 3, pp. 273–278.

C. Goswami, *Globalization Before Its Time: The Gujarati Merchants from Kachchh*, New Delhi: Penguin, 2016.

M. Goswami, *Producing India: From Colonial Economy to National Space*, Chicago: University of Chicago Press, 2004.

A. Grydejøj, "Island City Formation and Urban Island Studies", *Area* 47 (2015) 4, pp. 429–435.

M. Guangwen, "The Theory and Practice of Free Economic Zones: A Case Study of Tianjin, People's Republic of China", PhD dissertation, Ruprecht-Karls University of Heidelberg, 2003, http://www.eu-china.net/upload/pdf/materialien/meng_2003_theory_and_practice_of_free_economic_zones_china.pdf.

S. P. Gupta (ed.), *China's Economic Reforms: Role of Special Economic Zones and Economic and Technological Development Zones*, New Delhi: Allied Publishers Limited, 1996.

I. Hall (ed.), *The Engagement of India: Strategies and Responses*, Washington, DC: Georgetown University Press, 2014.

H. E. Haralambides and R. Behrens, "Port Restructuring in a Global Economy: An Indian Perspective", *International Journal of Transport Economics* 27 (2000) 1, pp. 19–39.

R. Harshe and K. M. Seethi, *Engaging with the World: Critical Reflections on India's Foreign Policy*, New Delhi: Orient Longman, 2005.

D. Harvey, "From Managerialism to Entrepreneurialism: The Transformation in Urban Governance in Late Capitalism", *Geografiska Annaler. Series B* 71 (1989) 1, pp. 3–17.

–, *Spaces of Capital: Towards a Critical Geography*, Edinburgh: Edinburgh University Press, 2001.

–, *Spaces of Global Capitalism: Towards a Theory of Uneven Geographical Development*, London: Verso Books, 2006.

S. Hazareesingh, "'Chasing Commodities over the Whole Surface of the Globe': Shipping, Port Development, and the Making of Networks Between Glasgow and Bombay, c. 1850–1880", Working paper, The Open University, 2007.

–, *The Colonial City and the Challenge of Modernity: Urban Hegemonies and Civic Contestations in Bombay (1900–1925)*, Hyderabad: Orient Longman, 2007.

–, "Interconnected Synchronicities: The Production of Bombay and Glasgow as Modern Global Ports, c. 1850–1880", *Journal of Global History* 4 (2009) 1, pp. 7–31.

G. Heuzé, "Labour Movements and Organisations in India", in: C. Jaffrelot (ed.), *India Since 1950: Society, Politics, Economy and Culture*, New Delhi: Yatra Books, 2012, pp. 425–444

A. Hilger and C. R. Unger (eds.), *India in the World since 1947: National and Transnational Perspectives*, Frankfurt am Main: Peter Lang, 2012.

G. M. Hiranandani, *Transition to Eminence: The Indian Navy 1976–1990*, New Delhi: Ministry of Defence (Navy) in association with Lancer Publishers, 2005.

W. Hui, "The Idea of Asia and Its Ambiguities", *The Journal of Asian Studies* 69 (2010) 4, pp. 985–989.
C. Hurtig, "The Restructuring of India's External Relations: 1971–1998", in: C. Jaffrelot (ed.), *India Since 1950: Society, Politics, Economy and Culture*, New Delhi: Yatra Books, 2012, pp. 183–193.
A. S. E. Iyer, "Co-operation Between and Assistance to Small-Scale units in Industrial Estates in India", in: *Industrial Estates in Asia and the Far East*, New York: United Nations, 1962, pp. 150–170.
C. Jaffrelot (ed.), *India Since 1950: Society, Politics, Economy and Culture*, New Delhi: Yatra Books, 2012.
P. Jain, "Japan-India Relations: Peaks and Troughs", *The Round Table: The Commonwealth Journal of International Affairs* 99 (2010) 409, pp. 403–412.
R. Jain, "India and SAARC: An Analysis", *Indian Journal of Asian Affairs* 18 (2005) 2, pp. 55–74.
R. Jenkins, L. Kennedy and P. Mukhopadhyay (eds.), *Power, Policy, and Protest: The Politics of India's Special Economic Zones*, New Delhi: Oxford University Press, 2014.
B. Jessop, N. Brenner and M. Jones, "Theorizing Sociospatial Relations", *Environment and Planning D: Society and Space* 26 (2008) 3, pp. 389–401.
H. H. Karrar, *The New Silk Road Diplomacy: China's Central Asian Foreign Policy since the Cold War*, Vancouver: UBC Press, 2010.
J. Keay, *The Honourable Company: A History of the English East India Company*, New York: Macmillan Publishing House, 1991.
O. Ken, "Bataan Export Processing Zone: Its Development and Social Implications", *AMPO: Japan-Asia Quarterly Review* 8 and 9 (1977) 4, 1–2, pp. 93–120.
N. Kenji, "Japan's Overseas Investment Patterns and FTZs", *AMPO: Japan-Asia Quarterly Review* 8 and 9 (1977) 4, 1–2, pp. 33–50.
L. Kennedy, "Large-Scale Economic and Infrastructure Projects in India's Metropolitan Cities: New Policies and Practices Among Competing Subnational States", Paper presented at the Fourth International Conference of the International Forum on Urbanism (IFoU), Amsterdam/Delft, 2009, pp. 1055–1065, http://newurbanquestion.ifou.org/proceedings/.
–, "Indian Federalism: Moving Towards a More Balanced System", in: C. Jaffrelot, (ed.), *India Since 1950: Society, Politics, Economy and Culture*, New Delhi: Yatra Books, 2012, pp. 249–270.
–, *The Politics of Economic Restructuring in India: Economic Governance and State Spatial Rescaling*, Abingdon: Routledge, 2014.
P. Khanna, *Connectography: Mapping the Global Network Revolution*, New York: Random House, 2016.
J. M. Kleibert, "Islands of Globalisation: Offshore Services and the Changing Spatial Divisions of Labour", *Environment and Planning A* 47 (2015) 4, pp. 884–902.
N. Klein, *No Logo: Taking Aim at the Brand Bullies*, 2nd edition, New York: Picador, 2002.
–, *The Shock Doctrine: The Rise of Disaster Capitalism*, New York: Metropolitan Books, 2007.
P. Knox and P. J. Taylor (eds.), *World Cities in a World System*, Cambridge: Cambridge University Press, 1995.
J. Kocka and H. G. Haupt, *Comparative and Transnational History: Central European Approaches and New Perspectives*, New York: Berghahn Books, 2009.
M. Kosambi, "Bombay and Poona: A Socio-Ecological Study of Two Indian Cities, 1650–1900", PhD dissertation, Stockholm University, 1980.

–, “Commerce, Conquest and the Colonial City: Role of Locational Factors in the Rise of Bombay”, *Economic and Political Weekly* 20 (1985) 1, pp. 32–37.

–, *Bombay in Transition: The Growth and Social Ecology of a Colonial City, 1880–1980*, Stockholm: Almqvist & Wiksell International, 1986.

N. Koyoma, “SEZs in the Context of Regional Integration: Creating Synergies for Trade and Investment”, in: T. Farole and G. Akinci (eds.), *Special Economic Zones: Progress, Emerging Challenges, and Future Directions*, Washington, DC: The World Bank, 2011, pp. 127–156.

S. D. Krasner, *Structural Conflict: The Third World against Global Liberalism*, Berkeley, CA: University of California Press, 1985.

M. Kudaisya, “‘The Promise of Partnership’: Indian Business, the State, and the Bombay Plan of 1944”, *Business History Review* 88 (2014) 1, pp. 97–131.

K. Kumar, “Nation-States as Empires, Empires as Nation-States. Two Principles, One Practice?”, *Theory and Society* 39 (2010) 2, pp. 119–143.

R. Kumar, *India’s Export Processing Zones*, New Delhi: Oxford University Press, 1989.

V. Kumar (ed.), *Committees and Commissions in India 1979*, vol. 17, part B. New Delhi: Concept Publishing Company, 1994.

A. Kundra, *The Performance of India’s Export Zones: A Comparison with the Chinese Approach*, New Delhi: Sage Publications, 2000.

H. Laurence, “Japan’s Proactive Foreign Policy and the Rise of the BRICs”, *Asian Perspective* 31 (2007) 4, pp. 177–203.

M. A. Lawrence, “The Rise and Fall of Nonalignment”, in: R. J. McMahon (ed.), *The Cold War in the Third World*, Oxford: Oxford University Press, 2013, pp. 139–155.

L. Lee, “Russia’s Engagement of India: Securing the Longevity of a ‘Special and Privileged’ Strategic Partnership”, in: I. Hall (ed.), *The Engagement of India: Strategies and Responses*, Washington, DC: Georgetown University Press, 2014, pp. 61–87.

H. Lefebvre, *La production de l’espace* [*The Production of Space*], D. Nicholson-Smith (trans.), Oxford: Blackwell Publishers, 1991 [1974].

M. Levien, “Regimes of Dispossession: From Steel Towns to Special Economic Zones”, *Development and Change* 44 (2013) 2, pp. 381–407.

I. Löhr and R. Wenzlhuemer (eds.), *The Nation State and Beyond: Governing Globalization Processes in the Nineteenth and Early Twentieth Centuries*, Heidelberg: Springer, 2013.

A. L. Lomax, *The Foreign Trade Zone*, Eugene, OR: University of Oregon, 1947.

L. Lüthi, *The Sino-Soviet Split: Cold War in the Communist World*, Princeton, NJ: Princeton University Press, 2008.

A. Mah, *Port Cities and Global Legacies: Urban Identity, Waterfront Work, and Radicalism*, Basingstoke: Palgrave Macmillan, 2014.

C. Maier, “Consigning the 20th Century to History: Alternative Narratives for the Modern Era”, *American Historical Review* 105 (2000) 3, pp. 807–831.

–, *Among Empires: American Ascendancy and Its Predecessors*, Cambridge, MA: Harvard University Press, 2006.

–, “Transformations of Territoriality, 1600–2000”, in: G. F. Budde, S. Conrad and O. Janz (eds.), *Transnationale Geschichte: Themen, Tendenzen und Theorien*, Göttingen: Vandenhoeck & Ruprecht, 2006, pp. 32–55.

–, *Once within Borders: Territories of Power, Wealth, and Belonging since 1500*, Cambridge, MA: Harvard University Press, 2016.

M. Mann, "India 1989: Overcoming the Post-Colonial State", in: U. Engel, F. Hadler and M. Middell (eds.), *1989 in a Global Perspective*, Leipzig: Leipziger Universitätsverlag, 2015, pp. 259–295.
P. Marshall, "Private British Trade in the Indian Ocean before 1800", in: A. Das Gupta and M. N. Pearson (eds.), *India and the Indian Ocean, 1500–1800*, Calcutta: Oxford University Press, 1987, pp. 276–300.
R. Marshall, *Emerging Urbanity: Global Urban Projects in the Asia Pacific Rim*, London: Spoon Press, 2003.
M. Maruschke, "Zones of Reterritorialization: India's Free Trade Zones in Comparative Perspective, 1947 to the 1980s", *Journal of Global History* 12 (2017) 3, pp. 410–432.
—, "Managing Shifting Spatial Orders: Planning Bombay's Free Port and Free Zone, 1830s–1980s", *Comparativ: Zeitschrift für Globalgeschichte und vergleichende Gesellschaftsforschung* 27 (2017) 3–4, pp. 21–40.
—, "Special Economic Zones and Transregional State Spatiality", in: M. Middell (ed.), *The Routledge Handbook of Transregional Studies*, London: Routledge, 2019, pp. 197–203.
J. Masselos, "Changing Definitions of Bombay: City State to Capital City", in: I. Banga (ed.), *Ports and Their Hinterlands in India (1700–1950)*, New Delhi: Manohar Publications, 1992, pp. 273–316.
P. I. Mathew, "India's Economic Relations with the Soviet Union During 1951–1976: A Study in Political Economy", PhD dissertation, University of Connecticut, 1979.
R. J. McCalla, "The Geographical Spread of Free Zones Associated with Ports", *Geoforum* 21 (1990) 1, pp. 121–134.
R. J. McMahon, *The Cold War on the Periphery: The United States, India, and Pakistan*, New York: Columbia University Press, 1994.
—, "On the Periphery of a Global Conflict: India and the Cold War, 1947–1991", in: A. Hilger and C. R. Unger (eds.), *India in the World since 1947: National and Transnational Perspectives*, Frankfurt am Main: Peter Lang, 2012, pp. 276–299.
— (ed.), *The Cold War in the Third World*, Oxford: Oxford University Press, 2013.
R. Mehrotra, "Remaking Mumbai", in: *Mumbai Reader'07*, Mumbai: Urban Design Research Institute, 2008, pp. 392–399.
—, "Twin City: Navi Mumbai Thirty Years Later", in: *Mumbai Reader'07*, Mumbai: Urban Design Research Institute, 2008, pp. 118–129.
M. Middell, "Kulturtransfer und Historische Komparatistik – Thesen zu ihrem Verhältnis", *Comparativ: Zeitschrift für Globalgeschichte und vergleichende Gesellschaftsforschung* 10 (2000) 1, pp. 7–41.
—, "Erinnerung an die Globalisierung? Die Portale der Globalisierung als *lieux de mémoire*. Ein Versuch", in: K. Buchunger (ed.), *Europäische Erinnerungsräume*, Frankfurt am Main: Campus-Verlag, 2009, pp. 296–308.
M. Middell and K. Naumann, "Global History and the Spatial Turn: From the Impact of Area Studies to the Study of Critical Junctures of Globalization", *Journal of Global History* 5 (2010) 1, pp. 149–170.
M. Middell, "What Is Global Studies All About?" *Global Europe: Basel Papers on Europe in a Global Perspective* (2014) 105, pp. 38–49, https://europa.unibas.ch/fileadmin/europa/redaktion/PDF_Basler_Schriften/BS105.pdf.
— (ed.), *The Routledge Handbook of Transregional Studies*, London: Routledge, 2019.
M. Miller, *Europe and the Maritime World: A Twentieth Century History*, Cambridge: Cambridge University Press, 2012.

G. J. Milne, *Trade and Traders in Mid-Victorian Liverpool: Mercantile Business and the Making of a World Port*, Liverpool: Liverpool University Press, 2000.

R. Mishra, *A Business of State: Commerce, Politics, and the Birth of the East India Company*, Cambridge, MA: Harvard University Press, 2018.

S. Mountfield, *Western Gateway: A History of the Mersey Docks and Harbour Board*, Liverpool: Liverpool University Press, 1965.

R. Mujumdar and B. Menezes, "Maharashtra: Institutional Politics and the Framing of Resistance", in: R. Jenkins, L. Kennedy, and P. Mukhopadhyay (ed.), *Power, Policy, and Protest: The Politics of India's Special Economic Zones*, New Delhi: Oxford University Press, 2014, pp. 239–271.

C. Mukerji, *Territorial Ambitions and the Gardens of Versailles*, Cambridge: Cambridge University Press, 1997.

R. Mukherjee (ed.), *Vanguards of Globalization: Port-Cities from the Classical to the Modern*, New Delhi: Primus Books, 2014.

D. Nagaiya, *Industrial Estates Programme: The Indian Experience*, Yousufguda, Hyderabad: Small Industry Extension Training Institute, 1971.

R. Nagpal, "Tariff Guidelines for Major Ports", *Indian Infrastructure* 15 (2013) 10, pp. 60–61.

S. Nair, "The Paradox of Mumbai Mills Land Sales", in: *Mumbai Reader'13*, Mumbai: Urban Design Research Institute, 2013, pp. 420–425.

B. R. Nayar, "When did the 'Hindu' Rate of Growth End?", *Economic and Political Weekly* 41 (2006) 19, pp. 1885–1990.

–, *The Geopolitics of Globalization: The Consequences for Development*, Oxford: Oxford University Press, 2007.

D. Nayyar, "India's Trade with the Socialist Countries", *World Development* 3 (1975) 5, pp. 273–298.

P. Neveling, "Structural Contingencies and Untimely Coincidences in the Making of Neoliberal India: The Kandla Free Trade Zone, 1965–91", *Contributions to Indian Sociology* 48 (2014) 1, pp. 17–43.

–, "Export Processing Zones and Global Class Formation", in: J. G. Carrier and D. Kalb (eds.), *Anthropologies of Class: Power, Practice and Inequality*, Cambridge: Cambridge University Press, 2015, pp. 164–182.

–, "Export Processing Zones, Special Economic Zones and the Long March of Capitalist Development Policies During the Cold War", in: L. James and E. Leake (eds.), *Negotiating Independence: New Directions in the Histories of the Cold War and Decolonisation*, London: Bloomsbury, 2015, pp. 63–84.

–, "Free Trade Zones, Export Processing Zones, Special Economic Zones and Global Imperial Formations 200 BCE to 2015 CE", in: I. Ness and Z. Cope (eds.), *The Palgrave Encyclopedia of Imperialism and Anti-imperialism*, Basingstoke: Palgrave Macmillan, 2015, pp. 1007–1016.

–, "The Global Spread of Export Processing Zones, and the 1970s as a Decade of Consolidation", in: K. Andresen and S. Müller (eds.), *Contesting Deregulation: Debates, Practices and Developments in the West since the 1970s*, Oxford: Berghahn Books, 2017, pp. 23–40.

D. Olivier and B. Slack, "Rethinking the Port", *Environment and Planning A* 38 (2006) 8, pp. 1409–1427.

V. Ogle, "Archipelago Capitalism: Tax Havens, Offshore Money, and the State, 1950s–1970s", *American Historical Review* 122 (2017) 5, pp. 1431–1458.

A. Ong, *Spirits of Resistance and Capitalist Discipline: Factory Women in Malaysia*, New York: State University of New York Press, 1987.

—, *Neoliberalism as Exception: Mutations in Citizenship and Sovereignty*, Durham, NC: Duke University Press, 2006.

D. Orenstein, "Foreign-Trade Zones and the Cultural Logic of Frictionless Production", *Radical History Review* (Winter 2011) 109, pp. 36–61.

Organisation for Economic Co-operation and Development, *The Competitiveness of Global Port-Cities*, OECD Publishing, 2014.

R. Palan, *The Offshore World, Sovereign Markets, Virtual Places, and Nomad Millionaires*, Ithaca, NY: Cornell University Press, 2003.

—, "International Financial Centers: The British-Empire, City-States and Commercially Oriented Politics", *Theoretical Inquiries in Law* 11 (2010) 1, pp. 149–176.

A. Palit, "NMIZs in India: Haunted by SEZs?", ISAS Brief 203, 17 June 2011, http://www.isn.ethz.ch/Digital-Library/Publications/Detail/?lang=en&id=130416.

J. S. Palsetia, *The Parsis of India: Preservation of Identity in Bombay City*, Leiden: Brill, 2001.

A. Panagariya, *India: The Emerging Giant*, Oxford: Oxford University Press, 2008.

H. V. Pant, "India and Iran: An 'Axis' in the Making?", *Asian Survey* 44 (2004) 3, pp. 369–383.

—, "India and US-Iran Imbroglio: Difficult Choices Ahead", *Indian Journal of Asian Affairs* 19 (2006) 1, pp. 25–38.

—, "India in the Asia-Pacific: Rising Ambitions with an Eye on China", *Asia-Pacific Review* 14 (2007) 1, pp. 54–71.

—, "China's Half-Hearted Engagement and India's Proactive Balancing", in: I. Hall (ed.), *The Engagement of India: Strategies and Responses*, Washington, DC: Georgetown University Press, 2014, pp. 111–128.

B. G. Park, "Spatially Selective Liberalization and Graduated Sovereignty: Politics of Neo-Liberalism and 'Special Economic Zones' in South Korea", *Political Geography* 24 (2005) 7, pp. 850–873.

A. K. Pasha, "India and the Gulf States: Challenges and Opportunities", in: R. Harshe and K. M. Seethi (eds.), *Engaging with the World: Critical Reflections on India's Foreign Policy*, New Delhi: Orient Longman, 2005, pp. 389–424.

U. R. Patel and S. Bhattacharya, "Infrastructure in India: The Economics of Transition from Public to Private Provision", *Journal of Comparative Economics* 38 (2010) 1, pp. 52–70.

J. K. Patnaik, "Indo-Iranian Relations", in: A. K. Pasha and R. Punjabi (eds.), *India and the Islamic World*, New Delhi: Radiant Publishers, 1998, pp. 84–94.

M. Pearson, *The Indian Ocean*, Abingdon: Routledge, 2003.

A. Pethe, V. Tandel and S. Ghandi, "Understanding Issues Related to Polycentric Governance in the Mumbai Metropolitan Region", in: *Mumbai Reader'13*, Mumbai: Urban Design Research Institute, 2013, pp. 240–261.

K. R. Pillai, "Rethinking India-Pakistan Relations: Challenges Ahead", in: R. Harshe and K. M. Seethi (eds.), *Engaging with the World: Critical Reflections on India's Foreign Policy*, New Delhi: Orient Longman, 2005, pp. 224–242.

P. Poiesz, G. J. Scholte and S. V. Ghandi, *Learning from Mumbai: Practicing Architecture in Urban India*, Rotterdam, 2013.

E. E. Pollock, "Free Ports, Free Trade Zones, Export Processing Zones and Economic Development", in: B. S. Hoyle and D. Pinder (eds.), *Cityport Industrialization and Regional Development*, Oxford: Pergamon Press, 1981, pp. 37–45.

O. Prakash, "The English East India Company and India", in: H. V. Bowen, M. Lincoln and N. Rigby (eds.), *The Worlds of the East India Company*, Suffolk: The Boydell Press, 2002, pp. 1–18.

V. Prashad, *The Darker Nations: A People's History of the Third World*, New York: New Press, 2007.

—, "India's Iran Policy: Between US Primacy and Regionalism", Working Paper Series 19, Assam Fares Institute for Public Policy and International Affairs, American University of Beirut, 2013, https://www.aub.edu.lb/ifi/international_affairs/Documents/working_paper_series/20131118_AI_WP_Indian_Iran_Policy.pdf.

E. Pratt, *The Bombay Wharves; How the Right of Way over Them Was Lost to the Public and the Commerce of the Port*, London: J. Weare, 1881.

S. Raghavan, "Between Regional and Global Interests: The Indo-Soviet Treaty of 1971", in: A. Hilger and C. R. Unger (eds.), *India in the World since 1947: National and Transnational Perspectives*, Frankfurt am Main: Peter Lang, 2012, pp. 326–345.

N. Rao, *Reshaping City Governance: London, Mumbai, Kolkata, Hyderabad*, New York: Routledge, 2015.

S. K. Rao, and R. Jaikumar, "Trade Plans and Production Cooperation", in: *Emerging Opportunities for India's Trade and Economic Cooperation with East Europe*, New Delhi: Indian Institute of Foreign Trade, 1977, pp. 103–114.

J. K. Ray and S. Chakrabarti, "Institutionalization of the Regional Space in South Asia", in: J. K. Ray (ed.), *Aspects of India's International Relations 1700 to 2000: South Asia and the World*, New Delhi: Peason Longman, 2007, pp. 429–480.

I. Rehman, "Keeping the Dragon at Bay: India's Counter-Containment of China in Asia", *Asian Security* 5 (2009) 2, pp. 114–143.

X. Ren and L. Weinstein, "Urban Governance, Mega-Projects and Scalar Transformations in China and India", in: T. R. Samar, S. He and G. Chen (eds.), *Locating Right to the City in the Global South*, Florence: Taylor Francis, 2013, pp. 107–126.

Y. Ren, "Architecture as Branding: Mega Project Developments in Beijing", *Built Environment* 24 (2008) 4, pp. 517–531.

"Revision of Development Plan (2014–2034)", in: *Mumbai Reader'13*, Mumbai: Urban Design Research Institute, 2013, pp. 37–135.

E. H. Rideout, "The Development of the Liverpool Warehousing System", *Transactions of the Historic Society of Lancashire & Cheshire* 82 (1930), p. 1–41.

N. Robins, *The Corporation that Changed the World: How the East India Company Shaped the Modern Multinational*, London: Pluto Press, 2012.

E. Rosen, *Making Sweatshops: The Globalization of the U.S. Apparel Industry*, Berkeley, CA: University of California Press, 2002.

A. J. Rotter, *Comrades at Odds: The United States and India, 1947–1964*, Ithaca, NY: Cornell University Press, 2000.

J. Ruet, "Thinking the Delhi, Hyderabad, Kolkata, and Mumbai Experience: Emerging Modes of Urban Governance and State Intervention", in: J. Ruet and S. T. Lama-Rewal (eds.), *Governing India's Metropolises*, New Delhi: Routledge, 2009, pp. 270–303.

V. Rymalov, *Economic Co-Operation Between the U.S.S.R. and Underdeveloped Countries*, Moskow: Foreign Languages Publishing House, 1962.

L. Sáez, *Federalism Without a Center: The Impact of Political and Economic Reform on India's Federal System*, New Delhi and Thousand Oaks, CA: Sage Publications, 2002.

I. Saint-Mézard, "A Quest for Power: India's Foreign Policy after the Nuclear Tests of 1998", in: C. Jaffrelot (ed.), *India Since 1950: Society, Politics, Economy and Culture*, New Delhi: Yatra Books, 2012, pp. 194–211.
O. Sanchez-Sibony, *Red Globalization: The Political Economy of the Soviet Cold War from Stalin to Khrushchev*, Cambridge: Cambridge University Press, 2014.
A. K. Sandoval-Strausz and N. H. Kwak (eds.), *Making Cities Global: The Transnational Turn in Urban History*, Philadelphia: University of Pennsylvania Press, 2017.
S. Sassen, "Spatialities and Temporalities of the Global: Elements for a Theorization", *Public Culture* 12 (2000) 1, pp. 215–232.
—, *The Global City: New York, London, Tokyo*, Princeton, NJ: Princeton University Press, 2001.
—, "Locating Cities on Global Circuits", *Environment & Urbanization* 14 (2002) 1, pp. 13–30.
—, *Territory, Authority, Rights: From Medieval to Global Assemblages*, Princeton, NJ: Princeton University Press, 2008.
—, "The Global City: Introducing a Concept", *Brown Journal of World Affairs* 9 (2009) 2, pp. 27–43.
—, "When Territory Deborders Territoriality", *Territory, Politics, Governance* 1 (2013) 1, pp. 21–45.
K. Sasuga, Katsuhiro, "Microregionalization Across Southern China, Hong Kong and Taiwan", in: S. Breslin and G. D. Hook (eds.), *Microregionalism and World Order*, Basingstoke, UK: Palgrave Macmillan, 2002, pp. 66–94.
P. Y. Saunier and S. Ewen (eds.), *Another Global City: Historical Explorations into the Transnational Municipal Moment, 1850–2000*, Basingstoke: Palgrave Macmillan, 2008.
J. C. Scott, *Seeing Like a State: How Certain Schemes to Improve the Human Condition Have Failed*, New Haven, CT: Yale University Press, 1998.
—, "Introduction to the Launch Issue", *TRaNS: Trans-Regional and -National Studies of Southeast Asia* 1 (2013) 1, pp. 1–4.
D. Shambaugh, *China Goes Global: The Partial Power*, Oxford: Oxford University Press, 2013.
O. P. Sharma, "India's Exports to the East European Countries: Issues and Prospects", in *Emerging Opportunities for India's Trade and Economic Cooperation with East Europe*, New Delhi: Indian Institute of Foreign Trade, 1977, pp. 30–102.
N. Shashikumar, "The Indian Port Privatization Model: A Critique", *Transportation Journal* 37 (1998) 3, pp. 35–48.
A. Shaw, *The Making of Navi Mumbai*, New Delhi: Orient Longman, 2004.
T. M. Shaw, J. A. Grant and S. Cornelissen (eds.), *The Ashgate Research Companion to Regionalisms*, Surrey: Ashgate, 2011.
—, "Introduction and Overview: The Study of New Regionalism(s) at the Start of the Second Decade of the Twenty-First Century", in: T. M. Shaw, J. A. Grant, and S. Cornelissen (ed.), *The Ashgate Research Companion to Regionalisms*, Surrey: Ashgate, 2011, pp. 3–30.
S. T. Sheppard, *Bombay*, Bombay: The Times of India Press, 1932.
J. Sidaway, "Enclave Space: A New Metageography of Development?", *Area* 39 (2007) 3, pp. 331–339.
L. Sklair, *The Transnational Capitalist Class*, Malden, MA and Oxford: Blackwell, 2001.
M. P. Smith, *Transnational Urbanism: Locating Globalization*, Malden, MA and Oxford: Blackwell, 2001.
T. Smith, "New Bottles for New Wine: A Pericentric Framework for the Study of the Cold War", *Diplomatic History* 24 (2000) 4, pp. 551–565.

F. Söderbaum, "Formal and Informal Regionalism", in: T. M. Shaw, J. A. Grant and S. Cornelissen (eds.), *The Ashgate Research Companion to Regionalisms*, Surrey: Ashgate, 2011, pp. 51–68
–, "Theories of Regionalism", in: M. Beeson and R. Stubbs (eds.), *Routledge Handbook of Asian Regionalism*, Abingdon: Routledge, 2012, pp. 11–21.
N. Somasekhara, "Industrial Estates in India", *Artha Vijnana: Journal of the Gokhale Institute of Politics and Economics* 8 (1966) 3, pp. 279–297.
J. A. Soulsby, "Shannon Free Airport Scheme: A New Approach to Industrial Development", *Scottish Geographical Magazine* 81 (1965) 2, pp. 104–114.
M. Sparke et al., "Triangulating the Borderless World: Geographies of Power in the Indonesia-Malaysia-Singapore Growth Triangle", *Transactions of the Institute of British Geographers* 29 (2004) 4, pp. 485–498.
P. J. Stern, *The Company-State: Corporate Sovereignty and the Early Modern Foundations of the British Empire in India*, New York: Oxford University Press, 2011.
D. Stone, "Transfer Agents and Global Networks in the 'Transnationalization' of Policy", *Journal of European Public Policy* 11 (2004) 3, pp. 545–566.
L. Subramanian, *Three Merchants of Bombay: Doing Business in Times of Change*, New Delhi: Penguin Books India, 2012.
R. J. F. Sulivan, *One Hundred Years of Bombay: History of the Bombay Chamber of Commerce, 1836–1936*, Bombay: Uchitha Graphic Printers, 1937. Reprinted 2012.
E. Swyngedouw, "The Mammon Quest: 'Glocalisation,' Interspatial Competition and the Monetary Order – the Construction of New Scales", in: M. Dunford and G. Kafkalas (eds.), *Cities and Regions in the New Europe: The Global-Local Interplay and Spatial Development Strategies*, London: Belhaven Press, 1992, pp. 39–67.
–, "Reconstructing Citizenship, the Re-scaling of the State and the New Authoritarianism: Closing the Belgian Mines", *Urban Studies* 33 (1996) 8, pp. 1499–1521.
–, "Neither Global nor Local: 'Glocalisation' and the Politics of Scale", in: K. R. Cox (ed.), *Spaces of Globalization: Reasserting the Power of the Local*, New York: Guilford Press, 1997, pp. 137–166.
–, "Globalisation or 'Glocalisation'? Networks, Territories and Rescaling", *Cambridge Review of International Affairs* 17 (2004) 1, pp. 25–48.
J. F. Taffet, *Foreign Aid as Foreign Policy: The Alliance for Progress in Latin America*, New York: Routledge, 2007.
T. Takeo, "Masan: An Epitome of the Japan-ROK Relationship", *AMPO: Japan-Asia Quarterly Review* 8 and 9 (1977) 4, 1–2, pp. 53–66.
–, "Free Trade Zones in Southeast Asia", *Monthly Review* 29 (1978) 9, pp. 29–41.
I. C. Taylor, "Spatial Development Initiatives: Two Case Studies from Southern Africa", in: T. M. Shaw, J. A. Grant and S. Cornelissen (eds.), *The Ashgate Research Companion to Regionalisms*, Surrey: Ashgate, 2011, pp. 325–338.
C. Tazzara, *The Free Port of Livorno and the Transformation of the Mediterranean World, 1574–1790*, Oxford: Oxford University Press, 2017.
–, "Capitalism and the Special Economic Zone, 1590–2014", in: R. Fredona and S. Reinert (eds.), *New Perspectives on the History of Political Economy*, Basingstoke: Palgrave Macmillan, 2018, pp. 75–102.
K. N. Thakur, "Project Report on Impact of Special Economic Zone (SEZ) on Birds in Uran, Maharashtra", MSc thesis, Mumbai University, 2010, http://awsassets.wwfindia.org/downloads/impact_of_special_economic_zone.pdf.

R. S. Thoman, *Free Ports and Foreign-Trade Zones*, Cambridge, MD: Cornell Maritime Press, 1956.
A. M. Thomas, "India and Southeast Asia: The Look East Policy in Perspective", in: R. Harshe and K. M. Seethi (eds.), *Engaging with the World: Critical Reflections on India's Foreign Policy*, New Delhi: Orient Longman, 2005, pp. 297–316
E. Thompson and G. T. Garratt, *Rise and Fulfilment of British Rule in India*, Allahabad: Central Book Depot, 1962.
L. Tillin, *Remapping India: New States and Their Political Origins*, London: C. Hurst and Co., 2013.
J. Toye and R. Toye, "The Origins and Interpretation of the Prebisch-Singer Thesis", *History of Political Economy* 35 (2003) 3, pp. 437–467.
C. R. Unger, "Towards Global Equilibrium: American Foundations and Indian Modernization, 1950s to 1970s", *Journal of Global History* 6 (2011) 1, pp. 121–142.
–, *Entwicklungspfade in Indien: Eine internationale Geschichte, 1947–1980*, Göttingen: Wallstein Verlag, 2015.
B. C. Upreti, "India's Policy Towards Its South Asian Neighbours: Constraints, Impediments and Perspectives", in: R. Harshe and K. M. Seethi (eds.), *Engaging with the World: Critical Reflections on India's Foreign Policy*, New Delhi: Orient Longman, 2005, pp. 203–223.
B. G. Van, "Survey on Duty-Free Export Processing Zones in Asian Region", *The Seoul National University Economic Review* 9 (1975) 1, pp. 126–244.
N. Vittal, "Free Trade Zones and Export Strategy", *Foreign Trade Review* 12 (1977) 3, pp. 396–414.
D. E. Wacha, *A Financial Chapter in the History of Bombay City*, Bombay: A. J. Combridge & Co, 1910.
D. Wall, "Export Processing Zones", *Journal of World Trade Law* 10 (1976) 5, pp. 478–489.
I. Wallerstein, "The Rise and Future Demise of the World Capitalist System: Concepts for Comparative Analysis", *Comparative Studies in Society and History* 16 (1974) 4, pp. 387–415.
J. J. Wang and D. Olivier, "Port-FEZ Bundles as Spaces of Global Articulation: The Case of Tianjin, China", *Environment and Planning A* 38 (2006) 8, pp. 1487–1503.
J. Wang, "The Economic Impact of Special Economic Zones: Evidence from Chinese Municipalities", *Journal of Development Economics* 101 (2013) C, pp. 133–147.
H. Weiss (ed.), *Ports of Globalization, Places of Creolisation: Nordic Possessions in the Atlantic World during the Era of the Slave Trade*, Leiden: Brill, 2016.
R. Wenzlhuemer, "The Ship, the Media, and the World: Conceptualizing Connections in Global History", *Journal of Global History* 11 (2016) 2, pp. 163–186.
M. Werner and B. Zimmerman, "Beyond Comparison: Histoire Croisée and the Challenge of Reflexivity", *History and Theory* 45 (2006) 1, pp. 30–50.
K. Y. Wong and D. K. Y. Chu, "Export Processing Zones and Special Economic Zones as Generators of Economic Development: The Asian Experience", *Geografiska Annaler. Series B, Human Geography* 66 (1984) 1, pp. 1–16.
M. H. Zérah, "Gouvernance métropolitaine et pilotage de réseaux techniques: le cas de la région métropolitaine de Mumbai (Bombay)", *Revue française d'administration publique* 3 (2003) 107, pp. 395–407.
–, "Une 'Vision Mumbai' pour transformer la ville ou la difficulté à (re)penser la gouvernance métropolitaine", *EchoGéo* 10 (2009), http://echogeo.revues.org/11389.

Libraries and Archives

British Library

India Office Records, General Correspondence, India Separate Revenue Department
B. Doveton and W.C. Bruce to L.R. Reid, 20 January 1834 (Z/E/4/14/D557, 1834–1837).
"Note prepared by the Secretary to Government in the General Department", 25 April 1834.
"Queries for Answers", Fort William, 19 May, No. 5. Govt. Dept. 1834.
Separate Department letter to the Court of Directors of the East India Company, 25 July 1834.

India Office Records, Bombay Presidency Acts
Act no. V. of 1870. An act for the levy of Fees for the use of the Government Bunders, Wharves, Landing Places, Piers and Hards in the City of Bombay.
Act no. I of 1873. The Bombay Port Trust Act of 1873. Acts of the Legislative Council of the Governor of Bombay, 1871–1874.
Act no. VI, 1879. An Act to consolidate the immoveable and other property vesting in the Trustees of the Port of Bombay, and certain other property on, or connected with, the foreshore of the Island of Bombay into one estate, and to vest the control and management of the same in one Public Trust; and for other purposes. Acts passed by the Governor of Bombay in Council in the years 1878–1880.

India Office Records, Bombay Port Trust Records
Bombay Port Trust, "Administration Report to 31st March 1874."
Bombay Port Trust, "Administration Report to the 31st March 1875."
Bombay Port Trust, "Administration Report to 31st March 1876."
Bombay Port Trust, "Administration Report to 31st March 1879."
Bombay Port Trust, "Administration Report to 31st March 1880."
Bombay Port Trust, "Administration Report to 31st March 1881."

Asia and Pacific Collection
Bombay Chamber of Commerce and Industry, 1864–1865, Annual Report.
Bombay Chamber of Commerce and Industry, 1867–1868, Annual Report.
Bombay Chamber of Commerce and Industry, 1870–1871, Annual Report.
Bombay Chamber of Commerce and Industry, 1871–1872, Annual Report.
Bombay Chamber of Commerce and Industry, 1872–1873, Annual Report.
Bombay Chamber of Commerce and Industry, 1873–1874, Annual Report.
Bombay Chamber of Commerce and Industry, 1875–1876, Annual Report.
Elphinstone Land & Press Company Limited, "Report of the Directors to the Shareholders at the First Annual General Meeting", 1860.
Elphinstone Land & Press Company Limited, "Report of the Directors to the Shareholders at the Second Annual General Meeting", 1861.
Elphinstone Land & Press Company Limited, "Report of the Directors to the Shareholders at the Third Annual General Meeting", 1862.
Elphinstone Land & Press Company Limited, "Report of the Directors to the Shareholders at the Fourth Annual General Meeting", 1863.

Elphinstone Land & Press Company Limited, "Report of the Directors to the Shareholders at the Seventh Annual General Meeting", 1866.
Elphinstone Land & Press Company Limited, "Report of the Directors to the Shareholders at the Eighth Annual General Meeting", 1867.

General Reference Collection
Maharashtra Economic Development Council, "Report on Free-Trade Zone in Maharashtra", 1964, reprinted 1970.
Maharashtra Economic Development Council, *MEDC: 1957–1977*, Bombay: The Council, 1978.

Central Secretariat Library

India Official Department, Annual Reports
Jawaharlal Nehru Port Trust, 2008–2009, Administration Report.
Jawaharlal Nehru Port Trust, 2010–2011, Administration Report.
Kandla Port Trust, 1958–1959, Administration Report.
Kandla Port Trust, 1962–1963, Administration Report.
Kandla Port Trust, 1963–1964, Administration Report.
Kandla Port Trust, 1964–1965, Administration Report.
Kandla Port Trust, 1971–1972, Administration Report.
Kandla Port Trust, 1977–1978, Administration Report.
Ministry of Commerce, Ministry of International Trade, Government of India, 1964, Administrative Report.
Ministry of Finance, Department of Revenue, Government of India, "Report of the Customs Reorganisation Committee", 1958.

Ministry of Shipping Reports
Ministry of Transport, Government of India, "Report of the West Coast Major Port Development Committee regarding the possibility of siting a major port on the coast covered by Kathiawar and Cutch", 1949.
Ministry of Transport, Government of India, 1955–1956, Annual Report.
Ministry of Shipping and Surface Transport, Government of India, 2007–2008, Annual Report.
Ministry of Shipping and Transport, Government of India, 1959–1960, Annual Report.
Ministry of Shipping and Transport, Government of India, 1968–1969, Annual Report.
Ministry of Shipping and Transport, Government of India, 1969–1970, Annual Report.
Ministry of Shipping and Transport, Government of India, 1971–1972, Annual Report.
Ministry of Shipping and Transport, Government of India, 1972–1973, Annual Report.
Ministry of Shipping and Transport, Government of India, 1974–1975, Annual Report.
Ministry of Shipping and Transport, Government of India, 1980–1981, Annual Report.
Ministry of Shipping and Transport, Government of India, 1981–1982, Annual Report.
Ministry of Shipping and Transport, Government of India, 1984–1985, Annual Report.
Ministry of Shipping, Government of India, 2006–2007, Annual Report.
Ministry of Surface Transport, Government of India, 1988–1989, Annual Report.

Ministry of Transport and Communications, Government of India, 1960–1961, Annual Report.
Ministry of Transport and Communications, Department of Transport, Government of India, 1958–1959, Annual Report.
Ministry of Shipping, Road Transport and Highways, Department of Shipping, Government of India, 2005–2006, Annual Report.
Transport Research Division, Ministry of Shipping and Transport, Government of India, "India Ports and Shipping Statistics 1970."

India Official Department

Ministry of Commerce and Industry, Government of India, "Report of the Committee Appointed under the Chairmanship of Shri P.K. Kaul", 1978.
Ministry of Steel, Mines & Coal, Government of India, "Report of the Review Committee on Electronics", 30 September 1979.

Indian Merchants' Chamber, F.E. Dinshaw Commercial and Financial Reference Library

Indian Merchants' Chamber, 1949, Annual Report.
Indian Merchants' Chamber, 1952, Annual Report.
Indian Merchants' Chamber, 1954, Annual Report.
Indian Merchants' Chamber, 1959, Annual Report.
Indian Merchants' Chamber, 1972, Annual Report.
Indian Merchants' Chamber, 1979, Annual Report.
Indian Merchants' Chamber, 1980, Annual Report.
Indian Merchants' Chamber, 1984, Annual Report.
Ministry of Commerce and Industry, Government of India, Resolution No. 64–LW (34)/49, "Report of the Export Promotion Committee", 1949.
Ministry of Commerce and Industry, Government of India, "Report of the Export Promotion Committee", 31 August 1957.

Other Reports

Board of Engineers for Rivers and Harbors, War Department and the Bureau of Operations, United States Shipping Board, *Foreign Trade Zones (or Free Ports), Analyzed with Special Reference to the Advisability of their Establishment in the United States*, Washington, DC, 1929.

Consulate General of the Kingdom of the Netherlands, Mumbai, "Building with Nature: Where Economic Development and Care for the Environment Go Hand in Hand", November 2013.

Department of Industrial Policy and Promotion, Ministry of Commerce and Industry, Government of India, "Concept Paper: Delhi-Mumbai Industrial Corridor", August 2007, http://www.dmicdc.com/frmDownloads.aspx?pgid=43.

Department of Industrial Policy and Promotion, Ministry of Commerce and Industry, Government of India, "India and Japan: A Winning Partnership", 2014, https://www.jetro.go.jp/ext_images/jetro/topics/pdf/1409_topics1_1.pdf.

Ernst & Young ShinNihon LLC, *Kaigai Kogyo Danchi Jigyo Tyosa Houkokusho* [Overseas Industrial Parks and Research Report], 2014, http://www.meti.go.jp/meti_lib/report/2014fy/001018.pdf.

International Labour Organization, "Employment and Social Policy in Respect of Export Processing Zones (EPZs)", 2003, http://www.ilo.org/public/libdoc/ilo/GB/286/GB.286_esp_3_engl.pdf.

Japan External Trade Organization, "'Look West,' with the Strategic Partnership Between India and Japan", Asia and Oceania Division, Overseas Research Department, September 2013, http://www.jetro.go.jp/ext_images/jetro/topics/pdf/1309_topics1_annexion3.pdf.

T. Kelleher, "Handbook on Export Free Zones", United Nations Industrial Development Organization, 1976.

McKinsey & Company, Inc., "Vision Mumbai: Transforming Mumbai into a World-Class City", 2003, http://www.visionmumbai.org/aboutusdocs/McKinseyReport.pdf.

Ministry of Economy, Trade and Industry, Government of Japan, "White Paper on International Economy and Trade 2014", 2014, www.meti.go.jp/english/report/data/gWT2014fe.html.

Ministry of Shipping, Government of India, "Maritime Agenda: 2010–2020", 2011, http://shipping.nic.in/showfile.php?lid=261.

Ministry of Shipping, Government of India, Annual Report, 2014–2015, http://shipping.nic.in/showfile.php?lid=2016.

Ministry of Shipping, Government of India, "Update on Indian Port Sector", 31 March 2015, http://shipping.nic.in/showfile.php?lid=2020.

Ministry of Shipping, Government of India, "Vision for Coastal Shipping, Tourism and Regional Development", 2015, http://shipping.nic.in/showfile.php?lid=1959.

Mumbai Metropolitan Region, Final Regional Concept Plan Report, May 2011, http://www.visionmumbai.org/images/projects/concept%20plan%20report_06May2011-final.pdf.

S. Perman, L. Duvillier, N. David, J. Eden, and S. Gruliau, "Behind the Brand Names: Working Conditions and Labour Rights in Export Processing Zones", International Confederation of Free Trade Unions, 2004.

Planning Commission, Government of India, *Maharashtra Development Report*, New Delhi: Academic Foundation, 2007.

T. J. Reeves and C. E. Bennett, "We the People: Asians in the United States", Census 2000 Special Reports, US Census Bureau, December 2004, http://www.census.gov/prod/2004pubs/censr-17.pdf.

Reserve Bank of India, "Report of the Working Group on Financing of Industrial Estates", Bombay: Reserve Bank of India, 1972.

J. P. Singa Boyenge, "ILO Database on Export Processing Zones (Revised)", International Labour Office working paper, Geneva, 2007.

The World Bank, "Project Completion Report", India, Nhava Sheva Port Project, Report Number 12189, 14 July 1993, http://www-wds.worldbank.org/external/default/WDSContentServer/WDSP/IB/1993/07/14/000009265_3960925200204/Rendered/PDF/multi_page.pdf.

United Nations Conference on Trade and Development, "Export Processing Free Zones in Developing Countries: Implications for Trade and Industrialization Policies", New York: United Nations, 1983.

United Nations Industrial Development Organization, "Guidelines for the Establishment of Industrial Estates in Developing Countries", Vienna: United Nations, 1978.

United Nations Industrial Development Organization, "The Effectiveness of Industrial Estates in Developing Countries", Vienna: United Nations, 1978.

United Nations Industrial Development Organization, "Industrial Estates: Principles and Practices", Vienna: United Nations, 1995, https://www.unido.org/fileadmin/user_media/Publications/Pub_free/Industrial_estates_principles_and_practice.ppd.

Newspaper Articles

S. Ashraf, "India and Pakistan Compete for Influence in Afghanistan", *East Asia Forum*, 25 April 2013, http://www.eastasiaforum.org/2013/04/25/india-and-pakistan-compete-for-influence-in-afghanistan/.

G. Aulakh, "Committed to Investing $5 Billion in Maharashtra: Foxconn", *Economic Times*, 17 February 2018, https://economictimes.indiatimes.com/news/economy/finance/committed-to-investing-5-billion-in-maharashtra-foxconn/articleshow/62953320.cms.

I. Bagchi, "India to Spread Tentacles into Central Asia via Iran", *Times of India*, 13 March 2012, http://timesofindia.indiatimes.com/india/India-to-spread-tentacles-into-Central-Asia-via-Iran/articleshow/12239197.cms.

S. Banerjee, "Major Infrastructure Boost for Navi Mumbai's JNPT Project", *Times of India*, 4 March 2015, http://timesofindia.indiatimes.com/city/navi-mumbai/Major-infrastructure-boost-for-Navi-Mumbais-JNPT-project/articleshow/46447679.cms.

N. Basu, "Chinese Industrial Parks to Have Same Incentives as SEZs, NMIZs", *Business Standard*, 1 July 2014, http://www.business-standard.com/article/economy-policy/chinese-industrial-parks-to-have-same-incentives-as-sezs-nmizs-114063001072_1.html.

R. Borah, "India's Challenges in Afghanistan Post-2014", *East Asia Forum*, 5 August 2013, http://www.eastasiaforum.org/2013/08/06/indias-challenges-in-afghanistan-post-2014/.

K. Bradsher, "Modi, in Davos, Praises Globalization Without Noting India's Trade Barriers", *New York Times*, 23 January 2018, https://www.nytimes.com/2018/01/23/business/modi-in-davos-praises-globalization-without-mentioning-india-trade-barriers.html.

Business Standard, "16 National Investment and Manufacturing Zones (NIMZs) to Boost Manufacturing Sector", 9 July 2014. http://www.business-standard.com/article/news-cm/16-national-investment-and-manufacturing-zones-nimzs-to-boost-manufacturing-sector-114070900694_1.html.

–, “Sagarmala: Concept and Implementation Towards Blue Revolution”, 25 March 2015, http://www.business-standard.com/article/government-press-release/sagarmala-concept-and-implementation-towards-blue-revolution-115032501253_1.html.

–, “Rajasthan to Have Second Japanese Industrial Zone”, 8 April 2015, http://www.business-standard.com/article/news-ians/rajasthan-to-have-second-japanese-industrial-zone-115040800931_1.html.

–, “Foxconn to Set Up Production Unit in Maharashtra for $5 Bn”, 8 August, 2015, http://www.business-standard.com/article/companies/foxconn-to-invest-5-billion-to-set-up-facility-in-maharashtra-115080800341_1.html.

–, “PM Lays the Foundation Stone for 4th Container Terminal of Jawaharlal Nehru Port Trust”, 11 October 2015, http://www.business-standard.com/article/current-affairs/pm-lays-foundation-stone-for-4th-container-terminal-of-jawaharlal-nehru-port-trust-115101100613_1.html.

–, “Japan to Set Up Financial Facility for ‘Make in India’ Initiative”, 12 December 2015, http://www.business-standard.com/article/news-ians/japan-to-set-up-financial-facility-for-make-in-india-initiative-115121200666_1.html.

D. R. Chaudhury, “Japan’s $12 Billion ‘Make in India’ Fund to Push Investments”, *Economic Times*, 13 December 2015, http://articles.economictimes.indiatimes.com/2015-12-13/news/69006246_1_pm-shinzo-abe-india-fund-oda.

–, “India and Iran Trying to Seal Chabahar Port Deal by January”, *Economic Times*, 17 December 2015, http://economictimes.indiatimes.com/news/politics-and-nation/india-and-iran-trying-to-seal-chabahar-port-deal-by-january/articleshow/50212231.cms.

–, “PM Narendra Modi Returns to Regional Diplomacy; Afghanistan-Pakistan Visit Drives Home Need for Cooperation”, *Economic Times*, 26 December 2015, http://articles.economictimes.indiatimes.com/2015-12-26/news/69317162_1_indian-pm-regional-cooperation-india-and-pakistan.

P. Doval, “Foxconn Plans to Make India Hub for Africa, West Asia”, *Times of India*, 14 January 2016, http://timesofindia.indiatimes.com/business/india-business/Foxconn-plans-to-make-India-hub-for-Africa-West-Asia/articleshow/50569582.cms.

Economic Times, “Reliance Industries Rewas Port: Nitin Gadkari Promises to Resolve Issues in a Month”, 7 June 2015, http://economictimes.indiatimes.com/industry/transportation/shipping-/-transport/reliance-industries-rewas-port-nitin-gadkari-promises-to-resolve-issues-in-a-month/articleshow/47574652.cms.

–, “India Makes Pitch for Chinese Investments in Special Economic Zones”, 15 October 2014, http://articles.economictimes.indiatimes.com/2014-10-15/news/55059512_1_indian-embassy-indian-ambassador-special-economic-zones.

–, “Twitter Launches Make in India Emoji”, 4 November 2015, http://economictimes.indiatimes.com/tech/internet/twitter-launches-make-in-india-emoji/articleshow/49659333.cms.

–, “Chinese Company to Get Lease of Gwadar Port’s Free Trade Zone”, 10 November 2015, http://economictimes.indiatimes.com/news/international/business/chinese-company-to-get-lease-of-gwadar-ports-free-trade-zone/articleshow/49740104.cms.

–, “Government Eyes Reclaimed Land from the Sea for Mumbai’s New Airport”, 16 November 2013, http://articles.economictimes.indiatimes.com/2013-11-16/news/44138236_1_navi-mumbai-new-airport-reclaiming-land.

–, “Cancelled SEZs in Maharashtra Will Have to Return Government Land”, 22 November 2015, http://articles.economictimes.indiatimes.com/2015-11-22/news/68484435_1_sezs-special-economic-zones-government-land.

S. Fazl-e-Haider, "China Set to Run Gwadar Port as Singapore Quits", *Asia Times*, 5 September 2012, http://www.atimes.com/atimes/China_Business/NI05Cb01.html.

M. Gadgil and P. R. Sanjai, "JNPT to Build Rs 10,000 Crore Satellite Port at Wadhwan", *Live Mint*, 22 December 2015, http://www.livemint.com/Companies/7K7QoESH7cOVCamaHQIiCL/JNPT-tobuild-Rs10000-crore-satellite-port-at-Wadhwan.html.

K. Ghoge, "Reliance SEZ in Raigad Gets One-Year Extension", *Hindustan Times*, 22 June 2011, http://www.hindustantimes.com/mumbai/reliance-sez-in-raigad-gets-one-year-extension/story-QrNnJmttzo8kiXRlQ2UOpM.html.

—, "CM asks SEZ Developers to Begin Projects in 3 Months", *Hindustan Times*, 16 August 2015, http://www.hindustantimes.com/mumbai/cm-asks-sez-developers-to-begin-projects-in-3-months/story-GcmbSbbJXe7gmbZaLeYjTI.html.

T. Gjelten, "In 1965, A Conservative Tried to Keep America White. His Plan Backfired", *National Public Radio*, 3 October 2015, http://www.npr.org/2015/10/03/445339838/the-unintended-consequences-of-the-1965-immigration-act.

S. Gupta and Sidhartha, "Korea, Japan Seek Industrial Zone in Rajasthan's Neemrana", *Times of India*, 21 July 2014, http://timesofindia.indiatimes.com/india/Korea-Japan-seek-industrial-zone-in-Rajasthans-Neemrana/articleshow/38772143.cms.

Hindu Business Line, "Investors Not Keen on SEZs Anymore; 57 to Surrender Zones", 10 February 2015, http://www.thehindubusinessline.com/economy/investors-not-keen-on-sezs-anymore-57-to-surrender-zones/article6878327.ece?ref=relatedNews.

Hindustan Times, "Foxconn to 'Make in India', Will Invest $5bn in Maharashtra", 8 August 2015, http://www.hindustantimes.com/business/foxconn-to-make-in-india-will-invest-5bn-in-maharashtra/story-8NNM9g8wqF5Nsj7XBgRxxL.html.

S. Jog, "Maharashtra Plans Another City, 50 km Off Mumbai", *Business Standard*, 4 October 2013, http://www.business-standard.com/article/economy-policy/maharashtra-plans-another-city-50-km-off-mumbai-113100300844_1.html.

—, "Maharashtra Maritime Board, JNPT plan all-weather port at Wadhwan", *Business Standard*, 19 May 2015, http://www.business-standard.com/article/companies/headline-maharashtra-maritime-board-jnpt-plan-all-weather-port-at-wadhwan-115051800481_1.html.

J. Johnson, "Attack on India's Economic Zone Plan", *Financial Times*, 24 September 2006, http://www.ft.com/intl/cms/s/0/151b19c0-4bfa-11db-90d2-0000779e2340.html#axzz3xQAYT0zA.

J. Johnson, "1 Million Workers. 90 Million iPhones. 17 Suicides. Who's to Blame?", *Wired Magazine*, 28 February 2011, http://www.wired.com/2011/02/ff_joelinchina/.

A. Khan, "New JNPT Terminal May Plunge 'Delicate' Coastline into Danger", *Indian Express*, 21 December 2015, http://indianexpress.com/article/cities/mumbai/new-jnpt-terminal-may-plunge-delicate-coastline-into-danger/.

P. Manoj, "A Turf War Could Potentially Spoil India's Port Tariff De-Regulation Plan", *Live Mint*, 26 July 2013, http://www.livemint.com/Opinion/FgtczAsa08XXlkH7DKo4tO/A-turf-war-could-potentially-spoil-Indias-port-tariff-dere.html.

—, "Chabahar Port Could Shape Global Strategy of India's State-Run Ports", *Live Mint*, 23 October 2014, http://www.livemint.com/Opinion/zcC4jzurlSBCFdgrisEa1L/Chabahar-port-could-shape-global-strategy-of-Indias-stater.html.

—, "Centre Considers Redefining Mumbai Port's Limits to Allow Reliance Port's Right of Way", *Live Mint*, 13 January 2015, http://www.livemint.com/Politics/jW5PdLJ7xz09EBE4wEWd5H/Centre-considers-redefining-Mumbai-ports-limits-to-allow-Re.html.

M. K. Mehta, "Govt to Free Up Mumbai Port Land for Development", *Times of India*, 4 June 2015, http://timesofindia.indiatimes.com/good-governance/centre/Govt-to-free-up-Mumbai-port-land-for-development/articleshow/47537120.cms.

J. Mukul and A. Paladhi, "Corporatisation of Ports Back on Track", *Business Standard*, 9 September 2014, http://www.business-standard.com/article/economy-policy/corporatisation-of-ports-back-on-track-114090800978_1.html.

G. Nataraj and A. Bhunia, "India and Japan Asia's Win-Win Partnership", *East Asia Forum*, 26 January 2014, http://www.eastasiaforum.org/2014/01/26/india-and-japan-asias-win-win-partnership/.

G. Nataraj, "India Should Get on Board China's Maritime Silk Road", *East Asia Forum*, 27 June 2015, http://www.eastasiaforum.org/2015/06/27/india-should-get-on-board-chinas-maritime-silk-road/.

A. Paladhi, "JNPT to Take 60% Equity in Iran Port Project", *Business Standard*, 15 December 2014, http://www.business-standard.com/article/economy-policy/jnpt-to-take-60-equity-in-iran-port-project-114121500048_1.html.

M. Phadke, "A Year on, Report to Develop Port Trust Land Gathers Dust", *Indian Express*, 19 November 2015, http://indianexpress.com/article/cities/mumbai/a-year-on-report-to-develop-port-trust-land-gathers-dust/.

S. Ramachandran, "India to Invest in Iran's Chabahar Port", *Central Asia-Caucasus Analyst*, 26 November 2014, http://cacianalyst.org/publications/analytical-articles/item/13099-india-to-invest-in-irans-chabahar-port.html.

A. Sarkar, "MbPT Land Oustees Spend Chilly Nights in the Open", *Indian Express*, 14 December 2015, http://indianexpress.com/article/cities/mumbai/mbpt-land-oustees-spend-chilly-nights-in-the-open/.

A. Sen, "One Year Extension for Navi Mumbai's Three IT/ITES SEZs", *Hindu Business Line*, 10 January 2016, http://www.thehindubusinessline.com/companies/one-year-extension-for-navi-mumbais-three-itites-sezs/article8089304.ece.

M. Shetty, "Finance SEZs Can Halt Rupee Trading Exodus: Finance Ministry", *Times of India*, 23 February 2015, http://timesofindia.indiatimes.com/business/india-business/Mumbaai-special-economic-zonesfinance-ministry/articleshow/46337112.cms?.

M. P. Singh, "The Japanese Connection", *The Hindu*, 6 April 2013, http://www.thehindu.com/business/Industry/the-japanese-connection/article4585093.ece.

K. C. Sivaramakrishnan, "Megacity Governance", *Business Standard*, 8 March 2009, http://www.business-standard.com/article/opinion/k-c-sivaramakrishnan-megacity-governance-109030800019_1.html.

K. Suneja, "India Expresses Interest in Preferential Trade Agreement with Iran Once Sanctions Are Lifted", *Economic Times*, 1 December 2015, http://economictimes.indiatimes.com/news/economy/foreign-trade/india-expresses-interest-in-preferential-trade-agreement-with-iran-once-sanctions-are-lifted/articleshow/49989768.cms.

Surabhi and A. M. Jigeesh, "Govt to Be Facilitator for Start-Ups: Jaitley", *Hindu Business Line*, 16 January 2016, http://www.thehindubusinessline.com/info-tech/govt-rbi-will-help-bankers-lend-more-jaitley/article8113541.ece?homepage=true.

The Economist, "Blacked Out", 21 September 2010, http://www.economist.com/node/17082677.

—, "Special Economic Zones: Not So Special", 4 April 2015, http://www.economist.com/news/leaders/21647615-world-awash-free-trade-zones-and-their-offshoots-many-are-not-worth-effort-not.

–, "Special Economic Zones: Political Priority, Economic Gamble", 4 April 2015, http://www.economist.com/news/finance-and-economics/21647630-free-trade-zones-are-more-popular-everwith-politicians-if-not.

Times of India, "Work on JNPT SEZ to Begin in Four Months", 20 August 2015, http://timesofindia.indiatimes.com/city/mumbai/Work-on-JNPT-SEZ-to-begin-in-four-months/articleshow/48562148.cms.

S. Tripathy, "Master Plan for Delhi-Mumbai Industrial Corridor First Zone Notified", *Times of India*, 28 May 2013, http://timesofindia.indiatimes.com/city/jaipur/Master-plan-for-Delhi-Mumbai-Industrial-Corridor-first-zone-notified/articleshow.

Websites

APM Terminals website, "Who We Are", http://www.apmterminals.com/about-us (accessed 28 June 2018).

Centre for Livable Cities Singapore website, http://www.clc.gov.sg/ (accessed 22 December 2015).

Cities Alliance homepage, http://www.citiesalliance.org/ (accessed 11 December 2015).

DP World website, "About DP World", http://web.dpworld.com/about-dp-world/ (accessed 28 June 2018).

Indian Council for Research on International Economic Relations website, "About ICRIER", http://icrier.org/abouticrier/about-icrier/ (accessed 17 September 2015).

Indian Institute for Foreign Trade website, "About IIFT", http://edu.iift.ac.in/iift/landing/index.html (accessed 17 September 2015).

Jawaharlal Nehru National Urban Renewal Mission website, http://jnnurm.nic.in (accessed 19 December 2015).

Jawaharlal Nehru Port Trust website, "Port Details", http://www.jnport.gov.in/AboutJNPT.aspx?id=3&cid=1 (accessed 22 February 2014).

Jawaharlal Nehru Port Trust website, "Terminals", http://www.jnport.gov.in/container.aspx (accessed 2 June 2018).

London First homepage, http://londonfirst.co.uk/ (accessed 10 December 2015).

London First website, "London as a World City", http://londonfirst.co.uk/our-focus/londons-economic-development-strategy/london-as-a-world-city/ (accessed 10 December 2015)

Maharashtra Industrial Development Corporation website, "About Us – History", http://www.midcindia.org/Pages/AboutUs.aspx (accessed 5 November 2015).

Maharashtra State Warehousing Corporation website, "Bonded Warehouses", http://mswarehousing.com/english/bonde-ware.htm (accessed 12 April 2015).

Make in India website. "Sectors", http://www.makeinindia.com/sectors (accessed 31 December 2015).

–, "About Us", http://www.makeinindia.com/about (accessed 30 December 2015).

–, "Electronic Systems", http://www.makeinindia.com/sector/electronic-systems (accessed 31 December 2015).

–, "Industrial Corridor", http://www.makeinindia.com/live-projects-industrial-corridor (accessed 31 December 2015).

–, "National Manufacturing", http://www.makeinindia.com/policy/national-manufacturing (accessed 30 December 2015).

–, "Media and Entertainment", http://www.makeinindia.com/sector/media-and-entertainment (accessed 31 December 2015).
Ministry of Overseas Indian Affairs website, "India and Its Diaspora", http://moia.gov.in/accessories.aspx?aid=10 (accessed 15 December 2015).
Mumbai First website, "Vision and Mission", http://www.mumbaifirst.org/vision.php (accessed 10 December 2015)
–, "Patron Members", http://www.mumbaifirst.org/patrons.php (accessed 15 December 2015).
Mumbai Metropolitan Region Development Authority website, "Who We Are", https://mmrda.maharashtra.gov.in/who-we-are (accessed 12 December 2015).
Mumbai Transformation Support Unit website "About Us", http://www.visionmumbai.org/aboutus.aspx (accessed 11 December 2015).
–, "Documents", http://www.visionmumbai.org/document.aspx (accessed 11 December 2015).
Narendra Modi website, "PM Launches 'Make in India' Global Initiative", 25 September 2014, http://www.narendramodi.in/pm-launches-make-in-india-global-initiative-6644 (accessed 8 January 2016).
Navi Mumbai Special Economic Zone website, http://www.nmsez.com/index.html (accessed 16 January 2016).
Prime Minister of India website, "Sagarmala: Concept and Implementation Towards Blue Revolution", http://pmindia.gov.in/en/news_updates/sagarmala-concept-and-implementation-towards-blue-revolution/ (accessed 29 December 2015).
Rewas Ports Limited website. "Promoters", http://www.rewasports.com/promoters.html (accessed 16 December 2015).
Royal HaskonigDHV website, "Eko Atlantic Nigeria", http://www.royalhaskoningdhv.com/en-gb/projects/eko-atlantic-nigeria/103 (accessed 29 December 2015).
–, "Reclaiming Jakarta's Future Pluit City, Jakarta", http://www.royalhaskoningdhv.com/en-gb/projects/s-projects-s-pluit-city-land-development-indonesia/2136 (accessed 29 December 2015).
Special Economic Zones in India website, "Operational SEZs in India", last updated 16 March 2018, http://sezindia.nic.in/cms/operational-sezs-in-india.php (accessed 28 June 2018).
–, "Approved SEZs in India", last updated 31 March 2015, http://www.sezindia.nic.in/about-asi.asp (accessed 9 January 2016).
–, "About SEZs", last updated 31 March 2015, http://www.sezindia.nic.in/index.asp (accessed 9 January 2016).
–, "Facilities and Incentives", http://www.sezindia.nic.in/about-fi.asp (accessed 19 December 2015).
–, "Fact Sheet on Special Economic Zones", http://sezindia.nic.in/upload/5b16778e5e714FACTSHEETupdationonSEZIndia.pdf (accessed 23 July 2018).
–, "List of State-Wise Exporting SEZs", 31 March 2015, http://www.sezindia.nic.in/writereaddata/pdf/ListofoperationalSEZs.pdf (accessed 19 December 19, 2015).
State Trading Corporation of India website, "Top Countries of India's Import and Export in US $ Million", http://www.stc.gov.in/WriteReadData/Countr_ImpExp_US.pdf (accessed 2 January 2016).
Twitter, "Make in India", https://twitter.com/makeinindia?lang=en (accessed 31 December 2015).

Wikipedia, "2012 Dhaka Fire", https://en.wikipedia.org/wiki/2012_Dhaka_fire (accessed 29 January 2016).

—, "Foxconn Suicides", https://en.wikipedia.org/wiki/Foxconn_suicides (accessed 29 January 2016).

World Cities Research Network website, "World According to GaWC 2008", http://www.lboro.ac.uk/gawc/world2008t.html (accessed 8 December 2015).

World Cities Summit website, "Narider Nayar", http://www.worldcitiessummit.com.sg/whos-coming/narinder-nayar (accessed 22 December 2015).

ZEC: Zona Especial Canaria/Canary Islands Special Zone website, http://www.zec.org/en/ (accessed 22 September 2015).

Index

https://doi.org/10.1515/9783110615135-010